Werner Zips, Manuela Zips-Mairitsch (Eds.)

Bewildering Borders

Legal Anthropology
and Indigenous Rights

edited by

Werner Zips
and
Manuela Zips-Mairitsch

Volume 4

LIT

BEWILDERING BORDERS

The Economy of Conservation in Africa

edited by

Werner Zips and Manuela Zips-Mairitsch

LIT

Cover Images

Front: The moral of the story in one shot: A mating lion couple, the iconic part of a rewilding project in a KwaZulu-Natal Private Game Reserve, at a "bewildering border" of fortress conservation; with a local community member on the backseat of an emerging economy of conservation.

Back: Postgraduate anthropology students of the University of Vienna researching "Ethnicity Inc." in the Little Hunter's Museum of //Xa/oba. As part of the evening programme, San demonstrate the art of fire-making before starting with choreographed and neo-traditional dances, such as the 'giraffe' and 'hyena' dance.

Copy-editing: Yolanda Hulse

Bibliographic information published by the Deutsche Nationalbibliothek
The Deutsche Nationalbibliothek lists this publication in the Deutsche Nationalbibliografie; detailed bibliographic data are available on the Internet at http://dnb.d-nb.de.

ISBN 978-3-643-91090-5 (pb)
ISBN 978-3-643-96090-0 (PDF)

A catalogue record for this book is available from the British Library.

Fresnostr. 2
D-48159 Münster
Tel. +49 (0) 2 51-62 03 20
Fax +49 (0) 2 51-23 19 72
E-Mail: lit@lit-verlag.de
http://www.lit-verlag.de

LIT VERLAG GmbH & Co. KG Wien,
Zweigniederlassung Zürich 2019
Klosbachstr. 107
CH-8032 Zürich
Tel. +41 (0) 44-251 75 05
Fax +41 (0) 44-251 75 06
E-Mail: zuerich@lit-verlag.ch
http://www.lit-verlag.ch

Distribution:

In the UK: Global Book Marketing, e-mail: mo@centralbooks.com
In North America: Independent Publishers Group, e-mail: orders@ipgbook.com
In Germany: LIT Verlag Fresnostr. 2, D-48159 Münster
Tel. +49 (0) 2 51-620 32 22, Fax +49 (0) 2 51-922 60 99, e-mail: vertrieb@lit-verlag.de

e-books are available at www.litwebshop.de

This book was funded by the Commission for Development Research (KEF) at the Austrian Agency for International Cooperation in Education and Research.

List of Figures

List of Images

List of Tables

Abbreviations

ABORNE	African Borderlands Research Network
ANC	African National Congress
AUBP	African Union Border Programme
BEE	Black Economic Empowerment
CAOM	Centre des Archives d'Outre-Mer
CBD	Convention on Biological Diversity
CBNRM	Community-Based Natural Resource Management
CCHA	Community-controlled Hunting Area
CGG	Community Game Guards
CHA	Controlled Hunting Area
CKGR	Central Kalahari Game Reserve
CSR	Corporate Social Responsibility
ECOWAS	Economic Community of West African States
ICH	Intangible Cultural Heritage
IEM	Integrated Ecosystem Management
IGO	Intergovernmental Organisations
IMP	Integrated Management Plan
IRDNC	Integrated Rural Development and Nature Conservation
ITD	Inter-Tropical Discontinuity
IUCN	International Union for the Conservation of Nature
IWGIA	International Work Group for Indigenous Affairs
IWP	iSimangaliso Wetland Park
IWPA	iSimangaliso Wetland Park Authority
JVA	Joint Venture Agreement
JVP	Joint Venture Partner
KAZA	Kavango-Zambezi Transfrontier Conservation Area
KZN	KwaZulu-Natal
KZNW	KwaZulu-Natal Wildlife
LCFN	Living Culture Foundation Namibia
LIFE	Living in a Finite Environment
LSDI	Lubombo Spatial Development Initiative
MCC	Millennium Challenge Corporation
MFDCM	Mouvement des Forces Démocratiques de la Casamance
MPA	Marine Protected Areas
NACSO	Namibian Association of CBNRM Support Organisations

NAGB	National Archives of the Gambia
NCCSP	National Climate Change Support Group
NG	Ngamiland
NNC	Nyae Nyae Conservancy
NNDFN	Nyae Nyae Development Foundation of Namibia
NNJC	Nigeria-Niger Joint Commission
OECD	Organisation for Economic Co-operation and Development
OMVG	l'Organisation Pour La Mise en Valeur de la Fleuve Gambienne
RBA	Rights Based Approach
SADC	Southern African Development Community
SNA	Senegal National Archives
SSBE	Small-scale Business Enterprise
TA	Traditional Authorities
TFCA	Transfrontier Conservation Area
THDT	Tsodilo Hills Development Trust
TPA	Transboundary Protected Areas
UKDM	Umkhanyakude District Municipality
UNDRIP	United Nations Declaration on the Rights of Indigenous Peoples
UNEP	United Nations Environment Programme
UNESCO	United Nations Educational, Scientific and Cultural Organization
UNWTO	United Nations World Tourism Organization
WHC	World Heritage Convention
WHS	World Heritage Site
WIMSA	Working Group of Indigenous Minorities in Southern Africa
WMA	Wildlife Management Area
WWF	World Wildlife Fund

Acknowledgements

A great many people and organisations have assisted in the various research activities that led to this book. We want to thank the University of Vienna, particularly the Faculty of Social Sciences, for the financial support of the projects in Namibia and South Africa. We are grateful to the Department of Social and Cultural Anthropology of the University of Vienna for the wholehearted facilitation of the field practices in these two countries. Furthermore, we thank the Head of the Department, Prof. Dr. Peter Schweitzer, for the Department's support of the editing.

This book would not have been possible without the generous grant of the Commission for Development Research (KEF). Special thanks go to this organisation and its Head, Prof. Dr. Andreas Obrecht, for the publication grant as well as for hosting the workshop of the *African Borderlands Research Network* (ABORNE) in September 2013 at the conference hall of the commission. In this regard, we thank the ABORNE Steering Committee and the network's coordinator, Dr. Wolfgang Zeller, for helping with the organisation of the symposion, along with Mag. Edith Neubauer. Sincere thanks also to the *European Science Foundation* for the support of the ABORNE network and our own participation.

We thank the Governments of Namibia, South Africa, and Botswana for greatly supporting our research, particularly the South African and Namibian Embassies in Vienna, Austria. We cannot thank enough the Nyae Nyae and N#a Jaqna conservancies and all local partners for getting involved in this research. Their collaboration over the years was indispensable for the publication of this volume. National agencies and NGOs, such as the *National Heritage Council of Namibia*, the *Museums Association of Namibia,* the *Living Culture Foundation Namibia* (LCFN) and the *Working Group of Indigenous Minorities in Southern Africa* (WIMSA), the *iSimangaliso Wetland Park Authority*, *Ezemvelo KwaZulu-Natal Wildlife*, and *Ditshwanelo – the Botswana Centre for Human Rights*, have greatly facilitated and supported this research. These, alongside numerous other local organisations and their officials, readily provided valuable background information through short seminars and talks to the participants of the field practices. We are very grateful to many individuals who took the time and energy to answer our countless questions and to guide us through their environments. The only reason why they are not mentioned by name is the realistic anxiety to forget important supporters.

Furthermore, we express our sincere thanks to all postgraduate students who contributed valuable empirical data to the findings presented in this book through their participation in the field practices in Namibia (2014) and South Africa (2016); particularly the members of the iSimangaliso research group: Sabina Mahr, Camilla Mittelberger, Grace Mosha, and Lena Nothdurfter.

Many thanks go to Jean Comaroff for her thoughtful comments on the draft manuscript.

Finally, we extend our deep gratitude to Yolanda Hulse for her careful copy-editing of this volume and her many valuable suggestions. The realisation of this book would simply not have succeeded without her relentless pursuit of improvement.

Preface

Peter Schweitzer

It is my great pleasure to introduce "Bewildering Borders", edited by my colleagues Werner Zips and Manuela Zips-Mairitsch. As indicated in the book's subtitle, it deals with "the economy of conservation" and, while less prominently advertised in the heading, with something one might call "the economy of culture". Regionally, all contributions to the book are situated in Africa, mostly in its southern part, but two contributions deal with West Africa. The genesis of the book is closely connected with the Department of Social and Cultural Anthropology of the University of Vienna. This connection includes the two editors, those authors who are past or present graduate students of the department, as well as the fact that a lot of the empirical material on which the book is based was collected in the course of two departmental field practices (*Feldpraktika*) led by the editors.

The title notions of the book – borders, borderlands, and boundaries – have a long history of serving as subjects of anthropological inquiries. Ethnicity studies from Barth (1969) to Wimmer (2013) have made use of the boundary, as a social border between groups, as an antidote to essentialising notions of the 'cultural stuff' ethnicity supposedly entails. An even older concept in the social sciences and humanities is the 'frontier'. Ever since the days of Frederick Jackson Turner (1861-1932), the author of the "frontier thesis" (Turner 1894), which attributed certain constituting elements of U.S. society – such as informality, a lack of interest in 'high' culture, a form of egalitarianism coupled with violence, etc. – to its shifting (western) frontier, which was imagined as the edge of 'civilisation' and 'wilderness'. Moving from North America to Africa, we come across Igor Kopytoff's "The African Frontier" (1987), which used the notion of the "internal African frontier" to promote a dynamic understanding of African history. While starting out from Turner's notion of the frontier, Kopytoff tried to overcome Turner's simplistic shortcut from the material conditions of the frontier to national psychology. Instead, he provided a model – heavily debated in the 30+ years since – that tries to accommodate similarity and difference within the context of the social and political reproduction of African societies. An approach that focused on the internal social and cultural dynamics within the continent's long history and has since been progressively replaced by an emphasis on the 'border' as a result of colonial and post-colonial politics. No matter how recent and artificial nation state borders in Africa and elsewhere are, their social, cultural, and ecological impacts cannot be denied.

Returning to the commodification of nature and culture in African contexts, "Bewildering Borders" follows the lead that was charted by John and Jean Comaroff's "Ethnicity, Inc." (Comaroff/ Comaroff 2009) ten years ago. The Comaroffs, starting out with materials from Southern Africa themselves, triggered debates in many parts of the world. The "identity economy" they analysed turned out to be most relevant in indigenous contexts and in 'remote' places, however. Being a northern anthropologist myself, the commodification of nature and culture, as described by the Comaroffs and others, seems very familiar. The Arctic, which figures primarily as 'wilderness' in popular imagination (Schweitzer et al. 2017), is also often conceptualised as home of the 'unspoiled indigenous' (a slot often filled by different Inuit societies). Issues of conservation, including the prioritisation of global environmental concerns over local and regional lifeways and subsistence practices, as well as a variety of examples for shared resource management arrangements, are as prominent in different parts of the circumpolar North as in the examples analysed in the present book. Thus, the question arises whether the similarities are connected to what the socio-spatial notion of 'remoteness' conveys, namely a somewhat peripheral or even marginal position. At the same time, 'remoteness' comes with the freedom of 'being out of sight' and can afford a variety of opportunities, whether in the field of eco- and/or ethno-tourism or in the realm of cultural revitalisation (cf. Schweitzer/ Povoroznyuk forthcoming).

Finally, one of the intriguing qualities of "Bewildering Borders" is the harmonious combination of research conducted by scholars with decades of experience with those of students, sometimes constituting their first publication. The conversation between youth and experience, between established authors and beginners, is an important precondition for the further development of scholarship and of our discipline. With this, I want to hand over the book to you, the reader, in order to connect it to your own experiences and draw your conclusions, and – most importantly – enjoy the read.

Foreword

David B. Coplan

The title of this important volume indicates a number of interconnected meanings: the authoritative re-creation of wilderness as 'conservation' and 'protection' (from its human inhabitants); the multiple contesting perspectives on the 'global' and the 'local'; what 'conservation' is for, what it should or can deliver, and to whom. The near Orwellian, Derridian (mis)representations of discourse and rhetoric. The tendency to locate and demarcate wilderness on the borders between neighbouring political states. The turmoil disturbing the peace of parks. The damage done to conservation projects by the host of illegal or legal business activities these projects themselves attract to borders and frontier areas. Rules and promises seemingly made to be broken. Us and them, whoever we are, on the eternally new African horizon. The almost painful intoxication brought on by the witches brewing of humanity with nature and the divine. All brought together in a dystopia of self-manufactured expectations, disappointments, reciprocal accusations and the common desire to be shown the money. No wonder the animals are frightened and bewildered; non-natives as well as natives, restless.

The original impetus for this book was a conference held under the auspices of the African Borders Research Network (ABORNE) at the University of Vienna at the end of September 2013, organised and chaired by the co-editors, in which I participated. I took a train from Basel so as to re-establish my sense of connection to mountains. In Austria, I played the role of an emissary from the austere, rocky fastness of Lesotho to a grand imperial capitol without an empire. The focus on wildlife conservation, tourism, and (aspirationally) community benefication was a novel one for ABORNE but not for the organisers, anthropological scholar-cinematographers Werner Zips and Manuela Zips-Mairitsch. They had been working in this domain for a number of years, which their editorship and contributions to this sure-to-be controversial collection demonstrate so convincingly. They clearly knew whereof they spoke, and here as editors have managed both to connect disparate cases, findings, and perspectives from the various contributors and to highlight some of the most fundamental and contentious issues facing programmes in Community-Based Natural Resource Management (CB-NRM) and Biodiversity Conservation in Africa. Chief among these, as the editors themselves ask, is whether CBNRM can be successful, or even possible, in the face of "neo-liberal conservation" regimes, and importantly therefore, what might be the "vital alternatives" (infra. p. 5).

Too often in the literature, argue the editors, critical scholars focus on the many ways pro-active conservationists are thought of as destined by the global economic regime to get it wrong, particularly with reference to the inclusion and empowerment of local communities surrounding the protected parks. Yet, despite the discontent, disappointment, and frustration of local community members reported in empirical social science research on African conservation areas and beyond, and discussed in great detail by the contributors to this volume, no local residents living in or adjacent to a conservation area have expressed anywhere the wish to have its status and legal protection revoked (infra. p. 12).

Perhaps it is time to inquire and then to specify more explicitly what we really want and can reasonably expect from wildlife tourism: If there are persistent complex problems, what are the solutions? How can multiple, sometimes admittedly conflicting values and goals be harmonised? What does success, not just evidence of failure, look like? What are the proper roles of government and local governance, since these are indispensable? What are the most preferable modes of participation for members of local communities? What forms should the well-intended involvement of outside sponsors, managers, and 'experts' responsibly and ethically assume? What are the outcomes that everyone involved can agree they desire? The case studies and analyses so impressively presented here do not answer these questions, but they do point ways forward, both for supportive scholarship in the field and for the broader objectives and management of the parks and wildlife tourism themselves. Zips and Zips-Mairitsch remind us all forcefully that the revitalisation and protection of both the natural environment and the economic viability of rural communities are what everyone involved are actively working toward. For this, all of us vitally concerned for the future of human and natural resources – the wealth of Africa's living beings – must thank the editors and contributors to this thoughtful collection. Following Bourdieu, they apply a "praxeological" approach to the inescapable strictures of the economy of conservation (infra. p. 11). And as we know, praxis makes perfect. Such work is a vital contribution to the rescue of humanity in nature, and to wildness, in which truly lies (thank you Henry Thoreau) the preservation of the world.

Pricing Nature and Culture
On the Bewildering Commodification of the African Frontier – an Introduction

Werner Zips and Manuela Zips-Mairitsch

"Many times, when we sit together and chat in the evening, we ask ourselves, why do people come from that far away, just to take our pictures. If they came from Windhoek, ok, but from overseas, we find it hard to understand. But, no matter, we are happy with the money they leave with us." (Zahavara Tjambiru 09.12.2013, interview)

"The living museum, it's now in our hands, so we are the ones, who will manage it, and we're having a management team, which is working with it. We are having the managers, the vice manager, we are having secretaries, the vice secretary, the treasury, and the vice treasury." (Henry /ui Nyani 12.09.2014, interview)

"We were moved, because people who moved us, were saying that when we stay here, we will finish the animals. I answered them by saying that our [great]-grand-fathers were staying here, but since that time the population of the animals didn't go down. But where you people are, there are no more wild animals." (Kgosi Molatwe Mokalake 05.09.2009, interview)

African borderlands have been called "theatres of opportunity". This notion, coined by Nugent and Ajiwasu (1996), draws on the artificiality of African boundaries owing their existence to external colonial interests and their remoteness from urban centres of postcolonial authority. In the vacuum of state power, African borders display a variety of paradoxes: Instead of just representing physical barriers, they have functioned more as conduits for the circulation of people, animals, and goods (Nugent/ Ajiwasu 2010: 540). Some of these 'theatres of opportunity' were reshaped in the last decades in form of (trans)frontier conservation areas, particularly in Southern Africa. With this face-lift, new theatrical stages for organised tourism adventures at the African frontier have been created at the turn of the millennium. These border spaces are marketed and framed as the last remaining true wilderness enclaves, and ecotourism promises performances of ancient cultures in close encounters with primordial 'Wild Africa'.

Wholeheartedly embraced by international campaigns for species and climate protection, conservation of biological diversity, and poverty alleviation of 'borderlanders' or 'remote area dwellers', the intertwined offering of culture and nature has gained strong momentum. Indigenous cultures are currently 'for sale' much the same as wilderness reserves are trademarked. Both the cultures and the reinvented pristine landscapes are increasingly advertised as exhibits of the African frontier, to become readily consumed by (theatre) patrons. This phenomenon has come under a growing critique related to its 'neoliberal commodification'. Catchwords, such as "Ethnicity, Inc." and "Nature^{TM} Inc." were coined to address the problematic and questionable consequences of the emerging conservation-tourism-development nexus. They refer to a 'rewilding' or in the double sense 'bewildering' African frontier, which is perhaps not a new fabrication, but certainly one of unprecedented dimension.

The growing literature on the topic is thoroughly multi-disciplinary – involving natural and conservation sciences, political economy, geography or ecology, social anthropology, development studies and international relations – but rarely interdisciplinary. This volume, introduced in the following chapters, may only suggest more cross-disciplinary exchange. Its anthropological foundation, however, proposes a more meaningful inclusion of 'borderlanders'. That is the people living at and with these boundaries, which may be inter-state (national borders) or intra-state (confined nature reserves). In any case, local communities are restricted by physical limitations of external making. At the same time, they undeniably open up new opportunities for impoverished frontier populations. Thus, new bottom-up initiatives of *Community-Based Natural Resource Management* (CBNRM) may potentially extend the 'theatres of opportunity' for larger sectors of 'borderlanders'. Their empowerment provides the background for the empirical studies of an emerging economy of African borderlands conservation in this volume.

The objective of this introduction is three-fold: first, to provide some background information on how this volume came about; second, to offer an outline of the two main common themes behind the re-naturalisation or 'bewildering' of African borders, i.e. the relatively new participatory concepts of conservation, mostly labelled *Community-Based Natural Resource Management* and the current discourses regarding 'neoliberal conservation' as an (empty) promise of integrated environmental protection and development; third, an overview of contributions and research projects, which form the compilation of papers in this volume.

1 Background of "Bewildering Borders"

The early beginnings of this book date back to a truly bewildering experience. In February 2002, the editors Werner Zips and Manuela Zips-Mairitsch visited the

Central Kalahari Game Reserve (CKGR) in Botswana for the first time. Upon entering the Reserve through the Matswere gate in the North-East, we were told by the park authorities that we were not supposed to drive beyond Piper's Pan in the middle section, about 80 kilometres from Xade (the formal entry post to the reserve and village of a San community). The surprising response to our inquiring why, was: "[...] because of the traffic". Puzzled by this answer – the CKGR was then a rarely visited conservation area hardly developed for tourism – we asked for more information until we were eventually told that "the people" were currently being moved out of the park by trucks. Of course, we had heard of earlier resettlements of the last remaining human inhabitants of the Central Kalahari, namely the various San communities for whom the reserve was originally proclaimed by the British colonial power in 1961 (Botswana Tourism n.d., online).[1] But, we were under the impression that negotiations were still under way and that such drastic measures would not be undertaken by a *coup de main*. Consequently, we were quite disillusioned by the announcement of the CKGR park wardens that the Botswana authorities were indeed prepared to face the national and international uproar over the internal displacement of 'their' indigenous peoples.

1.1 Setting the Research Agenda

However, this disturbing experience of getting privileged access to one of the most fascinating 'wilderness' regions on earth, kept and protected for posterity by the original dwellers, while these very owners were removed against their free will and informed consent, gave rise to a number of further research activities: First of all, the ensuing legal struggle for the right to ownership of the Central Kalahari, denied by the Botswana government. The results were published in the book "Lost Lands? (Land) Rights of the San in Botswana and the Legal Concept of Indigeneity in Africa" (Zips-Mairitsch 2013). When the San plaintiffs finally won most matters of their various claims in their law suit in the *Botswana High Court* in 2006 and could legally return to their (ultimately not lost) lands, they found themselves left alone with most precarious means of survival. To date, they are denied the right to hunt or gather on the legal grounds of the Botswana Government's conservation regime. It is truly perplexing and a challenge for them to come to terms with the official legal reasoning that prohibits hunting in the game reserve

1 According to the Botswana government, the so-called "Kalahari Desert", or rather dry savanna, was mainly inhabited by G/wi (47%) and //Gana (15.3%) but also Tsira and Hai/nu San communities as well as the relatively sedentary Sotho-Tswana communities of the Bakgalagadi (37.2%) (Zips-Mairitsch 2013: 291-292).

when it was their ancestors who ensured the survival of game in the first place, as one may gather from the third quote of the preamble.

Secondly, the current situation of the 'inconvenient indigenous' (Saugestad 2001) in Botswana (and beyond) motivated the editors of this volume to continue investigating the practices and strategies of displacement, eviction, and exclusion so often attached to nature conservation initiatives (West/ Igoe/ Brockington 2006: 257-260; Fabricius/ de Wet 2008; DeGeorges/ Reilly 2009: 742; Brockington/ Igoe 2006). But, even more importantly, it implicitly encouraged us to look for alternative concepts and practical attempts to enable inclusiveness within a legal framework of integrated *Community-Based Natural Resource Management* (CBNRM) schemes during our numerous visits to borderlands in Southern Africa, namely Botswana, Mozambique, Namibia, and South Africa. Our empirical research over the course of two decades, often combined with documentary film projects for various television networks, focused comparatively on the *Transfrontier Conservation Areas* (hereafter TFCAs) of *Kgalagadi Transfrontier Park*, *Great Limpopo Transfrontier Park*, */Ai-/Ais Richtersveld Transfrontier Park*, the *Kavango-Zambezi Transfrontier Conservation Area*, the (proposed) *Limpopo/Shashe Transfrontier Conservation Area*, the *iSimangaliso Wetland Park* in South Africa and the *Mozambican Ponta do Ouro Marine Protected Area* (as part of the envisioned greater *Transnational Lubombo Area*), the *Central Kalahari Game Reserve*, as well as smaller conservation areas, such as the *Madikwe Game Reserve* and the *Tembe Elephant Park*.

Most of these national parks or game reserves are located in African borderlands. Nevertheless, even where they were not positioned at national borders, for instance in the case of the *Central Kalahari Game Reserve* (CKGR), the framework of borderland research still appears adequate because of their functional border regimes. Access and permissions for temporary visits and residence are regulated by state law and controlled by park officials, operating as border guards. Even the citizens of a particular national state, including the former indigenous inhabitants and owners, are subject to these regulations of control and exclusion. In our view, it is important to note, that nature reserves exhibit sufficient traits to be adequately treated as borderlands, even if they do not touch on any state border. It should suffice in this regard to take the huge entrance gates of the CKGR modelled on actual border posts as an illustrating example. Some of these parks' borders are architecturally more impressive than most 'real' border posts of the respective countries. Analogous to these national border posts, the pre-paid access permits are checked at park gates just like visas in passports. Thus, the park's *Wildlife Department* officials are authorised to deny access to anyone without proper permits, thereby excluding former inhabitants of proclaimed conservation areas. Conservation efforts were historically directed against the interests of local people. For the better part of a century (starting with the earliest manifestation of the *Yellowstone National Park* in 1872), the key global concept was the protection of nature against people (Nustad 2015: 26). Over the past three decades, these top-down approaches have been increasingly questioned and widely replaced by a reinvention of so-called 'inclusive' or 'integrated' conservation efforts that involve local populations. It is of key importance to assess this now mainstream discourse empirically in terms of its fulfillment of development and poverty alleviation goals (Igoe 2006: 72).

In Southern Africa, a widespread and by now seemingly well-established consensus among scholars and practitioners of conservation and biodiversity protection advocates that any sustainable form of conservation depends intricately on an adequate inclusion of local communities, traditional authorities, and civil society. Yet, many grand visions of people-driven conservation are successful only on paper. And, often enough, this paper did not even take the formal dress of law or legally enforceable agreements and compliant documents. Perhaps similar to policies of *Black Economic Empowerment* in post-apartheid South Africa, participatory conservation empowerment lacks institutionalised guarantees. In this situation, window-dressings of equitable social and economic relations persist as order of the day. People-centred biodiversity conservation projects rarely stand the test against hegemonic realities on the ground (Igoe 2006: 72 pp.).

However, conservation ranks high on the agenda of sustainable development goals in Namibia, Botswana, and South Africa, which receive special attention in this book. Although it remains open to debate if post-colonial nature conservation in Southern Africa employs the same emperors in new clothes (Singh/ van Houtum 2002). Successful attempts to include communities in nature conservation practices appear quite exceptional if the growing literature on the social impact of so-called 'neoliberal conservation' is to be trusted in this regard (Igoe/ Brockington 2007: 445 pp.). Within a comparative framework, the Southern African countries referred to above seem to fare better in the realm of integrated or inclusive conservation. The papers in this volume will examine, if some models provide benchmarks for improvement and the further development of at least more sustainable initiatives, coined "Vital Alternatives" (with capital initial letters) by Dressler, Büscher, and Fletcher (2014: 250-253).

1.2 West Africa's Negligence of Conservation

West Africa, in contrast, has widely neglected the issue of conservation altogether. Political instability, widespread corruption, and limited interest in tourism development are among the main factors stated for the current disastrous West African conservation record (Adams 2004: 210, 231). Consequently, many states appear to be heading towards forfeiting their natural heritage once and for all. Elephants and lions will in all likelihood only show up as brands for national soccer teams such as the Ivory Coast "Elephants" or the "Indomitable Lions" of Cameroon. In the wild, both species appear on the brink of extinction in both countries. Their habitats are severely threatened, which makes future attempts of rewilding rather pointless.

Another regional example may illustrate one of a multitude of reasons for habitat loss and local species extinction: On many trips to the *Mole National Park* in northern Ghana (between 1994 and 2005), we learned about the complete lack of vehicles to control the park borders and patrol its interior to prevent poaching. 'Walking safaris' with armed rangers, conducted within the immediate vicinity of the single existing lodge and the *Park Rangers Headquarters*, were the only means of monitoring wildlife resources. During some full-day walking safaris we encountered traces of poaching everywhere, all in close proximity of the authorities. On the occasion of a few visits to the *Wildlife Department* (of the *Ghanaian Ministry of Lands and Forestry*) in the capital Accra, we found the parking lot full of four-wheel drive vehicles, usually donated by European donor agencies, as one could easily detect from the huge stickers on the cars' doors. Mole is one of the few protected areas in West Africa that still boasts a fairly great number of elephants and other big game, although lions are critically endangered, if not extinct (IUCN 2018: 6).[2] The lions' habitat in West Africa has decreased to about one percent of its original size, which attests to the dire conservation status of lions in West Africa (cf. Henschel et al. 2014; Henschel/ Hunter 2014).

It is much less the concern for natural habitats or wild animals that instigates conservation activities in the borderlands but cross-border social relations that

---

[2] The mission statement released by the *Ministry of Lands and Resources* (the successor to the earlier *Ministry of Lands and Forestry*) in the Ghana *Forestry Development Masterplan* (2016-2036) seems to have come to grips with the devastating biodiversity protection but may be (too) late for lions and other endangered species: "In supporting the development of the wildlife based industries, the FDMP will seek to build partnerships to promote the development of the wildlife based industries. It will enforce the ban on hunting and capturing of all protected wildlife species in Ghana whilst re-establishing the control over bushmeat hunting to bring these activities to a sustainable level" (Ministry of Lands and Resources 2016: 84).

appear 'bewildering' because of ongoing conflicts and a host of illegal activities. In this context, nature protection and even wildlife reintroduction projects, with their potential generation of ecotourism benefits, are increasingly considered as possible remedies against illegal cross-border trade and other informal economies in troubled borderlands, besides the machinations of militia groups. At least the idea of peaceful regional integration through the means of transfrontier conservation has been acknowledged by the *African Union Border Programme* (thereafter AUBP) and the *Economic Community of West African States* (thereafter ECOWAS) as an adequate policy to conform to the key vision of both organisations. For the AUBP (2017, online), the vision is quite obvious in this regard: "A united and integrated Africa with peaceful, open and prosperous borders." It is, however, likewise evident that the implementation of the AUBP, initiated in 2010, had other priorities than transfrontier conservation. This view is evidenced by the justification for the establishment of the AUBP paying little, if any, attention to conservation. Various other key incentives for the border programme are emphasised in lieu thereof:

> "To address the problems posed by the lack of delimitation and demarcation, which gives rise to 'undefined zones', within which the application of national sovereignty poses problems, and constitutes a real obstacle to the deepening of the integration process; To address cross-border criminal activities through pragmatic border management; To consolidate the gains made in the regional integration process, as demonstrated by the existence of the Regional Economic Communities (RECs) and of numerous large-scale cooperation initiatives; and: To facilitate the development of cross-border integration dynamics, which are sustained by local stakeholders." (ibid.)

From this statement, one may be tempted to conclude that it is the making of borders that appeals to the *African Union Border Programme* rather than the un-making targeted by the transfrontier conservation and/or peace parks' vision. However, the mission statement of the AUBP (ibid.) at least allows for alternative thinking: "The prevention and resolution of border-related disputes and the promotion of regional and continental integration, which constitutes a tool in the structural prevention of conflicts in Africa."

Regional integration was also the key objective behind the creation of ECOWAS in 1975. In its foundational treaty of 1975 (revised in 2015), "conservation of the environment" is at least mentioned once, in Article 27 (ECOWAS 2015: 19). Development on a decisive economic footing is, however, the main agenda, as stipulated in the *Vision 2020*:

"The idea is to make the ECOWAS Vision 2020 a people's document and make both the region's integration and development process people-centred and people-driven. This paradigm shift in attitudes and institutional orientation is vital if the region is to create an environment in which the business community and the general public will have a shared vision and work together to realize the development aspirations of the people and achieve equitable and broad-based growth, sustainable development and poverty eradication." (ECOWAS n.d., online)

This passage may stand *pars pro toto* for many analogous policy documents on development visions for Africa. Many mission statements and master plans use a vocabulary emphasising 'people-centred' and 'people-driven' development to invite private investors through the front door. 'Conservation for the sake of conservation' seems almost non-existent. We read this as a reminder that the so-called 'neoliberal' agenda for conservation in the majority of African contexts is formulated and implemented on the basis of prior governance instruments that provide the framework for environmental policies. Conservation governance thus emerges within ambivalent auspices, partly complying to predetermined economic prerogatives, partly struggling to establish space for manoeuvers against development expectations, but nevertheless attracting most of the blame (cf. Büscher 2013; Büscher et al. 2012; Brockington et al. 2008; Brockington/ Duffy 2011; Igoe et al. 2009).

Considering the comparative context this book sought to portray, the poor conservation record of many West African states affords a contrasting background for the remarkable transfrontier conservation efforts in Southern Africa (Henschel et al. 2014). These tend to get washed aside by a now popular anthropocentric critique of conservation by a growing number of social and political scientists. The sincere involvement of local people is of utmost importance on all accounts but should not create a false antinomy to the urgent protection of habitats, biodiversity, and wildlife. Since this volume dedicates a lot of space to the critique of 'neoliberal conservation' and development, apparent recent achievements, for instance in Namibia and South Africa, need to be emphasised on par, where- and whenever factual. Botswana, as the third country on the southern tip of the continent, justifiably boasts an exceptional conservation record since independence in 1966. More than 17 percent of Botswana's landmass is set aside for national parks and game reserves, which amounts to the highest percentage in Africa, and a further 20 percent are protected in the form of wildlife management areas. By employing a high-income, low-volume tourism policy, Botswana may be seen not only as a forerunner in biodiversity protection but also for ecotourism involving local communities (Maude/ Reading 2010: 109). During the last decade, the commodification of 'wilderness' areas has gained strong momentum, sometimes against the interests of indigenous people such as the San, in order to diversify the prevalent mining and cattle-farming economies. In unison with Namibia and South Africa, as mentioned above, Botswana stands at the forefront of transfrontier conservation initiatives, which are pursued in the region, not least for their projected contributions to regional integration and economic development through ecotourism.

It is no coincidence that West African national and regional organisations have recently been inspired by the establishment of transboundary conservation areas and transfrontier parks in Southern Africa (as Paul Nugent also notes for Senegal and Gambia, in this volume). Participatory environmental governance and resource management, including wildlife, forms an imperative beyond the window-dressing used in elitist development cooperation discourse by both parties, the donors and recipients (Hasselskog/ Schierenbeck 2017: 323 pp.). It, thus, needs theoretical parameters for meaningful assessments of community participation in the entire process starting from opinion-and will-formation to the informed, facts-based decision-making, and finally the implementation of consented strategies and policies.

2 Participatory Concepts of Nature Conservation: Some Theoretical Remarks

Effective participation and, perhaps most importantly, legal guarantees to secure land rights and access to adequate benefits from natural resources should be taken into account as key elements for a sound democratic basis of conservation governance. Inclusive procedures, according to discourse ethics, refer to rational decision-making based on argumentative plausibility and persuasion. Such a (procedural) parameter allows assessment of the entire process of consensus building. This procedural critical approach builds on discourse ethics (Habermas 1996; cf. Zips/ Weilenmann 2011: 15-18) to question the legitimation of actual conservation politics. It agrees with the now common critique of 'neoliberal conservation' governance as coalescing around dynamics of consensus, anti-politics, and marketing (Büscher 2013: xiii). Nevertheless, it aims to shift that critique to the procedural level of (ideally) unconstrained arenas of participatory nature conservation governance. Wherever absent in varying degrees the counterfactual paradigm sues for improved information of all concerned, adequate transparency, and discursive fora of opinion- and will-formation as a prerequisite for informed, facts-based decision-making. Therefore, a discourse-ethical parameter disagrees with the mere framing of 'neoliberal conservation' and aims to boost the rational involvement of local actors. This may be viewed as a pre-condition for the imperative of 'taking ownership', frequently invoked in developmental policies and their implementation strategies (cf. Hasselskog/ Schierenbeck 2017: 330).[3] It could also encourage a feasible change from marginalisation policies that lead to local passivity and indifference. The latter has been coined "anti-politics" or erasure of power (Ferguson 1990; Büscher 2010: 272; Wilshusen 2014: 148; cf. Taylor 2000: 238-274).

Within the critique of 'neoliberal conservation', anti-politics refers to the denial of politics, which is defined as the mediation and contestation of different interests and power struggles (Büscher 2013: 20). Sophisticated means of buying communities into acquiescence are rightly considered anti-political or anti-democratic, for that reason. The dissimulation of inequalities couched in the euphemist discourse of enabling conditions for a win-win conservation economy leads, indeed, to an erasure or camouflage of power relations (Wilshusen 2014: 153-155). But, consensus may be assessed critically on the basis of the procedural paradigm. The latter refers to an unconstrained discourse of opinion- and will-formation, potentially culminating in an informed decision based on argumentative persuasion (Habermas 1996: 107, 440).

In this way, it may be distinguished from the mere co-option of local communities, which is frequently misrepresented as free and informed consensus by policy-makers. The politics of top-down, market-based conservation draw legitimation from the marketing of such pretended inclusive arrangements of community-based conservation. This induced legitimacy, acceptance, and ownership can be contested empirically. Critical theory questions the existing power relations and differs in this respect from problem-solving theory (Ford 2003: 121; Büscher 2013: xiii). In this sense, restrictions and barriers to a meaningful participation of all concerned, particularly the immediately affected people living in or adjacent to conservation areas, are deemed truly 'bewildering' by critical discourse theory.[4] Therefore, it requires a change in the organisational structure of

[3] Discourse ethics focus on deliberative procedures based on the notion of communicative rationality and are, therefore, critical to the governmental recourse on mere formal procedures as highlighted by Hasselskog and Schierenbeck (2017: 327 pp.) for international development cooperation: "[T]he ownership ideal itself tends to guide aid to a great extent, and thus risks becoming more important than the actual contents of the aid. In addition, the heavy focus on form rather than content has resulted in recipient governments formulating programmes and policies according to required procedures with the aim to receive funding."

[4] For a detailed outline of critical discourse theory in relation to legal processes of decision-making, see Habermas (1996).

conservation agencies to turn local residents from subjects to partners, as Adams (2004: 213) maintains.

The most prevalent impediments to participation manifest as 'bewildering borders' for democratic self-determination. Such discursive obstacles reveal a tension between democratic participation as well as economic empowerment of local communities and the conservationist agenda of 'bewildering borders' through the reintroduction of wild animals in borderland nature reserves. Arguably, a profound structural and institutional change is necessary to intertwine conservation with democratisation. An emerging inclusive paradigm needs to process the conservation of natural resources, biodiversity, and entire biomes parallel to the discursive inclusion of those affected during the entire project planning and implementation. Without entirely dismantling the critique of 'neoliberal conservation', a discourse-ethical approach aims at a constructive engagement specifying and partly replacing the somewhat abstract condemnation of the obvious: the commodification, marketisation, and privatisation of conservation (cf. Fletcher/ Dressler/ Büscher 2014: 6). In this respect, reservations against the unspecified over-use of condemnatory words such as neoliberal, neoliberalism, and neoliberalisation appear reasonably justified. Particularly, as the precise meaning, the economic and social interests, as well as the mechanisms and effects circumscribed by these words are seldom adequately articulated, as Harding (2007: 455) bemoans in a different context: "In the absence of such clarity, the danger is that they continue to be used as catch-all terms of abuse by 'progressive' critics rather than concepts that are useful to empirical research."

An assessment of power relations in environmental politics, however, may not only focus on neoliberal or any other forceful structures of implementation but on these actual procedures of decision-making. In this view, the procedural costs (of time and energy) invested in consensus building on the basis of communicative opinion- and will-formation allow to measure the legitimacy of a political decision. Communicative rationality, seen as the procedure of meaningful political participation, is thus based on the critical parameter of an ideal pressure- and dominance-free speech situation (Habermas 1996: 107, 169-171). Through such a procedural paradigm, proclaimed *Community-Based Natural Resource Management* arrangements can be challenged on the discursive level. Ethnographically, this empirical approach means to ask for the communicative shares in conservation politics. Has an asserted communal consensus truly been based on the best reasons backed by arguments or merely induced by hierarchical and hegemonic practices? Such a critical analysis, it seems to us, lingers currently in the shadow of an all too self-evident and perhaps self-righteous broadside against 'the neoliberal conservationist' strawman, who appears pretty unimpressed by the blame of promoting the free market anyway.

3 Debating the Discourse of 'Neoliberal Conservation'

During the past decades, the model of biodiversity conservation in isolation of human disturbance, often labelled "fortress conservation" (Doolittle 2007: 704; cf. Adams 2003: 42), has come under increasing scrutiny for manifold reasons as discussed on empirical grounds in this volume (cf. Adams/ Hulme 2001: 10; Adams 2003: 42; Brockington 2002; Collet 1989: 144). A variety of factors contributed to a favourable environment for new inclusive conservation frameworks and (to a lesser extent) their respective practical implementations, namely recent developments in human rights, particularly the *UN Declaration on the Rights of Indigenous Peoples* (2007), the alleged governance strategies of democratisation, social, and economic transformation, as well as policies directed towards poverty alleviation. The related legal and political initiatives received various labels, such as "community-based natural resource management, community-based conservation, sustainable development and use, grassroots conservation and integrated conservation and development programmes" (Nustad 2015: 29).

The film and research projects referred to above, allowed us to interview a considerable number of beneficiaries in various designated areas for community-oriented conservation. Their first-hand experiences were, more often than not, no exception to the general discontent, disappointment, and frustration of local community members reported by empirical social science research on African conservation areas and beyond (discussed in great detail by the contributors to this volume). Yet, we are unable to recall a single formal interview or informal conversation, in which local residents living in or adjacent to a conservation area expressed the wish to have the legal protection of said area revoked. The main concern was less the alternative use of land for perhaps more viable forms of economic ventures but rather the augmentation of benefits for those residents directly affected. One important demand requested a strengthening of participation in all decisions with a special focus on what should be done to make conservation work for local populations (cf. Craig/ Davis 2005: 49-52).

Against these legitimate concerns, a rising number of academic critics from various disciplines appear to attack conservation as such for its presumably inherent capitalist alignment. In other words, for the relentless efforts of conservationists on the ground to 'sell' the agenda to national and global decision makers, who still rarely pay attention to the needs of biodiversity concerns, including the entire flora and fauna. Rhinos, cheetahs, wattled cranes, loggerheads (sea turtles), or fynbos are hardly ever referred to in the social science literature on conservation. We believe that in part this critique is not constructive enough to assist conservationists to swim against these strong currents. Quite aware of the inherent contradictions involved in the integration of conservation and development, we still reckon that conservation is getting a sweeping blow for the much larger economic forces it is susceptible to, just like so many – if not all – other fields of governance. The derogative label of 'neoliberal conservation' (Büscher 2013) may correctly target underlying processes of commodification that are quite obvious and incidentally acknowledged in most official contemporary conservation programmes. But, the self-explaining use of the label tends to reify the entire agenda into a strawman that perhaps unintentionally functions to identify conservation as the problem. It results in a deprecative view of conservation as almost inherently detrimental to social progress and liberation from exploitative structures.

The critique of 'neoliberal conservation', in our view, thereby abbreviates the critical analysis on several levels. First of all, it fails to pay sufficient attention to the on-going legal and political struggles in the local arena, including protests, negotiations, and various forms of passive and active resistance. Therefore, the potential local beneficiaries of conservation are not taken seriously enough, against the grain of the critique in favour of 'the people'. Secondly, the empirical time frame is often too narrow or consists of short-term observations. Such tempocentrism fails to concede enough time for the actual realisation of the proclaimed aims for inclusive conservation. This is less a matter of unfairness than of limited scope. Tempocentric critiques typically fall short to sue the powerful private and public sector selling conservation to civil society for the realisation of the projected future benefits from wildlife tourism development for a province, a particular state, or even for an entire region. Thirdly, the burning issues of protection of endangered species and biodiversity through preservation or recovery of suitable habitats that enable natural game behaviour become concealed behind anthropocentric motives. In effect, local stakeholders are positioned in opposition to the potentials of ecotourism, while a balanced empirical perspective should not overlook possible gains in democratic participation, self-determination, and economic benefits by overtly concentrating on the undeniable insecurities and inequities. Finally, comparative studies that aim to investigate best practices in search of the afore-mentioned "Vital Alternatives" are, for the most part, notably absent from the literature on 'neoliberal conservation'. The latter manifests itself in vague and all-too-fleeting remarks in standard works (cf. Büscher 2013: 228-232; Dressler/ Büscher/ Fletcher 2014: 250-253; Igoe/ Brockington 2006: 445 pp.).

A sound multi-disciplinary critique of current shortcomings of conservation initiatives for communities living in or adjacent to nature reserves might, however, meaningfully contribute to holding national and transnational agencies accountable for their often enough vain promises of development and empowerment. As is, the broad-brush indictment of so-called 'neoliberal conservation' fails to answer the following questions: How could the installation of conservation zones – transfrontier or not – improve the lives of large numbers of people within a short period of time? And could any other form of resource use – be it mining, commercial hunting, fishing, or agriculture – achieve such results, let alone sustainable results? The bashing of a conceived strawman of 'neoliberal conservation' may contribute to the authors' good conscience and well-being but in which way does it support the relentless and insubordinate efforts of those concerned and affected to take part in the decision-making and implementation of socially inclusive conservation in a meaningful way? And does it afford justice to conservation agencies and individual conservationists on the ground, who dedicate their professional commitment and a lot of compassion to make conservation work, not only for the natural but also the social environment – more often than not against the current of neoliberal control (or 'evaluation') mechanisms and imposed free market regimes?[5] These are some of the questions this volume seeks to address. Therefore, the individual chapters are thoroughly practice-oriented. Their common (praxeological) aim is to focus primarily on the actors and their practices within an emerging economy of conservation (cf. Bourdieu 1977).

From such a theoretical perspective, the responses of local communities and individual actors cover a wide range of attitudes or dispositions – from subordinate to resilient and ultimately resistant. On the one hand, the relational approach of a general economy of interests focuses on the objective power relations in the field of ('neoliberal') conservation. On the other hand, it investigates the generative, or even creative, capacity of the less powerful to have their interests not only heard but also respected and safeguarded within a reasonable time frame. It builds on concepts, such as habitus, the distribution of various forms of capital, and the historically accumulated divergent interests of local actors, to emphasise power

5 This closer examination differs from the defence strategies of self-ascribed green economists. Their charges of bias against critics may use similar claims for more constructiveness and fairness but this does not render such research standards spurious. Igoe's (2006: 76) attempt of self-immunisation (against criticism) does not release the eligible critical attitude towards conservation in general from equally well-established principles of academic impartiality. We, therefore, reiterate the need for constructive comparisons as a precondition to deconstruct the marketing lingua employed in the window-dressing of 'inclusive conservation'.

relations that are often enough partially unrecognised or misrecognised by less powerful actors. But, praxeology also uses ethnographic methods to unveil their conscious efforts to grapple with neoliberal capitalism and the superior powers behind the venture of the so-called "green economy" (cf. Wilshusen 2014: 127). In this sense, the potential of habitus as an *ars inveniendi* (constructed against mechanist social theory) shall be unfolded (cf. Bourdieu/ Wacquant 1992: 122). For this reason, the contributions build on ethnographic research in various African countries.

So-called 'neoliberal conservation', according to its critics, functions merely as a "green washing" strategy for capitalist accumulation (Büscher/ Fletcher 2015) or even as an integral part of neoliberal capitalism, thus turning conservationists into unwitting (secret) agents or even brokers of capital accumulation (Brockington et al. 2008). The critique challenges "[. . .] neoliberal conservation as an amalgamation of *ideology and techniques* informed by the premise that natures can only be 'saved' through their submission and its subsequent revaluation in capitalist terms" (Büscher et al. 2012: 4). As frustrating as the dominant imperative of 'if it pays, it stays' and its underlying assumption to 'save nature by selling it' may be for a critical political economy, a relational approach to conservation needs to account for 'indigenous and local' communities as well as conservationists on the ground (Adams 2004: 215 pp.; cf. Sullivan 2006: 128). If it takes the well-established interests of conservation seriously, it should also include the biopolitics of biodiversity protection and wildlife management. After all, it is quite a realistic scenario that even iconic animals such as lions, gorillas, and rhinos may not survive the 21st century as species living in the wild (cf. Adams 2004: 239 p.).[6]

The important praxeological dictum "the real is the relational" (Bourdieu/ Wacquant 1992: 97) defines a social field as a network, or a configuration of objective relations between positions. But the habitus (or cluster of dispositions) of individual actors does not function as a mechanistic habit to merely adapt to the given power structures, but evolves as a "[. . .] generative (if not creative) capacity inscribed in the system of dispositions as an *art*, in the strongest sense of practi-

6 As mentioned above, one of the most iconic African species, the lion, has disappeared in most of its former range throughout Africa (IUCN 2018; cf. Packer 2015: 296-300; Loveridge 2018: 252-263). To provide just another recent example: The last male Northern White Rhino died in March 2018 in a Kenyan conservancy. Poor conservation efforts and conflicts in Chad, Sudan, Uganda, Congo, and Central African Republic, some of the countries of its former habitat, were held responsible for the demise of the sub-species from a population of 2000 in the 1960s to its imminent extinction (Odula 2018).

cal mastery, and in particular as an *ars inveniendi*" (ibid.: 122). A praxeological theory seeks to escape the choice between objectivism and subjectivism. Therefore, it is hardly helpful to proclaim the less powerful actors (e.g. indigenous and local communities) in conservation governance as mere henchmen of corporate neoliberal conservation.[7] In this regard, it appears equally important to investigate the internal relations between divergent sets of conservationists (cf. Nustad 2015: 164-169).

If the self-identification of conservationists as progressive protectors of wildlife and biodiversity is deconstructed too unanimously, it fosters the danger of yet another inversion of perpetrator and victim (ibid.: 164).[8] Diversity is in dire need of a (relational) defence that includes and focuses on the relations of local communities to the environment, to conservation actors on all levels of environmental governance, and to their potential business partners for the marketing of the material and immaterial goods at their disposal (Comaroff/ Comaroff 2009: 139; Salomon et al. 2018). Instead of throwing resources into the hopeless task of developing increasingly rigid protection regimes, conservationists have begun to work with the economic, social, and cultural pressures that drive human consumption of wildlife and other natural resources (Adams 2004: 216). Therefore, this book reviews novel governance strategies of cooperation with local residents to find sustainable ways to derive benefits from species and ecosystems. Various multi-level and multi-sphere initiatives of conservation governance seek to overcome the dichotomy of strict preservation (coined 'fortress conservation') and the utilitarian imperative of 'use it or lose it'. Since ultimately, those wild species used, for instance in West Africa's extensive 'bushmeat trade', dissipate (Adams 2004: 215). These recent trends in environmental management are largely ignored or played down by the framing of neoliberal conservation (van der Duim et al. 2015: 4-10).

The critique of the presumed neoliberal hi-jacking of conservation, on the one hand, justifiably condemns 'green developmentalism' for creating the myth that the planet might be saved by the same unsustainable economic trajectories responsible for the severe degradation of biological diversity. On the other hand, it wantonly neglects or underrates local agency that more often than not plays havoc

7 The power of neoliberal capitalism is not specific to the field of conservation. After all, neoliberal imperatives have an impact on almost all social fields, not least on academia, where strategic career planning demands subordination to competitive publishing in high-rated journals (and many other forms of commodification, or even sell-out to external funding agencies).

8 The same may be said for the denunciation of the struggle for the recognition of indigenous rights as a "return of the native" (Kuper 2003; cf. Zips 2006: 28).

with unconsented and imposed conservation regimes. A conservation industry, oblivious to local people and their traditional authorities, likely faces fierce opposition, even if backed by state parties. It stands to encounter various forms of civil disobedience right up to acts of physical obstruction (e.g. against fences), and, most frequently, out-of-hand poaching. If diversity's chance of survival depends upon calculation of the prices for which it is sold to ecotourism, timber, oil, and mining companies, researchers, or pharmaceutical firms, then it is doomed, as McAfee (1999: 151) reminds us. Therefore, the focus, according to her, needs to shift from the top-down level to the bottom-up, i.e. the interactions of people on the ground with the global market:

> "Inevitably, as 'indigenous and local' communities interact with the world beyond the local, many will seek access to wider markets and 'Western' knowledge and technology. Whether these processes necessarily lead to major diversity losses depends upon the terms on which they take place: those of local peoples, or those of the 'globalized' market. The greater the political autonomy, access to information, and economic self-reliance of local and indigenous communities, the more likely it is that they will be able to influence these terms, and to adopt and invent mixes of old and new cultural forms and technologies that work with nature instead of at nature's expense." (McAfee 1999: 151)

In our view, this approach provides a parameter to evaluate integrated conservation and development initiatives as well as to pay close attention to the undeniable, intricate marketing strategies of greenwashing, exploitation of nature and people as 'ecological services', or 'ecological economics' (Nustad 2015: 165). The relational approach targets the age-old dichotomy between nature and culture to review the historically accumulated processes of inclusion and exclusion. Therefore, one of the main aims of this volume (and the various projects leading up to it) is to question CBNRM initiatives for their (lacking) communicative and institutional involvement of communities in order to establish empirical links between ecological sustainability, social justice, and economic empowerment.[9] This approach makes it imperative to examine the extent of conservation and development programmes that are really based on the (participation of) local communities, rather than imposed on them. The key task is less about the opposition between inclusion and exclusion, as most projects and governance strategies claim to be inclusive, but rather about the various levels of qualitative parameters for 'inclusion'. Meanwhile there is widespread consent among conservationists that the success of en-

---

9 Intra-community tensions, as for instance described by Robins (2001: 842), for the case of the Khomani San in South Africa are considered as common features of all political entities, and thus by no means denied by the outlined paradigm. Rather, the same discursive paradigm may be used to assess their eventual deliberative resolution.

vironmental policies depends on the motivation and volition of the communities living in and from the environment. And this correlates with their unrestrained inclusion in the public discourse as the key requisite of communicative rationality in democratic decision-making:

> "As a formation of opinion *and* will, public discourse is not merely a cognitive exercise but mobilizes reasons and arguments that draw on citizens' interests, values and identities. Political discourse thus brings in the citizens' actual sources of motivation and volition. It thereby generates a 'communicative power' that has a real impact on the formal decision making and action that represent the final institutional expressions of political 'will'." (Rehg 1996: xxviii)

A political economy of conservation, in this sense, asks about the recognition of local environmental knowledge, the respect for divergent histories and cultural concepts of authority, and of due process in opinion- and will-formation. This approach goes beyond the livelihood goals of local communities and borderland or frontier residents. Thus, community-based conservation is not just about the trickle-down of visible economic benefits to the broader population, which of course has become an important subject for the conservation policies of many African countries. Local involvement even transcends the important questions of distributive justice; in particular, how some of the new integrated and inclusive governance idioms attempt to lure away from the considerable benefits of the powerful and wealthy and the small crumbles left for the historically disadvantaged. The real crux for a sustainable economy of conservation, for both people and nature, lies in its democratic empowerment from below, not from above, as McAfee (1999: 152) plausibly argued two decades ago:

> "The conservation and sustainable use of biological diversity requires not only global plans and scientific priorities, but also a multiplicity of site-specific, information-intensive technologies relying heavily on inputs of local intelligence and planning to meet local and national needs. Further, strategies to save diversity must derive not only from assessments of economists, ecologists, and conservation biologists, but also from the economic and cultural importance of natural resources to the people who gather, farm, fish, hunt, worship, and otherwise live in direct interdependence with those resources, and who often have the most direct and longest-term interest in their conservation. At the same time, defenders of diversity at all levels must confront the larger political-economic trends that underlie its destruction, and the specific agents and beneficiaries of that destruction."

Abstract convictions deeming pretty much all conservation as (nothing but) neoliberal, in our view, tend to identify 'the market', or more precisely the utilisation of market-conscious environmental policies, as the problem. In some sense, the critique mirrors the (imperative) 'elevation of the market' within neoliberalism discourse in reverse, as the all-determinative evil. Thereby sacrificing valid concerns of local populations on the theoretical level of analysis. There is more than enough evidence that market forces have found their way into conservation to a degree unimaginable only a decade ago, triggered by a recess of public funding and a growing reliance on the private sector to make up for the shortfall, as Fletcher, Dressler, and Büscher (2014: 4) assert in the introduction to "Nature™ Inc.". But an economist reading of these processes of neoliberalisation eclipse the political arena of contestation. If utilising the tourism market to finance conservation efforts is turned into the problem, then the question, if and how local populations may benefit from it or organise on their own behalf, becomes obsolete. In this sense, the critique of the critical literature on neoliberalism, advanced in the context of urban studies, may apply to environmental issues, as well:

> "The elevation of the market over other modes of organization, its extension into other (or all) areas of social life, and a preference for free markets are certainly characteristics of neoliberalism, but they are the ones shared with broader pro-market stance. These principles each find a particularly radical and robust expression in neoliberal arguments, but they are not specific enough to identify neoliberalism as a circumscribed ensemble of theory and practice." (Palumbo/ Scott 2018: 2)

According to Palumbo and Scott (ibid.), the identification of neoliberalisation policies with the elevation/affirmation of free markets conflates neoliberalism's practices and policies with its intellectual self-understanding, thereby weakening its analytical usefulness. If the notion of "neoliberal" (conservation) is overgeneralised as a "sloppy synonym for capitalism itself, or as a shorthand for the world economy and its inequalities" (Ferguson 2009: 171), the critique indeed creates a strawman ready to be blamed for all possible failures. Perhaps its greatest shortcoming resides in the marginalisation of local agency against the factual constraints created by a global economy based on greed and maximisation of profits at any social and environmental costs.

While a systematic treatise of neoliberalism and its critique falls way beyond the scope of this volume, the prevalence of this analytic concept in the recent literature on conservation and development makes a discussion of its key assumptions on the ground of comparative empirical data indispensable. One of the main objectives of this book is precisely the focus on the agency of those concerned and affected by so-called 'neoliberal conservation'. This perspective includes attention not only to the defining characteristics of neoliberalism in actual conservation policies, strategies, and measures reordering the biophysical environment (cf. Castree 2010a) but also to apprehend possible counter-currents, for instance in social transformation policies, such as *Black Economic Empowerment* in South Africa, communal conservancies in Namibia, or the struggle of San communities in Botswana for their share in resource utilisation through tourism.

4 Short Overview of the three Parts of this Volume and their Research Background

The volume represents a collection of the results from three related research projects, initiated by the editors between 2013 and 2018, on the developmental economy of conservation in Africa. Its subdivision into three thematic sections corresponds to these origins in research, two of which derived from collaborative efforts with two separate teams of postgraduate researchers from the Department of Social and Cultural Anthropology at the University of Vienna. Both research projects happened within the framework of field practices, an important component of the postgraduate curriculum. The first included 18 postgraduate students spending a period of three weeks in January 2014 in northern Namibia, mainly in two locations: the N#a Jaqna and the Nyae Nyae conservancies. The second involved nine postgraduates for a period of four weeks in May/June 2016. It focused on various areas of the *iSimangaliso Wetland Park* in eastern South Africa. The third volume pillar emerged from the participation of the editors in the *African Borderlands Research Network* (ABORNE), a network started in 2009 and funded for five years by the European Science Foundation (until 2014).[10]

Part I of this book builds on the overall theme of the first field practice: *Life in a Living Museum – Conservation and Cultural Marketing in the Borderlands of Namibia and Botswana.* It contains one introductory chapter to the overall theme by the editors of this volume, two papers of field practice participants, namely Salomé Ritterband and Alicja Khatchikian, selected for this publication, and a detailed chapter by Robert K. Hitchcock, who had been involved in the establishment of the first Namibian conservancy and revisits its progress after more than two decades within a comparative framework to the governance of indigenous San communities in neighbouring Botswana.

Part II on the *"Wild Frontier" – Transnational Conservation and Resource Governance in West African Borderlands* contains two chapters from a workshop of the *African Borderlands Research Network* (ABORNE) organised by the volume editors in September 2013 at the University of Vienna. The contributions, written

[10] The latter forms the middle section of the book for content-related reasons.

by Paul Nugent and William Miles, deal with borderlands in West Africa (Senegal, Gambia and Nigeria, Niger) and, therefore, offer a comparative frame for the other empirical examples from Southern Africa.

Part III derives from the second field practice (mentioned above) that took place in May/June 2016 in the coastal region of South Africa. The theme of the research undertaking forms the topic of this third section: *iSimangaliso Wetland Park: South Africa's New Governance Model of Conservation and Development.* It offers a selection of five papers by participants of this field practice, namely Jennifer Kelleher, Christian Sterkl, Tibor Böhm, Patrick Cassidy, and Georg Bergthaler. Their results are discussed, summarised, and broadened to the perspectives of biodiversity conservation, wildlife management, empowerment, and education by a final chapter of the volume editors and organisers of the field practice.

In the following chapters of this introduction, we give a short overview on these three topics by paying close attention to the overall theme of 'bewildering African borders' in the name of an ever-emerging economy of conservation.

4.1 Life in a Living Museum – Conservation and Cultural Marketing in the Borderlands of Namibia and Botswana

All four papers in the first section of the book take a thorough look at the two largest conservancies in the district of Otjozondjupa in north-western Namibia, the Nyae Nyae and the neighbouring N≠a Jaqna conservancy. Both became prominent for a variety of reasons: They are run by San communities, who use a communal conservation scheme to market their cultural traits, including their hunting and gathering skills, to national, regional, and international tourists. They exploit the cultural economics of indigeneity for their livelihood and they experiment with lifeworld museums and cultural villages as stages for their performances.[11] In this sense, they offer a test case for the growing capitalisation of culture coined "Ethnicity, Inc." by Jean and John Comaroff (2009). The Nyae Nyae conservancy was the first of its kind and, therefore, provides one possible example for most follow-up projects in the Namibian border regions of Botswana, Angola, and South Africa.[12]

[11] It should be noted in this respect that cultural economics capitalising on preconceived notions of a primordial indigeneity form an uneasy alliance with empowering struggles for rights, among which intellectual property rights are but one item on the extensive list of indigenous rights formulated by the *United Nations Declaration on the Rights of Indigenous Peoples* (UNDRIP), adopted on 13 September 2007 (cf. Zips-Mairitsch 2013: 42-135).

[12] Since the content of this section is discussed in great detail in the first chapter to Part I (by

In the first chapter, the editors of this volume, **Manuela Zips-Mairitsch** and **Werner Zips**, offer a contextual introduction to this section and overview of the divergent concepts of borderland conservation in Namibia and Botswana. In particular, the chapter looks at how the Ju/'hoansi of Nyae Nyae and other San communities of the N≠a Jaqna conservancy have arguably commenced to rule their own destiny by positioning themselves in the 'modern world' instead of at its margins, as argued by Hitchcock and Biesele (2002).

In his contribution to this volume, **Robert Hitchcock** has an in-depth look at the divergent approaches of conservancies in Namibia and Botswana and the San communities' empowerment regarding conservation governance. The indigenous peoples of Southern Africa, including the Ju/'hoansi San of north-eastern Namibia and north-western Botswana, have been involved in ecotourism and heritage tourism activities since the 1970s. As global tourism and funding for tourism-related development expanded in the late 20th century and the new millennium, the opportunities for Ju/'hoansi and other groups to engage in tourism activities increased considerably. Various kinds of tourism programmes, including ecotourism and heritage tourism, were initiated among the Ju/'hoansi by non-governmental organisations, government ministries, international development agencies, and by Ju/'hoan communities themselves on both sides of the Botswana-Namibia border.

Based on assessments of some of these programmes, it is apparent that tourism has had mixed effects on individuals and groups in cross-border Ju/'hoan communities. While tourism has generated income for some local people and for the community-based organisations, the trickle-down effects have been limited, and many of the benefits have been captured by community elites. In Namibia, living museums and cultural villages were established in the two San-majority conservancies, N≠a Jaqna and Nyae Nyae, and the benefits of these programmes have mainly been limited to two communities, Grashoek in N≠a Jaqna, and //Xa/oba in Nyae Nyae. On the Botswana side of the border, because of changes in government policies with respect to land and *Community-Based Natural Resource Management*, the communities that were benefitting from ecotourism and cultural tourism in places such as the Tsodilo Hills, /Xai/Xai, and Dobe have seen declines in income and resources from private companies and individual tourists. Ecotourism and heritage tourism have had various kinds of impacts, some positive some less so, at the community, group, and individual levels in Namibia and Botswana, with some of the jobs and income going to community organisation

Manuela Zips-Mairitsch and Werner Zips), the introduction to the four chapters of Part I will be shorter than the ones for Part II and III.

management personnel and community elites. Ultimately, Hitchcock argues that having a broader-based system of benefit-sharing would ensure greater chances of poverty alleviation and more effective participation of a larger number of community members in tourism.

Salomé Ritterband's study analyses the commercialisation of cultural activities and traditional knowledge for tourism purposes in the Tsumkwe District where most of the Ju/'hoansi live. The processes of selling culture, performing for tourists, re-vitalising traditional life, and of using ancestral heritage for income are closely and decisively connected to visual aspects. She notes, that in general this process of commercialisation is a well-established and highly contested subject of anthropological interest and enquiry. Within this discourse, the exponential growth of the tourism industry and processes of globalisation are cited as the most precarious threats to indigenous populations, cultures, and traditions. Her chapter reflects on the use of attire, body adornment, and visual appearance as a realisation of tangible and authentication of intangible cultural heritage. Further, it examines the material culture of the Ju/'hoansi, casting light on how dress and accessories are relevant markers for ethnicity, identity, and social participation interconnected with hunting activities, family roles, and gender relations amongst the Ju/'hoansi.

The last study in this section by **Alicja Katchikian** examines how, as museological paradigms have evolved, the concept of living culture has emerged along with alternative ways for conserving intangible cultural heritage. Cultural villages and living museums derived from these notions and thought processes. Frequently criticised for blurring the lines between heritage and tourism, her study of institutionalised exposures moves beyond the dispute of cultural commodification to consider these initiatives in terms of performance. Herein the case of the *Ju/'hoansi San Living Museum* in Grashoek is elucidated as an archive and repertoire. That is, through the re-enactment of knowledge and culture, the San become carriers and transmitters of tradition while archive and repertoire coincide in a constant state of interaction embodied in the performance.

4.2 "Wild Frontier" – Transnational Conservation and Resource Governance in West African Borderlands

The two chapters of Part II derive (as mentioned above) from the Vienna workshop of the *African Borderlands Research Network* (ABORNE), funded by the *European Science Foundation* from 2009 to 2014. To a large extent, the inception of this volume is a result of the participation of its editors in this *Research Net-*

working Programme. A series of conferences, workshops, as well as winter and summer schools for post-graduates in Johannesburg, Bayreuth, Basel, Lisbon, St. Louis (Senegal), Edinburgh, Joensuu (Finland), and St. Petersburg brought together borderland researchers studying a tremendous diversity of topics, ranging from the historic genesis of African borders, border regimes, transborder relations, migration, mobility, and resource use, to the performance of borders by customs authorities, cross-border trade, corruption and other informal and/or illegal activities, renegotiations of borders, the African border as European frontier, transboundary governance systems, and regional integration – to name but a few of the more common themes (see ABORNE n.d., online).[13]

Although a conference trip at the first official meeting in Johannesburg (September 2009) led to the *Kruger National Park*, as part of the projected *Greater Limpopo Transfrontier* or *Peace Park*, the theme of transfrontier conservation appeared not to rank too high on the ABORNE priority list. The Workshop on *"Bewildering Borders" – Transnational Conservation and Resource Governance in Africa*, organised by Manuela Zips-Mairitsch and Werner Zips aimed at promoting a stronger focus on the important developments in transborder conservation cooperation. It was held in conjunction with the Department for Social and Cultural Anthropology of the University of Vienna and the *Commission for Development Research* at the *Austrian Agency for International Cooperation in Education and Research* in September 2013. The ABORNE Workshop created awareness for common patterns of African borderlands that were declared as conservation areas by different colonial powers.

The first chapter by **Paul Nugent** provides an elucidating history of missed opportunities, neglected borderland communities, and development failures in the borderlands of the Senegambia region. These forest habitats along the Gambia River were considered buffer zones by the French and British colonial entities. 'Borderlanders' sometimes belonging to the same ethnic groups, became part of the 'bewildering' colonial border policies. Their access to land, water resources, and forests was restricted by the creation of colonial borders and their reinforcement after independence. Nugent's key point highlights the fact that while governments have generally regarded the resources in question as zero-sum, and have tended to impose barriers to shared resource use, border populations have found ways of circumventing these boundaries, though not without considerable costs. The

[13] A great deal of borderland studies attest to the fact that borders may contribute to highly viable economic opportunities, for instance through the emergence of boomtowns triggered by circulation of people, animals and goods, referred to above (see e.g. Dobler 2009; Zeller 2009).

"regional integration from below" sustains at least the idea and perhaps ideal of the historical integrity of the greater Senegambian region. Renewed conservation efforts, picking up on experiences of *Community-Based Natural Resource Management* (CBNRM) across borders in Southern Africa, could build on the 'natural' integrative qualities of the Senegal and Gambia river systems that moved people, goods, and ideas across political division lines throughout the colonial period.

After independence "the idea of stitching together a 'natural region' that had been divided against the logic of nature itself" (Nugent in his chapter), was not attractive enough for Gambia, whose authorities feared a loss of power or, ultimately, being swallowed up by the embrace of the almost twenty times larger Senegal. Conservation and development stagnated in the border region that effectively encompasses Gambia as a whole. The only protected area in the borderlands to Guinea-Bissau, the *Niokola Koba National Park* in Senegal, is unfortunately no exception in this regard. It is almost the size of Gambia and is located at the Gambia River. However, it is quite inaccessible from Gambia due to a 'bewildering border'. Perhaps this may be a contributing cause to the general neglect of adequate conservation measures. Enlisted in 1981 as an UNESCO *World Heritage Site*, it had to be inscribed on the *List of World Heritage in Danger* in 2007 (UNESCO 2015).[14] During an extended visit in 2013 (at the occasion of the ABORNE St. Louis conference), the editors of this volume had the opportunity to get a good idea of the massive decline in biodiversity protection and wildlife numbers. From various conversations with guides, park wardens, and lodge staff at the few tourist enterprises in its surroundings, we got the impression that many species were on the brink of local extinction, including the two flagship animals: lions and elephants.

This grim picture of poor conservation efforts at *Niokola Koba National Park* reflects the situation of most protected areas in West Africa, where the situation is often even worse. The drastic neglect of protective measures and indifference to the requirements of wildlife management suggest a lack of will and vision as regards the sustainable utilisation of the last remaining 'wilderness' areas in this region. 'Conservation' practices overtly devoid of any economic perspective of a sustainable use through ecotourism somehow leave to wonder, if conservation in this and other parts of Africa is perhaps not 'neoliberal' enough, and accordingly

[14] The same source (UNESCO 2015) mentions an operation for counting the wildlife fauna by the *Direction of the National Parks* (DPN) of the Senegalese *Ministry of Environment and Sustainable Development*. Such counts should, however, be outsourced to independent agencies to avoid the common whitewashing of responsible authorities that all too often have cooked the numbers, e.g. in the form of (unrealistic) animal counts on paper.

considered unrewarding or useless by the public and private sector. Ecotourism in most West African countries still lingers in a nascent stage up to the present day. One does not have to play the devil's advocate for such a critical appraisal emphasising a lack of market initiatives (cf. Adams 2004: 208-210).

Regional comparisons in this regard probe into the different rationales and diverse experiences behind various conservationist resource governance models. It is important to reach out from academic exchange to the level of policy makers in the governance sector. The Vienna ABORNE Workshop succeeded in this regard through its involvement of representatives of the *African Union Border Programme* (AUBP), the *Economic Community of West African States* (ECOWAS), and the *International Union for the Conservation of Nature* (IUCN) (Zips and Zips-Mairitsch 2013). The second chapter in Part II picks up on the potentials and limits of re-spatialisation efforts in West African borderlands for local communities. It sheds some light on the problematic constructions of a 'community' in the developmental discourse, whereby more often than not it's a community from the 'outside' as opposed to the 'inside'.[15] Internal dimensions of power are at work in all local communities, from corporations to small family units of San (Robin 2001: 840 pp.; Wilshusen 2014: 22-24). Traditional authorities administer the land and its resources only to achieve the best possible outcome on behalf of or even for 'their subjects'. Thus, determining if and how nature conservation may contribute to an equitable distribution of possible economic benefits from (trans-)frontier area protection needs to take all possible power relations into account.

William Miles' study deals with the combat of climate change and desertification in the Niger-Nigeria borderlands. The imperative "Stop the Sahara!", quoted in his title, ironically points to failed political attempts of environmental governance in the past. He reiterates our earlier observation that game reserves in West Africa are often 'paper reserves' lacking infrastructure and anti-poaching protection. The author further emphasises that transborder cooperation between Nigeria and Niger may take experiences from other African regions as an example. He refers to folktale collections of earlier big game abundance in this border region to promote the visionary idea of biodiversity restoration, species reintroduction, and game reserve construction in the Nigerian-Niger borderlands. In his comparative analysis, this

[15] For this reason, the use of the notion of a "community" should be read in quotation marks throughout the entire volume. This appears important to note, since the authors do not share the vision of homogeneity sometimes cherished by development agencies. However, the term community is used consistently in this book to refer to local people on the ground, without suggesting their conformity, much less their unity (cf. Robins 2001: 833 pp.).

may be the most viable way to bring the already existing *Nigeria-Niger Transboundary Ecosystem Management Project* to life.

However, and against this somewhat utopian proposal, Miles, as a political scientist, has few misconceptions about the challenges such projects face, such as top-down management procedures, inconsistency of government policies, neglect of indigenous knowledge, use of inappropriate technology, and inadequate raising of environmental consciousness among the rural poor, to name a few. Joint governmental efforts pose a prerequisite to tackle the mutual ecological problems in both countries and to promote an integrated and sustainable ecosystem that may enhance livelihoods at the shared borderlands. Whether ecotourism could reasonably become part of the problem-solving cycle depends largely on the security situation. But, at this point the motive behind Miles' contribution is more about launching an alternative, more viable idea for the management of an artificial African border. It was arbitrarily created by colonial mapping in London and Paris and is considered impossible to control by both neighbour states at present. 'Bewildering' refers to a sense of recreating a wilderness for the double ends of ecological protection and economic development. Such conservation action could lead the way to the implementation of the common goals as laid down in *The Abuja Agreement* of 15 January 1990 and signed by the two states of Nigeria and Niger, which, notably, both owe their name to the same river. These goals refer explicitly to "transboundary control of desertification, promotion of conservation, rational utilisation and development of lands, water resources, flora and fauna" (Republique de Niger 2011: 108).

4.3 Benefits beyond Boundaries? The iSimangaliso Wetland Park as a Model for Inclusive Conservation and Development

The *iSimangaliso Wetland Park* (IWP) was declared South Africa's first *World Heritage Site* in 1999. Although it incorporated one of the oldest protected sites in Africa, its listing under *The World Heritage Convention Act* (Act 49) meant a fresh start on many levels. Riddled by the legacy of apartheid, the former *Greater St Lucia Wetland Park* was perceived as representative of the old model of nature protection against the interests of the (Black) majority.[16] Within the historic reality of South Africa, this meant that various parts under environmental protection were assigned as playgrounds for the privileged white minority. The Black

[16] The upper-case spelling of the adjective 'Black' is intended to clarify that the term is used as a signifier for a historical and social experience that cannot essentially be reduced to mere skin colour. Our use of this spelling is based on its increasing popularity among Black authors.

majority was excluded from all possible benefits and even denied access to the small town of St Lucia, which represents apartheid urban spatial development and planning in many ways. In stark contrast to its predecessor, IWP set the ambitious goal to transform itself into a "park for the people", *all* people that is. Under the decolonising renaming as *iSimangaliso* – meaning "land of wonder" in the Zulu language – the responsible IWP Authority attempted to forge nothing less than a 'wonderland' of integrated development of nature and society. Thus, IWP sought a paradigmatic change to break from the former concept of conservation as protection from people (Nustad 2015: 7).

The field practice (in May/June 2016) of the Department of Social and Cultural Anthropology (of the University of Vienna) had the overall research objective to find out whether and to what extent these aims have been achieved. Many of the theoretical questions and problems discussed in Parts I and II are revisited in great detail on the basis of data gathered in the course of this research, which included 9 postgraduate researchers. Five of their papers were selected for this publication. The contributions compiled on the basis of these data (and the considerable literature on IWP) focused less on the achievements in conservation and education than on the terms of local economic development and empowerment. Their main aim was to find answers to the question of whether this *Ramsar Convention* wetland park genuinely embodies a new vision of integrated wildlife protection and a rising apprehension of 'biodiversity with (the support of) people', as opposed to anachronistic approaches of 'nature conservation against people'. Based on the case study, the findings are consistently moderate in this regard. They seem to concur with the dominant view of extant literature (e.g. Büscher 2013; Nustad 2015; Igoe 2010; Igoe / Brockington 2006; Fletcher / Dressler / Büscher 2014) that the extension of national parks, game reserves, and so-called 'transfrontier peace parks' under the heading of "benefits beyond boundaries" are a mere window-dressing for continuing spatial politics of depriving the historically disadvantaged (Black) majority from their rights to land and resource utilisation.

Beyond doubt, this is a real threat and quite realistic scenario, nevertheless a final verdict appears premature. It will depend on concrete governance strategies and new institutional arrangements whether the proclaimed targets of poverty alleviation and empowerment of local beneficiaries are achieved within a reasonable time span. Critical social science studies may indeed contribute to hold policy makers accountable for their projected economic assurances. The key objective here is the promised generation of new viable forms of natural resource management. It is precisely this involvement with communities and empowerment that the five chapters examine from all possible angles against the backdrop of the slogan "benefits beyond boundaries". This motto for the overall empowerment agenda was taken from the theme of the *World Parks Congress* of 2003 and is currently promoted by international organisations such as UNESCO, the *International Union for the Conservation of Nature* (IUCN), and the *World Heritage Convention* (WHC) (iSimangaliso Wetland Park 2018a). Again, it appears easier to set a motto than to live up to its promises. There is a considerable danger that marketing slogans fuel great and often unrealistic hopes of the impoverished local populations. Transfrontier conservation initiatives define their vision of integrated nature conservation as double-minded to the promotion of peace as well as stability, on the one hand, and progress for local communities or even entire countries, on the other. IWP is no exception in the latter regard with its transboundary *Lubombo Spatial Development Initiative*, a regional development corridor involving South Africa, Mozambique, and Swaziland.

In first chapter of Part III, **Jennifer Kelleher** examines why the concepts 'protected area' and 'conserving biodiversity' are ambivalent. Her study determines that both are loaded terms that carry with them particular definitions of nature as well as the undermining of the power and participation of local communities and their forms of knowledge. By choosing a governance model that combines development and conservation goals and a rights-based approach, *iSimangaliso Wetland Park* attempts to address these very issues. The paper further explores the spectrum of power and participation of the communities surrounding iSimangaliso and assesses whether they are merely *stakeholders* or *rights holders*. In effect, the paper suggests that a rights-based approach should be about asserting agency in a way that reflects the needs of the communities. According to this author, it requires transparent local governance structures and a needs-based approach, supplemented by the identification of local knowledge and values.

This is followed by a socio-economic exploration of the challenges of nature conservation within a neoliberal capitalist system, and in particular, the potential effects of protected area nature conservation for the local inhabitants living in and around *iSimangaliso Wetland Park*. In this chapter, **Christian Sterkl** explicates why the reality of fencing off large expanses of land to protect vulnerable ecosystems from detrimental human intervention has given rise to a set of highly politicised problems. As the chapter resolves, the establishment and operation of nature conservation in South Africa is particularly challenging given its history of dispossession and socio-economic marginalisation. In a new democratic South Africa, where social equity and land reform are major considerations in policy development, nature conservation cannot afford to be viewed as channel for power, influence, and privilege. Giving consideration to these factors, Christian Sterkl analyses the strategies for social change and community empowerment as employed by IWP.

Continuing along these lines, the subsequent contribution by **Tibor Böhm** delves into the contentious role that 'traditional leadership' plays in South Africa. Though traditional leadership and the existence of chieftaincy are recognised under the *South African Constitution* (Act No 108 of 1996), they are considered highly controversial institutions of governance. Acting as middlemen and collaborators, first during colonial rule and later during apartheid, the perceived *traditionalism* of these institutions has been frequently questioned and criticised. His study looks into the roles that chiefs and traditional leaders play in dealings with iSimangaliso Wetland Park Authority and management. It questions the sphere of influence with regards to the administration and allocation of community resources. Further, it considers the representation of communities – externally as well as internally – and how to counter authoritarian power relations in communities through downward accountability.

Though *iSimangaliso Wetland Park* can point to a series of successes with regards to the conservation of its ecosystems, rewilding the park, promoting sustainable ecotourism in the area, and its co-management agreements, the park, as **Patrick Cassidy** is quick to note, still faces a complex and versatile range of stakeholders whose interests must be carefully considered and weighed in any and all decision-making processes. Conserving and protecting areas is an inherently political process and it requires skill to appease different interest groups without leading to preferential treatment. This chapter analyses the diverse and sometimes conflicting interests in the case of iSimangaliso and the park authority's response to dealing with these stakeholders. It advocates that while environmental conservation is crucial, adopting policies to follow this path should not marginalise certain interests and should not come at the cost of maintaining status quo socio-economic structures.

In the last contribution by the graduate student group, **Georg Bergthaler** breaks down why after becoming South Africa's first *World Heritage Site* in 1999, *iSimangaliso Wetland Park* shifted into the focus of domestic and international policy makers. As he details in his chapter, their objectives were two-fold: They sought to ensure the protection of the values and principles of the *World Heritage Convention* and to align their conservation measures with overriding strategies of tourism and poverty alleviation in the province KwaZulu-Natal. The research presented in his paper highlights the strengths and weaknesses of iSimangaliso's management in bringing together these objectives in an action plan that derives from *Community-Based Natural Resource Management*. To this end, the paper examines agency and participation in governance structures, collaborations, and entrepreneurial partnerships of and with iSimangaliso Wetland Park. It discusses how non-hierarchical collaborative management solutions should address and include all stakeholders and considers how to improve community empowerment.

The results presented by Jennifer Kelleher, Christian Sterkl, Tibor Böhm, Patrick Cassidy, and Georg Bergthaler in Part III, only touch upon the big vision of peace between neighbouring countries, inherent in transfrontier conservation initiatives. The contributions rather discuss some contradictions linked to the conceptualisation of peace parks by powerful national and transnational actors. Their main concern lies in the impact of transboundary agreements for local communities, and foremost the issues of inclusion in the process of will- and opinion-formation leading up to the decision-making processes and implementation of policies. The papers are, therefore, consciously anthropocentric, in accordance with the general topic of the field practice. However, these communal policies run parallel with a host of environmental governance strategies that form the basis of potential future benefits for the communities. Conservation is also about habitats, biomes, preservation of wildlife and flora, removal of alien plants, and the reintroduction of game species that formerly inhabited the area. These equally pivotal subjects, though not omitted entirely by Kelleher, Sterkl, Böhm, Cassidy, and Bergthaler, were treated of secondary importance. For this reason, they are supplemented with a separate article by the volume editors, Werner Zips and Manuela Zips-Mairitsch.

The 6th paper of Part III by **Werner Zips** and **Manuela Zips-Mairitsch**, therefore, has the main objective to throw actual conservation issues back into the discussion. It also attempts to set the record straight for a highly successful transformation project in the time span of less than two decades, starting from scratch. From a tempocentric perspective the shortcomings may appear obvious and well established by the voices of local residents. Their impatience is all but justified. Half a century of apartheid politics of systematic (legal) exclusion and contingent empowerment of the minority white landowners, who had grabbed the land from its former inhabitants at one point in history, require urgent and corrective measures. These lost decades created not only a blatant racist distortion of human society, but an utmost unequal land distribution. Notably they were preceded by centuries of anti-Black dispossession and comprehensive discrimination. However, conservation agencies, undermined by partial interests and flagrant underfunding appear to be the wrong end of the critical focus. At least, if correlated with the efforts of an IWP regular staff that currently counts just 35 employees (starting from just 16 in its first year of operation in 2002 with an increase to 41 in 2016).[17]

Could it be reasonably expected that this small organisation sets the record straight overnight? One may further question, which industry or business venture would in fact measure up with the expectations of more than half a million people (living in proximity to the park)? Or even lay the foundation to meet the requirements of fundamental change without adequate political support in the national arena? Should, then, the critique not be re-directed to provincial and national politics leaving the promises of change through conservation to an extremely understaffed organisation? And consecutively to the international community that redundantly claims sustainable environmental policies – or even "environmental justice" – but takes insufficient financial pains to assist in an agenda of global interest. These questions will be taken up from a great diversity of perspectives. The volume does not attempt to present a unified view on these conservation issues. In fact, the various chapters, particularly in Part III reflect the engaged, and sometimes even heated, debates in situ.

5 Summary and Outlook

The critique of neoliberalism adequately emphasises problematic aspects of manipulated consensus-building, the illusion of false or deceptive win-win situations through anti-political marketing, window-dressing in the form of "greenwashing" or "fair-washing", and competitive bidding for natural or cultural services (Büscher 2013: 18-28). But it mostly neglects the achievements of conservationists who have to live up to the limited means at their disposal (public funding, staff allocation, and general political support). Beyond doubt, the field of conservation is highly dependent on the overall field of power, but 'inhabited' by a great diversity of actors, who are in varying degrees resilient to the dominant forces. Some of these actors are the very individuals in leadership positions, who are targeted for their relentless efforts to make conservation work against the interests of quick capitalisation of natural resources. IWP is no exception, as it was saved, almost at the last minute, from the prospected mining of the coastal dunes (unsurprisingly with the intervention of the exceptional visionary Nelson Mandela).

17 We owe this information to Nerosha Govender, personal communication on 30th July 2018. Official figures are not easy to find.

Arguably, the accusation of facilitating, expediting, and even embodying the neoliberal agenda (e.g. Hansen 2014: 117) is highly questionable.

On the one hand, the various chapters of this volume, build on the now common critique of conservation. They carefully discuss the available literature, legal documents, political frameworks, interviews, and other resources on new inclusive conservation efforts. On the other hand, various contributions to some extent depart from the framing of neoliberal conservation, and rather question this critique as not only starting from the wrong end but also overlooking the conservation impacts on non-human life forms. Finally, some indictments are questioned as arguably tempocentric, given the short period and limited means of implementation. Until very recently, IWP was still literally under construction, in terms of institutional arrangements and infrastructure provisions. We trust that the various contributions to this volume provide a wide range of perspectives and possible analytical standpoints. Of course, social scientist positions do prevail, given the disciplinary background of most contributors in social and legal anthropology as well as political science.

One of the most important concerns of this book is clearly the inclusion and adequate participation of local communities, emphasising the needs of indigenous peoples. Many of whom lived in these territories, called them their home, and used their resources for their livelihoods. Their interests were clearly overlooked in the discourse and practices of nature conservation in the name of an abstract humanity. By this inversion of dispossessing the earlier inhabitants in the interest of a common national or even global good, sustainable conservation was rather harmed than helped. Therefore, while marginalised in earlier attempts of nature protection, this aspect is positioned in the foreground of this volume.

Thus, the volume wants to contribute to a growing awareness that sustainable conservation, especially in frontier and transfrontier areas, depends on the prior and informed consent of all people affected in order to reasonably claim a complex, systematical, and long-term understanding of sustainability. Otherwise, such claims will be increasingly seen as cheap talk and turned against the legitimate necessities of environmental protection from *homo oeconomicus*. On the basis of the empirical examples analysed in the various chapters, a plea often made by those affected by imposed conservation regimes will be given privilege. These voices, seldom listened to even in the critical literature, appeal to the urgent imperative of a return to sincere, inter alia long- and not short-term concepts of sustainability, as they were paradoxically often practiced by those dislocated from the areas their forefathers protected for posterity – in the name of nature protection.

Part I

Life in a Living Museum: Conservation and Cultural Marketing in the Borderlands of Namibia and Botswana

Inclusive Borderlands: The Cultural Marketing of San Communities in Borderland Conservancies of Namibia and Botswana

Manuela Zips-Mairitsch and Werner Zips

"There are a lot of wild animals, because it is far away and it's deeply in the bush. There was always an abundance of wild animals in the borderlands. So, our parents used to hunt the game and they told us that, if you don't hunt, then you will never know how tasty our meat is. And they eat meat a lot. We were fed with some bulbs and field-food, but we were also eating meat that time. I am happy that we can live like that in the conservancy." (!Kunta Boo 13.01.2014, interview)

"The life today, it seems to me, is almost a similar life as when I was a child. Because the things we used to do we are still doing today. We are still gathering and we are still hunting. But life has also developed new forms, yet very slowly. We didn't get help from our government so often, but we see that the outside people who are coming to film us and to photograph us, those people are those who are giving us means of development. So, I am very happy about that." (Xoan//a !Kunta 14.01.2014, interview)

"The members of the community are the members of the conservancy. They are the ones putting up the rules for the conservancy. They are the ones who apply the rules for the conservancy altogether. So, they sit together, discuss and decide the rules of the conservancy. What should be done inside the conservancy, what should not be done. They make the constitution of the conservancy. So, the conservancy is owned by the community. We are working together according to the constitution of the conservancy." (Kaqece N!ani 19.12.2014, interview)

1 Introduction

This chapter offers an overview on the divergent concepts of borderland conservation in Namibia and Botswana and a contextual introduction to the other three chapters of this first section by Robert Hitchcock, Salomé Ritterband, and Alicja Khatchikian. It reviews the Namibian borderlands conservancies, particularly the Nyae Nyae conservancy, the first of its kind, as an inclusive form of wildlife and natural resource management. Thereby, the Nyae Nyae provides an alternative example to top-down *Community-Based Natural Resource Management* (CBNRM) schemes still waged against indigenous claims to self-determination in neighbouring Botswana, particularly in the highly contested *Central Kalahari Game Reserve* (CKGR).

At the time of writing (March 2019) Namibia has 86 registered conservancies covering a land mass of over 166.045 square kilometres with approximately 228.000 residents (NACSO 2019). Therefore, almost 20 percent of its total size of 824.116 square kilometres fall under this fairly new model of community-based conservation. Nearly 10 percent of the total Namibian population of over 2.3 million live in and potentially benefit from the conservancy land ownership scheme governed by law, namely the *Nature Conservation Amendment Act* of 1996. These figures alone indicate a successful implementation of communal conservancies, if the steadily growing number may serve as such a yardstick. They are defined as: "[...] self-governing, democratic entities, run by their members, with fixed boundaries that are agreed with adjacent conservancies, communities or land owners. Conservancies are recognised by the *Ministry of Environment and Tourism* (MET), but not governed by the Ministry, which does, however, have powers to de-register a conservancy if it fails to comply with conservation regulation. Communal conservancies are obliged to have game management plans, to conduct annual general meetings, and to prepare financial reports. They are managed under committees elected by their members" (Ministry of Environment and Tourism 2018).

However, the number of conservancies alone says very little about the actual contentment of its beneficiaries and its positive impact on the conservation agenda. All four contributions to this chapter *Life in a Living Museum – Conservation and Cultural Marketing in the Borderlands of Namibia and Botswana* (including this one) explore the impact of the conservancy framework on the livelihoods, development ambitions, and personal life visions of those directly concerned. They all focus on the perspectives of their local inhabitants on the materialisation of their own interests. The key question in this regard is their active participation in the formulation and implementation of governance guidelines and the related issues of communicative inclusion, transparency, and adequate self-determination. The first two chapters (by Zips-Mairitsch/ Zips and Hitchcock) apply a comparative framework with Botswana, whereas chapters three and four (by Ritterband and Khatchikian) zoom into the tensions between local expectations and actual short-term benefits. Botswana has been criticised for its perhaps benevolent but nevertheless top-down approach towards CBNRM (cf. Mbaiwa 2012; Bollig 2003: 285; Suzman 2002: 3): "In Botswana, too, despite job creation related to wildlife activities, no empowerment is seen among the local people, as the management of the resources is entirely in the hands of the government" (Milupi/ Somers/ Ferguson 2017: 1130).

This state generally sought to apply one single model of CBNRM for the entire country. In contrast, the Namibian legal framework took the great ecological and social diversity of communal areas into account. Thus, the Namibian solution to integrated rural development and conservation avoided one of the most common lapses of *Community-Based Natural Resource Management* schemes in other African national states, i.e. to legislate an over-regulated, too narrowly defined governance framework (Owen-Smith 2010: 542). It appears to have learned the lesson from the fault-prone 'copy and paste approach' to CBNRM.

In comparison, the government in neighbouring Botswana decided to head into the opposite direction. The ban on wildlife hunting in Botswana with effect as of January 2014 and issued by the Botswana *Ministry of Environment, Wildlife and Tourism* ruled out subsistence and commercial hunting in controlled hunting areas (state land). Hunting on registered game ranches (private land) is not affected by the ban. Most of these wildlife management areas are situated in the Ghanzi district and along the Limpopo River in the Tuli region (Botswana Ministry of Environment, Wildlife and Tourism 2013). The differentiation corroborates local and indigenous populations' complaints that 'hunting for the pot' is sanctioned in the name of conservation, whereas private hunting enterprises in the interest of foreign exchange earnings are miraculously in line with biodiversity protection.

The hunting ban contradicts the goals of conservation and rural development, which the CBNRM programme was established to achieve. It reduces the benefits, such as income generation and employment opportunities of local communities from safari hunting, and stopped most of the community projects and development schemes due to a lack of funds. The *Wildlife Management Areas* (WMAs) and *Controlled Hunting Areas* (CHAs) constitute 22 percent of the country, as compared to 17 percent of protected areas in national parks and game reserves (Mbaiwa 2017: 52). It brought an end to the permissive *Unified Hunting Regulations* (Government of Botswana 1979), which provided for *Special Game Licenses.* Such licences, quotas and permits could be applied for by "[. . .] citizens of Botswana, who are principally dependent on hunting and gathering veld produce for their food" (Government of Botswana, *Wildlife Conservation and National Parks Act* 1992 (2008), Chapter 38: 01, Article 30). However, such licenses had to be secured from a licensing officer at the *Department of Wildlife* (ibid., Article 31), which proved extremely difficult, if not virtually impossible, for indigenous communities, such as the San inhabitants of the CKGR (cf. Hitchcock 1996: 55-60).

In practice, community trusts in *Wildlife Management Areas* had to team up with private safari operators to receive an income from commercial hunting. With the hunting ban, such revenues have almost completely dried up since photographic tourism is not feasible in many of these areas because of competitive disadvantages in higher game density national parks and game reserves. It has become a matter of a heated debate in conservation circles whether the benevolent shift to photographic tourism shows the anticipated positive effects on wildlife and the protection of biological diversity at all. According to Mbaiwa (2017: 51), the ban on safari hunting is reportedly reversing positive attitudes of local communities towards wildlife conservation, apparently leading to increasing incidents of poaching and conceivably affecting effective wildlife conservation negatively in the long run. All of this feeds into the argument that safari hunting through the CBNRM programme may encourage the development of positive attitudes of local communities towards wildlife conservation, notably in areas where ecotourism is either not feasible or undeveloped in terms of infrastructure.

2 Empowering Communities through Cultural Tourism

Cultural tourism proves much less profitable than wildlife tourism in the short run, particularly in areas too remote for most tourists. Private tourism companies are encouraged to enter into joint venture agreements with community trusts, but quickly pull out once they realise that the occupancy rates and turnover are insufficient to support a long-term investment. It is a very disheartening experience to visit the locations of community trusts that failed shortly after their inauguration or never took off ground (cf. Mbaiwa 2016b; Zips-Mairitsch 2013: 239 pp.; Bolaane 2001: 155 pp.). The rhetoric of empowering communities economically raises great hopes among rural people. They often contribute considerable manpower into building tourist accommodations in community camps, thereby reducing the financial risk of a private partner. One out of too many such first-hand encounters with declining tourist infrastructure and tremendous disappointment may be reported from the Botswanian village of Gudigwa, close to Seronga on the proposed Kavango-Zambezi transfrontier conservation corridor. In a detailed interview with Gontso Zero Ngorogwe, a culture guide of the *Bukakhwe Cultural Conservation Trust* (23.09.2005, interview), we learned about the ‘tragedy of commerce’ (as opposed to the ‘tragedy of the commons’). In this remote village in the Okavango Delta, almost the entire community helped to build eight fully furnished tourist huts, one traditional entertainment compound, a reception area, craft shop, restaurant, and bar. According to Gontso Zero Ngorogwe, some

40 people were trained for the cultural tourism venture but were unable to maintain their "ethno-prise" (Comaroff/ Comaroff 2009: 65, 144). When the private company pulled out after only half a year of fairly unsuccessful performance in 2004, operations were shut down and the infrastructure was left to rot (cf. Zips-Mairitsch 2013: 255 pp.).

In Namibia, conservancy committees are much less dependent on private investors. Rather, they team up with an umbrella organisation that offers access to specialised NGOs for particular management plans. Only then are private business partners recruited. Just two years after the legislation, the first four communal conservancies were gazetted by the *Ministry of Environment and Tourism* (MET) in diverse eco-zones, namely the Nyae Nyae in the dry east, the Salambala in the riverine north-east at the border to Botswana, the ≠Khoadi-//Hôas in the arid Kunene region in the north-west, and the Torra that spreads towards the Skeleton Coast. According to the *Namibian Association of CBNRM Support Organisations* (thereafter NACSO), these pioneer conservancies established a fairly flexible model for economic survival and growth in harsh rural settings. Where appropriate and compatible with the aims of bio-diversity and wildlife protection, communities were allowed to hunt. This was in stark contrast to pre-independence conservation regimes that regarded residents on communal land, who hunted game, as poachers (Owen-Smith 2010: 377 pp.). Now, hunting on conservancy land is governed by quotas, set by the MET on the basis of annual game counts carried out by the Ministry and conservancies with assistance from NACSO's *Natural Resource Management Working Group* (NACSO 2018: 1).

Communal areas in Namibia exhibit a great variety of eco-systems with culturally highly diverse ethnic groups. The legislation, therefore, had to be flexible enough to accommodate hunter-gatherers, nomadic pastoralists, crop farmers, and fishermen. The wide range of subsistence economies and social systems is reflected by a big difference in customary governance structures, including the divergent roles of traditional authorities. The *Nature Conservation Amendment Act* of 1996 consciously deviated from the pre-independence conservation ideology modelled on apartheid. It allowed communities to match the basic legal principles of communal conservation with their own needs and aspirations (Owen-Smith 2010: 542-544). For the first time in Namibian history, this paradigm of participatory conservation governance opted for a decisive rupture with the idea of "nature and wildlife protection against people" (cf. Adams/ Hulme 2001: 10). Thus, the long history of separating local communities from the environment and the use of its resources ended shortly after independence from South Africa in 1990. Ground-breaking legislation laid the foundation for a new approach to the sustainable use of natural resources in communal areas, as the following quote from a NACSO publication emphasises:

"Historically, conservation efforts generally separated people from wildlife, often alienated local communities from natural resource use and did not encourage compatible land uses in adjacent areas. Wildlife populations in communal areas had plummeted prior to Namibia's independence in 1990. Communal area residents had no rights to use wildlife, with even subsistence hunting considered illegal. This encouraged poaching, as wildlife had no legal economic value. Wild animals were seen as little more than a threat to crops, livestock and infrastructure, as well as community safety. After independence, far-sighted conservationists and rural developers sought to reverse the downward trend." (Denker 2011: 4)

The *Namibian Association of CBNRM Support Organisations* is an umbrella organisation, which unites different stakeholders. It was founded in 1996, the same year as the *Nature Conservation Amendment Act* that created the guidelines for conservancies was passed. This multi-sphere governance institution combines development NGOs with wildlife protection groups and rights-based community support organisations involved in the legal struggles of indigenous peoples and other local communities, mostly for land rights.[1] Its constitution lays out the principles for a partnership of both governmental and non-governmental institutions (including parastatal, community, business, etc.), that closely collaborate to practice, promote, and support *Community-Based Natural Resource Management* (CBNRM) activities in Namibia (NACSO 2002). It facilitates the establishment of tourism enterprises through joint ventures with the private sector for those conservancies with tourism potential. The *Nyae Nyae Development Foundation* that assists the Nyae Nyae and the N≠a Jaqna conservancies is also part of NACSO.

3 Flexible Legislation – Neither Gods nor Laws Must be Crazy

In fact, the legal-political conservancy framework allowed the San and other local communities living with and from wildlife to emerge as active designers of their own development. Before they evolved as political actors through organisations such as the *Nyae Nyae Development Foundation* of Namibia, they were mostly treated as objects of development by national planning institutions, quite similar to their relatives across the border in Botswana. These urban, often elitist promoters of 'modernity' considered local communities passive recipients of provisions in the double sense of legal regimes and basic supplies. Arguably, the pa-

[1] On the theoretical aspects of multi-sphere and multi-level governance and its implications for participatory concepts of inclusion, see Zips/ Weilenmann (2011: 15-19).

ternalistic attitudes conform to a habitus of a presumed obligation of the educated and wealthy elite to help the supposedly 'uneducated', pre-modern 'remote-area dwellers', as the San were officially referred to before their resettlement to small towns outside game reserves.[2]

The case of the San communities in Kaudwane, New Xade and Xere, relocated from the *Central Kalahari Game Reserve* to the park's borders in neighbouring Botswana, is a telling example in this regard. Once a week a truck arrives at the local police station with food rations, other alimentations, and pension funds. The once self-reliant Kalahari inhabitants are thus turned into objects of charity in total dependency. While the San communities in the Namibian Kalahari conservancies of the Nyae Nyae and N≠a Jaqna are entitled to destine their agency as indigenous conservationists.[3] In this sense, the conservancy legal framework takes the idea of *Community-Based Natural Resource Management* seriously and aims to provide a new standard for self determined development and conservation (Jones et al. 2015: 23 pp.). Nyae Nyae was founded as the initial communal conservancy in Namibia in 1998 on the legal basis of the *Nature Conservation Amendment Act* of 1996. It came into existence with the strong support and guidance of anthropologists and other social scientists, who have worked in the area for many decades (Hitchcock 2015: 12).

This paradigmatic model for community-based conservation showcases a long history of development and interactions with non-governmental organisations, national institutions, and international agencies (cf. Biesele/ Hitchcock 2011). Scholars and filmmakers such as John Marshall (and family), Claire Ritchie, Megan Biesele, and Robert K. Hitchcock contributed significantly to the enormous body of knowledge on many aspects of the San communities' lifeworlds and methods of subsistence in the area now known as Nyae Nyae. The film "The Gods Must be Crazy" (Uys 1980) gave rise to their international fame and recognition. All of this contributes to the successful branding of the conservancies as 'authentic' arenas for indigenous lifestyles, foremost hunting and gathering. Therefore, a lot of attention and funding was and still is designated for ensuring the viability and sustainability of the Nyae Nyae (with its predominant Ju/'hoansi popula-

2 A quote by the former President of Botwana, Festus Mogae, is quite revealing in this regard: "[...] a certain extremist NGO ... has relentlessly attacked this country because of our long-standing, non-negotiable commitment towards ensuring that all of our citizens, including remote-area dwellers of whatever ethnicity, gain access to the benefits of development in the form of schools, clinics and additional opportunities, to become part of our modern mainstream economy" (Festus Mogae, cited in IRIN 2004, online).

3 Notably, many San communities in Namibia were also previously relocated from national parks such as Khaudom or Etosha (cf. Dieckmann 2001).

tion) and the neighbouring N≠a Jaqna conservancy (with its diverse !Xun, Khwe, Hai//om, and Ju/'hoansi inhabitants). In the early stage pre-dating the gazetting of the conservancies, wildlife was reintroduced to the Nyae Nyae region by the *World Wildlife Fund* (WWF) under the *Living in a Finite Environment* (LIFE) project. The conservancy actively took part in the conception and adoption of a suitable set of rules for commercial safari and subsistence hunting (Biesele/ Hitchcock 2011: 208-209).

A recent report based on extensive research by Robert K. Hitchcock (2015) presents a fairly optimistic outlook, but nevertheless offers numerous recommendations to ensure and improve the lasting success of these two flagship conservation management schemes. On their website, the *Nyae Nyae Development Foundation of Namibia* (NNDFN 2017, online) addresses current issues that potentially threaten the integrity of conservancies. Without legal enforcement of court orders protecting their land rights, various communities feel threatened by illegal grazing of encroaching pastoralist groups. Notwithstanding these and other concerns, Hitchcock's contribution to this volume emphasises the empowering achievements of conservancies. His in-depth comparison between divergent approaches in Namibia and Botswana to community conservation assesses the feedback of San communities to conservation governance. In the past, both countries required local people to vacate their lands once these were declared protected areas, such as national monuments and game reserves. In case of their refusal, they were more often than not forcibly resettled. Such forced relocations of indigenous populations generally inflict material and psychological harm, as has been widely documented on a global level (Brockington/ Igoe 2006: 449).[4]

Yet, in most cases the restricted access to natural resources had negative implications not only for those directly concerned but also for the successful protection of wildlife, which was thereafter commonly considered 'fair game' for poaching by those excluded from hunting and other forms of resource utilisation. The ensuing lack of incentives to conserve wild animals and habitat resulted in the deterioration of the natural environment and the alienation of entire communities who were turned into dependents of welfare policies. His empirical findings led Hitchcock to the well-balanced conclusion – presented in his contribution to this volume – that it may well be time to employ a diversified strategy for conservation, development, and tourism. An approach that is not based on restricting the local people from the benefits of their natural and cultural environments or their

4 See also Dowie (2009) on the hundred years of conflict between global conservation and "native peoples".

intangible heritage, in the form of traditional ecological knowledge (Craig/ Davis 2005: 32-39, 56; cf. Rozemeijer 2001). The Namibian conservancies appear to provide adequate means for community conservation based on the full participation of those concerned in the opinion- and will-formation leading up to sustainable decisions (Biesele/ Hitchcock 2011: 208-209; Jones et al. 2015: 34 pp.).

The other two chapters in this first section question the different strategies for (self-)marketing cultural traits in response to the increase of tourism in the area. San communities in both conservancies bank on their self-destined performance culture to secure a livelihood from eco- and ethno-tourism. Visitors interested in indigenous culture and wildlife pay readily for a variety of performances and transmission of indigenous (ecological) knowledge. These cultural and at the same time creative, artistic expressions, therefore, became a pivotal resource for the San in re-shaping the relationship with their environment. Salomé Ritterband and Alicja Khatchikian analyse emerging indigenous practices to capitalise on their cultural skills and intellectual properties. Their scope is less a critique of the 'neoliberal commodification' of culture in tourism, than a close study of the indigenous explorations of the emerging cultural market. The local communities appear to search for meaningful and acceptable ways for themselves to cash in on the global demand for 'authenticity', without selling out to the hackneyed clichés produced and reproduced by the primitivism brand of 'native' cultural tourism (cf. Fillitz/ Saris 2013).

It is of utmost importance for the San to respond, react, and reflect on how their performances are perceived by their 'clients', as the tourist groups sent by tour operators or other tourism enterprises are generally referred to. They are also very much concerned with the divergent views of "correct representations" of their own cultural heritage and ask themselves to what extent they may deviate from preconceived perceptions of an "original tradition" passed on by their ancestors (cf. Ritterband 2018: 188-194). Their idea of tradition appears much less static than many preconceived notions of a 'traditional culture', frozen since time immemorial. These static images are created by outsiders who construct 'the other' as counterpart to modernity. The interviews and observations during the University of Vienna field practice on cultural villages and living museums, in which Ritterband and Khatchikian participated, confirm the active shaping of self-representations. Many actors in the visited locations consciously reflect on intercultural encounters and inquire about expectations of their 'clients'. These careful observations of the observed reveal interpretive tensions with the tourist gaze of 'othering'. San performers, who refer to themselves as "actors", are reluctant to present themselves as living fossils of the early beginnings of mankind

(Ritterband 2018: 248). They have their own view of the exotic consumerism involved in ethno-tourism and have their means of deconstruction – not least by means of their humour and mimicry of the implicit evolutionist bias and prejudiced primitivism (see Katchikian, in this volume). "Ethnicity, Inc.", as examined by Comaroff and Comaroff (2009: 148), is not a one-way street, but rather tends to expose the stranger's desire for difference:

> "It also makes clear the obscene undersides of a commerce in exotic, exciting, but ultimately safe, encounters with the dispossessed and desperate 'others' of the earth. And the fact that, in the traffic in difference, culture-as-commodity may expand onto even the most inhospitable of terrains. In one form or another, Ethnicity, Inc. can turn up, if not everywhere, then almost anywhere. For, existentially speaking, it appears to be driven by a burgeoning desire at once to endorse difference and to transcend it, the desire to touch for an instant the elusive otherness that we are too late, too settled, too detached fully to embrace."

4 The Cultural Economics of "Ethno-prises"

"Ethnicity, Inc." refers to the commodification of culture within (neoliberal) market contexts. It draws attention to the underlying question of how the stakeholders of ethno-enterprises shape their own conceptualisations, practices, strategies, and economic ideas for marketing their own 'traditional culture'. This process involves new bottom-up modes of interaction with national and international NGOs. In contrast to top-down development delivery, the highly discursive arena of communal cultural entrepreneurship coined "ethno-prises" tends to promote the renegotiations of gender, the generational divide, and the internal leadership structures, including the procedures of decision making, participation, and the distribution of income generated through cultural performances. In short, it may encourage community self-determination instead of its presumed sell-out. Empirical assessment will determine which consequences prevail. Therefore, such 'ethnic productions', whether susceptible to neoliberal marketing or not, envelop an entire spectrum of economic, social, and cultural opportunities and threats. Unwanted consequences linked to the emergence of a local consumer economy are by no means negligible. Soon after the living museum in Grashoek had generated its first entrepreneurs, it began to attract 'outsider' businesses, in particular Shebeens that sell alcohol. The negative effects for an unprepared local community are part of the cultural economics in conservancies. Identity businesses that build on ethnic cultural capital become intertwined with the capitalisation of nature (cf. Comaroff/ Comaroff 2009: 65-85).

This new space of economic ventures poses considerable cognitive conundrums for indigenous actors. The encounters with 'strange peoples' (the ethno-tourists) are not new to them but their active role in shaping this intercultural exchange is to some extent. It is challenging for them to read the interests of their clients. Since their global customers' expectations are never quite straightforward, the performance of culture in living museums and cultural villages generally transpires in a communicative space of ambivalence with ample potential for misunderstanding (cf. Ritterband 2018: 172-236).

It is remarkable that San performers in the Nyae Nyae and N≠a Jaqna conservancies explicitly welcome the active participation of their audience. This interactive involvement may be partly owed to the training of *The Living Culture Foundation Namibia*, a German-Namibian organisation responsible for the creation of the Living Museum of the Ju/'hoansi-San in Grashoek and the *Little Hunter's Museum* in //Xa/oba.[5] But, in Doupos, a Ju/'hoansi-San settlement with a self-designed cultural village, the alteration of passive consumers to participants appears to be an idiosyncratic choice. Doupos is arguably the most accessible and best-known village out of 36 traditional territories (n!oresi) for hunting and gathering groups in the Nyae Nyae conservancy. There, a situation defined by the exotic gaze of most ethno-tourists is regularly transformed into an intercultural exchange on equal footing across language barriers. The process of cultural commodification thus converts cultural capital into economic capital, and vice versa. When the San tour guides appear with their pre-made 'menu of traditional services' that lists fixed prices, their 'clients', who anticipated time travel into the early beginnings of mankind, might be disillusioned, but they use this awakening creatively to open up a new space of contemporaneity.[6] At least some unavoidable contradictions involved in the marketing of ethnicity or indigeneity are potentially resolved in an intercultural learning process revived from the inside. So-called trance or healing dances and other activities offered for strangers ideally lose their inherent otherness (Ritterband 2018: 210-222; Zips 2018: 18-20; cf. Keeney 2013: 80).

Perhaps surprisingly, the staged scenario does not necessarily lead to a mimicry of commodified indigeneity but enables San performers to renegotiate their identity, even within their self-perceptions. Of course, not all visitors are

---

5 It should be noted that the naming of the Living Museum as "Little Hunter's Museum" appears unfortunate in the light of its reference to an adamant stereotype: the small body height of San people. The problem lies less in physical appearance than in their recurring use as a defining characteristic.

6 Compare the documentary film "A Living Museum – Ethnotainment in Namibia" (Manuela Zips-Mairitsch and Werner Zips), Austrian Television (ORF) and 3sat, Vienna 2015, 52 min.

prepared to overcome their possible cultural bias and expectations within one encounter (von Stauss 2012: 86-87). Essentialist notions of absolute difference are not easily cured by one healing dance. But, the constructions of otherness do not end at this point. Ironically, over the past two decades since the formation of the cultural village in Doupos the San family around the famous healer and local leader !Kunta Boo developed their own assessments of visitors according to national differences, thus breaking the Western monopoly of categorisation. In a lengthy conversation between our field practice student group and the men and women of the hunting and gathering "Bushwalk performance group", ascriptions of national mentalities were treated humorously and tentatively. The San appeared to test their (empirical) findings against our own views of 'national mentalities'. This observation points to the huge difference between the contracted staging of "Bushmen dance shows" in touristic settings of hotels and restaurants (including so-called cultural villages adjacent to lodges and campsites) and the self-designed choreographies in performance spaces of existing villages, described by Ritterband and Khatchikian in this volume (cf. Butler/ Hinch 2007: 323).[7]

5 Managerial Ownership of Cultural Heritage

The difference between the (mostly) exploitative contracting of dance groups and the self-representations in the examples discussed in this volume lies not only in the agency but also in the managerial ownership of cultural heritage. Doupos and the two San living museums provide unique examples of economic self-determination. The *Ju/'hoansi Living Museum* in Grashoek, for instance, operates as a business enterprise. Although marketed as an "authentic open-air museum", its organisational structure is that of a company. A passage from an interview with Henry /ui Nyani (11.01.2014, interview), the first tour guide of the *Ju/'hoansi Living Museum* in Grashoek, may provide evidence of the entrepreneurial self-confidence of the self-employed owners:

> "The living museum, it's now in our hands. So, we are the ones who manage it and we are having a management team, which is working with it. We employ a manager, a vice manager, secretaries, vice treasurer and the tour guides. I'm the first tour guide, but there are other tour guides and actors. So, the whole enterprise is in our hands. When the visitors book an activity, they have to pay according to the programme price list. We experience a lot of changes, because now we pay for our kids so that they can go to school and we are

7 See also the film portrait on the healer !Kunta Boo in Doupos, Nyae Nyae conservancy: "The Great Shaman – Healing in the Kalahari" (Manuela Zips-Mairitsch and Werner Zips), Austrian Television (ORF) and 3sat, Vienna 2015, 52 min.

having a little bit of income also. With these earnings we can buy food for our kids and a little bit of food for ourselves. But before, when there was no living museum, there were no jobs available for us."

Henry /ui Nyani is also a highly prolific master of ceremony, who eloquently mediates the day programme of (neo-)traditional activities to visitors, which sometimes involve 50-60 San actors (as was the case during our University of Vienna field practice on site). On the figurative level, those San actors are also masters of (their) re-enacted ceremonies. They are able to reflect and decide on their choreography and to change it – if necessary – just like actors would in other more formal settings. Their fairly spontaneous performances clearly go beyond the constraints of an ascribed passive ethnic commodification. These re-enactments neither adhere to an exoticised or fictitious past. Rather, the professional participants consider themselves active members in a process of will-formation and decision-making on the actual forms, practices, and visions to represent their historical experiences, skills, and competences.[8] However, and perhaps most importantly, there is a decisive difference to "Bushmen Shows" (so common throughout the region): here they act on their own account economically. This includes their responsibility for and control over the (cultural) economics that are sometimes labelled 'neoliberal' (Koot/ van Beek 2017: 139). In our view, the potential of (self-)liberation from poverty and the mere passive role as contractors and recipients of limited earnings in the tourism economy should not be ignored (cf. Hall/ Patrinos 2012).

The decisive question may be less if a certain practice corresponds to a specific (neoliberal) format, but rather, if the economic outcome complies with the interests of those involved. An overall economy of interests, as called for by Pierre Bourdieu (cf. Bourdieu/ Wacquant 1992: 115-120), may effectively protect against premature categorisations. In this sense, the indigenous actors are now becoming "stars of their own show" (Zips 2018: 15). These practical expositions of their intangible heritage evoke dynamic representations of 'culture and tradition', not given or dictated to them by outsiders but to a large extent projected, developed, and owned by themselves. Ownership in this case appears much less imposed by the neoliberal reconstitution of a protected area, but rather by conscious communicative deliberations, that do not necessarily fall short to acknowledge risks and unintended consequences. This makes a difference for the critical assessment of economic instrumentalisations of intangible cultural heritage and

[8] We here use the terminology of Jürgen Habermas (1996: 107) to refer to a critical parameter of participatory natural resource governance. Critical discourse theory, in our view, provides a highly sensitive and empirically established framework for the assessment of inclusive governance and leadership structures.

natural resources, that Büscher (2013: 205) aims to expose, but perhaps overgeneralises (against the empirical background of his study of the Maloti-Drakensberg Transfrontier Project in South Africa and Lesotho):

> "[T]he 'refashioning of cultures', according to the 'spirit of the time', through ecotourism is a more subtle, disciplinary process whereby marketing works to stimulate demand from clients (tourists) in response to which local people have to start behaving like entrepreneurs, to live up to this demand, for instance by providing so-called authenticity."

On the basis of the marketing rhetoric used in travel brochures selling a nostalgia trip to ethno-tourists, this spirit of time appears indeed neoliberal. Outsiders who organise tours to the "last hunters and gatherers" generally stimulate the popular demand for romanticised images of primitivism (Büscher 2013: 203). Yet, in our view, it also depends on 'the spirit of time' nurtured by those concerned with the performance of culture. For an adequate analysis on this intercultural level, the abstract figure of a neoliberal anonymous is not enough. We rather suggest a procedural paradigm to question the communicative participation of the actors (in the double sense of social and aesthetic actors) in the entire process of opinion- and will-formation as a prerequisite for participatory decision-making (Biesele/ Hitchcock 2011: 205; cf. Habermas 1996: 170).

Such a comprehensive framework allows for and even compels to attempt a historic reconstruction of the genesis of community-based development projects. In the case of the two San living museums in Grashoek and //Xa/oba and the cultural village of Doupos, reviewed in the chapters of Part I, not a single interview referred to an imposed or patronised act. Notwithstanding the logistical and material support of NGOs, such as *The Living Culture Foundation Namibia*, the established cultural enterprises comprise much more than the occasional derogatory labels as "Ethno-theme parks" or even "human zoos" insinuate (cf. Comaroff/ Comaroff 2009: 11-21). In many ways, these cultural businesses build on the substantial self-determination of their participants (Zips-Mairitsch/ Zips 2015, film; Ju/'hoansi Living Museum 2018, online). Concurrently, the benefits are considerable in terms of capacity building, job creation, and tangible income creation, as Kaqece N!ani, one of the traditional counselors in Tsumkwe, summarises (in an interview on 14.01.2014):

> "The community profits from the conservancy in the way that there are people employed. The conservancy is having projects like water-tanks construction. The community members are maintaining the village water-points and also controlling the wildlife at the waterponds for game. They are maintaining these water sources as well. Then, there are devil's claw coordinators. It is a medicine, which the communities are harvesting in wintertime.

So, we are having a devil's claw coordinator, an agricultural coordinator. That one, his duty is to provide seeds and other support to the villages so that they can also have their own fields, where they plant maizemill, beans, groundnuts, melons and so on. The agriculture is based on these decisions. And we are also having the buffalo-rangers. Those ones are taking care of the buffalo camp, they maintain the fence, they care about the electricity of the fencing, they patrol and see whether there are poachers. Because at the buffalo camp we also have rhinos. The buffalo rangers are very important people and so are the community game-rangers. Those ones are at the village, they are doing fixed patrols to see which animals are in the area and so forth. So, community rangers and buffalo rangers, they are the main project beneficiaries, because we are receiving income just because of these animals. They count the animals and ask for hunting quota from the Ministry of Environment. Without the counting of the animals, the Ministry would not permit commercial hunting. Before the quota to be set up, they do a full-moon game count, where at each and every waterhole, there must be two people. They start at the same time and they count 48 hours. Then they come back, give the data for all species, for instance how many elephants plus minus are in the whole Nyae Nyae, how many Roan antelopes, how many Kudus. And the Ministry of Environment is giving the quotas accordingly. Then, if tourists come, they are supposed to pay the entrance-fee into the conservancy, the filming-fee and fees for the trophy-hunting, all this money is divided within the community. Some money goes to the members for their benefit, cash will be paid out according to their services. Other parts of the money go to the operational purposes of the conservancy, like to fill up the vehicles, pay the staff, maintain the office. So, I think the community is getting benefits from all this."

Obviously, neither the substantial self-determination through governing bodies, such as the management board of the Nyae Nyae conservancy, nor the tangible benefits accounted for in the quoted interview passage suggest either an ideal form of inclusive governance or a perfectly equitable model for one and all. Undoubtedly, meanings of various 'typical' hunter-gatherer activities (such as tracking or hunting) have now changed (and continue to change) under the influence of outside forces, as Koot and van Beek (2017: 144) emphasise. It really depends on the standard of comparison used in the final evaluation of CBNRM projects, such as the Nyae Nyae conservancy. From numerous interviews conducted between 2009 and 2014, including the University of Vienna field practice, it would appear that many individuals we spoke to actually experience an uplift or empowerment through the conservancy strategies for development. This observation somewhat contrasts with other, more critical reviews that detect an increasing domination by outside forces, which are then academically sued for enforcing involuntary acts of acquiescence or adaptation under pressure from former hunters and gatherers:

"Such changes are based on new relationships that have evolved in their environment, for example with a private tourism operator, trophy hunters, tourists, the government,

NGOs, expatriates, donors and consultants, who all in their own way dominate a part of the *Ju/'hoansi*'s environment, mostly based on goals and values in the global political economy." (Koot/ van Beek 2017: 145)

In their book "Ethnicity, Inc.", Jean and John Comaroff (2009) gave various examples of commercialisation or 'indigenous' entrepreneurship, including entire communities. Their careful weighing of opportunities and threats linked to an ever-expanding global economy of "Ethnicity, Inc." seems to come to the conclusion that it all depends: On the one hand, culture is certainly in danger of becoming a copyrighted possession in the growing hegemony of the global intellectual property regime. Reification to a mere heteronomous product appears as the natural role for those unable or unwilling to get the upper hand in the ensuing process of collective commodification. The entrenched colonial imagery may then be readily employed by the branding industry of ethno-tourism and its media derivatives. On the other hand, indigenous peoples and other collectives may consciously materialise their cultural experiences, traditions, and ecological knowledge. Thus, their self-marketing could potentially provide means to counteract long-standing structures of expropriation and exclusion from viable markets. Dispossessions of their lands and legal prohibitions of subsistence economies, such as hunting and gathering, backed by state sanctions robbed many self-reliant groups of their basic means of existence: "[...] in many desperate poor parts of the world, the attenuation of other modes of producing incomes has left the sale of cultural products, and of the simulacra of ethnicized selfhood, one of the only viable means of survival" (Comaroff/ Comaroff 2009: 139).

6 An Emerging Complementarity of Wildlife and Human Lifeworlds

In the context of the Namibian conservancies, the protection of intangible cultural heritage and traditional ecological knowledge becomes intertwined with the protection of habitats, nature, and wild animals (Ministry of Environment and Tourism 2018; cf. Craig/ Davis 2005: 54). Conservancy committees and wildlife councils, enacted by Section 24A and 24B of the *Nature Conservation Amendment Act* of 1996, represent, perhaps, new forms of conservation governance that abstain from a strict division of nature from humans. These local organisations treat the environment as integrative for the survival of some local communities. In turn, these landowners even consider themselves as part and parcel of the protected area (cf. Alden Wily 2003: 36 pp.). In contrast to the "fortress conservation" concept of a "pure, pristine natural environment" undisturbed by human interference, the

Namibian conservancies allow for hybrid types of conservation and novel institutional arrangements (Jones et al. 2015: 23).[9]

According to earlier concepts of nature protection, aptly coined "fortress conservation" (Adams/ McShane 1996; Adams/ Hulme 2001: 10), the foundation of a national park or game reserve almost always meant the practical dispossession and often displacement of people living on its land and off its resources. This was based on a presumed necessity of non-human interference to conserve wildlife and biodiversity. Forced removals were substantiated with the professed naturalist explanations of positive impacts on conservation, such as the expansion of the country's conservation estate. They were further legitimised with insistences of reduced consumptive use and decreased land deterioration, especially in high-biodiversity areas from which people were relocated (cf. Brockington 2002: 3-11; see also Zips-Mairitsch/ Zips 2017: 368 pp.). However, no evidence of negative impacts on conservation prior to people's relocation could be found in any of the cases studied, and no lasting impacts were evident (Fabricius/ de Wet 2002: 144).[10] For those affected in almost all cases of national park or game reserve declarations in Southern Africa (and beyond), the involuntary eviction meant not only profound symbolic losses but also their entire economic deprivation:

> "Conservation displacement, like other forms of displacement, compromise two processes (i) the forced removal of people from the[ir] homes; and (ii) economic displacement, the exclusion of people from particular areas in their pursuit of a livelihood." (Brockington/ Igoe 2006: 425)

Today, those communities potentially affected in Southern Africa (and beyond) are, therefore, quite immune to the 'sweet talk' of community participation and empowerment or joint management, which they suspect is a rhetorical strategy of the public and private sector to disguise its main agenda of wildlife protection geared to attract tourists with the myth of 'authentic wild Africa'. Many of those aware of the dramatic consequences of a long history of displacement and forced denial of resource access associate the idea of wildlife reserves with being forced off their land and deprived of their way of life (Metcalfe 2003: 10). Such appealing terms as economic community empowerment through ecotourism do not necessarily lure many of the communities concerned into believing that exclusive game

---

9 On so-called "fortress conservation" and its implications for indigenous peoples see Zips-Mairitsch (2013: 259).

10 Indigenous peoples are well aware of the irony that they are removed from wildlife areas against factual evidence that they were responsible for the preservation of biological diversity since generations, as the interview with Kgosi Molatwe Mokalake (05.09.2009), quoted in the preamble of the introduction to this volume shows.

lodges include considerations for their well-being. There is, rather, a widespread understanding that wildlife tourism and hunting for food appear to exclude each other, as, for instance, most San communities in Southern Africa painfully experienced. Many governmental institutions declared their relationships with nature as backward or archaic and therefore an unwanted survival of an anachronistic past. These governmental attitudes towards commercial conservation aggravated local sentiments against the lure of environmental protection and development initiatives. With the result that such promises of an unconditional mutual advantage and guaranteed improvement of their livelihood were no longer bought at face value by local entities (cf. Magome/ Murombedzi 2004: 116).

The negative impacts of fencing off huge areas for conservation and the protection of livestock production, particularly the cattle industry in the case of Botswana, were more than obvious. Animal counts of ungulates who depended on cut off migration routes indicate that the fences cutting through the Kalahari were the major causes for the loss of hundreds of thousands of wildebeests, hartebeests, zebra, and other species in just two decades from 1978 to 1999 (Mbaiwa/ Mbaiwa 2006: 19; cf. Perkins/ Ringrose 1996; Perkins/ Stuart-Hill/ Kgabung 2002). They were therefore aptly coined "fences of death" by foreseeing critics (Owen/ Owen 1980). Could the few Kudus or Gemsbok hunted per annum by the remaining San inhabitants of the Kalahari really matter that much? Especially if compared to the massive losses of various ungulate species caused by animal husbandry protection measures? A statement by the Botswana NGO *Kuru Family of Organizations* trying to protect the interests of San communities dispossessed of their lands in various national park sites of the Kalahari (including what is today the *Kgalagadi Transfrontier Park*) provides a telling answer in this regard:

> "For thousands of years people have been practicing [Community-Based Natural Resource Management] CBNRM by using their natural resources in a sustainable way. But, when National Parks and Game Reserves were set up, hunting for subsistence became poaching and local people were alienated from managing the resources on which they had previously depended." (Kuru Family of Organizations 2004: 2)

Against the backdrop of these negative examples in other countries of the region, Namibia opted to pioneer a new approach to integrated rural development and nature conservation. This particular scheme originated in the arid Kunene region in the north-west of Namibia. Owen-Smith describes in his brilliantly written 600 pages book "An Arid Eden. A Personal Account of Conservation in the Kaokoveld" (2010), how *Integrated Rural Development and Nature Conservation* (IRDNC), as an NGO and a programme came into existence after a long struggle against top-down conservation policies of exclusion. The author is the current co-director of IRDNC, one of the founding personalities behind this promising paradigm of conservation and development that integrates the interests and needs of local communities, and, perhaps, the key figure behind the alternative Namibian model for CBNRM. The mission statement of IRDNC (n.d., online) offers the imperatives in a nutshell:

> "IRDNC strives to improve the lives of rural people by diversifying the socio-economy in Namibia's communal areas to include wildlife and other valuable natural resources. We believe this will secure a long-term place for wild animals outside of national parks, and significantly reduce future pressure on these areas. We also aim to build up the capacity of rural Namibians, and to assist them to develop a civil society whose members can sustainably manage and benefit from their local natural resources."

Benefitting in the above sense includes controlled hunting, in both forms, as subsistence hunting with or without cultural hunting performances for tourists, such as in the Nyae Nyae conservancy and commercial trophy hunting, which makes up for one of the major sources of income in communal conservancies (including the Nyae Nyae). Trophy hunting is perhaps the most contentious, at least as far as animal rights activists and a great number of strict conservationists are concerned (cf. Adams 2004: 220-223). However, the critique of such resource utilisation often applies a strong double bind that delegitimises supervision and control by state bodies and NGOs as hegemonic domination, on the one hand, and accuses private businesses of luring indigenous communities into commercial ventures, on the other (cf. Naidoo et al. 2016: 634). The Ju/'hoansi of the Nyae Nyae we interviewed had quite a number of complaints against the government, like (justifiably) most indigenous communities, but never considered the Namibian *Ministry of Environment and Tourism* as their "landlord", as Koot and van Beek (2017: 142) would have it.

Instead of propagating questionable ideas of an 'unspoiled nature' with 'unspoiled cultures' dwelling within, these new governance approaches depart considerably from ongoing processes of marginalisation, disempowerment, development paternalisation, and so forth (Jones et al. 2015: 35). We therefore propose a discourse-critical parameter of due process in opinion- and will-formation based on equitable procedures of inclusion of all concerned with possible decisions and their implementation (cf. Habermas 1996: 129 pp.), instead of a comparative framework based on an ideal or idealised past of free, independent hunters and gatherers (Koot/ van Beek 2017: 145). Even well institutionalised conservancies, such as the Nyae Nyae, may still be considered as scanty forms of participatory governance as far as their intrinsic empowerment factor is concerned. However, they certainly allow for much more inclusive modes of natural resource management than the established forms of 'conservation against people', which commonly offers hardly anything apart from a few unreliable handouts to the former inhabitants and protectors of the environment:

> "Conservancy means first and foremost an obligation to conserve the natural resources like plants and animals. The real logic and purpose of a conservancy is not to restrict the environment at our grace. Because the constitution of the conservancy states it clear that a village is not supposed to have for instance more than hundred cattle, which would interfere with the wild animals. We want to keep the livestock limited so that the wild animals can have more space to roam freely. In the last years before independence, outside hunters came at their will and they shot animals as they wished. The community didn't get any money from commercial hunting, all the money went to the government. Then the Nyae Nyae conservancy came in and readjusted it, so that we can now benefit from the hunting. And also control it ourselves and take care of it." (Kaqece N!ani 14.01.2014, interview)[11]

To some extent conservancies do acknowledge the long histories of the co-existence of humans, animals, plants, and the natural landscapes to form integrated and integrating living environments (cf. Nustad 2015: 169). Although perhaps in an early, and still imperfect or nascent stage, these conservancies intend to combine the politics of empowerment, conservation, and development in a complementary mode of land use (NACSO 2016: 9). In a number of Namibian conservancies, the governmental support of joint venture partnerships with private investors beaconed novel models for community involvement in tourism. All of these have strengths and weaknesses in terms of asset ownership, business advantages, and risks. Yet, they also provide options for rural communities to regain control over the natural resources on their land (cf. Jones et al. 2016: 25-36). Taking the perspectives of those concerned into account, it appears premature and mono-dimensional to slander the potentials of self-reliance entrepreneurship as mere development rhetoric. The projected complementarity of conservation and development is explicitly predicated upon the balanced and sustainable management of natural and cultural resources made available to local communities. It projects a growing utilisation of cultural and natural resources through wildlife

[11] This development complies with the core of the UNESCO *Man and the Biosphere Programme* (MAB), which strives to improve the overall relationship between people and their environment (See: www.unesco.org/mab/wnbrs.shtml on Biosphere Reserves). Sadly enough, the establishment of a Biosphere Reserve was one of the sixteen recommendations for the *Central Kalahari Game Reserve* in Botswana but the government opted for the "least preferable" of all options for those directly concerned, which was the relocation of the San (cf. Zips-Mairitsch 2013: 280 pp.)

management and the self-designed commodification of cultural capacities. But, yes indeed, all this most certainly appears to be a far cry from the lifeworlds of hunters and gatherers in days long gone by.

The existence of wildlife is a fundamental resource for the cultural services at offer in the conservancies. However, success on hunting trips with tourists is rather the exception than the rule. Wild animals may be tricked by the San hunters, but much less so in the company of unaccustomed tourists. Still, the performance of a hunt, successful or not, is always considered as culturally rich, if //Xa/oba's visitors' book is to be trusted. This success depends overwhelmingly on the alternative acceptance of an 'impure nature', where people live and interact with the environment. Therefore, the once negative image of a 'wilderness lost due to human interference' has become the imprint or foundational principle of communal conservancies. 'Impure' in this context takes on new meaning of a true and impressive wilderness area peopled by local communities, its original inhabitants, custodians, and ultimate preservers.[12] Human interference, once considered contradictory to nature protection, is now increasingly considered as a prerequisite for sustainable conservation. The natural environment of Namibian conservancies has, thus, been re-evaluated as an indispensable resource for the performances of hunting skills. Nevertheless, it is much more than a mere setting for cultural performances. Within the interactive scenario encompassing the indigenous San, the visitors and animals, plants and other natural features, the intimate relationship between humans and their surrounding nature comes to the fore. Its empowering potential lies in the qualification of the San performers as creative directors of the event. They are the producers of their own show, in which they picture themselves as an integral part of nature (Ritterband 2018: 201-207; see also Zips-Mairitsch/ Zips 2015, film).

According to their experiences, failures and setbacks are always involved in the art of tracking on a hunt. However, their attitudes on hunting take into account that a successful hunt depends on the 'willingness' of the animals being hunted and the tacit support of other natural forces. The perspectives of San and other indigenous communities intricately refer to these non-human 'actors', not least by evoking their spirits (cf. Katz 1982: 13). Hunting and healing dances materialise the spiritual connection to the animal world, particularly for the performers themselves. Thereby, they deny a strict dichotomy between the tangible and intangible

---

[12] Koot/ van Beek (2017: 144) rightly distinguish between the historical indigenous safekeeping of an environment and the modern notion of conservation: "The way that hunter-gatherers consider themselves as custodians of their environment is very different from the scientific notion of conservation and the two should not be confused."

world (Günther 1999: 186 pp.; cf. Keeney 2010: 60). At the same time, their creative play with 'immemorial tradition' as part of their intangible heritage wreaks havoc with static concepts of authenticity. In this sense, Ju/'hoansi and other San communities in Namibia take on an active role in the "politics of authenticity" (cf. Fillitz/ Saris 2013: 14 pp.).

7 Conclusion: Almost like Christmas …

For a long time, the authoritative evaluations of authenticity were seen as prerogatives of much more powerful actors than San and other indigenous communities. National state institutions, such as museums, ministries, and universities, alongside international institutions and NGOs, determined the authentic quality of intangible and material culture and art. The self-designed re-enactments of 'traditional' cultural expressions by contemporary San performers in Namibian conservancies make their 'intangible heritage' very much tangible, not only for others but also for their younger generations (≠Oma/ Thoma 2002: 39-41). We were intrigued to learn from Xoan//a !Kunta, a leading personality, medicine woman, and daughter of the famous healer !Kunta Boo in Doupos, that the community decided to celebrate Christmas Day in 'the traditional way'. This meant to get together in the cultural village, built for the staging of 'traditional culture' for tourists, and to partake in traditional games and dances, dressed in the traditional way. Little did it matter to them that Christmas and the birth of Jessu Kriste (as they refer to Jesus Christ) was not celebrated at all in the olden days (cf. Günther 1999: 91).

The experiential journey on Christmas Day implicitly questions the now common critique of neoliberal cultural and ecological economics as imposed commodification. Such a reading may be adequate in many circumstances, where indigenous, ethnic, or ethnicised cultures are forced or co-opted to play the roles of exotic others from a past evolutionary time period (Urry 2002: 139-140). But inclusive and integrated schemes of conservation and development governance may also contribute to the (self-)empowerment of local communities to gain control over their heritage and the means as well as the limits of its marketing. Under certain conditions – and the Namibian conservancy model may be deemed quite advanced in this regard – the indigenous actors do not just fall victim to the global market of "Ethnicity, Inc." but use their cultural capital to take their destiny into their own hands, or at least try to get a more self-designed hold of it. Potentially, the occurring entrepreneurial agency could provide an enabling medium of self-governance to re-shape long-established power relations in conjunction with the material basis of indigenous land rights (WIMSA 2010: 12; cf. Mbaiwa 2016a).

Such emancipatory initiatives often overlooked and sometimes deliberately ignored by the contemporary critique of eco- and ethno-tourism as nothing but neoliberal acquiescence and subordination, in fact provide a comparative framework against which other regional developmental policies directed against indigenous cultures might be critically contextualised.

On various visits to San communities in neighbouring Botswana over many years (from 2000 to 2014), we became unwitting witnesses of the (symbolic) sacrifices of dignity, self-esteem, and even mere hope for the future caused by paternalistic governance attitudes for indigenous peoples. This appears to provide the more realistic or pragmatic frame of comparison, in terms of time and space, than the ideal of ageless or 'typical' hunters and gatherers free from outside interference. For those San entitled to return to the CKGR by the ground-breaking High Court decision of 2006 (see Zips-Mairitsch 2013: 322-358), Christmas meant the temporal visit of their children and grandchildren on school holidays from the resettlement villages outside of park's borders. The village of Mothomelo, forcibly deserted in 2002, came alive with crowds of kids and young people visiting their relatives during Christmas holidays in 2013 (as we were able to witness on this occasion). However, apart from that, we were told, there is little to celebrate. Left without noteworthy means of economic livelihood, subjected to new legal provisions banning hunting and gathering, as well as prohibiting animal husbandry within the game reserve, the entire community depends on handouts from occasional individual travellers; most of whom leave them behind, standing at the roadside in huge dust clouds, swirled up by their 4x4s. In the absence of alternative income sources from organised ecotourism, the once self-reliant factual owners of the Kalahari are turned into involuntary beggars for food and money, as one of the residents complained bitterly.

In contrast, perhaps for the first time in their more recent colonial and post-colonial history, the Ju/'hoansi of Nyae Nyae and other San communities of the N≠a Jaqna conservancy have arguably commenced to rule their own destiny by positioning themselves in the 'modern world' instead of being positioned at its margins (cf. Hitchcock/ Biesele 2002). These conservancies present institutional arrangements and legal arenas for emerging inclusive modes of nature and wildlife governance. Though most certainly still quite imperfect (as Robert Hitchcock elaborates in this volume based on sound empirical and historical data), they enclose new spaces of agency for local (at least partial) owners of land. In this regard, the conservancies appear much less as vanguards of an essentialised authenticity projected by some tempocentric critics. Explicit legal frameworks, which included their participation in the process of opinion- and will-formation, may prove better means of protection against the use and abuse through commercial enterprises by outsiders marketing a prescribed ageless authenticity than the dependence on good (governmental) will. It is, in our view, precisely this dependence, which makes the appeal to the public sector highly problematic. Notwithstanding the adequate criticism of private sector exploitation policies through exotic branding and other means of alienating commercialisations, not all CBNRM initiatives including market considerations are necessarily and merely neoliberal. The following three chapters in Part I shed light on both the opportunities and achievements as well as the contradictions and ambivalences of community conservation and cultural (self-)marketing in Namibia and Botswana.

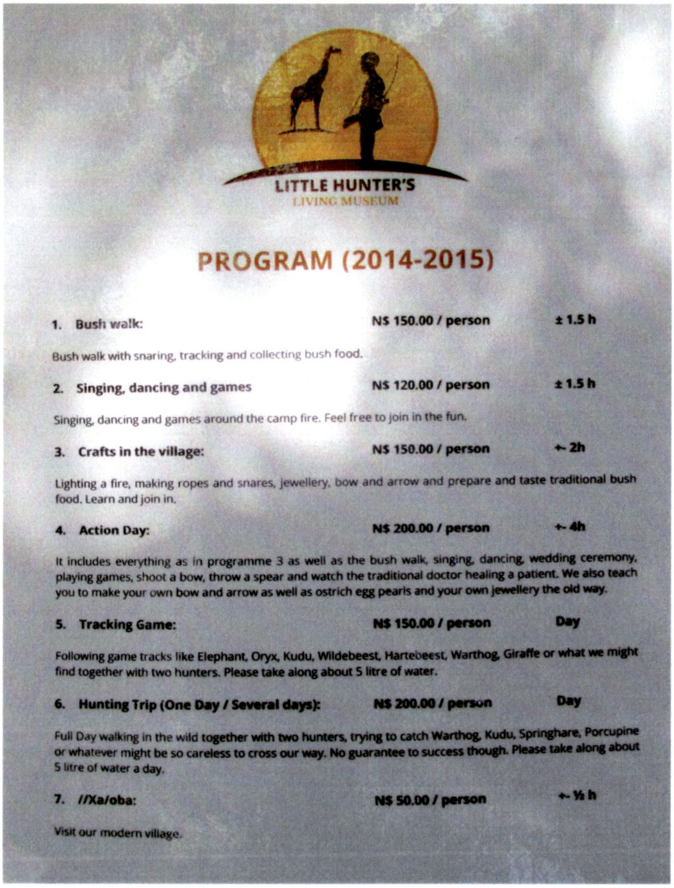

Ecotourism, Heritage Tourism, and Community-Based Development in a Southern African Borderland

Robert K. Hitchcock

1 Introduction

Many of the issues facing indigenous peoples today are the result of global processes, including economic development, the trans-border movement of people, services, goods and information, short-term and long-term environmental change, and competition for resources (de la Cardena/ Starn 2007; Hall/ Patrinos 2012; Bodley 2015). Another global process, the efforts of indigenous peoples to promote economic opportunities and empower themselves socially and politically through tourism has the potential of redressing some past injustices and ameliorating present circumstances (Aicken/ Ryan 2005; Johnston 2006; Whyte 2010; Fletcher/ Pforr/ Brueckner 2016; Wachira/ Karjala 2016: 409-410). In this paper, I address issues that relate to various kinds of tourism and indigenous peoples in a borderland region of Southern Africa.

In the past several decades, the Ju/'hoan San and other indigenous groups in Southern Africa have been able to benefit from Community-Based Natural Resource Management (or CBNRM) projects that have tourism as a component (Rozemeijer 2001; Mbaiwa 2003, 2004, 2005, 2008, 2016a, 2016b; Jones 2010; Jarkko/ Moswete/ Monare 2014). Some of this tourism is *ecotourism*, defined by the World Conservation Union (the IUCN) as "environmentally responsible travel and visitation to relatively undisturbed natural areas in order to enjoy and appreciate nature and any accompanying cultural features, both past and present that promotes conservation, has low visitor impacts, and provides for beneficially active involvement of local populations." Much of the tourism in Southern Africa revolves around ecotourism, which includes both nature-based recreational tourism and photographic tourism (for discussions of ecotourism, see Wearing/ Neil 1999; Stonza 2001; Stonza/ Durham 2008).

In addition to ecotourism there is cultural tourism, sometimes called ethnotourism (Guenther 2002). Cultural tourism can be defined as tourism that is concerned with a society or region's culture, especially the lifestyles, traditions, values, rituals, religion, art, ideas, and behaviours of that society. A sub-type of cultural tourism is heritage tourism, which enables visitors to see places that are significant from a cultural, archaeological, historical, architectural, and/or religious standpoint (see, for example, Kirshenblatt-Gimblett 1998; Sorensen/ Carman 2009; Staiff/ Bushnell/ Watson 2013). Heritage tourism may also include an element of searching for or exploring one's ethnic or cultural roots. A tourist, for our purposes, is an individual who has left his or her normal place of residence and has gone to a new place in order to gain new experiences, insights, and information.

It is estimated that 37% of contemporary tourism comprises cultural tourism according to the World Tourism Organization in 2017 (UNWTO, online). A significant portion of this tourism is heritage tourism, whereby people visit culturally significant places such as the pyramids of Giza in Egypt, the temples and residences of Angkor Wat in Cambodia, Great Zimbabwe, or the Taj Mahal in India. In Botswana, cultural tourism makes up approximately one fifth of the tourist visits to the country, according to the Department of Botswana Tourism in the Ministry of Environment, Wildlife, and Tourism (December 2016, personal communication). In Namibia, cultural tourism comprises approximately 25% of all tourist visits to the country (Namibia Ministry of Environment and Tourism March 2017, personal communication). There were 1.4 million tourists who came to Namibia in 2015 (Republic of Namibia 2017: 30); the number of tourists who visited Botswana in 2015 was 1.527.614 (Botswana Central Statistics Office 2016). In both Namibia and Botswana, many of the tourists interviewed said that they came to see 'the Big Five': lion, elephant, leopard, Cape buffalo, and rhinoceros. Some of these animals, notably elephants, are tied to water, some of which is developed using artificial water points (boreholes, windmills, and diesel or wind pumps (see, for example Rispel/ Lendelvo 2016, on the situation in Nyae Nyae, Namibia).

Both Botswana and Namibia have World Heritage Sites (WHS) that include extensive rock art, archaeological sites, and other valuable cultural heritage resources (Dowson 1991; Pager 1993; Keitumetse/ Nthoi 2009; Campbell/ Robbins/ Taylor 2010; Giraudo 2011; Mbaiwa 2016a). Tourists have visited Namibia specifically to see specific ethnic groups, notably the Himba in Kunene Region (Jacobsohn 1990; van Wolputte/ Hoorelbeke/ Bleckmann 2015) and the San in the Otjozondjupa and Zambezi Regions (Taylor 2012; van der Burg 2013). Some of the tourists who visit north-eastern Namibia and north-western Botswana come there purposely to visit the Ju/'hoansi San. The Ju/'hoansi, along with their relatives the X'ao-//'aen, number some 11.000 people on both sides of the Botswana-Namibia border (Dieckmann/ Thiem/ Hays 2014: 23, table 3.2; Hitchcock 2015, 2017, field data Botswana). Some tourists have said that they come to this area because they have seen films such as "The Gods Must be Crazy" (Uys 1980) or documentary films such as John Marshall's "A Kalahari Family" (2003) and Adrian Strong's "Bitter Roots" (2011). These films have commented on both the costs and benefits of tourism as it affects the San. The film "Ghostland" by Simon Stadler (2016) depicts Ju/'hoan reaction to tourists.

Interviews of tourists in the northern Kalahari suggest that films and documentaries influenced their decisions to visit the people of the area and had some impacts on their perceptions. Also important were well-known books such as Elizabeth Marshall Thomas' "The Harmless People" (1958) and her more recent book "The Old Way: A Story of the First People" (2006). In some cases, tourists said that they visited these places and people because they were intrigued by advertisements of the tourism departments of the two countries and private tourism companies such as Wilderness Safaris, Abercrombie and Kent, Natural Habitat Adventures, and Micato Safaris. A few tourists said that they had heard of the Living Culture Museums of Namibia and wanted to visit the Ju/'hoansi Living Museum in Grashoek and the Little Hunter's Museum in //Ao/oba (data obtained in June-July 2017).

One of the issues that adventure tourists sometimes react to is the presence of safari hunters and their clients. From the standpoint of the conservancy management committees, the safari hunting, which is conducted by private safari hunters who have contracts with the conservancies, is valuable economically, generating income, jobs, and meat from the kills (for a discussion of safari hunting in communal conservancies, see Naidoo et al. 2016; Angula et al. 2018).

The United Nations World Tourism Organization (UNWTO) and the World Bank both see tourism as a major means of promoting economic growth, improving livelihoods, and alleviating poverty (OECD 2009; Christie et al. 2014; UNWTO, n.d.). Tourism represents an important source of income and employment for the nation-states of Namibia and Botswana. In the case of Namibia, tourism makes up 4% of the Gross Domestic Product. From the standpoint of employment, tourism represents 5% of the total number of people employed. In the past 5 years tourism made up 19% of all jobs created (National Planning Commission, Government of Namibia employment data 2016).

According to the World Tourism Organization, Namibia ranks third in Sub-Saharan Africa in terms of tourism's contribution to the economy (see Government of Namibia 2012; UNWTO n.d., online). Tourism is ranked second in the list of priorities for Namibia in its current development plan (NDP 4, Republic of Namibia 2012). According to the Namibian National Development Plan 5 (Government of Namibia 2017), there are a number of challenges facing Namibia's tourism development, including lack of social and physical infrastructure in some rural areas, lack of skills on the part of some members of the population, and a lack of a service-oriented culture. The National Tourism Growth and Development Strategy (NTGDS) and Namibia's latest national development plan (NDP 5; Republic of Namibia 2017: 30-31) both aim to resolve these difficulties and to promote sustainable tourism.

The government of Botswana, in its 10th National Development Plan, sees tourism as an important engine for economic growth in the country (Republic of Botswana 2009a: 195-201). Tourism represents approximately 2.5% of the Gross Domestic Product of Botswana. The government admits, however, that in global terms Botswana does not stand out as a well-known and sought-after tourism destination (Republic of Botswana 2009a: 162). In the first decade of the new millennium, tourism provided some 23.000 jobs (Republic of Botswana 2009a: 195). Tourists spent P 5.1 billion during the NDP 10 period.[1] It was decided by the Botswana government that greater emphasis needed to be placed on cultural tourism in order to diversify the tourism industry and increase the benefits to local people (see Republic of Botswana 2009b).

In the 1990s, Botswana embarked on a nation-wide Community-Based Natural Resource Management programme, part of which focused on the formation of community-based organisations and the development of tourism (Rozemeijer 2001). As will be shown below, the CBNRM approach in Botswana has gone through some changes, some of them due to policy shifts (e.g. Republic of Botswana 2009b, c) and decisions of the district councils, supported by the central government, that have sought to capture more of the resources of the community trusts in the past 5 years (Poteete 2009; Hoon 2012; Hitchcock et al. 2015; Mbaiwa 2012).

In the balance of this paper, I consider the community-based institutions that have been established in Namibia and Botswana in order to take advantage of the presence of natural resources and tourists. While the two countries are known for their wildlife-related tourism, cultural and heritage tourism are also being encouraged by both governments (Government of Botswana 2009a, b, c; Government of Namibia 2012; Saarinen/ Moswete/ Monare 2014). Tourism-related institutions that exist in Namibia are conservancies and in Botswana they are known as community trusts or community associations. There are also national level non-government organisations that deal with tourism.

In Namibia, there were 82 communal conservancies as of July 2017 (NACSO, online), which together cover 54.3 % of the communal land in Namibia.[2] Commu-

1 The Exchange rate for the Botswana Pula in December 2015 was P 1 = US$ 0.09.

2 Since their inauguration, the trend to register communal conservancies has endured. Their num-

nal land in the country, according to government figures, comprise 298.200 km^2, or 36% of the total area of Namibia. In Botswana, community trusts are found primarily in what are known as Wildlife Management Areas (WMAs) which make up 129.450 km^2 or 22.2% of the total area of the country. Both countries have protected areas found within communal areas, which are considered to be state land. In Namibia, the conservation areas cover 116.000 km^2, or 14.03% of the country. In Botswana, national parks, game reserves, and monuments make up 101.535 km^2 or 17.4% of the total land in the country.

A major issue facing the people living on communal or state land is that they do not have legal control over their areas, so they cannot use the land as collateral for loans for local-level development purposes nor can they exclude outside groups or individuals from coming in to these areas and utilising the resources.

2 Communal Conservancies in Namibia

The government of Namibia established conservancies in the country in the late 1990s. The idea behind conservancies was to allow people in communal areas access to the benefits from wildlife. A conservancy in the communal areas of Namibia, under the *Nature Conservation Amendment Act* of 1996 (Republic of Namibia 1996) has resource rights to the benefits from wildlife and tourism.

The oldest communal conservancy in Namibia is the Nyae Nyae Conservancy, established in February 1998. The Nyae Nyae Conservancy, which is 8.992 km^2 in size, is located on the Namibia-Botswana border in the north-eastern part of the country in Otjozondjupa Region, which is 105.460 km^2 in size. Just to the west of Nyae Nyae is the N≠a Jaqna Conservancy, which was established in July 2003. At 9.120 km^2, N≠a Jaqna is the largest communal conservancy in the country and is more diverse in its ethnic composition than Nyae Nyae (Hohmann 2003; Hitchcock 2012; NACSO 2014).

Nyae Nyae and N≠a Jaqna are the only two communal conservancies in which San peoples are in the majority (Ju/'hoansi in the case of Nyae Nyae, and !Kung, !Xun, Khwe, Hai//om, and Ju/'hoansi in the case of N≠a Jaqna). Nyae Nyae has had a long history of development and interactions with non-government organisations and international agencies (Biesele/ Hitchcock 2013). Nyae Nyae is also one of the best-known areas in the world where local people derive a significant portion of their livelihoods from hunting and gathering. It is thus of great interest to tourists, journalists, filmmakers, researchers, and development workers.

ber has increased to 86 conservancies in less than two years, covering by now a total land mass of more than 166.000 km^2.

Currently, conservancies cover some two thirds of the communal land of Namibia (298.200 km^2 or 36.07% of the country's total land which is 826.680 km^2 in extent). Some of these conservancies have been quite successful, generating both income and jobs for their members (Jones 2010; Weaver et al. 2010; Integrated Rural Development and Nature Conservation 2011; Gargalo 2015; Mosimane/ Silva 2015; Naidoo et al. 2016). Namibian communal conservancies derive their funds from a variety of sources, including tourism, safari hunting, collection of high value medicinal plants, and payments from organisations that come to do films and other kinds of work. Some of the communal conservancies employ staff members, who receive salaries for their work. The conservancy management committees, who in most cases are unpaid, oversee the business of the conservancies. In 2016, the Nyae Nyae Conservancy generated over N$ 6 million for its members, some of the funds derived from safari hunting, some from tourism, some from the sale of high value plants, and some from payments by researchers and filmmakers.

Some of the work of the communal conservancies involves the following:

- High-end Tourism: Private companies are given leasehold or freehold rights over blocks of land for ecotourism purposes, as seen, for example, in the Kunene and Zambezi Region where tourist lodges were established.
- Safari Hunting Tourism: Private companies are given hunting rights as joint venture partners (JVPs) in communal conservancies; this is done through a competitive bidding process.
- Community-based development (CBD) approach: Local communities receive funds generated from tourism, safari hunting, and other activities such as sales of non-timber forest products (NTFPs) for local development.

Funding for conservancies in Namibia has come from a number of different sources, including international donors such as the World Bank, the U.S. Agency for International Development, the Millennium Challenge Corporation (MCC), the European Union (EU) as well as the Namibian government. Some conservancies in Namibia have the backing of local non-government organisations such as the World Wildlife Fund, Integrated Rural Development and Nature Conservation (IRDNC), and the Nyae Nyae Development Foundation of Namibia (NNDFN). The Nyae Nyae Development Foundation of Namibia, which was established in 1981, provides support and technical assistance for both Nyae Nyae and N≠a Jaqna (Biesele/ Hitchcock 2013; Hitchcock 2015a).

These conservancies are in remote areas and are located along a calcrete road which is over 280 km from the nearest large town in Namibia (Grootfontein). Both of the conservancies have benefitted from tourism, Nyae Nyae much moreso than

N≠a Jaqna. They have both had their challenges when it comes to the operations and viability of the community-based organisations established in the two areas (Hohmann 2003; Hitchcock 2012; Welch 2013). Boundary disputes have occurred between the two conservancies but generally these have been resolved. There are both similarities and differences between these two conservancies, which are summarised in table 1. Nyae Nyae has a greater abundance and diversity of wild animals and fewer people than does N≠a Jaqna.

Tsumkwe District West(N≠a Jaqna)	**Tsumkwe District East (Nyae Nyae)**
N≠a Jaqna Conservancy (2.000 members)	Nyae Nyae Conservancy (1.350 members)
9.120 km^2, 25 villages, 7.000 people	8.992 km^2, 36 villages, 2.700 people
Date of establishment: July 2003	Date of establishment: February 1998
!Kung, !Xun, Khwe, Hai//om, and Ju/'hoansi San, Kavango, Herero	Ju/'hoansi San
Not allowed to hunt	Subsistence hunting allowed
No use of traditional or modern weapons allowed	Use of traditional weapons, including bows and arrows with poison
No snares or traps allowed	Can use traditional snares
Cannot use dogs to assist in hunting	Cannot use dogs to assist in hunting
No mounted hunting allowed (horses, donkeys)	No mounted hunting allowed (horses, donkeys)
Ambush hunting is not allowed	Ambush hunting is allowed
Limits on all animals – no hunting	Limits on types of animals to be hunted
Quota set by Ministry of Environment and Tourism (MET), MET obtains meat for the villages	There is a quota for 'own-use' subsistence hunting, for safari hunting, and for the Traditional Authority
Some safari hunting done with a concession-holder (Eden Trophy Hunting)	Some safari hunting done with a concession-holder (SMJ Safaris) and a sub-contractor (Camelthorn Safaris)
Problem animal (predator) control done by MET	No shooting of predators by local people; problem animal control by MET
Resource management by N≠a Jaqna Conservancy members at the village level and traditional leaders and managers	Resource management by Nyae Nyae Conservancy and local *n!ore kxaosi* (Ju/'hoan territorial overseers)

Tsumkwe District West(N≠a Jaqna)	Tsumkwe District East (Nyae Nyae)
Tourism encouraged; Omatako Rest Camp run by the N≠a Jaqna Conservancy; Grashoek Ju/'hoansi Living Museum and Campsite and local level involvement in tourism, some returns from lodges in other areas	Tourism encouraged, done in conjunction with communities and the Conservancy Management Committee; 2 community campsites; Hunters Living Museum at //Ao/oba provides funds to the Nyae Nyae Conservancy (10% of income)

Table 1: Comparison of Natural Resource Management and Utilisation Strategies
Note: Data obtained from the N≠a Jaqna and Nyae Nyae Conservancy management committees, the Nyae Nyae Development Foundation of Namibia, the Ministry of Environment and Tourism (MET), and fieldwork.

The Nyae Nyae Conservancy saw the translocation of wild animals into the area by the World Wildlife Fund under the Living in a Finite Environment (LIFE) Project which was implemented in the period between 1995 and 2002 (Biesele/ Hitchcock 2013). These two conservancies are among the most successful in Namibia in terms of income and democratic decision-making. Both face major challenges, however, including widespread poverty, difficulties in financial management and record keeping, and incursions of people with livestock from outside of the region who have brought in livestock and are constructing fences and attempting to establish cattle farms (Begbie Clench 2015; van der Wulp 2016). These land use conflicts have affected the environments, the livelihoods of local people and the viability of tourism and community-based activities in the conservancies.

Nyae Nyae Conservancy is located in the Kalahari Desert region of northeastern Namibia and is part of the borderlands of Namibia and Botswana. The Ju/'hoansi who occupy Nyae Nyae and adjacent Dobe–/Xai/Xai in Botswana are, like a number of other indigenous peoples in Africa and around the world, a transboundary population.

The Nyae Nyae Conservancy's eastern boundary consists of the Botswana-Namibia border. The border fence was constructed in 1964. To the south of both conservancies is what is known as Namibia's 'red-line' veterinary cordon fence which runs east-west and separates the communal areas of the country from areas to the south, much of which is made up of commercial farms (Miescher 2012). The red-line fence is significant for a number of reasons, not least of which is the fact that livestock raised north of the fence cannot be sold to the European Union because of foot-and-mouth disease (FMD) restrictions. The fence represents a settlement border, as well, with what used to be known as Hereroland lying to the south of Nyae Nyae and N≠a Jaqna. There is also a veterinary cordon fence that runs north-south on the eastern boundary of N≠a Jaqna.

The two San majority conservancies have traditional authorities (TAs) who work in co-operation with the government of Namibia and the two conservancy management committees. TA Tsamkxao ≠Oma of the Ju/'hoansi in Nyae Nyae became one of the first San Traditional Authorities in Namibia in 1998, and Glony Arnold, the !Kung Traditional Authority in N≠a Jaqna became the !Kung TA in March 2015, replacing her father, John Arnold, who had died in 2012. The Traditional Authorities are consulted on matters involving land use and business development in the two conservancies and they play important roles in dispute-resolution and information dissemination. The Ministry of Environment and Tourism in Namibia and the Ministry of Environment, Wildlife, and Tourism (MEWT) in Botswana both consult local authorities and value their inputs.

The Otjozondjupa Regional Land Board based in Otjivarango in Namibia is the organisation in charge of land allocations along with the Ministry of Land Reform (MLR, formerly the Ministry of Lands and Resettlement (MLRR). Wildlife and tourism-related matters are handled by the Ministry of Environment and Tourism (MET). The Ministry of Environment and Tourism also handles the competitive bidding process in which private companies vie with one another for the hunting and safari tourism rights in communal conservancies. The management boards of the conservancies also play a role in the selection process for joint venture partners (JVPs). The bidding processes have not been without difficulties, however, and sometimes communal conservancies are told by the Ministry of Environment and Tourism that they have to go back to the drawing board and start the bidding process all over again. The communal conservancies get training from the MET and from non-government organisations in how to go about dealing with the leasing process.

An evaluation of the Nyae Nyae and N≠a Jaqna conservancies was carried out in June-August 2015 (see Hitchcock 2015a), with follow-up work in June-July 2017. Part of the focus of this evaluation, which also looked at the Nyae Nyae Development Foundation of Namibia, the organisation that provides support to the two conservancies, was on the economics of the two conservancies, including the benefits derived from tourism. Both conservancies attract tourists, most of whom come to Tsumkwe, the administrative centre of the district, before heading off to see places such as the Nyae Nyae Pans near /Aotca (Gautscha) or Khaudum National Park north of Tsumkwe next to the Botswana border (see figure 1).

There are no lodges or other formal tourist facilities in Khaudum at present, but there are camping sites that have water and in a few places, observation posts

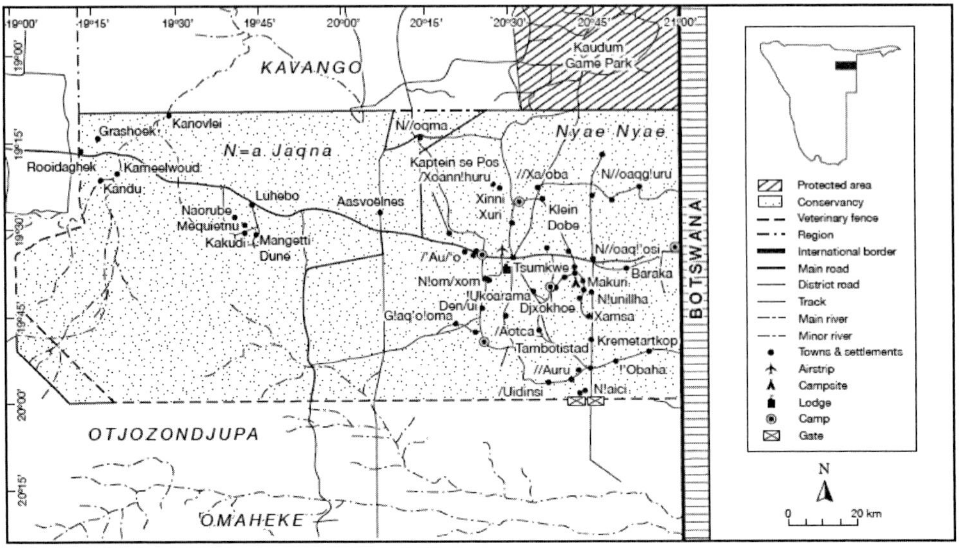

Figure 1: Nyae Nyae and N≠a Jaqna Namibia

for game viewing. An assessment of the numbers of visits to Khaudum in 2014 was that there was a total of 902.

Tsumkwe itself has a school, a clinic, a petrol station, a community centre, a police station, a municipal courthouse, several small general stores, and craft shop located next to the Nyae Nyae Conservancy office. Tsumkwe Lodge, now run by The University Centre for Studies in Namibia (TUCSIN), offers cabins and campsites for tourists. Some of the tourists who come to Tsumkwe are self-supporting, driving four-wheel drive vehicles and carrying camping equipment, food, and water. Safari company clients also come to the area to stay at Eden Game Farm, which is next to the western border of the N≠a Jaqna Conservancy. Others go to SMJ Safaris camp near Khaudum National Park or to the hunters' camp of Camelthorn Safaris near Baraka, a few kilometres east of Tsumkwe.

Tourists who visit the Tsumkwe area have another choice where they can stay, Nhoma, a tented camp near a San village located to the north of Nyae Nyae and outside the boundaries of the two conservancies. It is run currently by Arno Ouisthuizen. Tsumkwe Lodge is visited regularly by tourist groups, including ones from Club Med, which brings as many as 20-25 tourists several times a year. Other tourism companies, including one from Spain, bring smaller groups of tourists (8-12) to Tsumkwe. There are also self-driving tourists who stay at the Tsumkwe Lodge.

Some of the tourists who come to Tsumkwe Lodge are taken to two Nyae Nyae communities to the south of Tsumkwe, Du Pos and Mountain Pos. At present, there are no arrangements between either of these lodges (Nhoma and Tsumkwe) and the two conservancies in terms of paying a percentage of their profits to the conservancies. On the other hand, Nanofasa, a relatively recent arrival on the tourism scene in the area (2011), does provide funds to the two conservancies and has had some success in promoting community-level development in Nhoma and at //Xau/oba, though the operation is in flux because of issues involving land tenure as of July 2017.

Tourism can also pose risks both for the tourist and his or her hosts. This can be seen in the case of an Australian tourist who was saved from a bush fire in southern Nyae Nyae on 28 August 2012. As it turned out, three of the five Ju/'hoansi who were accompanying her burned to death in the fire, and two others were severely injured. The selfless actions of the Ju/'hoansi got considerable media coverage in Namibia, South Africa, Australia, and the United Kingdom. The two surviving Ju/'hoansi, always self-effacing, did not want to take credit for their efforts.

Namibia has a Living Culture Foundation (LCFN), which provides support to living museums and cultural villages in the country (Zips 2015). Two of these living museums are found in the Tsumkwe District: (1) Living Museum of the Ju/'hoansi San at Grashoek, established in July 2004, which is in N≠a Jaqna Conservancy, and (2) the Little Hunter's Museum of the Ju/'hoansi San which is based in //Xa/oba in the Nyae Nyae Conservancy, established in March 2010. When the Little Hunter's Museum of the Ju/'hoansi began, there were less than 40 people living in the village; there are now over 220. As shown in table 2, there are living museums and cultural villages found in several countries in Southern Africa including Namibia, Botswana, and Zimbabwe. In addition to the two Ju/'hoan living museums, Namibia also has living museums in Damaraland and in Zambezi Region in which Damara and Mafwe communities are involved. In 2014 the Living Museum of the Ju/'hoansi and its campsite had a business manager, a crafts manager, and 6 groups of performers. The total number of people who benefitted from Grashoek was 80 people.

Name of Living Museum or Cultural Village, Date of founding	**Location**	**Population Size**	**Activities undertaken by residents and visitors**
Living Museum of the Ju/'hoansi San, Grashoek, July 2004	Grashoek, N≠a Jaqna Conservancy, Otjozondjupa Region, Namibia	250 people, !Kung and Ju/'hoansi San	Dances, gathering trips, guided walks, camping, crafts manufacture and sales
Little Hunter's Museum of the Ju/'hoansi San, March 2010	//Xao/oba, Nyae Nyae Conservancy, Otjozondjupa Region, Namibia	220 people, Ju/'hoansi San	Dances, hunting trips, gathering trips, guided walks, crafts manufacture and sales
Nanofasa, 2011	Nhoma, Nyae Nyae area, Otjozondjupa Region, Namibia	250 people, Ju/'hoansi San and some Khwe and !Kung	Dances, hunting trips, gathering trips, guided walks, crafts manufacture and sales, including high quality sandals
The Living Museum of the Damara, February 2010	8 km from Twyfelfontein, a World Heritage Site, 2007, Namibia	No data, total population of Damara 100.000	Cultural village, traditional life, bush walks, dancing, singing
The Living Museum of the Mafwe, February 2008	22 km north of Kongola, Zambezi Region, Namibia	Singalawe Village nearby, 21 people work at the Living Museum	Cultural village, traditional life, bush walks, dancing, singing, crafts
The Living Museum of the Mbunza, October 2011	14 km west of Rundu, Kavango East Region, Namibia	Samsitu Lake, Kavango Region, 115.447 total in region	Cultural village, traditional life, bush walks, dancing, crafts
The Living Museum of the Ovahimba, November 2016	40 km north of Opuwo on C43, road to Epupa Falls	Kunene Region	Cultural village, traditional life, bush walks, camping, crafts
N/a'an ku sê, wildlife sanctuary and cultural village	30 km east of Windhoek	3.200 ha wildlife sanctuary	Cultural village, wildlife viewing, bush walks, dancing, healing
/Xai/Xai Community, Botswana, October 1997, size 20 km^2	/Xai/Xai, North West District, Botswana	500 people, Ju/'hoansi San and Mbanderu (Herero)	Dances, hunting trips, gathering trips, guided walks, crafts manufacture and sales

Name of Living Museum or Cultural Village, Date of founding	Location	Population Size	Activities undertaken by residents and visitors
Tsodilo Hills World Heritage Site, 2001, size 225 km^2	Tsodilo Hills, North West District, Botswana	350 people, 100 Ju/'hoansi San, 250 Mbukushu	Dances, guided walks, crafts manufacture and sales
Dqae Qare Game Farm, 1998, size 75 km^2	Ghanzi District, Botswana	40 people, Naro San	Dances, guided walks, crafts manufacture and sales, plant identification
D'Kar Village, 1986, size 30 km^2	Ghanzi District, Botswana	1.200 people, Naro San, Bakgalagadi, Herero	Museum, cultural centre, art project, art and crafts manufacture and sales
Manxotae, 1975, size 4 km^2	Central District, Botswana	800 people, Tshwa San, Kalanga, Bamangwato	Involvement in Nata Bird Sanctuary
Dlamini, Zimbabwe, 2011, size 0.5 km^2	Tsholotsho District, Matabeleland North Province, Zimbabwe	130 people, Tshwa San, Ndebele, Kalanga	A cultural village and craft sales to tourists
Liphofung Cave and Museum, February 1998, size 4.5 ha	'Muela Region, Lesotho	150 Bashoto in a nearby village, Community Conservation Forum (CCF)	Cultural museum, crafts, guided rock art walks, pony trekking

Table 2: Living Museums and Cultural Villages in Southern Africa

Data from the N≠a Jaqna Conservancy and the Living Culture Foundation of Namibia reveal that individuals involved in the tourism programme were making approximately N$ 4.290 per year per person. The Grashoek Living Museum was thus one of the largest employers and providers of funds to people in the N≠a Jaqna Conservancy, giving N$ 15.000 to the N≠a Jaqna Conservancy in the 2014-2015 period (Hitchcock 2015a). The Grashoek Living Museum generated as much as N$ 500.000 per annum.[3] In the past year (2015-2016), however, there have been some intra-community splits in Grashoek over who in the village gets to participate in the living museum and tourism activities.

Numerous activities are demonstrated in the living museums, including fire making, plant processing, craft manufacture, gathering of wild food and medic-

[3] The Namibian Dollar in December 2015 was equivalent to US$0.064.

inal plants, hunting and tracking, hut building, and plant identification. Dances, some of which represent healing dances, are performed by groups of village residents. There are also traditional activities that are done rarely for tourists, such as arrow poison manufacture, since it is potentially dangerous and the Ju/'hoansi poison-makers want to ensure that their secrets about the manufacture are kept to themselves (Chaboo et al. 2016). Tourists do, however, frequently ask about the manufacture and use of arrow poisons.

The Little Hunters' Museum of the Ju/'hoansi San (also called //An Tsia Tju /o) at //Xa/oba was founded and is managed currently by !Amace N!aici. The museum pays 10% of its profits to the Nyae Nyae Conservancy. Some of the village members also work for SMJ Safaris which is located to the north and west of //Xa/oba. At the time, I visited the Little Hunter's Museum in July 2015, the residents had just been given some elephant meat by one of the hunting companies operating in Nyae Nyae. According to !Amace N!aici, the living museum has several benefits, including generating income for the village and its members, providing employment, and facilitating the maintenance of Ju/'hoan culture. The practicing of traditional activities is important 'so that Ju/'hoan children do not forget', as !Amace N!aici put it in the film on Living Museums done by Werner Zips and Manuela Zips-Mairitsch (2015). He also said that the presence of the Little Hunter's Museum has served to attract other projects, including a tracking academy operated by Cybertracker (Cybertracker n.d., online; see also Liebenberg 1990, 1992, 2006). The presence of the tracking activities has focused attention on the Ju/'hoansi and their skills and abilities to find animals and make their way around the northern Kalahari landscape (Stander et al. 1997; Biesele/ Barclay 2001; Hitchcock 2017a).

Ju/'hoan women are as skilled as men at recognising tracks, and the exchange of information between men and women while tracking contributes substantially to greater effectiveness in the procurement of prey. As Biesele and Barclay (2001: 78) note, women on hunts share signals with men. Tracking knowledge also helps ensure the safety of individuals since people can recognise signs of predators and the presence of other people, some of whom may represent potential threats. Several Ju/'hoansi in Botswana mentioned the importance of tracking skills in determining the presence of game scouts of the Department of Wildlife and National Parks intent on seeking people obtaining wildlife illegally. They also noted that the tracking skills made them aware of tourists coming to their villages, which had potential economic benefits for them. Communal conservancies in Namibia that promote tracking of high value animals have demonstrated that they can produce benefits for the conservancy management committees and the members of those conservancies (Ndlovu/ Utete/ Kimaro 2014; Hitchcock 2017b).

3 The Living Museums and Cultural Villages

An analysis of the activities that take place in the living museums reveals that some gender division is associated with specific activities. Activities that men tend to do more than women are fire making, smoking bees out of trees to obtain honey, skin tanning, tracking, and hunting, while women tend to engage more frequently in the making of grass huts, jewellery manufacture, and wild plant gathering. Both men and women take out groups of tourists, as can be seen in one of the films of Werner Zips and Manuela Zips-Mairitsch (2015). Sometimes the tourists pay the treasurer or manager of the living museum directly, while in other cases, they may engage individuals for specific activities such as nature walks who they pay directly, usually N$ 100 – N$ 150 per person.

In addition to the two living museums in the Nyae Nyae and N≠a Jaqna Conservancies, there are also some campsites that are operated by local communities. One of these is the Omatako Rest Camp, which is operated by Omatako Village in N≠a Jaqna Conservancy. Another is Makuri in the Nyae Nyae Conservancy (Wiessner 2003). In addition to the benefits provided by these community campsites to the conservancy management committees, funds from the campsite also go to the villages with which they are associated.

Tourists also pay individuals for specific activities such as trips to the Nyae Nyae Pans near Gautscha, which can be arranged through the Tsumkwe Lodge. These trips cost N$ 350.00, not including tips. There were two Ju/'hoansi who were based at Tsumkwe Lodge who took tourists to the pans and other places. A total of 10 Nyae Nyae Ju/'hoansi were Community Game Guards (CGGs) for the Nyae Nyae Conservancy, and there were 7 such game guards in the N≠a Jaqna Conservancy in 2014-2015. A dozen Ju/'hoansi were employed as hunting assistants and guides by the two safari companies operating in Nyae Nyae. Approximately a dozen Ju/'hoansi had jobs at Tsumkwe Lodge where they also received training of various kinds (Hitchcock 2015a). Nanofasa Conservation Trust was employing four San cobblers and three San trackers, and a !Kung San assistant in March 2017.

Besides the tourists who visit the living museums at Grashoek and //Xa/oba, there are also those who visit Tsumkwe on their way to Khaudum National Park or who are driving east toward Botswana, crossing the border at the Dobe Border

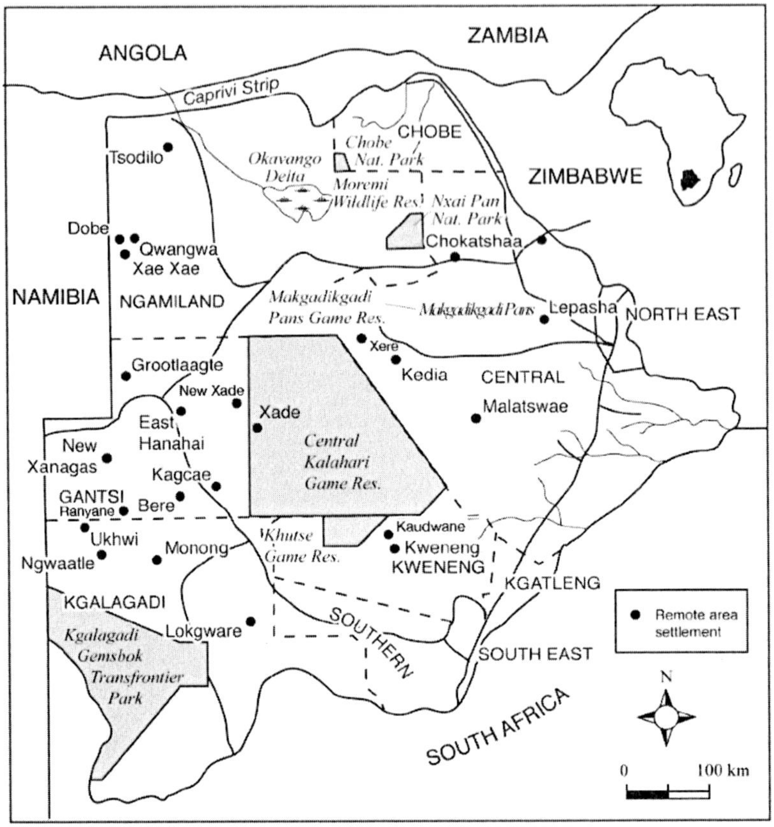

Figure 2: Map of Remote Area Settlements in Botswana

Gate and going on to places such as /Xai/Xai, G/wihaba, the Tsodilo Hills, or the Okavango Delta (see figure 2).

Once across the Botswana-Namibia border tourists often have a very different experience than they do in Namibia, due to the ways that the government of Botswana and private companies deal with cultural tourism and heritage tourism.

4 Cultural and Heritage Tourism in Botswana

The Botswana government prefers not to use the model village or living museum approach. Instead, much of the current tourism at the community level is leased out to private companies which have joint venture agreements (JVAs) with community trusts. There are no living museums or cultural villages that are separate from local communities in Botswana except for a few private sector operations.

Unlike Namibia, the communities that have joint venture agreements do not set up separate facilities for tourists. Tourist-related activities are carried out directly in villages such as /Xai/Xai or Dobe (Mbaiwa/ Sazuke 2009; Garner 2012; Hitchcock et al. 2015). Botswana in the past focused on high cost, low volume tourism which was oriented mainly toward protected areas.

In the 1970s, 1980s, and 1990s, the government of Botswana tended to shy away from cultural tourism, in part because government personnel felt that cultural tourism was exploitative and tended to favor specific ethnic groups over others, something that Botswana government officials were concerned about (Wily 1975, 1979). In the 1970s, for example, Botswana would not allow photographs of people in traditional dress such as men in leather breechcloths carrying bows and arrows or spears. In recent years, this attitude has changed, and one now sees representations of traditional dances and cultural festivals such as the Kuru Dance Festival, held most recently in late August 2015 at Dqae Qare Lodge in Ghanzi District. Individual dance groups such as the G/wihaba Dancers from /Xai/Xai are paid for their participation in the dance festivals, as they are when they go to Gaborone for cultural festivals held on Independence Day on the 30th of September every year. These cultural festivals have been promoted heavily by the former president of Botswana, Lt. General Seretse Khama Ian Khama.

It is important to note that the conservancies and community trusts have a variety of procedures and rules by which they operate. Some of them provide funds only for community events such as funerals and they pay for medicines such as anti-retrovirals for people with HIV/AIDS and provide blankets and food to needy people. One of the problems that community-based organisations face is that members do not always agree about the ways to handle issues such as the use of community trust funds. In the case of the /Xai/Xai (Cgae Cgae) Tlhabololo Development Trust in Botswana, the distribution of benefits was done by household groups, which differs somewhat from that of the Namibian conservancies which provide individual member benefits once a year, usually at Christmas time.

In the case of Tsodilo Hills in Botswana, there are differences of opinion as to whether the Tsodilo Hills Development Trust (THDT) gets any funds from the World Heritage Site or the Botswana National Museum which oversees the hills. There are also disagreements over how to handle high-value areas within community trusts. In /Xai/Xai, Botswana, for example, there are arguments among trust members over what to do about important places such as G/wihaba, a set of caves with important gathering and cultural resources. The president of Botswana wants to turn it into a private concession area and give a private company the rights to establish a lodge there, something that people in /Xai/Xai are opposed to. They would prefer to see a lodge run by the community (Hitchcock et al. 2015). However, since the hunting ban was imposed in Botswana in January 2014, there is a great deal of uncertainty over the future of community trusts, with some Botswana government officials pushing hard for all the trusts to be turned over to private Batswana-owned companies.

Another problem with ecotourism and heritage tourism projects is that they tend to have differential and sometimes negative gender-related impacts. Hunting-related activities tend to favor males, as do those projects that have employees that serve as guides. Often, males are more familiar with English, Afrikaans, German, or Spanish and thus they interact more with the safari hunting clients. In some cases, women do get jobs, notably working as cooks in safari camps or as cleaners in tourism lodges. Women make most of the craft items that are sold to tourists. But in general, males tend to benefit more from tourism development than females in communal conservancies in Namibia and community trusts in Botswana. An area where women tend to outcompete men is in the procurement, processing, and sale of high value plant products such as Devil's Claw (*Harpagophytum procumbens*). Adult females and males and sometimes children take part in dance festivals such as the ones that occur at /Xai/Xai and at the Dqae Qare Game Farm in Botswana.

One of the ways that ecotourism has been promoted in Namibia and Botswana has been on private farms that support wildlife, including predators such as cheetahs and leopards and ostriches. One example is Okonjima in Namibia, which is a private farm which operates partly as a large cat conservation project and tourism operation. Another example of such a game farm is Dqae Qare Game Farm, which is owned by the Naro San of Kuru Development Trust of D'Kar in Ghanzi District. Dqae Qare is situated about 21 km north of Ghanzi town in western Botswana. This game farm, which is 7.500 hectares in size, is operated as both an ecotourism and cultural tourism project. Tourists can visit and stay at the game farm, which has an Afrikaner-style guesthouse and a set of huts where people can camp. About two dozen people from D'Kar and elsewhere work at Dqae Qare. The game farm offers not only food and lodging but also the opportunity to interact with local San and have what the Dqae Qare website calls "the Bushman Experience" (Dqae Qare n.d., online). As the website and brochures on Dqae Qare put it:

"For those wishing to delve a little into our traditional life style, we offer the "Bushman Experience" which is the opportunity of living with us in the veld and learning from the masters themselves. Practice the techniques developed long ago to allow us to survive the harsh environment of our homelands. You can build your own grass hut, track game by reading the messages they leave in the sand, gather your food from the veld, start your own fire with traditional sticks, make jewelry from ostrich eggshell beads, learn to play our games and participate in our traditional dances." (ibid.)

Interviews of people who have visited Dqae Qare reveal that many of them enjoyed the opportunity to see how people made a living in the Kalahari and to learn about various aspects of local cultural traditions and practices. They appreciated the fact that the game farm project was multi-purpose in nature, that is (1) to promote greater understanding of the environment and local societies, (2) to preserve traditional knowledge, (3) to create employment and generate income, and (4) to give local people the opportunity to manage a business of their own. For the past several years, the Kuru Dance Festival, an important multi-ethnic cultural festival, has been held at Dqae Qare, where as many as 2.000 or more people gather to watch the dancing of people and community groups from across Southern Africa. There have been arguments about whether Kuru and other cultural festivals in Botswana have economic, cultural, and social benefits and whether these performances have allowed communities and individuals to 'cash in or sell out' (Rupoo 2016).

It is important to emphasise that there are controversies and conflicts between conservation and development in Southern Africa, with some policy makers favouring strict preservation of habitats and wildlife and other natural resources while people at the grassroots level favour a community-based conservation and development approach that allows local people to benefit from natural resources. To take one example, when the Tsodilo Hills became a World Heritage Site in 2001, there was a land rush of people from outside of the hills who wished to get land allocations near Tsodilo (Giraudo 2011). This followed the relocation of the Ju/'hoan village away from the hills in 1994-95, for which the Ju/'hoansi were paid a compensation fee of P 17.500 (Alec Campbell 1995, personal communication) (at the time, 1995, the exchange rate was P 2.76 to US$ 1).

The Ju/'hoansi at Tsodilo continue to feel that they were treated differentially and unfairly by the National Museum, the North-West District Council, and other Botswana government agencies. One of their main complaints has to do with the fact that the Mbukushu village remains close to the southern entrance of the Tsodilo Hills, while the Ju/'hoan village was relocated several kilometres to the South. Their new location meant that they had less access to the tourists who visit Tsodilo. A comparison of economic returns of the two villages shows that the Mbukushu village earned approximately three times what the Ju/'hoan village earns from tourists. It should be noted, however, that the Ju/'hoan craft producers tend to make more money than do the Mbukushu as their crafts are more highly valued by tourists. Part of the difference between the two villages arises from the fact that the Mbukushu have a better command of English than do the Ju/'hoansi and can serve as guides to the rock paintings and archaeological sites.

One of the problems faced in the past by communities in both Botswana and Namibia was that once protected areas such as national monuments and game reserves were established, local people were required to vacate them, and then their access to resource within the protected areas was limited (Dieckmann 2007; Hitchcock 2015b; Sapignoli 2015). The declaration of an area as part of a transfrontier conservation area or a World Heritage Site does not guarantee that people will not be excluded from those areas. This can be seen in the case of the Tsodilo Hills and there are indications as well that some of the communities in the recently declared (July 2014) Okavango World Heritage Site have been told to resettle and to restrict activities such as resource collection and livestock grazing inside of the boundaries of the World Heritage Site (Mbaiwa 2016b). It should be noted, however, that both Tsodilo and the Okavango World Heritage Sites allow mineral and gas exploration activities, including hydrological fracturing ("fracking") by private companies for which local communities receive no benefits whatsoever.

Both Namibia and Botswana are placing more emphasis today on the establishment and operation and management of transfrontier conservation areas and are promoting transboundary cooperation on issues such as wildlife conservation, tourism, and anti-poaching. A transfrontier conservation area (TFCA) is defined in the SADC Protocol on Wildlife Conservation and Law Enforcement (Southern African Development Community 1999) as a component of a large ecological region that straddles the boundaries of two or more countries encompassing one or more protected areas as well as multiple resource use areas.

Southern Africa is a world leader in the area of community-based conservation and integrated conservation and development projects (Hanks/ Myburgh 2015). Some of the transfrontier conservation areas are also called "peace parks" (see Büscher 2013). These TFCAs have existed since the late 1990s; one example is the Kgalagadi Transfrontier Park which is administered by both Botswana and South Africa. In 1998, the ≠Khomani San won an out-of-court settlement over benefits from the Kgalagadi Transfrontier Park including co-management rights and a portion of the gate receipts from the park. The ≠Khomani also received six farms covering an area of some 40.000 hectares where local people engage partly in food and craft production and in cultural tourism (Mboti 2017).

The Botswana-Namibia border area is part of what is known as the Kavango-Zambezi Transfrontier Conservation Area (KAZA) (400.000 km^2) which includes the Nyae Nyae and N≠a Jaqna Conservancies and the /Xai/Xai and Tsodilo community development trusts in Botswana (for an assessment of KAZA, see Cumming 2008). It should be noted that from the conservancy and community trust standpoints, the KAZA transfrontier conservation area has provided relatively few direct benefits in terms of funds to the community-based organisations, most of the funds going to either the governments or the non-government organisations working with them. There are plans, however, to expand tourism activities and to set up mechanisms to channel funds to communities more effectively.

Questions have been raised about whether tourism has had more positive impacts than negative in communities in both Namibia and Botswana (Garland 1994, 1999; Schalken 1999; Mbaiwa/ Sakuze 2009; Koot 2013, 2015; van der Burg 2013). A significant question raised by both tourists and other observers is the degree to which living museums, cultural villages, and community campsites are authentic expressions of local culture (see, for example, Garland/ Gordon 1999; Zips 2015). An assessment of places that tourists visit are now conservancies and community trusts (see table 3 for data on conservancies in Namibia and community trusts in the North-West District (Ngamiland), Botswana).

Name of Conservancy or Community Trust and date of establishment	**Controlled Hunting Area Number, Size (square kilometres)**	**San Population and Total Population and Composition**	**Activities undertaken by residents and visitors**
Nyae Nyae Conservancy, February 1998	No. 1 of 84, 8.992 km^2	2.700 people, Ju/'hoansi San	foraging, farming, crafts, livestock, tourism, safari hunting
N≠a Jaqna Conservancy, July 2003	No. 29 of 84, 9.120 km^2	7.000 people, !Kung, !Xun, Khwe, Hai//om, and Ju/'hoansi San, Kavango, Ovambo, Herero	foraging, farming, crafts, livestock, tourism, safari hunting
/Xai/Xai (/Kae/Kae, Cgae Cgae), Tlhabololo Trust, October 1997	NG 4, 9.293 km^2 and access to NG 5, 7.673 km^2 (16.966 km^2 total)	Ju/'hoansi San 425 (of 500, 80%), Herero (Mbanderu), Tawana	foraging, farming, crafts, livestock, tourism, JVP
Dobe Community Development Trust, 1999	NG 3, 5.760 km^2	Ju/'hoansi San 350 (of 550, 63%) in Dobe, Herero, Tawana	foraging, farming, crafts, livestock, tourism
Jakotsha Community Trust, 1999	NG 24, 530 km^2	Mbukushu, Herero and G//anikwe San, 10.000 people, multiple villages	Community tourism, *makoro* (canoe) poling, basketry and other craft sales

Name of Conservancy or Community Trust and date of establishment	Controlled Hunting Area Number, Size (square kilometres)	San Population and Total Population and Composition	Activities undertaken by residents and visitors
Khwai Development Trust (KDT), 2.000	NG 18, 1.815 km^2 and NG 19, 180 km^2	Bugakwe San, Tawana, and Subiya, 360 people, 1 village	Ecotourism, craft sales, work at safari lodge, Tsaro, and leased out hunting quotas to a JVP
Mababe Zukutsama Community Trust, 1998	NG 41, 2.045 km^2	Tsegakhwe San, 400 people, 1 village,	Ecotourism, leased out some of the hunting quota to a JVP
Okavango Community Trust, 1995	NG 22, 580 km^2, NG 23, 540 km^2	Bugakwe, Wayeyi, Mbukushu, G//anikwe, Dxeriku, Batawana, 2,200 people, 5 villages	JVP Safari hunting, photo-based tourism, crafts, foraging
Okavango Kopano (Mokoro) Community Trust (OKMCT), 1997	NG 32, 1.223 km^2	Bugakwe San, Wayeyi, Mbukushu, 800 people	Community tourism, craft sales, natural resource marketing (palms)
Teemashane Community Trust, 1999	NG 10 and NG 11, ca. 800 km^2	Mbukushu, Wayeyi, Bugakwe San, G//anikwe San, 5.000 people	Community tourism, campsite, cultural trail, craft sales
Tsodilo Community Development Trust (TCDT), 2006	NG 6, 225 km^2	Mbukushu, Ju/'hoansi San, 250 people	rock art guiding, community tourism, craft sales

Table 3: Conservancies in North-Eastern Namibia and Community Trusts in the North-West District (Ngamiland), Botswana
Note: Data obtained from the Ministry of Environment and Tourism, Namibia, the Nyae Nyae Development Foundation of Namibia, the Ministry of Environment, Wildlife and Tourism, Botswana, and from Cassidy et al. (2001: A-38, table A 30; see also NACSO 2014, www.nacso.org.na; JVP stands for Joint Venture Partnership; NG stands for Ngamiland)

Detailed studies of only a few of these community-based organisations have been carried out. The /Xai/Xai Tlhabololo Trust in Botswana is one example. This community trust is the oldest in Botswana, having been founded in October 1997. /Xai/Xai is located in a community-controlled hunting area (CCHA) known as NG (Ngamiland) 4, which is 9.293 km^2 in size. People at /Xai/Xai also have rights to wildlife in NG 5 (7.623 km^2 in size). The total area to which the people of /Xai/Xai had access to was 16.916 km^2 in area. This /Xai/Xai NG 4 and NG 5 area is relatively comparable in size to the area of the two communal conservancies in Namibia, which together cover an area of 18.112 km^2. The difference between the two areas on opposite sides of the border that is so significant is the fact that the two Namibia conservancies have 61 communities and a town (a municipal area) (Tsumkwe), while /Xai/Xai is a single village.

Unlike Nyae Nyae, at /Xai/Xai, there are members of two ethnic groups who are on the board of the community trust, Ju/'hoansi and Herero. There are significant differences of opinion at /Xai/Xai between the Ju/'hoansi and the Herero about how the trust should operate. In recent years, the Herero have tended to dominate the decision-making in the /Xai/Xai Trust. The Ju/'hoansi of /Xai/Xai, especially Ju/'hoan women, sell arts and crafts and take part in dances and other cultural activities when safari operators bring clients to the area, which is usually for a period of 3 to 4 days. Local people demonstrate gathering of wild plants while men show how they hunt, track, and trap. Individuals are usually paid directly for these activities. The safari operators who work in the /Xai/Xai area say that they prefer to pay people who work for them directly rather than providing money to the /Xai/Xai Trust, because they do not feel that the /Xai/Xai Trust is accountable and that it only benefits the people directly associated with it.

Some of the funds generated by the /Xai/Xai Tlhabololo Trust were reinvested in community-level projects, including the construction of a trust office, a community hall, two campsites, and an air strip. Fees were supposed to be paid by visitors to the NG 4 and NG 5 areas, with the revenues going to the trust. According to interviews by Masilo-Rakgoasi (2002), most people in the /Xai/Xai community felt that they did not benefit directly from the investments of the /Xai/Xai Trust. They did admit to getting some money through craft sales, participation in dances, and taking people out on hunting, gathering, and animal tracking trips.

An important benefit that the people of /Xai/Xai received from the community trust's operations was the production of game meat by safari hunting clients which added to the protein levels of households. At the same time, it should be noted that there was a sense in the /Xai/Xai community that the distribution of the meat was inequitable, with adult males, some of them Herero, getting the majority of the meat, and women, children, and the elderly getting smaller portions if any meat at all. This meat benefit is no longer available to members of the /Xai/Xai Tlhabololo Trust or to other community trusts that had joint venture agreements with safari operators in Botswana because of the hunting ban and changes in Botswana government policies toward community trusts.

There were other disagreements among residents of /Xai/Xai as to the ways in which benefits were distributed (Garner 2012; Hitchcock et al. 2015). This was particularly the case with jobs and income, a significant portion of which reportedly went to the trust management committee and to the Herero in the village. The Ju/'hoansi at /Xai /Xai said that greater emphasis should be placed on the promotion of culturally oriented community-based tourism since, in their opinions, heritage tourism tends to provide benefits to a wider portion of the population including women, children, and the elderly.

There is a problem of social exclusion, or what some community members might define as discrimination, in some of the community trusts in Botswana. One of the reasons that there are difficulties in the community-based organisation in the /Xai/Xai area is due, in the opinion of Masilo-Rakgoasi (2002), to the lack of sufficient grassroots mobilisation of the full range of community members in CBNRM. Part of the problem relates to language difficulties. In Botswana, the majority of CBNRM-related business and community-level discussions are held in Setswana, one of the two national languages of Botswana (along with English) which many members of the communities do not speak well. This means, in effect, that the elderly and those who have had less opportunity to learn other languages besides their mother tongues are not able to participate as extensively in the deliberations of the community-based organisation; they also have greater difficulty in obtaining information on community trust, district council, and Botswana government plans and policies because of language issues.

Important conclusions that were drawn by members of the community trusts in Botswana were that the government did not trust them to make their own decisions, and that government agencies, district councils, and private companies wanted to gain additional access to the funds being generated by the community trusts from tourism and other activities.

5 Conclusions

Tourism is seen as a potential generator of income for local communities, and as a way to increase public participation in the national and global economies.

In spite of the rhetoric about public participation and the benefits of tourism which are supposed to accrue to local populations, more often than not tourism serves to dispossess local people and has only limited social and economic benefits and many risks (Butler/ Hinch 1996; Hitchcock/ Brandenburgh 1990; Duffy 2002; Aicken/ Ryan 2005; Minority Rights Group International 2007; Brondo 2013). These risks include various types of exploitation, which exacerbate social problems such as alcohol abuse, due to alcohol being provided to local people by tourists and tourism companies. Disease, including sexually transmitted diseases such as tuberculosis and HIV/AIDS have increased due to extensive contact, some of it between tourists and local people.

Tensions between people due to inequalities in access to resources provided by tourists and tourism companies have increased. Women have complained that they have lost out to men in terms of having access to employment and income generating activities related to tourism. On the other hand, some adults and children pointed to the value of tourism in encouraging young people to learn how to hunt and track, since these skills can be used in the ecotourism and safari tourism industries. Some of these problems could be seen especially in the early days of tourist visits to Tsumkwe after Namibian Independence in March of 1990, and in Botswana in places such as the Okavango Delta and the Tsodilo Hills, which became popular tourist destinations. Cultural tourism can influence people's identities and feelings of self-worth in both positive and negative ways (Tomaselli 2012; Bolaane 2013, 2014; Mbaiwa 2016a). At the same time, tourism can serve to promote and maintain indigenous cultural knowledge and can serve to reinforce social identities which are valued highly at the local level.

In some parts of the world, including Namibia and Botswana, 'indigenous' identity has taken on added political and economic significance due to its use to claim title over blocks of land, certain types of resources, development assistance, or recognition from states and intergovernmental organisations (IGOs). Indigenous organisations, local leaders, and advocacy groups all maintain that it is necessary to gain not just *de facto* control over land and resources, but also *de jure* (legal) control. The advantage of having private land is that benefits flow more directly to the owners, and they have control over decision-making about wildlife management (Lindsey et al. 2013). Another way to do this is to negotiate binding agreements with states, and yet another is to seek recognition of land and resource rights through the courts (see Sapignoli 2012, 2015; Zips-Mairitsch 2013). A problem facing the San and other indigenous peoples in Namibia is that the process of turning common property rights in communal areas into nationally recognised legal rights is complex since the government of the nation-state claims that all communal land is state land (Mendelsohn et al. 2009; Government of Namibia 2012; Melber 2014).

While ecotourism and heritage tourism activities have been able to generate at least some income for people in Namibia and Botswana, problems pertaining to inequities in the distribution of benefits have led to some local-level conflicts. There is an open question as to whether ecotourism and CBNRM projects have enhanced the balance between conservation and development. Some groups in the communities where CBNRM activities have taken place have had less chance to participate than others in decisions regarding the trust management and operations. In addition, some community members receive less economic and social benefits from the tourism-related activities than others. As a result, those excluded have questioned the legitimacy of the leadership of the communal conservancies and the community trusts. Several individuals to whom I spoke said that they wanted to form their own small-scale business enterprises (SSBEs) rather than rely on the community-based institutions. This is in part because the important goal of poverty alleviation has generally not been achieved as much as was hoped through Community-Based Natural Resource Management and tourism activities.

It is interesting to compare the economic returns to people in different CB-NRM projects in Namibia and Botswana. In areas where there is a combination of safari hunting and photographic tourism, relatively sizable returns are generated for the conservancies and community trusts. Community-Based Natural Resource Management projects based solely on photographic tourism are not necessarily less viable economically than those where there is a combination of safari hunting and cultural tourism, but safari hunting tourism is far more profitable (Naidoo et al. 2016). Hunting tourism with private companies bringing in safari clients provides a variety of benefits to local communities, including employment, opportunities to sell crafts, promotion of cultural identity, and emphasis on valued cultural traditions, as seen, for example at /Xai/Xai among the Ju/'hoansi (Horton 2014; Hitchcock et al. 2015).

The benefit distribution situation points to a difference between the two countries. In Botswana Xai/Xai and other community trusts no longer receive income from safari hunting operations due to the 2014 hunting ban (Hitchcock et al. 2015; Onishi 2015), whereas the two communal conservancies in Namibia receive several million Namibian dollars plus meat for the community members in return for the rights of safari companies to operate in those conservancies (Hitchcock 2015a; Naidoo et al. 2016; Nyae Nyae Development Foundation of Namibia 2016, personal communication). From a sustainability perspective, the Ju/'hoansi and the NGOs working with them tend to see ecotourism involving photography and cultural tourism as having greater long-term benefits as long as the community members have decision-making power and an equitable share of the benefits.

It is clear that in both Botswana and Namibia, tourism contributes in various ways to communities, but it also exacerbates social, economic, and environmental conflicts. These conflicts are not lost on the tourists who come to visit these places. The San, Mbukushu, Herero, Kavango, Tswana, and others see conflicts between conservation and development as they are being pursued in Botswana and Namibia. The governments of the two countries are attempting to ensure that there is harmony between the various groups present at tourism destination sites, though this is not easy to do from a distance. Questions arise around favouritism. The tourism site residents ask why conservation and development appear to be geared more toward helping certain groups more than others, and why does tourism tend to favor the wealthy more than the poor? They point to the evidence seen in the benefit distribution data in communal conservancies and community trusts in the two countries. Local communities in Namibia and Botswana are pushing increasingly for sustainable tourism that not only benefits the state, the companies, and the tourists but also the host communities.

Tourism has had a mixed reputation in Southern Africa as well as other parts of the world. On the one hand, it is presented as having enormous local-level benefits (Christie et al. 2014), it also has a number of costs (Crick 1988; Haratsebe/ Moswete/ Saarinen 2016). It is not surprising therefore, that both analysts and local people see tourism as being 'good, bad, and ugly.' The differential effects of tourism benefits on the communities in Namibia and Botswana have been remarked on by both community members and researchers. It is interesting to note that one of the benefits of research in tourism-affected areas is that mapping has been done of traditional territories, producing data that have been employed by indigenous peoples in their efforts to document their land use and resource management history in land claims cases (see, for example, Vermeylen/ Dovies/ van der Horst 2012; Hitchcock/ Biesele 2013; van Der Wulp 2016).

One of the general conclusions that can be drawn about the impacts of tourism on remote area populations, especially ones without much experience with outsiders, is that the effects of tourism are often fairly negative at the outset, especially in terms of the impacts of availability of alcohol, some of which is brought in by tourists or tour operators. There are also environmental impacts of tourists, as seen, for example, in the Nyae Nyae region of Namibia in the 1980s and 1990s, when tourists would use large amounts of firewood, leave trash, and swim in the water reservoirs that provided drinking water to local people. The Nyae Nyae Conservancy attempted to establish tourism regulations in order to reduce these problems, but many of the tourists who visit the area do not stop at the Nyae Nyae Conservancy headquarters where they can get a briefing on what to do when they visit the villages in the Nyae Nyae area. Some of the tourists also disregard representatives of the communities who come out from the villages to their camping places and ask them to treat the areas where they are staying with respect.

While governments and international organisations such as the World Conservation Union (IUCN), the World Bank, and the World Tourism Organization (UNWTO) and many environmentally oriented non-government organisations such as World Wildlife Fund and Conservation International endorse ecotourism and heritage tourism, it is clear that a great deal of work needs to be done to ensure that conservation and development programmes involving tourism are as beneficial to local people as they are to wealthy international organisations, governments, private companies, and the tourists whose visits the governments, and private companies, and local communities seek.

There is no question that some of the community-level development that has occurred in north-eastern Namibia and north western Botswana is supported by ecotourism and heritage tourism. A major problem in Botswana is that the government has sought to reverse its original community-oriented policy and to get private sector operators to work in the communities who then tend to capture the bulk of the funds, leaving little for local level development by community-based institutions. One might hope that the private companies would follow a pattern of Corporate Social Responsibility (CSR) like some of the mining companies operating in Botswana and Namibia do.

The most effective means of promoting conservation and sustainable community-based development is one that allows local people to benefit from the natural and cultural resources that are there and which gives them incentives to conserve the wild animal, plant, fish, and other species while obtaining resources that are useful for their livelihoods and employment opportunities. In the face of increasing human pressures on the environment in Southern Africa, it may well be time to employ a diversified approach to conservation, development, and tourism, one that is not based on keeping local people from exploiting and benefitting from their natural and cultural environments and their heritage.

Acknowledgments

Earlier versions of this paper were presented at The University Centre for Studies in Namibia (TUCSIN) Conference on 'Heritage and Cultures in Modern Namibia,' Tsumkwe, Namibia 20-21 August 2015 and at the 115th annual meetings of the American Anthropological Association, 17 November 2016. Some of the funding for the research upon which this paper is based was provided by the Norwegian Agency for Development Cooperation (NORAD), the Danish International Development Authority (DANIDA), and the International Work Group for Indigenous Affairs (IWGIA), the Ford Foundation, and the U.S. Agency for International Development (USAID), and Brot für die Welt (Germany). I wish to thank the Nyae Nyae Development Foundation of Namibia, the Nyae Nyae Conservancy, the N≠a Jaqna Conservancy, the /Xai/Xai Tlhabololo Trust, and the Botswana National Museum office in Tsodilo for their help. I also thank Kallie Nannie, N!aici, !amace, Steve /Kunta, Tsamkxao ≠Oma, Leon Tsamkxao, Rosinah Masilo-Rakgoasi, Poppy Monyatse, Charlie Motshubi, Axel Thoma, Ute Dieckmann, Megan Biesele, Richard Lee, Maria Sapignoli, Lara Diez, Margie Jasobsohn, Polly Wiessner, Michael Painter, Sonia Arellano-Lopez, Arthur Albertson, Ben Begbie-Clench, Dries Alberts, Stacey Alberts, Stasja Koot, Melinda Kelly, John Hazam, Ryan Klataske, Mike Main, Willem Odendaal, Larry Robbins, Mike Murphy, and the late Alec Campbell for their many contributions. I appreciate the opportunity afforded to me by Werner Zips and Manuela Zips-Mairitsch to reflect on living museums, cultural villages, and tourism. I am deeply grateful to the governments of Namibia and Botswana for permission to carry out this work. And last but by no means least, I thank the people in the communities, living museums, and cultural villages who provided me with information and who were so willing to share their opinions.

Re-Inventing the Traditional Self: Body Adornment in the Performance of Cultural Heritage in the 'Living Museums' and 'Cultural Villages' of North-Eastern Namibia

Salomé Ritterband

1 Introduction

We arrived at the traditional village of Doupos, in the Nyae Nyae Conservancy in north-eastern Namibia, after having crossed several water puddles, rocks, and spiny bushes. About 200 metres and one lake separated the 'modern' from the 'traditional' village, where the cultural performances took place. The Ju/'hoansi, a subgroup of the San people, were waiting in everyday clothes between the nine traditional straw huts on a sandy place in the middle of a very wide green scrubland, and welcomed us very warmly with big smiles. The first staging was performed by us, a group of seven novices and two experienced anthropologists. One tent, two tables, several chairs, backpacks, luggage, and much more, came out of our two adventure-cars with rooftop tents. We prepared our sleeping places, set up the dining table, sprayed each other with mosquito-protection, applied sun screen against the intense ultraviolet rays, put on heavy shoes, big hats, took our bags, our water bottles, and, of course, our cameras. The villagers of Doupos were standing and sitting on their 'stage', some meters away from the camping site, observing and commenting on our actions. When we were ready, we joined them, and negotiated the price and the time for a traditional healing dance. They went to the modern village, where they actually lived, and after 45 minutes came back in traditional attire, wearing animal skins, jewellery, and walking barefoot through the bush. Suddenly they ignored us, while we stood around observing them, filming, taking pictures, and commenting as they prepared their re-enactment, making fire, positioning themselves in a circle, wrapping rattles around their legs, warming up their voices, and rehearsing their clapping. Slowly, the performance of the Ju/'hoansi began.

The Ju/'hoansi belong to the Ju/'hoansi San people, who live in Southern Africa. Their number is not precisely known, although WIMSA – the Working Group for Indigenous Minorities in Southern Africa – estimates that around 6.000

live all over Namibia (Biesele/ Hitchcock 2011: 6). The physical appearance of the San, their remarkable language including four click sounds (ibid.: 5), the hunter-gatherer lifestyle, and their image as people from the past, living in harmony with nature, have attracted anthropologists and scientists since the 19th century. They have inspired romanticising literature and movies, and motivated – often evolutionist – ethnological research (Barnabas/ Finlay 2012: 78). This has resulted in the San becoming one of the most 'explored' indigenous societies worldwide (Zips-Mairitsch 2013: 22). The ethically and gender discriminating term 'bushmen' was used until the 1960's and was then officially replaced with 'San', a relatively neutral Nama term that refers to their gathering-activity (ibid.: 156). I will therefore use this latter term although I am aware of the fact that this group is too inhomogeneous to have a common history, experience, and culture (ibid.: 158-159). Since this paper is about a special group within the San I will more often use the term Ju/'hoansi.

In the past, the San suffered violence and marginalisation from neighbouring groups, and later from the national state (Biesele/ Hitchcock 2011; Zips-Mairitsch 2013), as has happened to so many minority indigenous societies around the world. Nowadays, a global tendency towards cultural commercialisation for touristic purposes can be observed among many indigenous communities. With few alternative sources of income, some of the Ju/'hoansi in Namibia also got involved in the tourism industry and are guided by larger programmes with the aim to empower them. Cultural tourism is based on the concepts of "otherness, and the discovery of the unusual and exotic, through adventure" (von Stauss 2012: 86), relies on the touristic desire for authenticity (MacCannel 1999), and is structured by the "romantic gaze" (Urry 2002: 43) of travellers. Cultural tourism includes the creation of attractions arranged on purpose, the preservation of heritage, history, and 'tradition', and the marketing of experiences, which are often claimed to be 'authentic' (von Stauss 2012: 86). One specific form here is indigenous tourism, in which either their culture serves as a touristic offer, or – what is less often the case – the project is managed by indigenous people themselves (Goodwin 2007: 84). Since tourism is such a huge and fast-growing industry, it is unavoidable to consider its implications. It seems to be a common concern that tourism and global dynamics threaten or exploit local people and traditions. Although this is, unfortunately, certainly the case in some places, it is also relevant to illustrate cases of alternative cultural tourism, considering opportunities, and challenging creative interpretations of heritage not only as negative side effects. For these reasons, I am intrigued by the strategies and actions the Ju/'hoansi apply to perform cultural activities for tourists.

The research took place in Otjozondjupa, in the north-eastern part of Namibia, and more specifically in the Tsumkwe District, where most of the Ju/'hoansi live. We visited four villages, for a few days each: Grashoek, //Xa/oba, Doupos, and Djohkoe. The Living Museum in Grashoek, and //Xa/oba, the Little Hunter's Museum, are part of the Living Culture Foundation Namibia (hereafter LCFN), Doupos is a Cultural Village. Together with Djohkoe, the last three mentioned are part of the Nyae Nyae Conservancy – the first such conservancy built on communal land in Namibia (Biesele/ Hitchcock 2011: 206). Conservancies are areas of land, on which communities become collective managers over territory and wildlife, and that combine nature conservation and human development (ibid.: 199-200). Tourism was further recognised as an important potential source for economic growth and since the 1990's the Community-Based Natural Resource Management (hereafter CBNRM), combines the three fields. The power of decision lies with the Ju/'hoansi living there, who further offer touristic activities in Cultural Villages (van der Burg 2013: 11). About 700 km southwards in the N/a'an ku sê Lodge, located between the capital city and Windhoek airport, tourists with restricted time and a tight programme can enjoy an adapted version of the 'traditional' activities of the Ju/'hoansi. The Living Museums, also situated in the Tsumkwe District, are part of the project LCFN, which was initiated by Werner Pfeifer, a German-Namibian. He himself describes the concept as open-air-museums, in which actors re-enact their culture like in times before colonisation, accentuating the fact that it is not their way of living anymore. The foundation offers them aid and training, but no economic help (Pfeifer 09.01.2014, interview).

The Ju/'hoansi organised themselves and reconstructed their costumes, tools, and huts, using their cultural heritage as a tool for generating income (ibid.). They offer different established activities for paying visitors that aim to show the 'authentic' cultural life of their ancestors, including bushwalks, hunting trips, crafts in the village, dance and game performances, storytelling, and healing dances with differing durations, intensities, and interactions. In the course of this paper, I will often refer to these as 'performances', which include the observation of people's everyday interactions forming a staged self (Goffman 1959), and are based on complex phases of preparation (Schechner 2013), the use of the body and its behaviours, the conscious or unconscious manipulation of specific gestures and actions, including embodied cultural practices (Bourdieu 1982), the transmission of cultural heritage through performance (Taylor 2003), incorporated (re-)identification with (re-)learned 'traditions' (Comaroff/ Comaroff 2009), as well as the explicit staging of choreographed acts for monetary contribution.

Performance studies differentiate between "'is' and 'as' performance" (Schechner 2013: 37), and between ordinary life and "special events" (Lewis 2013: 5). In the Living Museums, this dichotomy refers to the distinction between specific staged acts and the performances in everyday life. At the intersection of touristic cultural commodification and performance, MacCannel coined the term "staged authenticity" (1973: 595-596). The discussions on 'authenticity' and 'staged' culture in touristic activities are controversial and open to critique, so I am not interested in judging to what extent this happens, but rather in analysing the creative interpretations of this by the Ju/'hoansi themselves.

The processes of selling culture, of performing for tourists, of re-vitalising traditional aspects of life, and of using ancestral heritage as a tool for (economic) survival, are crucially connected to the visual aspect. As soon as visitors come to experience cultural activities, the Ju/'hoansi put on their traditional attire, and, in general, adapt their visual appearance to the expectations of the tourists. Material and visual culture seem to serve as a 'proof' for 'authenticity', probably connected to the inherent notion of museums exhibiting tangible objects (Kidd 2011). My main question, therefore, is about the role body adornment plays in the construction of an image during the performance of commodified cultural activities in the cultural villages and living museums of north-eastern Namibia.

The Ju/'hoansi have been widely researched in the past but the ongoing topics of commodified culture and indigenous tourism raise new and interesting questions. The empirical data for this paper were collected during a fieldwork expedition organised by the University of Vienna in January 2014, which took us to four different villages in the Tsumkwe District. They had different styles of performance and costumes, which gave us the opportunity to compare them with each other. A second field research was conducted together with my colleague, Josef Wukovits, in August and September 2014, when we spent three weeks in the village of Doupos. I can thus compare two very different approaches: A more touristic perspective, when in January we mainly experienced the performances as an audience and as short-time travellers, and the perspective from the backstage-area in August, from where we observed the 'actors' go on stage, heard the singing from the distance, and saw them coming back some hours later. We further participated in some private activities arranged for us. Based on participant observation, informal talks, interviews, and the theoretical frame found in the literature, I will discuss the aspect of cultural commodification in the context of performance, with a focus on costumes and traditional clothes. In the first part of this paper I shall concentrate on the activities and performances of the Ju/'hoansi in the course of cultural commodification, and briefly analyse the concepts of culture, heritage, and authenticity in the context of Namibia's tourism and museum approaches. In the second part, I will consider traditional clothing as a relevant element of 'authentic' performances and have a closer look at their production, meaning, and use.

2 Selling 'Culture' in the Tourism Context

"The culture, in the Living Museum, it brings us more guests and also some income. Because in our village, we don't have any job that the government is offering us. The only thing is that we can show our culture, that is where we get our income for ourselves, clothes for the kids, and also the support for the school. We get it from the culture, which the guests come to see here in the Living Museum." (Henry /ui Nyani 11.01.2014, interview)

The above citation of the main guide and manager of the living museum in Grashoek shows the importance of the income that the Ju/'hoansi generate through visits of tourists. They offer pre-established activities and sell self-made crafts, another relevant factor of income (Biesele/ Hitchcock 2011). It has become a global trend to replace the sale of labour through the sale of culture, according to Comaroff and Comaroff (2009: 11). Although tourism is not the main source of income for the San (Biesele/ Hitchcock 2011: 211-226), direct and visible cash is generated mainly by the visits of travellers, as many interviewees told us. Several people explained that the earned money enables them to buy modern clothes, shoes, food, cattle, and further material for the manufacturing of jewellery, and to pay school fees and transport to the clinic if necessary (Cwi //ao / Dabe //ao 13.01.2014, interview; Henry /ui Nyani 11.01.2014, interview; Komtsa Daqm 16.01.2014, interview; Tsemkgao Daqm 17.11.2014, interview; Xoan//a Cgaesje 13.01.2014, interview; /Gao N!aice 11.01.2014, interview).

The quote from the interview further illustrates the interconnection between income and culture. Comaroff and Comaroff (2009) see the future, if not even the survival of certain ethnic groups, in the commodification of culture for tourism. They suggest that this does not necessarily imply the destruction of certain customs, but more so a revival, rediscovery, or even creation of new traditions. The Ju/'hoansi have realised that in order to generate more income and attract tourists, they have to make use of their culture, shape it, and adapt it to what they think tourists would like to see. Simultaneously, they have to consider how they want to represent themselves. An interesting aspect of culture for the purpose of this research is its connection to property and saleability. Layton and Wallace ask the question whether culture can be sold as a commodity at all (2006). It has often and generally been claimed that cultural identity is not tangible and can, therefore, not be marketed; a claim that negates a connection between economy and culture (Comaroff/ Comaroff 2009: 22). The Comaroffs challenge Bourdieu's differentiation between cultural and economic capital, claiming that in the course of cultural commodification the two merge (ibid.: 33).

For the Ju/'hoansi of the Tsumkwe area, 'culture' is closely related to traditional knowledge and the past. They often associate it with hunting and gathering activities, the religion of their forefathers, traditional clothing, and the content of touristic performances (!amace N!aice 16.01.2014, interview; Tsemkgao Daqm 17.01.2014, interview; N!ae Komtsa 17.01.2014, interview; Kxore Erna /ui 13.01.2014, interview). Henry /ui Nyani, one of the most eloquent people we met in the course of our field practice, explained what 'culture' means to him:

> "Culture is the meaning, that you are the person who stays in the bush. You know exactly how to stay there, to survive in the field. [. . .] Culture is the history. The history about the old things, and the things which we are teaching the children." (11.01.2014, interview)

Culture serves as more than just a basis for bush survival: "I also learn them how to use their culture, and how to do things so that they can survive with the guests", as /Gao N!aice (11.01.2014, interview) explained in reference to workshops he gives to other San people in South Africa on their common cultural heritage and on how to use it in the context of tourism. In the interviews, culture was often mentioned in the context of income and of sharing their knowledge with guests and visitors: "[. . .] if they [the San people] are not ashamed to wear the traditional clothes they can come and join the culture, so that they can get their income" (Henry /ui Nyani 11.01.2014, interview).

The Ju/'hoansi offer a range of different activities in their villages at more or less fixed tariffs paid by visitors: "Tourists they are coming to see our traditional culture and they would like to learn. [. . .] Doing things like hunting and singing and playing games. And also how we make crafts" (Komtsa Daqm 16.01.2014, interview). In the opinion of the Ju/'hoansi, tourists or visitors come to the villages to learn about their culture and ancient traditions, so their main activity consists in explaining and performing them. There are bushwalks that demonstrate the gathering of plants and roots, and how to survive in the bush and to make fire; tourists can also go on a hunting trip with the men. The Ju/'hoansi further offer interactive singing and dancing activities, as well as workshops on how to produce artefacts like bows and arrows or make jewellery. The experience of healing dances is very intense and the audience is asked to observe rather than to participate. They further ask for money for being photographed, for giving interviews, and they charge a fee for camping. In addition, a varied number of performance styles were developed in the different projects of the Ju/'hoansi San involved in cultural tourism: from highly commercialised acts for short-time tourists with restricted time performed in safari lodges, to adapted performances in traditional clothes in the 'natural' environment of the San and animating tourists to participate, up to intense and longer experiences with deeper involvement of the visitors.

The Ju/'hoansi adapted their ancient traditions, rebuilt huts, reproduced traditional clothes, and acquired knowledge about plants, roots, and healing techniques from their elders to present the cultural re-enactments as 'authentic' as possible (Pfeifer 09.01.2014, interview). The Comaroffs claim that the main dialectic in the commercialisation of ethnicity lies in the incorporation of identity and at the same time the commodification of culture. Dealing with their heritage every time tourists ask for it leads to a re-identification with culture and traditions (Comaroff/ Comaroff 2009: 21). According to Diane Taylor (2003), the body serves as storage of memory and history that can easily be transmitted to other bodies in forms of performance – thus passing on intangible cultural heritage. Nevertheless, some adults had to re-learn the movements of some activities by listening to descriptions and stories from the elders. A binary process took and still takes place in cultural villages and living museums – traditional knowledge was and is unconsciously incorporated during each (touristic) performance and is combined with active research among the elders, who verbally transmit information of their heritage.

The main motivations for participating in cultural performances, according to interviews given to us by the San, were on the one hand the financial benefit in times of big financial struggle, and on the other hand the possibility of keeping their traditional culture alive and especially teaching it to their children. The San working in cultural institutions are aware of the interest, and proud to show their cultural heritage to visitors and travellers: "I choose to take you as my family, to teach you my language, to teach you my skills, how we are living" (!amace N!aice 16.01.2014, interview). In Werner Pfeifer's opinion, the performances for tourists are just a job, with the traditional clothes serving as working uniforms (Pfeifer 22.01.2014, interview). The protagonists observed and interviewed seemed to really enjoy performing, to be happy to teach the visitors bits and pieces of their culture, and to exchange views (Kxore Erna /ui 13.01.2014, interview; N!ae Komtsa 17.01.2014, interview; !Kunta !amace 17.01.2014, interview), although the levels of identification with the performed traditions may differ between individuals and the generations involved. While children have a quite playful approach to the cultural activities that surround them on a regular basis, teenagers partly seemed to distance themselves from the traditions of their forefathers. For young adults the cultural heritage obtains a new relevance, as it can be used as a potential source of income (Tsemkgao Daqm 17.01.2014, interview). The adults and the older generations might still have practiced traditional activities on a daily basis, and their cultural knowledge is more deeply embodied. Several interview partners in Doupos, Grashoek, and the Little Hunter's Museum told us that it does not make a difference for the healing dances if visitors watch or if they do not (Komtsa Daqm 16.01.2014, interview; !amace N!aice 16.01.2014, interview).

In tourism, putting oneself in a 'good light' is a necessary marketing strategy. Tourism workers, therefore, consciously and unconsciously construct their own commodified personae, which consist of various roles that are used according to the situation (Bunten 2008). A stakeholder in the tourism industry can choose from a set of different identities according to the required premises in the context and the people they find themselves with (ibid.: 381, 389). Goffman (1959) argues that the aim of a good performance is a convincing representation of oneself. By taking control over one's own body, the individual can manage the situation, displaying his identity and status, and thus be able to influence other individuals (ibid.: 17, 26-27). There is also the strategy of playing a different role than the 'real' one, and the audience can decide whether or not to believe the act (ibid.: 28-31). I was especially impressed by the living museum in Grashoek – the most professionalised of all – when the English speaking guide Henry /ui Nyani picked us up at the campsite, with a very polite smile, and hospitable manners, and invited us to follow him to the "cultural adventure".

Comparing oral statements from the interviews and the observations I made, especially during my second stay, it was interesting to find a contradiction between the way the San talked about their heritage in front of a recorder and how I experienced them during a longer stay without explicit touristic cultural performances. While explanations given during interviews show a strong identification with the 'traditions' performed, during daily life people rarely went into the bush for gathering, hunting, or for medicinal plants. This can be linked to Bunten's (2008) concept of the commodified persona in tourism, according to which persons construct their own convincing 'ethnic' appearance; although, in this case, the anthropologists represent a particular audience of their own for the narrative performances of the San.

3 Heritage Performance and Museum Re-enactments

Museums are one aspect of Namibia's attempt to reinforce development and cultural safeguarding through tourism. The idea of statically showing traditional objects in an exhibition was carried from European travellers to Namibia and is not an adequate representation of Namibia's intangible cultural heritage (or ICH) (Silvester 2011: 2). It raises the question of how 'lived' culture can be preserved and shown in a way that people and identity, not objects, are in the focus of museum work; there is a demand for lived practices which has led to a changing perspective of the role of museums in the past years (Alivizatou 2001: 84, 93; cf. Binter 2014). The style of presentation shifted from the exhibition of static objects – for a long time considered observable data from the past (Kidd 2011: 29) – to a place of experiences and encounters (Jackson/ Kidd 2011: 1). More events have entered the stage, and the use of performances has become important, building upon the concept of 'edutainment' (Jackson 2011: 1).

Cultural villages and living museums exist through the use and performance of intangible cultural heritage, instead of exhibiting material culture in the way traditional museums do (Jackson 2011). Both concepts obtain information about the traditions shown from oral knowledge and therefore present it mainly on an intangible basis (Dürrschmidt 13.08.2014, interview). The legal possession of intangible cultural knowledge by indigenous people has become a matter of concern since in the past it had often been appropriated by others (Layton/ Wallace 2006: 31). Through acknowledged ownership of their own heritage culture can become a resource and a hope for indigenous communities (ibid.: 53). At the same time, its commodification is a starting point for controversial discussions. The literature repeatedly claims that in tourism, which is often said to be practiced by ignorant and superficial people, traditional activities and artefacts are shown 'artificially' and 'staged'. The term 'performance' itself implies the sense of artifice and spectacle (Taylor 2003: 13).

Schechner's (1982) differentiation between 'is' and 'as' performance is relevant in the context of heritage museums. He claims that everything can be studied 'as' performance, whereas an event 'is' performance when the historical and social context or tradition mark it as such – it is further framed, enacted, presented, and highlighted, like dances or rituals (Schechner 2013). The way in which the Ju/'hoansi present themselves to tourists through speaking, gesturing, and clothing can be related to Goffman's (1959) description of performance in everyday life or to Schechner's concept of 'as' performance; but there are also more specific situations of acting. In living museums a tour guide does 'as' performances that are rarely recognised as 'is' performances in the classically staged sense (Kidd 2011: 24).

The explanations during the bushwalks in Grashoek, Doupos, and the Little Hunter's Museum resemble situations of intended acting, showing situations of traditional hunting and gathering. The hunting experts, who often did not speak English themselves, performed with big gestures and facial expressions, in a very exaggerated, humoristic, and yet understandable way. They routinely paused to let the English speaking guides translate their words. The guides detached themselves from the scene and described it, reminiscent of a voice-over commentary in a movie. The Ju/'hoansi performers explicitly included humour and jokes. They would always laugh when we tasted bitter fruits from the bush, and performances including the building of a bird-trap, or the chasing of an imaginary animal, should inspire the audience to smile. There are also 'is' performances in heritage sites that are clearly marked as such, with the use of specific stages, props, costumes, and specific choreographies. In contrast to theatre, in shows in living museums there is no applause at the end of an act and no word-by-word script (Schechner 1982: 97). Moreover, the acting is supposed to look as if the actors were not performing (Kidd 2011: 24).

While theatre is explicitly marked as a make-believe performance, restored villages try to act as 'realistic' and 'authentic' as possible, and to disguise their artificiality (Schechner 1982: 96). The performed dances and games are considerably shorter than their traditional ones and last around ten minutes each. They are performed on a stage, representing a physical frontier between 'us' and 'them', and are accompanied by short explanations in English explicitly devised for the visitors. The audience is allowed to participate in a regulated way in some of the dances. The actors claim that the performed healing dances, lasting about two hours, are 'authentic'; although we were told that a 'real' one would last for around twelve hours. The connotation of 'staged' has aroused fears among experts and tourists alike about the 'alienation' of traditional activities. Cultural performances in the museum context further raise unwelcome associations of *Völkerschauen* and raise questions about the purpose of cultural performances in general (Alivizatou 2001: 86). Heritage performances have become a matter of contested and controversial negotiations between communities (ibid.: 70).

The knowledge about traditional activities is a prerequisite for being able to participate in cultural performances and is acquired in a life-long process. Intangible cultural heritage is partly stored in the bodies (Taylor 2003) and is further learned through the observation and practice of participating in traditional activities – with or without tourists. According to Schechner (2013), a good performance is achieved when the individual has successfully incorporated a role. The habitus is incorporated through the repetition of patterns, movements, and gestures until they become naturalised (Lewis 2013: 15). But habitus is also subject to change – a constant selection takes place to adapt to specific situations. Habitus is not a mechanical process, but a constant re-creation. Although habits are seen as embodied structures that are difficult to change, there can be a certain extent of experimentation (ibid.: 95).

I was able to observe that in Grashoek, where the performance group was accustomed to and well organised for visiting tourists, the dance performances seemed to be routinised show, with integrated explanations and shortened, tailored to the spectators' attention span. In the Little Hunter's Museum, where visitors are less frequent, the dancers were discussing the various steps of a performance, animating each other to participate in the dance, and negotiating about the 'right' explanations to tell the tourists. In Doupos and Djohkoe, where the healing dance lasted for 11/2 to 2 hours, the routine aspect was less visible since in the first village the sick person treated really suffered from pains in the foot. People were talking among themselves, not to the spectators, and the gestures and movements seemed to be generated in the spur of the moment instead of being systematically performed. On the other hand, our presence was undeniable, since we had chosen the moment for the dance, we illuminated the dancers with our spotlights for filming, and we certainly influenced the dance in one way or another. Through this indirect participation it seems that cultural dances and other activities retain their vitality and are constantly adapted and renewed.

Working in cultural tourism does not only imply the understanding and embodiment of traditional knowledge, but also includes more specific behaviours and expertise needed for the explicit interaction with visitors. The Ju/'hoansi have, with the help of the LCFN or the NNC, constructed specific programmes adapted to touristic interests. Strict authenticity rules are meant to guarantee a historically correct representation of heritage, including the shortening of activities, and the selection of special and exciting procedures to make them more interesting for tourists. The Ju/'hoansi received further instruction in photographing, and the guides must be fluent in English so they can make use of specific attitudes and behaviours, and, with humor and hospitable manners make the visitors feel comfortable.

The dichotomy between cultural performances and everyday life is constantly challenged by the presence of the children. During the second field research, I observed that the kids spent most of the day playing in the village and the nearby bush, with no one actively looking for them or asking where they were. They themselves decided what to do next or if to pay us a visit. With us, the children spontaneously and regularly decided to stage specific "special events" (Lewis 2013: 5) and "as if" (Schechner 2013: 90) performances, practicing the staged acts they regularly observed and attended with their parents. The approach to traditional learning among the Ju/'hoansi is playful: Children observing, imitating, and then practicing the knowledge until it can be performed in front of visitors. The children used us to actively practice the things they learned, and were the driving force behind the organising of bushwalks, hunting trips, and singing evenings for us. Playing in the village or using Josef Wukovits and me as 'tourists-for-practice', they imitated the activities while laughing and experimenting but at the same time kept a professional attitude. This shows the learning and re-interpretation of traditional activities by the younger generation through embodying some acts and continuing to develop the performance of preserved, and at the same time, transformed 'culture'. Children incorporate the habitus through observation, imitation, and practice until a series of structured patterns is embodied and can then be applied in the varied performances of each individual (Bourdieu 1982).

A relevant aspect to keep in mind during the experience and the analysis of the situation is that a performance is always based on the interaction between audience and performers (Korom 2013: 2). Acting happens through the communication between the actors on the stage and with the observers (Goffman 1959: 9); just as the production of culture is systematically constructed by the interaction between producers and consumers (Comaroff/ Comaroff 2009: 25). This relationship becomes visible in two processes. Firstly, cultural performance would not take place without the visitors directly or indirectly asking for it and the Ju/'hoansi wanting to comply with their wishes. Secondly, as mentioned in the introduction, the Ju/'hoansi are not the only ones performing things unusual for the audience. We as visitors were similarly acting on our 'stage' and with our 'costumes'. In this context, Korom asks who is performing for whom in the field since anthropological work itself can be seen as an act of performance (Korom 2013: 4).

Performances disappear the moment they are made. When a performance genre is exported or presented to tourists, changes happen. According to Schechner, the original might be "the totality of previous performances, on which performance is based, and incorporated in oral tradition" (Schechner 1982: 49). There is no fixed 'true' performance, only the incorporated interpretation of it; even its documentation is already an interpretation (ibid.: 49-50). Heritage performance is less about the correct recreation and remembrance of the past, it is about a collective rethinking of it, and at the same time, it is a situation that creates memories and common identities in itself. Through a collective negotiation of old memories new ones are constructed and loaded with meaning (Smith 2011: 78-80). According to Kidd, many participants and spectators feel a deeper sense of how the 'past' might have looked like through performances on heritage sites. Especially from an educational point of view, experiencing the past gives a completely new perspective as opposed to reading about it in books or looking at objects, even if we know that it is only a mere re-production of a re-invented past (Kidd 2011: 27). Werner Pfeifer, the founder of LCFN, is fascinated by the idea of actually experiencing the historical situations, seeing people in activity, and being able to touch the tools – as a teacher he would like history lessons to work like that (Pfeifer 09.01.2014, interview).

4 Performing 'Authenticity'

The touristic visit of 'bushmen' – as the San are still referred to in some tourism agencies or in everyday speech – is associated with notions of authenticity and a "last-chance glance" (Garland/ Gordon 1999: 271). The tourists desire 'authentic' and intimate experiences. They want to see the backstage, and to be able to experience the 'real thing'. Since the cultural managers – the performing ethnic populations – know about the tourists' wishes, according to MacCannell (1999), they sometimes produce an artificial stage 'behind the scenes' which he calls "staged authenticity" (ibid.: 595-596). There they generate experiences for the visitors. In the course of a growing tourism industry in Namibia, the Ju/'hoansi are placing themselves in a new light as modern tourism agents, although at the same time they demonstrate 'traditional' activities to the visitors (Garland/ Gordon 1999: 267, 272).

The question of authenticity is delicate and controversial but does play a major role in the context of tourism as tourists look for it in the communities they visit (Garland/ Gordon 1999; MacCannell 1973). Authenticity is a socially constructed, subjective, and dynamic concept. Although I do not think that the extent of authenticity should be judged or examined arbitrarily, this question seems to evoke animated discussions both in the minds of tourists and the tourism stakeholders responding to it. Tourists have different views and expectations which in turn influence the construction of tourism sites and performances, some of which are specifically arranged for the satisfaction of the visitors. The Living Culture Foundation Namibia itself uses notions of authenticity to sell its projects:

"The San focus on showing their original lifestyle. They present the old, almost forgotten culture in traditional dresses in the midst of their reconstructed 'nomad-village' from the ancient days. The San of the Living Museum set a high value on presenting the hunter-gatherer culture as authentic as possible." (LCFN n.d., online)

It is striking to see how the San deal with matters of 'authenticity' without explicitly calling it such and being influenced to varying degrees by outside implications and demands. At the living museums of the Ju/'hoansi – and let us not forget that they were founded by a white German-Namibian – a series of strict rules guarantees the exclusive use of pre-colonial elements, forbidding 'modern' tools. Each performing group of the museum has a group leader, who is responsible for quality control. They have extensive knowledge about traditional objects and behavioural patterns, and apart from preventing fights and rudeness in the group and dealing with alcohol abuse, or begging, they also control the 'authenticity' of the costumes and props. Every performer carries the required traditional tools with him and does not bring any unfitting modern accessories into the museum area (Henry /ui Nyani 13.01.2014, interview; Dürrschmidt 09.01.2014, interview). It is also not allowed to carry plastic bags, radios, food, or water bottles to the performance of traditional activities, as Tsemkgao Daqm explained to us:

"No drinking at the museum area, also no water. When the tourists come and even go out for hunting, you don't have to carry any food, only the tourists have to carry food. You can show the tourists only bush food, how you did it in the past." (16.01.2014, interview)

In the less institutionally organised cultural villages, the rules are not that strict and the perception of tradition is more lax. During the activities 'modern' props can be seen under and on traditional costumes, for example a neon green string thong under a worn animal skin skirt, and a plastic bottle carried inside the traditional gatherer leather bag. This represents a contrasting point of view concerning the perception of what really is traditional for the Ju/'hoansi according to the specific historical periods living museums and cultural villages rely on. Authenticity is to a large extent related to past and ancestral heritage because of its nostalgic and sentimental connotations (MacCannell 1999: 82). At the same time, the concept of performing one's past implies the activity of 'staging', which contradicts standards of 'authenticity' per se, although restored villages try to hide their artifice behind the pretence of 'tradition'. The tourism agents decide whether to choose a specific period of history that will best depict their interpretations of cultural authenticity and traditions. Alternatively, tradition can be considered as a dynamic development, incorporating new elements and changing through time. Zips argues against the notion of tradition related to the concept of 'cultural purity', but rather considers its derivation from the Latin term *traditio* that relies on the dynamic transfer of knowledge (2001: 186). For Sebastian Dürrschmidt and Werner Pfeifer from the LCFN, the performances and used objects accurately have to correspond to the time before colonisation; they both seem to perceive 'tradition' as opposed to 'modernity'. The cultural villages instead chose a more variable approach as I observed with regard to jewellery worn locally that used coloured glass and plastic beads, which were evidently imported, and partly replaced the traditional beads. Tsemkgao Daqm, a guide at the Little Hunter's Museum, as well as Smallboy, a touristic guide for Doupos, criticise that the colourful beads of Doupos are not part of the traditional body adornment of the Ju/'hoansi and should not be allowed in the 'traditional' village (Tsemkgao Daqm 16.01.2014, interview; !L/ae Tsemkgao "Smallboy" 01.09.2014, interview).

The concept of authenticity was first raised in the context of museums where experts and professionals were concerned with determining whether objects were 'fake' or not (Cohen 1988: 375). Fillitz and Saris (2013: 10-13) ask for the criteria of authenticity, and argue that objects become 'authentic' through their singularity when they are 'uncontaminated' by outside factors and when specific materials, techniques, and knowledge about the (traditional) production and consumption of the object in question are documented. Commodification often seems to be a characterisation for 'inauthenticity', and modernity is viewed as an 'enemy' affected by Western influences (ibid.: 375). Many museums have tried to deal with this issue by establishing objective criteria of how to measure and categorise levels of authenticity. While MacCannell accuses tourists of believing to experience authenticity while the events are only 'staged', Wang points out that authenticity is a much more complex issue than the mere difference between the 'original' and the 'imitation' (Wang 1999: 351-352). The constructivist approach recognises authenticity as a social construction and perception, a result of one's own imagination, stereotypes, and expectations. Authenticity is not quantifiable and there is no such a thing as an 'original' (ibid.: 351). In this view, what tourists look for is "symbolic authenticity" (ibid.: 351, 356), labelled by signs and symbols that are associated with the authenticity of an object or activity. In postmodern approaches, 'inauthenticity' is not considered a matter of concern because the notions of 'real' or 'false' are not relevant anymore.

Wang proposes the concept of "existential authenticity" (1999: 351-352) which involves the reception and feelings of the touristic audience. In this form of 'authenticity' tourists are not concerned with the extent of it but only with their own state of being. This approach concentrates on the personal making of an authentic self-experience, in contrast to the judgment whether an object or a performance is 'authentic' or not (ibid.: 360). In this context, Zhu, in contesting the concept of 'existential authenticity', argues that the process of 'becoming' is more relevant than the state of 'being', and criticises Wang for focusing too much on the self-reflection of a person (Zhu 2012: 1498). Zhu takes up the already existing concept of performative authenticity, based on the idea of Bourdieu's embodiment. Through ritualised performance, the body integrates personal memory and physical settings (ibid.: 1499-1500).

The understanding of authenticity has moved from a static and measurable unit to its subjective perception during an experience. In living museums and cultural villages, a creative and performative approach to heritage, the past, traditions and authenticity is used. The own subjective experience, the atmospheric scenery, the beautiful landscape, and, most of all, the interaction between the tourists and the Ju/'hoansi performers are ultimately seen as more important than the judgement whether the dance is 'real' and 'authentic' or performed. The aim is to transport the actors and the audience into an imagined and re-created situation, which at the same time has the scope to transmit cultural knowledge to the spectators; instead of mourning the loss of 'authentically' re-enacted cultural activities. And considering the results of performance studies one can understand that there is never an exact replication of a former performance but rather a flexible re-interpretation of it.

5 Behind the Scenes

Most studies on performance focus mainly on the act itself and scarcely consider the rest of the process, which is without question relevant as a whole. In some situations, the phases before the show are much longer and more important for the participants than the actual performance (Schechner 1982: 16). Training, workshops, rehearsals, and warm-up take place as preparations before the performance, and cool-down and aftermath happen afterwards (ibid.: 16). Goffman's (1959) differentiation between front and backstage can be used to explain the lack of consideration for the phases before and after the public performance: The Euro-American convention does not allow outsiders to enter or see the backstage and private area. According to this theory, the performance is prepared in the backstage where no audience is allowed, whereas in the front stage the audience and the performers meet, the latter carry with them the necessary props and costumes and play a routine (ibid.: 34, 231).

The survival of some ethnic minority groups depends to a considerable extent on the success of the commodification of culture. For that matter, the image presented has to please the tourists' expectations and often consists of a primitive and 'exotic', homogenised construct (Comaroff/ Comaroff 2009: 26-27). Unfortunately, the image of indigenous tourist agents has been distorted and stereotyped for a long time. It is, therefore, relevant to reflect on the extent to which indigenous peoples can produce and manage the images themselves and how the categories 'traditional' and 'modern' are applied (Butler/ Hinch 2007: 323-324). Although tourists get to see the Ju/'hoansi mainly in their constructed traditional environment, Smallboy – a tourist expert of the East Tsumkwe Area – is convinced that it is important to explain how the San live when they are not performing for tourists (01.09.2014, interview). Komtsa Daqm, a guide of the *Little Hunter's Museum*, describes the tourists' demand for the traditional ways of living:

> "[Some,] they are interested to go to the modern villages. But many of them are interested in the traditional culture. When they come, they want to see hunting. Or they want to see people dancing and see people doing things in the traditional way." (17.01.2014, interview)

Sebastian Dürrschmidt explains that the LCFN offers training to adapt certain traditional ceremonies to the taste of Western tourists with limited time at their disposal (09.01.2014, interview). We experienced that the healing ceremony was shortened to a 'bearable' duration for tourists who would possibly be 'bored' during a longer performance. So the performance of the 'traditional' is again adapted to the taste of the visitors to make it more entertaining and easier to understand. The trainers of the LCFN followed the San on their gathering walks, gave them hints about what would be interesting to tell, and suggested some exciting activities, like demonstrating how to build a trap. A tour should not only be informative for the spectators but also entertaining and exciting (ibid.).

As in a theatre, the Ju/'hoansi prepare to perform for arriving visitors. This happens firstly through the adaptation of the visual appearance, putting on what is defined by the San themselves as traditional clothing, and secondly through the physical preparation of the stage. The actors start their warm-up with clapping, singing, and adjusting last accessories on their bodies. The sandy ground of the performing area is stamped and fireplaces are installed, making use of modern accessories stored in the straw huts if necessary. The area for the bushwalks, which are restricted to a certain area near the parking lot, is prepared by burying bush food in advance, which is then systematically discovered together with the tourists. This became clear when !Kunta Boo and his daughter Xoan//a !Kunta, the leaders of the cultural performances, spent the whole day looking for water roots in faraway areas to put them into the new ground where they usually would not grow.

According to MacCannell (1999), tourists long to see the 'real' life of the visited people and therefore try to get a glimpse of what Goffman (1959) defined as backstage. Although the separation between front and backstage is not necessarily supposed to be physical, in the case of the living museums and cultural villages of northern Namibia it is clearly visible. The Ju/'hoansi have separate 'modern villages', where they live, and 'traditional villages', where the activities take place. During the second field research, I never attended the touristic presentations and this gave me the strong sense of waiting in a backstage area until the performers returned. Observations made in the cultural village of Doupos showed that while cooking, washing, and producing crafts are central in the inhabitants' lives, the activities for tourists held outside the villages – that interrupt daily work and break the routine – are not necessarily part of ordinary everyday life. When tourists arrived, the news would immediately spread through the village and make everyone drop their daily activities, jump into traditional attire, and sometimes walk, sometimes run, into the traditional village and the performance area. The arrival of the tourists marked a complete break in their everyday life routines and led everyone to run around and prepare, even if climate conditions such as strong wind made it difficult.

These isolated events present a frequent, although not so predictable, activity because the inhabitants are often informed at the last minute. The arrival of tourists and the clearly accentuated cultural acts correspond to what Lewis' (2013: 5) called "special events" or Schechner (2013: 37) defined as marked "is" performance, and are clearly separated from everyday life. Preparations, such as making clothes and carving tools, are nevertheless included in the daily activities. Elements of traditional knowledge are moreover clearly present in the modern village: Traditional songs are constantly chanted during everyday tasks, and traditional dancing moves are made to contemporary music from Southern Africa played in the yards by young people. In the cultural villages and living museums, the backstage, meaning the modern village and modern clothes, is not hidden from the tourists. Tourists are allowed to visit the village where people actually live and where they sit around calmly without trying to explain or hide something. If the guides are caught by surprise, they welcome the visitors in T-Shirts and jeans.

Both concepts of touristic villages, with their physically separated performance areas, were established to protect the Ju/'hoansi from visitors randomly intruding into their private spheres and to avoid non-regulated exploitation or embarrassment (Dürrschmidt 13.08.2014, interview). According to Wang (1999) and Urry (2002), 'staged authenticity' is partly practiced to avoid invasive on-lookers and to help protect the community from being disturbed. While the most sensational concepts – very commercialised short cultural acts – may be least intrusive for the San, anthropologists who live with the people for a long time and want to experience the 'real' and daily life might be most disturbing (Urry 2002: 151). To regulate the number of the visitors who come to the modern villages of the living museums, the Ju/'hoansi offer paid tours to these villages, which are not very detailed or instructive. Werner Pfeifer explained that the people in the living museums are not enthusiastic about tourists walking into their backstage or private sphere but, thinking of the economic benefit, they included this offer in their programme (22.01.2014, interview). In my opinion, this activity is neither staged nor performed – it rather shows that the Ju/'hoansi do not hide how they live today but want to keep people at arm's length from their living sphere.

A vast majority of interviewees, especially in the cultural village of Doupos, did not explicitly differentiate between activities performed with or without visitors, although the presence of people from a different background automatically brings about changes. In contrast to Grashoek, hunting is allowed in the Nyae Nyae conservancy, where it is included in the touristic programme. In Doupos and the Little Hunter's Museum they explained that they also hunt with traditional bows and arrows when tourists are not there (Dabe //ao 14.01.2014, interview; Komtsa Daqm 17.01.2014, interview). Cwi //ao explained that they would usually go longer distances to increase the chance of hunting a big animal but, as he explains, tourists are sufficiently "happy" to see "something traditional" closer-by (13.01.2014, interview). Even !Kunta Boo, the traditional healer of Doupos, does not see a difference if tourists are watching a healing ceremony:

> "It is the same, whether you perform for a tourist or you heal. It is the same, because people are still singing and you are still dancing. [...] My experience is that it is still the same. The performance for the tourist or to heal people is the same" (13.01.2014, interview).

In informal talks, we were told that a healing dance could last for the whole night, while for us, the visitors, it was always much shorter. Moreover, in the living museums they interrupted the dance with short explanations, which clearly shows that they adapted the activity to the audience. When tourists come, they can 'order' a dance at a specific time, but I assume that a 'real' healing dance takes place when required or decided upon by the community. Probably most of the interviewed actors wanted to demonstrate the 'authenticity' of their activities and claimed that there was no difference with or without our presence.

The separation between a 'real' backstage and a performed front stage is much more complex and multifaceted, as described by Goffman and MacCannell. The backstage is where the modern life takes place. It is not necessarily hidden by the villagers but also not explicitly shown. On the front stage a traditional show is performed that, according to Werner Pfeifer, does not exist as such anymore, but is still claimed to be part of the everyday life by the interviewed people of Doupos. Observations made clear that traditional activities and the performances done in the museum area were seldom taken into the living area by the professional performers. In my opinion, the Ju/'hoansis' wish to separate their performances for others from their 'modern' lives does not specifically derive from the effort to create exact 'authenticity' but rather from the need to keep separate the two areas of their lives for their own protection. As much as the San enjoy doing traditional activities, irrespective of whether they practice them in their daily lives, the performances are considered a money generating business and seen as a good alternative for young people to the work in the cities (Pfeifer 22.01.2014, interview).

6 Costumes – the Material Aspect of Performances

The processes of selling 'culture', performing for tourists, re-vitalising 'traditional' aspects of life, and using ancestral heritage as a tool for (economic) survival are crucially connected with the visual appearance. As soon as visitors announce themselves, people look for their costumes and put on traditional garments. Dress and body adornment in general include clothes, fabrics wrapped around the body, jewellery, body painting, and all forms of body decoration that serve to express one's identity (Eicher/ Roach-Higgins 1979: 7). In the context of cultural performances, objects are regarded as visible testimonies from the past. Therefore, they are often used in touristic acts to impress the audience, combining material items with living and intangible interpretation (Kidd 2011: 29). Not only do tourists, as a consequence of their gaze, expect specific costumes as proof of 'authenticity' but the state of Namibia itself uses clothing as a basis for determining a 'real' San as 'hunter and gatherer' when it comes to hunting rights (Biesele/ Hitchcock 2011: 47). Considering paid cultural activities of the Ju/'hoansi as their official job, the traditional costumes in the tourism context may serve as working uniforms, and are an essential tool to construct a 'traditional' or 'authentic' experience for visitors. Bunten (2008) states that the uniforms, worn by the tourist guides in the course of the construction of a commodified persona in tourism, are provided with symbolic markers and adapted to tourists' expectations to clearly differentiate them from the travellers (ibid.: 386-387). Wearing traditional clothes is, therefore, essential in the eyes of the Ju/'hoansi:

> "It is very important for them to wear the traditional clothes, because the tourists would really like to see it, so tourists don't want to see the clothes they are making, because the clothes are coming from them. So, they want to see something different and also want to see the San Ju/'hoansi people wearing their own clothes. That is why it is important for them to wear it in front of the tourists." (Tilxo Dabe 14.01.2014, interview)

Schechner (1985) sees costumes and masks as relevant constitutors to performances on the stage as well as in everyday life, helping to shape a person pretending to be someone else. Costumes are used to transform the actor into the role he is playing; changing costumes here serves to put on a temporary identity and to create an adequate "[. . .] mood that can be communicated to and participated in by their audience" (Eicher/ Roach-Higgins 1979: 9, 11). Eicher describes how traditional dress can be manipulated for touristic purposes and is used to construct a specific ethnicity: "[A]rticles of dresses become selected, characterized, incorporated and transformed by a group that has had contact with others" (Eicher 1995: 3). Ethnic dress helps position individuals in time and space and preserves traditional heritage while at the same time incorporating changes and new elements (ibid.: 4-5). Dress can mark the differentiation between everyday life and rituals, such as weddings, funerals, and traditional dances; since certain costumes are associated with specific music or other activities (Eicher/ Roach-Higgins 1992: 9, 18). The touristic re-enactments can be regarded as 'special events', for which the Ju/'hoansi possess specific costumes. However, their making is an integral part of their everyday life.

The shape and material of the clothes influences the bodily behaviour and serves specific functions connected to the activities of the Ju/'hoansi. Clothing becomes part of the person or its extension and can even change the mobility of people (Keali'Inohomoku 1979: 80). The shape of clothes, jewellery, shoes, and props affect the physical movements and match the dance steps, and, therefore, are sometimes necessary to perform specific movements. Clothes do have an influence on the behaviour but are also made to fit the embodied habit that Bourdieu defined as "hexis" (1982: 283). For dancing activities, the Ju/'hoansi put on foot rattles, made out of seeds and filled with ostrich eggshell pieces, to regulate the rhythm of their movements and melodies. The traditional clothes are intrinsically connected with the body behaviour of the Ju/'hoansi. For example, each time they sat down on the sandy ground, the men spread the leather pieces of their pants to protect their bottom. Clothes are especially relevant when it comes to the traditional activities of hunting and gathering. On the one hand the colours serve as camouflage, so that the wearer remains undiscovered by animals (Tilxo Dabe 14.01.2014, interview; !L/ae Tsemkgao "Smallboy" 15.01.2014, interview), and on the other hand they "prefer the traditional clothes, because it is very light and makes no noise" (!amace N!aice 16.01.2014, interview), and their lightness facilitates fast running (Kxore Erna /ui 13.01.2014, interview). Little consideration has been given in classic anthropology to the study of dress, although it is a relevant tool for detecting cultural connections and embodied behaviour (Schwarz 1979: 23).

The Ju/'hoansi described how they waited for tourists who could arrive anytime; then they would have to get dressed very quickly to welcome them (Tsemkgao Daqm 16.01.2014, interview). Komtsa Daqm describes that it is quite stressful to change when tourists come because they often do not have much time (18.01.2014, interview) and they were told that tourists do not like to wait (van der Burg 2013: 72). If they are surprised by visitors, they would greet them in their everyday, 'modern' clothes because they recognise that not every tourist necessarily has to see them in their traditional adornment (N!ae //ao 16.01.2014, interview). I had the impression that it is not strictly forbidden for them to present themselves in modern clothes, but for formal activities, traditional clothes are required – for the correct re-enactment and to appear with the right garments in front of tourists. The villagers feel obliged to wear traditional clothes in the traditional village – as stated above, quality controllers in the living museums make sure that no modern elements are taken into the museum area. Tilxo Dabe, inhabitant of the cultural village of Doupos, explained to me that she does not have a problem to show herself in modern clothes and to be photographed in those but it is not allowed by the head man Boo !Kunta to wear them in the huts area (Tilxo Dabe 14.01.2014, interview). In the perspective of the actors, there is a strong separation between the attire for performance and the clothes worn when tourists are not present: "We do have a difference between the both. When we are dressed like this, we don't perform. We just wear our own clothes for each day. But when it's for culture, we have to use the ones for culture" (Xoan//an Cgaesje / !uu Cgaesje 13.01.2014, interview).

An exception to this more or less strict separation between 'traditional' and everyday activities in living museums and cultural villages was Djohkoe. This village did not have a designated place for traditional performances and they did not possess traditional costumes either but upon our arrival we found an old price list in one of the houses. Here the healing dance was performed after being booked for a fee, but not in a traditional village and with a mixture of modern clothes and traditional jewellery; only the female healer wore traditional attire. In this case, the stage, the props, and the costumes were missing, and the dance was probably closer to the one they practice for themselves every fortnight, as they told us.

In this context, it was interesting to ask if the Ju/'hoansi wear the traditional clothes for healing dances and hunting and gathering activities, even without the tourists' presence. People's statements were varied and undecided. Some told us with conviction that it is only possible to perform those activities in traditional clothes (Cwi //ao 13.01.2014, interview; Kxore Erna /ui 13.01.2014, interview), whereas others said that today they also dance and hunt in 'modern' clothes (!uu Cgaesje / Tilxo Dabe 13.01.2014, interview; Cwi Quinten Gerrie 13.01.2014, interview). Most of the people, however, claimed that this depended on the prevailing mood and that it did not matter which clothes they wore for which occasion (Xoan//a Cgaesje / !uu Cgaesje 13.01.2014, interview; Tilxo Dabe 14.01.2014, interview; Kxore Erna /ui 13.01.2014, interview; Tsemkgao Daqm 16.01.2014, interview). According to Werner Pfeifer, the traditional clothes are never worn in the 'modern' area because people prefer modern clothes, and because the production of traditional attire is so elaborate and work-intensive (Pfeifer 22.01.2014, interview). While I was staying in the 'backstage' area of Doupos, I never observed people dressing traditionally without the tourists' presence and they mostly changed in the last second on their way to the performance area. Only the elders wore some traditional accessories combined with modern outfits. The Ju/'hoansi get new clothes from shops in the towns of Tsumkwe and Grootfontein, the nearest cities, but it is a problem to have sufficient money and find transportation to go and buy them (Henry /ui Nyani 13.01.2014, interview). Modern clothes are the most wanted items from the visitors, and the San regularly asked for our clothes.

7 Possessing Traditional Attire

Let me briefly describe the traditional body adornment of the Ju/'hoansi. The clothes of the people we visited are mostly made of treated animal skins. Traditionally, the men wear short and wrapped pants called *tjona*, made out of springbok skin. It covers only the genitals and a thin string of leather goes up the bottom with two bigger pieces hanging from it. The women do not cover their upper body and their leather pieces are larger, reaching down to the knees like skirts, but moving around when walking or dancing. Their clothes are made out of springbok, duiker, and steenbok skin. In some of the villages, the traditional leather pieces are further decorated with eggshells or coloured beads in the shapes of small geometrical figures. The children wear either nothing or a very short apron made of leather. To cover the whole body or for sleeping, the San use blankets made out of the leather of larger animals, like kudus or red hartebeests (Cwi Quinten Gerrie 13.01.2014, interview; Tilxo Dabe 14.01.2014, interview). The leather pieces are softened and dyed red with a special liquid from a tree (Dabe //ao / Cwi //ao 13.01.2014, interview). They further wear leather bags to carry collected plants or fire sticks. All visited Ju/'hoansi owned remarkable jewellery – necklaces and headbands. For the cultural performances in the living museums they are made in the traditional way: out of ostrich-eggshells in different shapes and colours, seeds, or carved wood. For daily life, all Ju/'hoansi wear self-made jewellery out of glass beads according to the individual's taste and creativity.

The choice of clothing depends on the position of an individual in their environment, and on their interaction with other players and nature. Schwarz sees clothing as the connection between the socio-cultural and natural environment and the human body (1979: 29, 31). The traditional clothing of the Ju/'hoansi has a strong connection to their habitat; it is adapted to the requirements of the bush, and the materials are traditionally directly provided by nature. Originally, crafting jewellery was connected to gathering, as they used materials from the bush. The possession of traditional clothes, made of animal skins, depended to a great extent on the activity of hunting. Until today, the young hunters of Doupos underline the importance of being hunters (Tsemkgao Daqm 16.01.2014, interview) and the importance of hunting to provide traditional clothing:

> "In our traditional clothes – when you are not hunting, you will not have the skins to make your traditional clothes and most of all – to have traditional clothes you have to hunt. If you are not hunting, maybe – even if you are big – you will just stay like a small kid and don't make anything." (Dabe //ao / Cwi //ao 13.01.2014, interview)

They have to hunt the animals themselves, otherwise it will not have the same value (ibid.). This is even confirmed by Cwi Quinten Gerrie who grew up in Tsumkwe, a smaller town nearby, and who does not possess traditional attire: "If I want it, I can buy it. But I want to make it myself" (13.01.2014, interview). In the past, if someone was not a hunter himself or married to a hunter they had to hope for the help of relatives. Today, as hunting is either not allowed or not as common as before, many people told us that their clothes were inherited from their grandparents (Kxore Erna /ui 13.01.2014, interview; !amace N!aice 16.01.2014, interview; Tsemkgao Daqm 16.01.2014, interview).

The manufacturing of body adornment is connected to gender relations within the village structure. The production and creative process of crafting is a constant aspect of daily routine and also serves as a recreational activity among women of all ages, who often sit together on blankets around a fire and create jewellery, chatting together and occasionally interrupted by smaller children who need care. The men are busy with the making of carved and wooden objects and souvenirs, and support the women with the manufacturing of wooden beads. The making of craft and jewellery is essential: On the one hand as a relevant part of the income (Suzman 2001: 43-44) and on the other because Ju/'hoansi women always wear a lot of jewellery themselves. In the making of leather clothing, men are responsible for hunting and further for the removal of the hair, softening, and dying of skin. It is, therefore, up to them if their wives get a new piece of clothing, as Xoan//a !Kunta, daughter of the traditional healer of Doupos, states (14.01.2014, interview). The woman's role instead is "making it very nice" (ibid.), decorating the skin with eggshell-decorations and beadwork, or sewing together small bags (Dabe //ao / Cwi //ao 13.01.2014, interview; Tilxo Dabe 14.01.2014, interview; Xoan//a !Kunta 14.01.2014, interview; Tsemkgao Daqm 16.01.2014, interview).

In Grashoek, //Xa/oba, and Doupos, the possession of traditional clothes or the knowledge about their production is a prerequisite for participation in the touristic activities (Henry /ui Nyani 13.01.2014, interview; !amace N!aice 16.01.2014, interview; !uu Cgaesje / Tilxo Dabe 13.01.2014, interview). This is demonstrated by the following quote:

> "All of us we can do it. But we wonder about the clothes – so if you don't have the clothes, better you leave to give others the chance, the ones who have it. That's why you only saw a few of us yesterday [during the performance]. And the rest of them, they don't have the clothes of the culture. Because one has to be nice, that's why they use traditional, because that is their culture." (!uu Cgaesje, Tilxo Dabe 13.01.2014, interview)

In Grashoek – where hunting is not allowed anymore – the Living Culture Foundation Namibia provides goatskins for the actors to make their clothes (Henry /ui Nyani 11.01.2014, interview). Paulina Tsauses, shop manager of "G!hunku Crafts – San Handmade" in Tsumkwe, explained that the conservancy provides the villages with ostrich eggs to manufacture jewellery, purchased from a farm in South Africa since it has become very difficult to find them in nature today (04.09.2014, interview). This shows the connection between traditional hunting and gathering, and new possibilities of production through (inter-)national networks of tourism. Interestingly, people from Doupos – where hunting is still allowed – occasionally buy traditional clothes in a Craftshop in Tsumkwe, which trades these goods with neighbouring communities and sells them in a back room, reserved for local people (Cwi Quinten Gerrie 14.01.2014, interview; Cwi //ao / Dabe //ao 13.01.2014, interview; Xoan//a Cgaesje / !uu Cgaesje 13.01.2014, interview). The rarer the production materials have become, the more the value of traditional dress has increased. Consequently, the fragility of the clothes has become a delicate problem. The skins break easily when they are old, particularly from water in the rainy season, or when dogs rip them up:

> "Yes, if it's broken, it is a big problem. For example, now when you guys are coming, you must hide from yourself, you are scared of your friends, you have to help yourself. That's why we must care for those skins, it is a very big problem. Even the dogs, they can eat those skins and afterwards when you find it and people know, you will start suffering." (Cwi //ao / Dabe //ao 13.01.2014, interview)

Another reason for not participating in the cultural performances is that some are ashamed to wear the traditional clothes in front of tourists (Henry /ui Nyani 13.01.2014, interview). The Ju/'hoansi police officer Willem Gaiseb speaks of the embarrassment of the younger generation with respect to wearing traditional clothes. Since throughout history the San have been oppressed by other ethnic groups, he speaks of children being ashamed to say: "I'm a San" and who feel uncomfortable walking around in skins today in the streets of Tsumkwe (Willem Gaiseb 14.01.2014, interview). The healer's wife N!ae //ao in Doupos explains that people are proud to wear their traditional clothes in front of tourists today, but would not wear them in front of other ethnic groups because they somehow feel uncovered (N!ae //ao 16.01.2014, interview). As Josef Wukovits and I observed, the younger men who lived in Doupos were not as used to wearing traditional costumes, as evidenced on a walk one morning. Josef Wukovits and I were dressed up in skins and beads, and the adults convinced the boys to accompany us on this improvised bushwalk. !Kunta borrowed the tjona of his uncle but kept his pink, green, and orange underpants on underneath, to feel less exposed. The guide of the Little Hunter's Museum Komtsa Daqm felt shy and ashamed wearing a tjona at the beginning but as the museum project advanced so did his pride, since wearing tjonas demonstrates his identity as a Ju/'hoansi (16.01.2014, interview). Others, too, defined their costumes as markers of being Ju/'hoansi that differentiate them from other groups who do not wear traditional clothes anymore (Xoan//a Cgaesje / !uu Cgaesje 13.01.2014, interview; Cwi Quinten Gerrie 14.01.2014, interview; !amace N!aice 16.01.2014, interview). Comaroff and Comaroff describe this effect as commodification of culture, giving new pride and consciousness to one's own heritage (Comaroff/ Comaroff 2009: 9). People in the cultural villages or living museums are nowadays proud of their ethnic identity and demonstrate it by wearing traditional clothes. Interestingly, as soon as the Ju/'hoansi wore their traditional clothes in front of us they behaved like professional performers – their commodified persona in correspondence with the adequate visual appearance.

8 Conclusion

The Ju/'hoansi of north-eastern Namibia made use of their culture to gain economic profit from it, offering different established programmes for paying visitors. Through Community-Based Natural Resource Management, the San were able to combine economic benefit from touristic activities with wildlife conservation and the active involvement of the local people (Zips-Mairitsch 2013: 254, 261). The acts performed by the Ju/'hoansi cover a range of activities with the aim to show the 'authentic' cultural life of their ancestors, including bushwalks, hunting trips, crafts, dance and game performances, storytelling, and healing dances with varying degrees of interaction and duration. The performances were adapted to assumed touristic expectations, the actors were trained by local and German organisations, to assess the 'traditional' activities, and arrange them into an enjoyable and exciting way for the visitors. Specific authenticity rules regulate the acts, traditional costumes and environment are a prerequisite for the performances, and the performers were trained for the interaction with tourists. The knowledge used and transmitted during the touristic activities has been embodied through life-long training, explicitly appropriated for the purpose of the performances and further complemented with specific knowledge for the tourism business. Through creative and experimenting re-interpretations of old traditions, the cultural performances are each time re-created and experienced through the interaction with the audience. Reinterpreting, rehearsing, and parodying the performances of the professional actors, the Ju/'hoansi children practice the *Intangible Cultural Heritage* of their parents. The strongest aspect for the tourists is the 'experience', being transported and absorbed by all kinds of activities – either observing or actively practicing. Judging the extent of 'authenticity' therefore loses its relevance in the context of heritage performance. The tourism performances are part of the life of the Ju/'hoansi and can happen any time, they usually interrupt the ordinary routines and take place in a separate area. The performances are often seen as a job, therefore the change of physical space marks the separation between different activities in their lives. However, it is important to know about the real circumstances in which the Ju/'hoansi live to avoid stereotyped images alleging a pristine and traditional lifestyle.

An important activity that takes place in the backstage is the changing of appearance through costumes, jewellery, and props. As soon as tourists arrive, people change into traditional attire; from a touristic perspective, those clothes seem to guarantee an authentic experience, since costumes are used to transform the actor into the role he is playing (Eicher/ Roach-Higgins 1979: 9, 11). Dress and jewellery are part of material culture, which is used in addition to intangible cultural activities to foster what is claimed to be 'authentic' by an insider and an outsider view (Kidd 2011). Clothes are relevant markers for ethnicity, identity, and social participation, and are interconnected with hunting activities, family, and gender relations among the Ju/'hoansi. In their actually lived-in village, traditional clothes were seldom worn, and 'modern' clothes are the most wanted items San wish from the visitors. Traditional clothes nevertheless have a relevance for the performance of 'traditional' activities, since they were developed for specific movements and circumstances. Further, the possession of traditional clothes is a condition for being able to participate in tourism activities and, because of their fragility, they are treated with respect.

The dichotomy between nature and culture has caused negative impacts throughout Africa by building conservation parks, which include the protection of nature and game and exclude the indigenous population from their ancestral lands. People were considered a threat to the environment and were allowed to live on it only as attraction for tourists (Zips-Mairitsch 2013: 83). Native indigenous people living on the territory were often not involved in the planning and organisation of nature parks, although their participation and knowledge would have been extremely important (Zips/ Zips-Mairitsch 2007: 38-40). Most development programmes in the Tsumkwe District further used a top-down attitude (cf. Zips-Mairitsch 2013: 251). The Nyae Nyae Conservancy today embraces the protection of fauna and flora by the people living on the territory, giving them the possibility to profit through activities with tourists, but demanding from the visitors a respectful approach to the nature and the hosting communities. Although tourism is statistically seen not the main part of income – which is by contrast given by the conservancy and most of all, state pensions and jobs (Biesele/ Hitchcock 2011: 211) – for the Ju/'hoansi involved, it is considered an important factor for financial security, according to the interviews I have made. In my opinion both projects – the LCFN and the NNC – give the Ju/'hoansi the possibility to actively manage and influence their own images.

The visitors often travel from far to see and meet the Ju/'hoansi – tourists as well as scientists. The people of Doupos are today further called upon to cooperate with other San groups in South Africa, teaching them their traditional techniques of making fire, and manufacturing jewellery with ostrich eggshells (!L/ae Tsemkgao "Smallboy" 01.01.2014, interview). I therefore tend to see the Ju/'hoansi as experts for their culture, whether 'authentic' or not, embodied or not, preserved or not. Through processes of learning from their parents, as well as through study and exchange with other groups, the San are nowadays teaching and performing as professionals and the traditional clothes and props serve as tools for their acts. The knowledge of their culture is a basis for tourism business and has heightened the self-esteem of many participants. The Ju/'hoansi in the Living Museums and Cultural Villages in the borderlands of north-eastern Namibia have actually become professionals in handling their culture, and are sought-after experts invited to travel, to share their traditional knowledge, and their emerging entrepreneurial skills. Perhaps this is a major difference to their kin on the other side of the border in neighbouring Botswana (cf. Zips-Mairitsch 2013).

Throughout this paper I have analysed the strategies and the materials the Ju/'hoansi apply to adapt their cultural heritage to the creation of informative and yet entertaining experiences for tourists. I have focused on the costumes as tangible objects used during the performance of traditional re-enactments. They serve to create an adequate mood for the audience, and foster the performers' role. They are so relevant for the performance that they are included in the rules that regulate the acts and are a condition to be able to participate. The production of traditional garments is connected with hunting and gathering skills, and specific knowledge about their manufacturing. Nowadays, many of the materials have become less accessible and have to be supplied by other sources. The eggshells are imported from South Africa, while the 'traditional' Kudu skins – that have partly become goat skins today – are provided by the LCFN. The colourful beads used in some of the villages have their origins in the Czech Republic and are loved by Ju/'hoansi women. Although the remote location of the Ju/'hoansi communities corresponds to the image of the 'pristine' indigenous, which is applied in touristic marketing, the visitors, the performers themselves, and the materials used, place the San in a clearly cosmopolitan and global field.

Between Archive and Repertoire: The Ju/'hoansi San Living Museum in Grashoek

Alicja Khatchikian

1 Introduction

In 2007, Namibia signed the UNESCO Convention on the Safeguarding of the Intangible Cultural Heritage (hereafter ICH), strengthening the 2005 Heritage Hunt campaign initiated by the Museums Association of Namibia in partnership with the National Heritage Council. Embedded within a larger policy commitment to preserve national heritage and cultural diversity in Namibia, the project seeks to create a database of heritage sites based on public nomination and research to be added to the inventory of national heritage sites outlined by the National Heritage Council. Indeed, the project aims to diversify the notion and representation of Namibian heritage by encouraging greater recognition of sites of historical and cultural relevance to local communities.

While no less than seventeen African countries were celebrating their fiftieth anniversaries of political independence in 2010, Africa's last colony, Namibia, celebrated its twentieth jubilee of independence after more than a century of enforced economic, cultural, and racial segregation. The aftermath of independence in 1990 was, therefore, deeply marked by a will to redefine the notion of 'Namibianess' and its political aesthetics (Akuupa 2011: 41-42). Accordingly, the notion of museum and its environment has been changing and increasingly challenged by new museological paradigms and curatorial forms (see Kreps 2009) that consider various aspects of the heritage they present in terms of "living culture" (Silvester 2011). Amongst others, cultural villages and living museums were initiated in Namibia and Southern Africa as alternative ways for safeguarding the intangible cultural heritage and to foster cultural tourism under the paradigm of Community-Based Natural Resource Management.

Nevertheless, criticism repeatedly highlights the differences between heritage discourse and the tourism industry. On the one hand, advocates of these institutions support their role as cultural custodians and claim that they enable communities to benefit directly from their cultural resources while strengthening the vitality of their cultural heritage and its transmission to younger generations. On the other, critics sustain that commodification of culture may affect and distort its authenticity, draining rituals of meaning and transforming cultural practices into mere "staged performances" (Silvester 2011). The idiosyncrasies of tourism agendas lie at the core of this discussion: While these forms of heritage intervention and sustainable development may offer financial support to the communities they engage, they seem to fail at grasping the diversity and dynamism of contemporary Namibian cultural heritage by promoting an image of minority groups as "timeless" and "primitive" (Akuupa 2014, interview). Furthermore, as ≠Oma and Thoma (2002) maintain, communities involved in such projects might benefit financially from them, yet completely lack information about the tourism industry and its potential impacts on their community life. Therefore, the debate about living museums does not only entail issues of representation and authenticity but also evolves in terms of transparency and agency.

Highly aware of the complexity of these issues within the heritage discourse and taking distance from the authenticity debate (Fillitz/ Saris 2013), this paper does not seek to answer the question of whether new institutions, such as living museums, contribute to preserving cultural diversity or rather transform them into mere commodities. Differently, largely drawing from memories, field notes, and ethnographic material collected in January 2014 between Windhoek and the Ju/'hoansi San Living Museum in Grashoek, it attempts to frame living museums in terms of "ritual" (Duncan 1995) and "scenario" (Taylor 2003). By analysing the content and quality of experience displayed, performed, and embodied within their spaces, living museums are framed within the field of performance studies.

I here use the term performance as in Taylor (2003), i.e., a performance scenario that cannot be reduced to the discursive and narrative realm but rather unfolds its performative and non-discursive expressions. From this perspective, performances *of* and *within* the living museum environment become both corporeal and spatial acts of transfer: As a liminal space of encounters between different physical, temporal and cultural spaces, the living museum bridges past and future, archive and repertoire (Taylor 2003: 58). This takes place by re-enacting the living past through the embodied experience of its present and future possibilities (Lepecki 2010: 31; Schechner 1985). Therefore, like Lepecki investigates contemporary dance and performance art, I look for creative values in those re-enactments of traditional knowledge as a "will to archive" that "derives neither exclusively from 'a failure in cultural memory' nor from 'a nostalgic lens'" but rather refers to a "capacity to identify in a past work still non-exhausted creative fields of 'impalpable possibilities'" (Lepecki 2010: 31).

2 The Will to Redefine Museums in Namibia

According to the project coordinator for the Museums Association of Namibia, Jeremy Silvester (2011), Namibian museums are mostly associated with the image of spaces where visitors encounter objects and texts that highlight selected features of Namibia's history and environment. In their classical understanding, museums indeed relate to the preservation and display of objects belonging to several different temporal and spatial realms in one unique site. French philosopher Michel Foucault coined the term "heterotopia", describing such spaces as "capable of juxtaposing in a single real place several spaces, several sites that are in themselves incompatible (...) something like counter-sites, a kind of effectively enacted utopia in which the real sites that can be found within the culture are simultaneously represented, contested, and inverted" (Foucault 1986: 24). These spaces are neither reproduced nor invented anew: Heterotopic places exist and are formed in the grounding of society. The Foucauldian museum thus operates on the cultural practice that converts a *place* into a *space* (see Taylor 2003: 66; italics in original).

Nonetheless, Namibian scholar, Michael Uusiku Akuupa, argues that the selective process through which these features, objects, and sites are chosen and given significance does not reflect local values in the context of their time, partly explaining why Namibian state museums have failed in engaging with local narratives.[1] While in West and East Africa, he sustains, museums were redefined as "spaces for reconciliation", considering the history of each place and its meaning through time (Akuupa 2014, interview), Namibian museums' narrative is still strongly influenced by the context of both colonial rules: The apartheid wounds seem to remain open as German cannons silently stand next to ancient rock art pieces at the Alte Feste[2] in the city centre of Windhoek.[3]

[1] "In Kavango, for instance, in Rundu, there is a state museum that never opened. Why? (...) The other one in Okahandja, a military museum, also never opened. One must read these facts critically. State's narrative is based on nationhood; however, does nationhood as a value make sense for its citizens? Why are citizens not curious about exploring these buildings? (...) Can we look at museums as nation-building means?" (Akuupa, personal communication, Windhoek 2014).

[2] The Alte Feste, now a historical museum in downtown Windhoek, is a fortress designed by captain Curt von François as headquarters for the Regional Command and the Imperial Schutztruppe during the German colonisation of South-West Africa (1885-1914).

[3] "Our society survived a long period of colonial time. South Africans occupied us enforcing upon us the notion of race. Only two classes existed in Namibia: whites and non-whites. If you were white, you were civilised, human; if you were non-white, you were simply 'non'" (Strauss, personal communication, Windhoek 2014).

As Akuupa (2011) importantly highlights, the passage from the *One Namibia, One Nation* narrative to the post-apartheid *Unity in Diversity* slogan mirrored a caesura in Namibian governmental cultural policy. The recognition and value of the diverse Namibian cultural repertoire as one and many rather than "dissonant heritage" (Silvester 2011) thus emphasised the inadequacy of existing museological models in Namibia. That is, since signing the UNESCO Convention on the Safeguarding of the Intangible Cultural Heritage (2003), there has been growing attention to the importance of intangible cultural heritage in Namibia, and museum agents acknowledged the importance of working together with the communities whose culture they represent (Silvester 2011).

Current museological debate is concerned with "how museums can supplement their conventional tasks of curating and preserving tangible culture (objects and collections) with activities devoted to curating and preserving intangible, living cultural expressions", such as performances, skills, knowledge, and its practices (Kreps 2009: 194). Similarly, Namibian museums are facing the challenge of linking those objects to the music, dances, oral traditions, craftsmanship, and intangible knowledge they embody by entrusting their curatorial aspects to the communities they belong to.

In order to preserve and respect the ICH domains, as listed in Article 2(2) of the Convention (UNESCO 2003, online), one governmental strategy was the (re)introduction of the annual hosting of cultural festivals at local, regional, and national level.[4] At the same time, the establishment of new museological paradigms, such as living museums and cultural villages in Southern Africa, prompted the inclusion of new actors into the heritage arena and offered both educational and touristic spaces through which local communities could subsist while practicing their own cultural heritage. As ≠Oma and Thoma (2002: 40) describe, "[i]t may seem ironic that catering to tourists for economic gain could have a positive impact on the cultural revival of San communities, especially among San youth who have lost interest in their heritage, yet it does have a positive impact in many respects. Tourism elevates the position of elderly community members as the teachers of San traditions." However, they continue, "communities that emphasize the income-generating potential of their culture risk further undermining it if they perform cultural practices exclusively for the sake of tourists" (ibid.).

[4] For deeper insight into cultural festivals in Namibia, I refer to the doctoral work of Michael Uusiku Akuupa (2011). His PhD thesis investigates the formation of "national culture" in post-apartheid Namibia by focusing on the Kavango case. Akuupa's historical approach sustains that cultural festivals were not introduced in 1995 but rather *re*-introduced after being discontinued in the passage from South West Africa to independent Namibia.

The authenticity debate surrounding these forms of cultural tourism is undeniably critical and activities engaged in living museums are often thought of as unauthentic 'staged performances'. In fact, while in the arts authenticity has been formulated as a category (Dutton 2003), from an anthropological vantage authenticity constitutes a specific discourse but cannot be taken as an independent analytical category (Fillitz/ Saris 2013).

In the debate on authenticity in arts, Denis Dutton (2003) distinguished between two analytic categories of authenticity, i.e., *nominal* and *expressive*. Nominal authenticity deals with the empirical facts related to a work of art, determining how the work came to be. Expressive authenticity relates to how much the work of art possesses original or inherent authority, how much genuine expression and passion the artist or performer put into the artwork according to his/her individual "artistic self" (ibid.). Therefore, while nominal authenticity includes values and beliefs of specific artistic and historical tradition embodied in an artefact, expressive authenticity "is seen as committed, personal expression", a form of truthfulness towards the self (ibid.). Dutton's philosophical departure on the use of "authentic" in aesthetics revolves, nonetheless, around the question: *"Authentic as opposed to what?"* (ibid.; italics in original).

From an anthropological vantage, Thomas Fillitz and Jamie A. Saris (2013) highlighted how an anthropological debate on authenticity needs to first acknowledge its non-existence as an analytical category: Even though "anthropology has had, from the beginning, what one might call a professional interest in, and connection to, authenticity," current anthropological insights argue that "authenticity and inauthenticity need to be understood as part of the same process of situated social actors engaging culturally salient ends" (Fillitz/ Saris 2013: 2). "It is therefore somewhat regrettable that recent anthropological work on this most protean but very socially relevant category has tended to move in an analytical direction, trying to get a handle on the defining features of authenticity" (ibid.: 3).

The authenticity debate is never-ending as far as we allow the existence of an *authentic state* of culture and enforce upon it the rule of comparison. The term 'performance' is similarly tackled: Acknowledging to the San the right to speak their values and truths implies to entrust their artistic selves (Dutton 2003). However, besides authenticity, the limits of heritage agenda also need to be discussed. I therefore share Kirshenblatt-Gimblett's interest in the meaning of safeguard, which, in UNESCO terms, often "requires highly specialized skills that are of different order from the equally specialized skills needed for the actual performance" (Kirshenblatt-Gimblett 2004: 55; Kearney 2009). Safeguarding measures and heritage interventions, she continues, often "reveal how different the professional heritage enterprise is from the heritage that is to be safeguarded" and eventually collide with the tendency of heritage politics to create "metacultural productions" that freeze the internal cultural dynamics of the communities they claim to represent (Kirshenblatt-Gimblett 2004: 59-61).

Two interconnected questions can thus be raised: How deeply does the living museum engage with safeguarding and preserving and to what extent does it simply provide employment possibilities? Further, why should these two aspects be necessarily conflicting?

3 Doing Heritage, Living Culture

> "I think of museum as a place with four major characteristics: it collects; it curates; it preserves; and it educates. Those purposes are so universal, so in grant. The main question is how can we reconcile the livingness of culture with its memory. Yet, I believe past, future and present exist at once. It cannot be otherwise. Then, perhaps, living museums are also possible." (Strauss 2014, interview)

When asked for an opinion about living museums, André Strauss[5] hesitated at first. From his long-time experience as Deputy Director of the Namibian Government and former President of the National Art Gallery in Windhoek, he wondered how the livingness of the San could reconcile with their ancient cultural memory and how such an effort may affect the means of collecting, curation, preservation, and education. Then, as soon as he contemplated the overlapping presence of past and future in their livingness, Strauss entered the field of possibilities that Diana Taylor terms *scenario*. Before entering this scenario, I shall introduce Grashoek, the Ju/'hoansi San Living Museum and some of the activities engaged in it.

Located in the north-eastern Otjozondjupa Region within the N≠a Jaqna Conservancy since its establishment in 2003, Grashoek is a small village of the Tsumkwe district with no more than three hundred inhabitants according to local sources. Some of them are Ju/'hoansi San or !Kung, as they mainly refer to themselves. To this regard, it should be mentioned that diverse groups of hunters and gatherers that have recently labelled as "the San" had no shared identity in the past. However, as the Comaroffs sustain, the fact that the San identity is a comparably new social construction does not reduce the omnipresent ethnic identification: "Their putative presence in the past has sedimented into an assertive, future-

5 I wish to thank Ms. Tharacky Namupala, Regional Education Advisor for the "Working Group of Indigenous Minorities in Southern Africa" (WIMSA) in Windhoek for providing me his contact.

oriented ethno-corporation. [. . .] 'San' has become a term of self-reference" (Comaroff/ Comaroff 2009: 96).

Not surprisingly then, Grashoek has neither historical nor symbolical meaning for its inhabitants. Founded in 1990, the village was established as a result of the relocation policies in post-apartheid Namibia. It simply gathered different families from the surrounding villages.[6]

Scattered over an area that stretches, according to local sources, "from over there up to the other side," Grashoek looked rather spare to my eyes when I first visited. As Memory Simasiku, pre-primary teacher at the governmental Grashoek Primary School, points out, "the only modern buildings here are the school and the teachers' homes" (Simasiku 2014, personal communication). The school year had just started when I arrived in Grashoek and most classes were waiting for both students and teachers to reach the village. On the one hand, Memory explains, school education is still widely considered of secondary relevance within the community, hence it is likely that parents register their children throughout the whole first term. On the other, teachers assigned to Grashoek coming from different regions of the country frequently complain about general conditions in the village and ask for reassignment.[7]

Most inhabitants live in handmade clay houses with sheet iron metal roofs and share the overall area as communal space; few fences around the housing areas protect them from the donkeys, which move noisily and freely. At the centre of an apparently bare expanse, a sign "Reception" stands on a signpost beneath a big tree. Six hundred meters away from Grashoek, the living museum of the Ju/'hoansi San engages in its activities based around eighty inhabitants of what is referred to as "the modern village".

Since its foundation in 2004, by Namibian tour guide Werner Pfeifer and San teacher Ghau N!aici, the museum has been locally run by San people with the long-lasting background support of the Living Culture Foundation Namibia (hereafter LCFN), a non-profit, German-Namibian organisation consisting of the Windhoek-based LCFN and its German partner organisation in Tangermünde.

According to the organisation's official website, the LCFN provides professional support to the community throughout the process of building the living

6 For deeper insight into the legal debate about San's land rights in Southern Africa, see Zips-Mairitsch 2013 and Useb 2002.

7 During my stay in Grashoek, a male teacher from the Caprivi region had just arrived to visit the school and meet its director. After a short round, he started complaining about the precarious school conditions (e.g. the lack of a library; the rooms' size) and the boredom of everyday life in the village. He firmly stated he was not going to teach there.

museum, mostly advising on price structures, activity programmes, and staff organisation. Furthermore, the organisation is responsible for promoting and advertising six different museums[8] by providing, amongst others, a platform on their website as well as professional signboards for each of them. Interestingly, they clarify that signboards remain property of the foundation, as they reserve the right to remove them "should the museum fail to adhere to their requirements" (LCFN 2014, online). Collaborators of living museums are encouraged to follow and respect certain etiquettes and behavioural rules within the museological space, such as wearing traditional clothes, engage only with traditional dance and music, and speak their own language. Along with self-responsibility, low financial input, and participation, authenticity is listed as one of the core values of the programme. Disciplinary measures are contemplated in case of misleading behaviours (e.g. alcohol consumption) in the form of temporary or permanent exclusion from the project.

The museum area or 'campsite', as it is called by local people, consists of three rudimentary camping sites, each equipped with a shower and a dry toilet. There is no running water, electricity or mobile network in the camping area. If not equipped with one's own provisions, one needs to carry water in tanks from Grashoek. For a mobile network, one needs to reach the veterinary fence two kilometres away. Similarly, electricity is a luxury that only teachers can directly benefit from.

Once you know the route, there are different shortcuts to the campsite from the village, but tourists will enter and exit the living museum from the same path, first encountering the camping area and then, possibly, the village. One of the first things they will notice is the craft shop: There, together with different kinds of handicrafts, the official menu and the list of prices for each activity is advertised on posters. Only few meters away from the shop, the museum space silently exists: Three traditional hay huts stand in the middle of a sandy area surrounded by bushes and mangetti trees; fire leftovers lay on the soil with what remains from some sweet monkey oranges. A few young and older women sit on the ground, chatting and laughing under the shadow while waiting for the activities to start.

When tourists arrive, this apparently empty space becomes the main stage of the living museum. The area is completely out of range of mobile networks; therefore, it is not always possible to arrange meetings in advance. The system works efficiently though: Immersed in nature and silence, as soon as inhabitants hear a car from the village they will run to the campsite and change into traditional

8 The sixth one, the Ovahimba Living Museum, was inaugurated in 2017.

clothes. Generally, one of the nominated museum guides welcomes visitors while the group prepares. Dressing traditionally in the living museum means wearing a leather loincloth for men and a leather skirt for women. Women may have some leather clothing wrapped around their shoulders but their breasts are exposed. Traditional clothing also includes different types of ornaments, bracelets, necklaces, and hunting equipment.[9] They seldom make their own dresses these days, even though they know the procedure. The leather mostly comes from Springboks and Did-diks, as Erna illustrates while showing me her grandmother's dress:

> "We take all the animal body out; then dry the skin under the sun. After it dried, we prepare some water… You know, we have some water roots. We take a big water root, squeeze the water out and wash the skin. When the skin is still a bit wet, we start softening it. We mix the skin with *kiaat*, a tree which falls and we cut it into pieces. We make it soft like powder and put it on the skin." (Kxore 2014, interview)

Erna is the only female guide of the living museum in Grashoek for two main reasons, which she highlights.[10] Firstly, most women are shy with strangers and not proficient enough in English. Women and elder generations are more likely to speak Afrikaans, whereas children and youngsters receive education exclusively in English since pre-primary school. Still, communication at the campsite is constantly moderated by the guides. The group at the museum is varied in terms of sex and age: children are not part of the official team – basically meaning that they do not benefit financially from the project – but they often join parents and grandpar-

[9] Noteworthy information regarding hunting permits in the area is unclear among locals. They generally claim that hunting is forbidden by governmental law since 2002. Other sources (Taylor 2008) sustain that, "in order to obtain a hunting license nowadays, you need to own a high-powered rifle, a safe to store it in and a fridge to store the meat, all expensive items that the San would never be able to afford." As reported by UNDP in 2012, "the N≠a Jaqna Conservancy has a contract with a trophy hunting agency that in turn imports game animals each year. […] Tourists pay high prices to hunt in the area and a good portion of that money goes back into the conservancy." Furthermore, "[w]hen trophy hunters make a kill, they are not allowed to take the whole animal; the hunter is allowed to remove the head […], but the main part of the animal goes to the conservancy as meat." Apparently, trophy hunting does not seem to oppose one of the leading objectives of the N≠a Jaqna Conservancy, i.e., the re-establishment of game population. Yet, since the conservancy was founded in 2003, locals in Grashoek are not officially entitled to hunt. Still, in the Nyae Nyae Conservancy, 150 kilometres away approximately, they are advertised as *traditional* hunters in the Living Hunter's Museum of the Ju/'hoansi-San in //Xa/oba, close to Tsumkwe.

[10] Erna //ui Kxore is a 29-year-old Ju/'hoansi San woman. Erna is her Christian name. As she explains, most of them have one since they are Christian and their Ju/'hoansi names are often too difficult for foreigners. She is married to Khau Morris //oce, Treasurer of the Ju/'hoansi San Living Museum in Grashoek, and mother of four young children. Two colleagues and I were hosted by them during our stay in Grashoek.

ents when off from school and collaborate in dances, games, and crafts marking. Secondly, roles in the museum are not exclusively assigned, even though men are primarily involved in activities related to hunting, its knowledge and tools, fire making and healing practices while women are engaged in dancing, singing, and jewelry making.

Our first day at the campsite starts with the so-called "Action Day", an approximately five-hour overview of the main practices and activities they offer to show the "original lifestyle of the traditional hunter-gatherers San." The "Bushwalk" engages mainly men and consists of tracking and collecting bush food, starting a fire traditionally (i.e., rubbing two sticks into one another, one representing the male and the other the female), and preparing snares and ropes for the hunt. We walk around the main area with two men, a hunter and the guide. A few women follow our path, grab something off the ground, and give the men some bush potatoes and sour plums.

The following craft and jewelry making activity engages both men and women: While men construct bows and arrows, women use ostrich eggshells and other natural elements to create colourful necklaces and bracelets. "Each of them has a meaning," comments Erna, including beauty and decoration, healing power and protection. After a lunch break, they join again for a shorter version of the elephant-healing dance and the so-called "wild melon dance". Women and youngsters particularly enjoy this game: While women sing and dance passing on a monkey orange with a quick hand move, men watch them and eventually try to steal the orange to stop the game. Those not actively involved sit on the sand next to the rest of the audience and watch their fellows while passing a pipe, chatting and commenting. When the activities are over, visitors are guided back to the entrance and are welcomed to the craft shop.

Once the cars are finally gone, the group of Ju/'hoansi San walk back to the village: Some leave a bag with their clothes on their way to the museum, some directly go home and then change to T-shirt, trousers, and dresses. Exhausted by the heat and the intense day, we also walk back to our tents.

4 Between Scenarios

When talking about rituals, healing, and hunting knowledge, one of the most recurring questions I heard myself and my colleagues asking was: "Do you *still* do it in the village? Do you actually do it *so*?" In fact, I recognise such questions as naïvely judgmental, taking for granted that museum equals past and tradition while village stands for present and modernity in a contrasting rather than concurrent way.

The relation drawn by Diana Taylor (2003) between archive and repertoire finds a singular counterpoint in the space of the living museum, namely the archive made of "supposedly enduring material (i.e., texts, documents, buildings, bones)" and the repertoire enacted and embodied "ephemeral, non-reproducible knowledge" (Taylor 2003: 19-20). According to Taylor (2003), the repertoire is always embodied and manifested in performance, in action, in doing. However, as she highlights, "[m]useums have long taken the cultural Other out of context and isolated it [. . .] behind glass" (ibid.: 66). Yet, people are not mere objects of cultural transmission and preservation but subjects, living agents in the heritage enterprise above all (Kirshenblatt-Gimblett 2004: 58).

When confronted with the question of whether tradition presented in living museums merely represents 'a business' for San people or rather has an everyday relevance for his community, Komtsa Daqm[11] looked quite surprised and answered straightforwardly: "We live our culture" (Daqm 2014, interview). Similarly, being invited to draw themselves and their houses, 6th grade children of the Grashoek Primary School, whose parents are involved in the living museum, spontaneously used both blank pages and drew themselves in the village as well as at the campsite, wearing both leather clothes and T-shirts. In this regard, it seems more and more evident that issues regarding representation and authenticity in living museums are largely raised outside the community itself.

From a different perspective, if we focus on the activities and practices enacted *within* the living museum, the museum environment can be considered both as a space of encounter and encounter of spaces between text and body, knowledge and practice, the ephemeral and the tangible, fictional landscapes and corporeal bodies – archive and repertoire – that are activated whenever the Ju/'hoansi San meet the visitors. As Carol Duncan writes (1995: 2), any museological environment prompts visitors to enact a performance of some sort, whether visitors would describe it as such or not. That is, visitors gain a certain quality of knowledge from the museum experience: Some might enjoy the activities as mere entertainment and experience; some believe that this is how San people still actually live; others might develop deeper insights that require intellectual effort and critical thought. In other terms, spectators also have their subjective position and impact.

[11] Komtsa Daqm is a tour guide at the Living Hunter's Museum of the Ju/'hoansi in //Xa/oba, Namibia.

As the space of the museum is activated, the encounters double, triple, overlap: The transfer happens simultaneously and multilaterally. Not only is knowledge transmitted and shared between San and tourists but also *among* them. The museum provides a platform for encounter and exchange between at least three generations that they extremely value. Kxao Moses ≠Oma and Axel Thoma (2002) highlight that, "although some San youth still refuse to admit openly that their cultural practices have social value, they are prepared to learn more about such traditional skills such as the ability to identify animal tracks, the knowledge of edible bush foods, and the use of medicinal plants because they have recognized that these skills will enable them to generate income." While the need for economic gain is indeed enormous within the community, living museums have positive impacts on the cultural revival of San communities in other terms (≠Oma/ Thoma 2002).

As a matter of fact, children do not practice traditional dances or games except in the space offered by the living museum or during the annual cultural festivals. Despite the fact that the youngest generations have been born and raised in an environment that visibly differs from the one presented by the living museum, it should be acknowledged that they believe in the contemporary relevance of those values and inherently perceive them as part of who they are. A practical example relates to hunting: Although hunting has been forbidden in the Grashoek area for over a decade, San are highly interested in practicing this knowledge and believe in its future possibility:

> "The most important thing we should teach our children is hunting. [. . .] In the future, we might get licenses for hunting. Then, we will start hunting again by using our traditional weapons." (Khau 2014, interview)

The risk might be that, under the trap of what is commonly understood as 'development', the San remain suspended within a frame that depict them as 'too underdeveloped' to be modern, yet 'too developed' to be traditional. This contradiction is reflected in the living museum in a situation that John Marshall dubbed as "a plastic Stone Age" (in Hitchcock/ Biesele 2002): A sort of heterotopia that functions as a broken mirror reflecting Western expectations for the wild and primitive San.

Nevertheless, while the negative influences of tourism on San communities are widely discussed, the opportunities such an experience can provide in raising awareness of their skills and aspirations lacks critical consideration (≠Oma/ Thoma 2002). Therefore, in trying to grasp the impalpable possibilities[12] the living

[12] Lepecki attributes the expression "impalpable possibilities" to Brian Massumi (2002).

museum can offer, the performance *of* it should be considered, just as the practices displayed *within* its space. Not only does the living museum environment embody and give form to the ephemeral but it also reflects what André Lepecki defined as a "will to archive" or "will to re-enact," that is, "a capacity to identify in a past [work] still non-exhausted creative fields" (Lepecki 2010: 42).

The notion of performance as re-enactment is not a novelty in the field of anthropology. Amongst others, Richard Schechner's conceptualisation of twice-behaved behavior[13] represents a milestone in the field of performance and ritual studies. According to Schechner, performance does not inherently exist individually but is rather behaved, passed through, rehearsed, and rearranged 'transindividually' (Schechner 1985: 35-36). More recently, Lepecki further investigated the intimate connection between an act and its re-enactment, a behaviour and its restoration. The link between archive and re-enactment implies that "each 'will' acts upon the other to re-define what is understood by 'archiving' and what is understood by 're-enacting'"; this continuous redefining action is carried out, he continues, through a common articulator – the body (Lepecki 2010: 42).

Even though Lepecki refers to the dancer's body, I here consider the body of the living museum both as 'dramatis personae' ("the Ju/'hoansi San") and as a space the museum occupies. While living in the village of Grashoek among its inhabitants, its presence was highly perceivable even outside its spatial delimitation: The museum has a role in their everyday life; it is present in their everyday talk as well as in the way they organise their routines. I contemplated the nature of its presence, often asking myself whether it was intrusive or rather intimate for them and concluded that there is no binary response. The living museum does not exist as a separate entity from Grashoek: There is no *there* there nor *here* here but rather an *in-between* (Taylor 2003: 72).

Merely considering the living museum in Grashoek as an example of 'staged authenticity' would therefore fail in looking at it from a local perspective. Yet, the ritual cannot be detached from its scenarios, the act from its carriers, the performance from its bodies. As Lepecki (2010: 31) poetically expressed, "the body is archive and archive a body." In the living museum, archive and repertoire exist at once as the scenario enables the simultaneous and continuous transfer between (doing) heritage and (living) culture.

13 "Performance behavior isn't free and easy. Performance behavior is known and/or practiced behavior – or "twice-behaved-behavior," "restored behavior" – either rehearsed, previously known, learned by osmosis since early childhood, revealed during the performance by masters, guides, gurus, or elders, or generated by rules that govern the outcomes, as in improvisatory theatre or sports" (Schechner 1985: 118).

5 Conclusions

I frankly admit that the idea of a 'San-body' in a 'San-space' blurrily existed in my mind before being in the field. Nonetheless, I soon recognised those images were biased by an understanding of museum and body as a "primitive scenario"[14] (Taylor 2003). As soon as I arrived in Grashoek, I started reflecting upon the existence of two apparently different bodies and separated spaces – the museum and the village – and began perceiving those bodies and spaces as neither different nor separated. As I moved from the campsite to the village, that feeling increased and points of co-existence and convergence between spaces became more tangible and evident.

If we do not account for its living connotation, the museum in Grashoek is fully representative of what any other ritual site is generally considered, as Duncan argues (1995: 10): It is structured in a space that is "carefully marked off and culturally designated as reserved for a special quality of attention," wherein "a certain decorum" is also expected. The depth and quality of shared knowledge within that specific space depends on its audience, as "some individuals may use a ritual site more knowledgeably than others – they may be more educationally prepared to respond to its symbolic cues" (ibid.: 12). As she continues, "to control a museum means precisely to control the representation of a community and its highest values and truths," and not everyone is socially, psychologically, and culturally pre-disposed to access them (ibid.: 8-12).

Nevertheless, by simply integrating the 'living' connotation to a classical understanding of museological space, ambivalences rise. Namely, as Kirshenblatt-Gimblett (2004: 58) highlights, living archives "do not assert a person's right to do what they do, but rather their role in keeping the culture going on [for others]", hence performers are mere carriers, transmitters, and bearers of tradition rather than active agents and interpreters of culture. Differently, by acknowledging the San the right to speak their values and their *on-going* (rather than still) relevance, we actively include the most evident means through which they are archived and expressed: the body.

The conundrum of living museums primarily tackles its living connotation and its corporeality: Critics strongly argue against the 'primitive' and 'timeless' image

[14] "The 'primitive' body as object reaffirms the cultural supremacy and authority of the viewing subject, the one who is free to come and go" (Taylor 2003: 64). Therefore, the "body-as-primitive-scenario" serves to the narrative of heritage by presenting traditions as "staged subnational cultural expressions within the supranational framework" rather than as "highest values and truths" (Kirshenblatt-Gimblett 2004: 58; Duncan 1995: 8-12).

the San people present of themselves and of their bodies whereas in 'modern' villages communities live and dress differently (Akuupa 2014). Even though I partly share this position, a series of questions could be raised. Amongst others: Why do we recognise a 'will to re-enact' in dance or performance as art whereas we reduce it to 'staged authenticity' when dealing with cultural memory? Why do we tend to believe that what the San do in the living museum is not what they did in the past?

If we look at the living museum and Grashoek exclusively in terms of 'front stage' and 'backstage' respectively, we are still trapped in the authentic-unauthentic dichotomy. On the contrary, by considering the Living Museum *in* Grashoek in its unity, the curtain between stage and audience, front and back starts to blur (see Quick 2012) and may only appear in our understanding. Even when "the tendency has been to banish the repertoire to the past", archive and repertoire exist at the same time in a constant state of interaction (Taylor 2003: 21). Lepecki identifies their point of convergence in the space of the body: The performance scenario is the medium through which archive and repertoire are expressed and express their will to re-enact.

The problematisation of the San body indeed remains central when dealing with living museums: Once acknowledged the contemporaneity of their truths and their possibilities, we also need to update and confront with the livingness of their bodies. Consequently, the heritage debate cannot merely revolve around expressions of authenticity and representation; rather, it should identify and investigate the points of convergence and interaction between conservation and renewal (Nas 2002: 142), and their meanings among the communities they primarily relate to.[15]

[15] I would like to highlight the recent publication of a code of ethics for researchers written by San people of Africa. Available online: http://trust-project.eu/wp content/uploads/2017/03/San-Code-of-RESEARCH-Ethics-Booklet-final.pdf

Image 1: Dabe Dahm and //'Ao Kxao, Mountain Post.

Image 2: "Traditional hunters" from Doupos.

Image 3: Ghanzi Trailblazers, Botswana.

Image 4: Performers on a Kalahari farm.

Image 5: Standard San performance.

Image 6: Bushwalk, Ghanzi Trailblazers, Botswana.

Image 7: Kxao ≠Oma.

Image 8: Kxao ≠Oma and Dabe //Ao.

Image 9: Dabe //Ao, Kxao ≠Oma, and Boo !Kunta.

Image 10: Hunting trip.

Image 11: Tsumkwe, Nyae Nyae Conservancy.

Image 12: Djxohkoe, Nyae Nyae Conservancy.

Image 13: Tsumkwe, Nyae Nyae Conservancy.

Image 14: Cultural village of Doupos.

Image 15: !amace !Kunta with anthropologist in Grashoek Living Museum.

Image 16: //'Ao Kxao.

Image 17: San hunting performers.

Image 18: //'Ao Kxao and Kxao /Ai!ae, Mountain Post.

Image 19: N≠aisa N!ani, ≠Oma !Kunta, and Xoan//a Cgaesje.

Image 20: Boo !Kunta, Xoan//a !Kunta, and N/ae !Kunta.

Image 21: Kxao ≠Oma.

Image 22: N/ae !Kunta, //'Ao Kxao !Kunta, and Boo !Kunta.

Image 23: Healing dance, Doupos cultural village.

Image 24: Boo !Kunta during healing.

Image 25: Staged healing dance.

Image 26: Little Hunter's Museum of //Xa/oba.

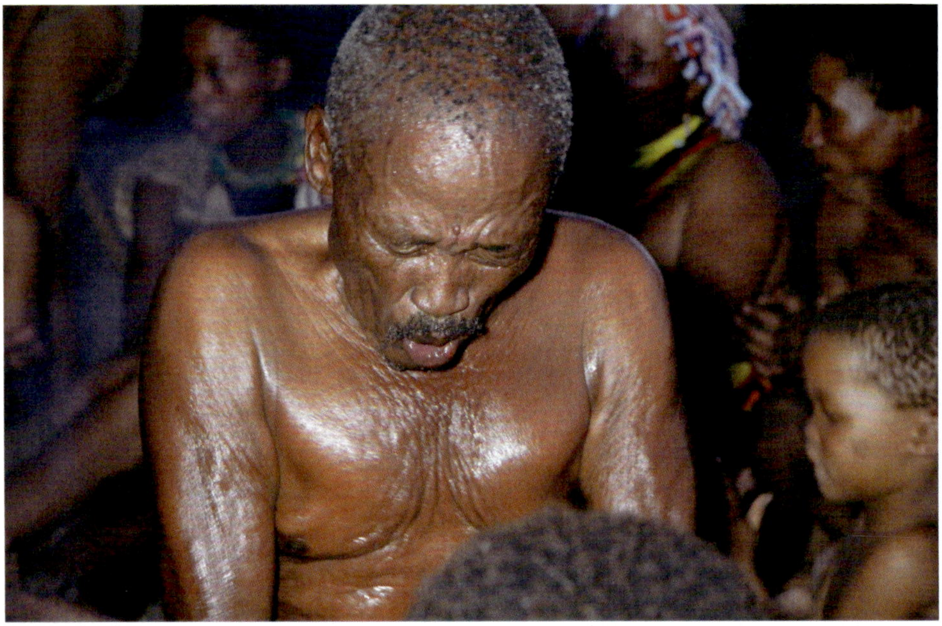

Image 27: Boo !Kunta, healing dance.

Image 28: Young San actors teaching visitors.

Image 29: Boo !Kunta.

Image 30: Hunting team from Mountain Post.

Image 31: !amace !Kunta in a hideout.

Image 32: Justice Manxiweni Zikhali, Sangoma.

Part II

"Wild Frontier": Transnational Conservation and Resource Governance in West African Borderlands

Seeing the Trees for the Wood: The Environmental and Human Consequences of Partition in the Senegambian Borderlands

Paul Nugent[1]

The economic history of West Africa has conventionally been told as a tale of the development of cash crop agriculture, and the associated development of migrant labour, within spaces defined by colonial borders. What is less often included is the simultaneous moulding of the environment to create wilderness, particularly in border regions where forests were often deployed as buffer zones. The manner in which the Upper Gambia was partitioned between the British and the French ultimately killed off its potential as a viable waterway to the interior. This did not substantially change after the creation of the l'Organisation Pour La Mise en Valeur de la Fleuve Gambienne (OMVG) in 1978. At the same time, the Lower Gambia was turned into a barrier between northern Senegal and the Casamance by virtue of the British (and later Gambian) refusal to bridge the river. After a discussion of competitive policies pursued by the colonial regimes of the Gambia and the Senegal, the chapter considers some of the continuities into the independence period. It looks at migratory flows, in which border crossings became established as the norm; the instrumentalisation of the Gambia River in the politics surrounding trade and transport; and the insertion of forest resources into the dynamics of insurgency in the Casamance. Current hopes for binding the Senegambia together as a 'natural region' rest on the development of cross-border tourism, thereby turning the wilderness into an economic resource, and the bridging of the lower reaches of the Gambia River in order to facilitate trade. However, both of these remain points of contention amongst actors in the Gambia and the Casamance who are worried about what a greater Senegambia would mean in practice.

1 The author would like to thank the Institute for Advanced Study (IAS) in Princeton where the author was a member over 2015/16. It draws extensively on a forthcoming manuscript entitled *Boundaries, Communities and State-Making in the Senegambia and the Trans-Volta: The Centrality of the Margins*.

1 Introduction

In 1907, the Acting Governor of the Gambia, Brandford Griffith, wrote to the Governor-General of French West Africa concerning the case of a Jola man from the riverside town of Kartong who had allegedly been arrested for chopping down a tree in the Senegalese border village of Séléty with the intention of making a pirogue. Griffith's understanding was that the offence arose from the fact that he was not in possession of the appropriate licence. The Governor was not querying the decision per se, and merely wished to ascertain if it was necessary for money to be sent across the border to pay any resulting fine.[2] Merlin's response was that the only person who had been arrested for felling a tree was actually a native of Séléty. However, local administrators believed that there was some confusion with a different case involving one Sécou from Thionk Essyl in Buluf who had taken up residence in Kartong after he became sick.[3] When Sécou returned to Thionk Essyl to make a pirogue, he was seized by villagers there for felling a tree without their permission, while a relative of his was apprehended over some stolen cows that had been sent to him for safe keeping in the Gambia.

The knotted plot lines can stand for so many others in the administrative archives of the two countries. But what is most significant about this case is two levels of ambiguity: firstly, about what it meant to be 'indigenous' (had Sécou forfeited his rights of local citizenship in Thionk Essyl when he moved to Kartong?) and secondly, about who had the right to regulate access to forest resources (was it only the French authorities or did local communities retain residual rights?). Such questions have continued to recur in different forms down to the present day, and as such make a fitting starting point for this article.

Having begun this account at a very micro-level, we also need to be cognizant of other scales and temporalities. Boubacar Barry (1998) has made a plausible case for considering the deeper historical integrity of a greater Senegambia centred on the Senegal and Gambia River systems that circulated people, goods and ideas over time and through space. The underlying "geographic cohesiveness" was, he maintains, reflected in a longstanding demographic, economic and political interchange (Barry 1998: 3). Barry goes on to argue that the slave trade locked the greater Senegambia into the Atlantic trading system before the Europeans for-

2 Senegalese National Archives (SNA), 1F14 "Relations Avec le Gambie: Reclamations Particulières (1905-1910)", Acting Governor Brandford Griffith, Bathurst, to Governor-General de l'AOF, Dakar, (11 November 1907).

3 SNA 1F14, Henri Merlin, Governor General of l'AOF, Dakar, to Governor of the Gambia (9 Feb 1908), and Résident du Fogny à Bignona to L'Administrateur Supérieur à Sedhiou (8 Jan 1908).

mally dissected the region towards the end of the nineteenth century. In this article, I consider some of the long-term consequences of the partition, but along a foreshortened time-line and a reduced spatial ambit. I am concerned with the question of how borders affected access to resources in the Gambia, the Casamance and to some extent Guinea-Bissau, over a hundred-year period. The resources in question are water, forests, farmlands and pasturage, all of which were integral to the daily lives of people in this segment of Barry's greater Senegambia.

2 Colonial Borders and Resource Use

After the colonial partition, the two great river systems came to assume a rather different function to their historic role as regional connectors. The Senegal River demarcated the boundary between Mauritania and Senegal, even if both were placed under French control and were administered from St. Louis. The northern and southern borders of the Gambia were drawn mostly at a distance of 10 kilometres from either side of the riverbank, while the eastern limits were derived from the arc of a circle drawn from the riverside town of Yarbutenda. In the first case, the Senegal River constituted the border, while in the second colonial space was enfolded around the lower reaches of the Gambia River. It is the second case, which has received much less academic treatment that concerns us in this paper.[4]

In view of its high degree of navigability, there were good reasons why the British and French authorities might have wanted to co-operate in exploiting the potential of the Gambia River as a commercial artery.[5] Moreover, livelihoods in the Gambia River basin, which was framed by the bodies of water that fed into the Gambia, depended on a shared ecological system. In the lower reaches of the River, proximity to the Casamance River and its tributaries created a closely interconnected ecological zone. Along the coast and for some hundred miles up the Gambia River, the water was saline which meant that wetland rice systems depended on elaborate water management techniques. Further upriver, it was possible to produce both paddy and upland rice alongside the cultivation of other grains (notably millet and maize) and vegetables, using both river waters and runoff. Moreover, the lands that lay in proximity to the Gambia and Casamance Rivers provided rich grazing at crucial times of the year. Finally, wood from the forests was used across the sub-region as a source of household fuel, for housing and

4 On the Senegal River, see Searing (1993), Barry (2012), and for the more recent period Adams and So (1996) and Alam (2012).

5 The Senegal River was only fully navigable for commercial craft during the rainy season when the water levels were at their highest.

fencing (essential given the high concentration of cattle) and for the construction of the pirogues that were used both for fishing and transportation. The practical question that arose was how far the colonial authorities were interested in facilitating shared access to these resources across their common boundaries. The short answer is that they hardly treated this as a pressing concern – indeed, they generally treated resources as zero-sum not just in respect of African usage, but in terms of trans-boundary flows more generally. Nevertheless, borderlanders themselves found ways of exploiting ecological niches in ways that frequently bypassed official controls – and often created a more rational use of resources in the process.

3 Partitioned Senegambia: A Perpetual Misunderstanding

3.1 The Gambia as a Blocked Artery

In Phillip Curtin's classic text, *Economic Change in Pre-colonial Africa* (1975), he writes of how African traders either sent their trade to the British trading post at Bathurst, at the mouth of the Gambia River, or deflected it to rival European ports on the basis of current market information. However, this flexibility became increasingly circumscribed as the Europeans asserted control over the trade routes and began the process of formally staking out territory. To the south of the Gambia River, Luso-African trading networks were long established, but the Portuguese lacked the capacity to translate trade into colonial claims once the Scramble began in earnest. The British might have profited at their expense had the metropolitan government not been so lukewarm about extending sovereignty beyond the narrow confines of Bathurst. By the time the British felt compelled to take action, they had been effectively encircled by the French.[6] A series of agreements formalised the borders between the Gambia and Senegal and Senegal and Guinea-Bissau respectively. The 1889 Franco-British agreement defined the Gambia/Casamance border as follows:

> "To the south (left bank) the line, starting from the mouth of the San Pedro [Allahein] shall follow the left bank as far as 13°10' of north latitude. The frontier shall thence follow the parallel which, starting from this point, goes as far as Sandeng (end of the Vintang creek, English map). The line shall then trend upwards in the direction of the Gambia, following the meridian which passes through Sandeng to a distance of 10 kilom. from the river. The frontier shall then follow the left bank of the river at the same distance of 10 kilom. as far as, and including Yarbutenda." (Brownlie 1979: 215)

6 I deal with this in greater detail in Nugent (2018), ch.3.

A Boundary Commission formally demarcated the border in 1891, at about the same time as military action was taken against the 'warrior marabouts', Fodé Sylla Kombo and Fodé Kaba, who had sought to defend their autonomy by playing the British and the French off against each other.

The French never ceased to believe that the British would eventually tire of governing a colony that consisted of a narrow strip of land on either side of a riverbank – especially as the principal trading firms were French and the dominant currency was the French silver 'dollar'. However, successive offers of an exchange of territory fell through, in part because of sustained African opposition in Bathurst (Mahoney 1963). From the French standpoint, the British position was perverse because the authorities in Bathurst seemed reluctant to invest in making the Gambia a paying proposition. Worse still, they seemed determined to frustrate the French at every turn, knowing full well that the *mise en valeur* of the Casamance – which was always considered as a potential breadbasket for the rest of Senegal – depended on closing up the space across the Gambia. On the one hand, the British refused to grant the French rights of passage along the river, in effect killing off the utility of the French stretch of the Gambia.

In retrospect, the British position seems self-defeating, given that an increased volume of traffic along the Gambia River would have accrued to the benefit of the port of Bathurst and would have enabled the authorities to maximise the revenue from import and export duties alike. On the other hand, the British refused to agree to the construction of a bridge across the Gambia River that would have facilitated trade between Dakar and the Casamance, but which could have been of some utility to the Gambia as well. The British stance is only really explicable in terms of a sensitivity to French territorial ambitions which made it necessary to avoid entering into a position of dependency. What this meant is that the Gambian authorities concentrated on the development of a series of wharf towns along their stretch of the river that funnelled Gambian groundnuts to Bathurst and consumer goods the other way, but without seeking to exploit the potentialities of the basin more broadly. Moreover, the British did something rather unusual in the annals of colonialism and forgot about building roads – at least until the 1950s.

For their part, the French looked to the railway that passed from Dakar through Tambacounda en route to Bamako as a means of short-circuiting the trade along the Gambia. In addition, because the upper stretches of the Gambia River were now severed from the lower reaches of the river, the French inherited a 'dead' space. Their response was to create a classic 'bewildered zone', in the shape of a reserve and then in 1954 the Niokolo Koba National Park. This conformed to a common pattern in which national parks and forest reserves were located along borders: In order to create buffer zones between colonial entities, as well as *cordon sanitaires* to block the transmission of animal diseases such as sleeping sickness by removing both people and cattle from the equation. To this day, it is striking how many national parks and forests are located in border regions – not least in the Senegambia.

In the aftermath of the Second World War, the French authorities believed that fiscal distress in the Gambia meant that the time was opportune to reopen negotiations. The imperative of creating better transport links between the Casamance and Dakar assumed a heightened importance in post-war development thinking. The Gambian authorities did consent to the construction of the trans-Gambian highway in the early 1950s, but this was only likely to make a substantive difference if the notoriously poor and unsafe ferry crossings were upgraded. French requests to be permitted to operate their own service were rebuffed on the grounds of national sovereignty. In 1955, the two sides did reach an agreement on modernisation of the roads and an improved ferry service to be run entirely from the Gambian side, as well as a negotiated agreement on tariffs.[7] However, the promises were never properly kept which meant that significant transport bottlenecks continued into the independence era – and remain a contentious issue to this day.

3.2 Migration and Demography

Alongside the lack of agreement over the development of an integrated transport network, the two sides actively competed for ownership of population. The so-called Marabout-Soninke wars in the western Mandinka states, which dominated the first half of the nineteenth century, followed by slave raiding against Jola populations in the second half, had depopulated the areas in closest proximity to Bathurst. It therefore became a priority for the Gambian administration to entice population out of French territory. These came as seasonal migrants, or 'strange farmers' (Swindell/ Jeng 2006), but the Gambian authorities always hoped to settle them permanently. The inducement was lower taxes and the promise of easy access to farmland, which the chiefs were expected to facilitate. The French response was to discourage permanent settlement, as one Commissioner noted:

---

[7] CAOM (Aix-en-Provence), Affaires Politiques: 1AFFPOL/2184/1, A. Chataigner, Consul de France in Bathurst, to Ministre des Affaires Etrangeres (12 December 1955). The final agreement in March 1956 included "a categorical assurance that the proposed new ferry will give an efficient service" and "that there will be no discrimination in the charges paid by the Gambian and non-Gambian users of the proposed new ferry service." CAOM, Affaires Politiques: 1AFF-POL/2184/1, "Agreement Concerning the Construction of the Trans-Gambian Road and Matters Incidental Thereto and Concerning Arrangement for the Ferry Service", signed 10 March 1956.

"Immigrants as far as can be seen must come from French territory and the French have never concealed the fact that they regard emigration to this country with disfavour. Families attempting to move over are usually deprived of everything but the clothes they stand up in; many no doubt would like to come to a country where taxes are low, and where there is neither conscription or forced labour, but they are deterred by the risk they run of losing all their possessions; most who have crossed have come over at night."[8]

Nevertheless, the French authorities did permit seasonal migration for the reason that the 'strange farmers' would use their earnings from sharecropping on Gambian groundnut fields to pay their head taxes in Senegal. And, of course, the French authorities were not above poaching their own settlers from Guinea-Bissau. The Senegalese authorities also facilitated the relocation of population from the relatively high-density zones south of the Casamance River towards the more lightly populated areas along the Gambian border. What neither the British nor the French authorities fully anticipated was the frequency of border-hopping. This consisted, on the one hand, of Jola migrants moving back and forth across the line in search of the optimal mix of land for paddy rice production, grain farming and pasturage. On the other hand, migrants gravitated towards border locations where there was ambiguity as to where one colony ended and the next began – often in the hope of avoiding taxes.

Although their failure to find common ground is striking, the two sets of authorities were in agreement that it was unacceptable for populations to drift back and forth across the border. Hence, everyone was expected to have a primary community where they paid either their yard tax (to the British) or head tax (to the French). In 1945, French officials noted that farmers from the Gambia were quietly moving across the international border to cultivate on their side. The official policy was that they would either have to settle, in which case they were liable for *l'impôt*, or they would be treated as migrants who would pay the reduced *impôt flottant*, but without residence rights. Whereas the British and the French authorities in partitioned Togoland agreed that land rights remained unaffected by the border – which meant that someone living on one side could access farms on the other – the Senegambian authorities were much less accommodating. People were, in effect, required to choose which side of the line they wished to live and farm on, while chiefs were required to monitor compliance. The possibility that a farm might cut across the border was not entertained because land was accessed through chiefs who derived their jurisdiction from the respective colonial author-

8 E.B. Leese, Commissioner of South Bank Province, to Colonial Secretary, Bathurst (4 February 1932), National Archives of the Gambia (NAGB) CSO 3/204, "Review of Policy with Regard to the Strange Farmers".

ities. The authorities also attempted to create a no-man's land, and at one point even talked about planting a hedge along the border to render it more visible to the naked eye.

However, the quest for greater certainty was continually undermined as migrants successfully exploited the opportunities that came with mobility. Hence, in the inter-governmental correspondence that survives, one comes across many cases of uncertainty as to where exactly particular individuals were resident. Moreover, the constant shuttling of population back and forth across border spaces had led to a situation by the early 1940s where it was often unclear in which colony particular villages were located. The ambiguities remained unresolved before independence because both governments were worried that they might forfeit territory if the issue was tackled head on. In the case of cattle, there were agreements that permitted cattle to graze on lands on the other side of the line. But rustling was rife and once cattle crossed the line, it became very difficult to secure their return. Moreover, the French authorities believed that cattle that were ostensibly sent for grazing were being sold on the Gambian side. Hence, the French *douaniers* often insisted on the payment of export duties on cattle before they crossed the border. Inevitably, this led to attempts to evade the French Customs controls altogether.

One consequence of the narrowness of the Gambia, the obsession with maximising groundnut production and the demographic one-upmanship is that the colony ran a perpetual food deficit. The 'strange farmers' contributed labour to the groundnut fields, but they also added to the population that needed to be fed. This led to the practice of the government lending food on credit to farming communities, which was eventually terminated in the 1930s (Swindell/ Jeng 2006). The deficit might have provided an opportunity to develop a trade in paddy rice from the Casamance in the direction of the Gambia. In practice, the French authorities displayed little interest in such a possibility. The allotted role of the Casamance was to supply northern Senegal, but since this was not feasible while the Gambia continued to cut the colony in two, this prospect was consigned to some indefinite future. This did not exactly create a 'dead space', but it foreclosed the economic potential of the Casamance. In the meantime, rice imports from Asia supplied Dakar with most of its requirements. The Gambian authorities equally imported much of their rice through Bathurst, but it was an open secret that considerable quantities leaked across the southern border. During the Second World War, when international shipping was severely disrupted, the Gambia depended heavily on a clandestine trade. A report from 1944 noted:

"War conditions have naturally brought shortages of many important commodities, but compared with other countries, the Gambia has been very fortunate and there has practically been no real hardship. The supply of cotton goods was excellent and was bartered against groundnuts, coos and rice. The high quality attracted many French farmers in frontier areas to bring their produce into the Gambia, although it is believed this was frowned on by the French authority." (NAGB ARP 34/2, Divisional Annual Reports 1944)

The same report indicated the source of much of the rice was Portuguese Guinea:

"There has been a good deal of trade with Portuguese Guinea from the Kombo area, especially during the rainy season. The principal imports were rice, coos and flour, but it is to be regretted that much of the property for which they were bartered consisted of service stores stolen from the army and the Royal Air Force." (ibid.)

Much of this trade was carried out by pirogues that plied the routes from Portuguese Guinea to the Gambia, often via Kartong.

3.3 Forest Resources

On both sides of the border, the authorities became concerned with what they regarded as the mounting threat of forest degradation. The short-lived rubber boom along the Gambia/Casamance border at the start of the colonial period, which culminated in the wholesale destruction of wild vines, seemed to underline the dangers of unregulated exploitation. This took little account of the ways in which Mandinka and Jola communities actually related to the forests. Amongst the Mandinka, the Soninke rulers who had been defeated by Muslim reformers in the nineteenth century had been closely associated with the forests. Converts to Islam therefore gave the forests a wide birth, regarding them as the repositaries of malign spirits. A striking exception was Cheikh Mahfoudz, a Mauritanian marabout, who established his religious base in the Narang forest, along the border with the Gambia, precisely in order to demonstrate his mastery over such forces. To this day, people farm at a safe distance from the forests and do not seek to exploit them for firewood. Amongst the Jola of the Casamance, by contrast, converts to Islam continued to participate in initiation rituals that were performed in the forests (Mark 1992: chs. 2-3). The Jola had their own reasons for wishing to protect the forests, and the seizure of Sécou attests to their efforts to do so without reference to the colonial authority.

Be that as it may, the French authorities believed that there was a need to intervene to protect the forests from "abusive use by natives".[9] This led to the passage

[9] The then Governor of French West Africa quoted in 1933, in Ribot (1993: 563).

of a code in 1935 that placed forests under state control and introduced permits for the production of charcoal above a specified quantity. Moreover, responsibility for managing designated forest reserves was vested in a Forestry Service in 1936, which acquired reputation for rigid enforcement (Ribot 1993: 563-564). The French authorities did not liaise with their British counterparts over forestry policy, and kept a close watch lest firewood disappear over the border into the Gambia. Given that a number of the forest reserves were located in close proximity to the border, this was always a distinct possibility.

The picture that emerges, therefore, is one in which the Gambian and Senegalese authorities scarcely considered joint management of resources as something worthy of active consideration. However, it was in the interests of the Gambian authorities to look the other way when foodstuffs, cattle and firewood crossed border in breach of French Customs regulations. According to a zero-sum calculus that ran deep in official thinking, Senegal's loss was the Gambia's gain.

4 The Post-Independence Years

There was a brief period at the end of the 1950s when the border between the Senegal and the Gambia might have lost much of its practical significance. The Gambian state was running a significant fiscal deficit, which the British government was not willing to cover in perpetuity. The administration therefore encouraged Gambian politicians to open negotiations with their Senegalese counterparts over the terms of closer association. The rationale was that while Senegal might absorb some of the costs of administering the Gambia, the possibility of connecting the Casamance to the rest of Senegal would make this an attractive proposition. In Dakar, the idea of stitching together a 'natural region' that had been divided against the logic of nature itself was a very attractive one. But in practice, the Gambian authorities proved more concerned with rendering their country viable as a distinct entity than transcending the border. Indeed, the very existence of border flows was what enabled the Gambia to reproduce itself as an independent country.

4.1 The Gambia as a Developmental Problem

By 1960, there was an acceptance in Bathurst that the dog-in-the manger approach of days gone by had hobbled the Gambia. As one official expressed it: "The separation of the Gambia from its hinterland has progressively retarded the economic development of the country."[10] Provided the Senegalese and Gambian authorities could agree on a distribution of the revenues, it was thought that there might be much to recommend closer economic integration. In 1962, the governments of the Gambia and Senegal jointly approached the United Nations to request a technical mission to assess the options. The van Mook report argued that the existing dispensation was indeed as detrimental to the interests of the Gambia as to Senegal:

"For Senegal it means a partial isolation of the Casamance, even though the transgambian road has eased the access to the southern province. It poses the problem of guarding a customs frontier of inordinate length that can easily be crossed at many places. It finally deprives southern Senegal and the adjoining countries of the full use of the splendid waterway and harbor of the Gambia river. For the Gambia, it means that the part of the river basin which forms the main agricultural asset of the country cannot be fully and rationally exploited and that Bathurst cannot become the port of a much wider area, which its natural advantages entitle it to be."[11]

The report posited three alternatives: outright integration of the Gambia into Senegal; a looser association that would protect the legal personality of both countries but set up a central authority to oversee common functions; and a loose entente in which the countries would agree to co-operate on matters of common interest. Although the mission broadly favoured the second alternative, the Gambian government was reluctant to agree to anything as binding as a Customs union, which was what the Senegalese really wanted. The most that could be achieved, therefore, was the agreement to two treaties of cooperation, one covering foreign policy and another covering defence and security – to which a third accord was added later on covering the integrated management of the Gambia River Basin. This meant that shared resource use was formally on the agenda, but the years that followed were marked by limited and fitful progress. The greatest success lay in resolution of outstanding border anomalies, most notably the confusion over the eastern limits of the Gambia.[12] There were also some steps taken to create structures for the management of the resources of the Gambia River Basin following the creation of *l'Organisation Pour La Mise en Valeur de la Fleuve*

[10] K.G.S. Smith, Officer Administering the Government of the Gambia, Bathurst, to Macleod, 9 September 1960, in Gambia House of Representatives, *The Financial Position: Exchange of Despatches Between the Governor and the Secretary of State for the Colonies*, Sessional Paper 11 of 1960 (Bathurst: Government Printer).

[11] The Gambia, *Report of the Alternatives for Association Between the Gambia and Senegal* (by Hubertus J. Van Mook, Max Graessli, Henri Monfrioni and Hendrik Weisfelt, Appointed Under the United Nations Programme of Technical Assistance), Sessional Paper No. 13 of 1964, p. 6.

[12] Although the OMVG agreement was only signed in 1978, there were understandings as early as 1971 (Griffiths, 1994: 71-72).

Gambienne (OMVG). The OMVG accord of 1978 included an agreement in principle to construct a bridge across the Gambia with financial assistance from the European Development Fund (Touray 2000: 80-81). This project would have satisfied a longstanding Senegalese ambition. However, the Gambians held out for a bridge-cum-barrage that would permit irrigated rice cultivation along the river by preventing the passage of salt water upriver (ibid.). These agreements had failed to come to fruition prior to the creation of the Senegambian Confederation in 1981.

The underlying problem was that the priorities of the governments remained as divergent as ever. On the one hand, the Gambian authorities turned a blind eye to illicit cross-border trade that benefited the exchequer and supported the livelihoods of many Gambians. On the other hand, both governments embraced development planning in ways that took the primacy of the border as an immutable given. Hence, the governments produced parallel sets of plans that aimed to promote irrigated rice production, but without any effort at co-ordination. Equally, both governments planned to promote tourism, as a compliment to the embattled groundnut sector, but in a manner, that was competitive rather than complimentary. The Gambia set out to attract beach tourists and birdwatchers, whereas the Senegalese combined a Club Med enclave in 1974 with village *campements* that were supposed to allow Europeans to enjoy the 'authentic' African experience in the Casamance. An integrated tourism policy might well have used Banjul airport as the hub and facilitated movement across the border. However, the Senegalese chose to construct their own airport near Cap Skirring. The net effect was that tourists were not encouraged to visit the other side of the border and hardly did so. It is only in the very recent past that there has been an attempt to investigate something comparable to the transfrontier parks of Southern Africa.

4.2 The Issue of Migration

Despite significant impediments to cross-border cooperation at the inter-governmental level, the populations of this part of the Senegambia continued to exploit the opportunities for mobility. In 1975, there were 54.500 foreign-born persons living in the Gambia, which amounted to 10.6 per cent of the total population and accounted for 55 per cent of the population growth over the period. Although the Gambia exported population to Senegal, it remained the net recipient of immigrants to the tune of 100.000 people between 1963 and 1973. By contrast, Senegal was a net recipient of 70.000 immigrants between 1961 and 1971 (Zachariah/ Condé 1981: 45).

But focusing on the borderlands throws up even more striking patterns. In the Gambia, Banjul proper was not the primary magnet for migrants. It was settlements in the Kombos – especially Serrekunda (Kombo St. Mary) and Brikama (Kombo Central) – that witnessed the most spectacular growth. Given that their markets were heavily oriented towards Senegal, their demographic boost is indicative of the enhanced importance of cross-border trade. In many ways, the standard narrative of urbanisation is in need of significant revision. In Senegal, the Cap Vert region (including Dakar) attracted 37.977 'lifetime' immigrants from other countries, but the Casamance accounted for no fewer than 101.402 people – or nearly half of total immigration into Senegal. The greatest contributor to this growth was Guinea-Bissau (71.470), but it is striking that the 15.881 Gambians who moved to the Casamance far outnumbered the 1.680 who relocated to Dakar. This is telling us something about the ways in which populations continued to exploit different niches.

One of the attractions of the Casamance was that it had more land suitable for the farming of paddy rice and the rearing of cattle. Migrants from Guinea-Bissau – especially Manjagos but also Balantas and Mancagnes – continued to cross the border into the Casamance to farm and to fish, and many subsequently made their way to the Gambia. The 1983 Gambian census recorded 14.100 Manjagos, most of whom were to be found in the Kombos. The village of Marakissa is predominantly Manjago, with a strong Christian identity, but the latter also became a visible presence in many other settlements, including Darsilami, which is located right on the border (Frederiks 2003: 73).[13] While the liberation war in Guinea-Bissau displaced many people, the Gambian authorities were aware of the fact that the line between migrants and refugees was distinctly blurry. It was a not uncommon practice for people to maintain one foot on either side of the border, being formally resident on one side of the line, whilst keeping relatives and rearing cattle on the other side. In the event of a political crisis, people simply moved over to join relatives without invoking the status of refugee. Needless to say, one of the key resources was the border itself. The fact that Sine-Saloum was the second choice of destination for Gambians (8.657) strongly suggests that economic activity was the primary attraction there as well – especially at a time when the groundnut economy was in decline (Zachariah/ Condé 1981: 40). What we can conclude is that if the resource could not physically be moved (e.g. a forest), bor-

13 Kunkujang was another Manjago settlement in the Gambia. Balantas were more thinly spread, but were to be found in towns like Kartong, which had a close trading relationship. Interview with Alhaji Demba Jabang, Kartong (Gambia), 4 June 2004.

derlanders travelled to the resource, whilst remaining careful to retain access to other accumulated claims such as farming land.

4.3 The Issue of Forest Management

The prolonged Sahelian drought of the late 1960s and 1970s placed severe pressure on agrarian systems across the Senegambia region. It manifested itself, amongst other things, in declining returns from groundnut production and the salinisation of the rice fields. There was also mounting concern expressed by governments on both sides of the border about the effects of population pressure on the long-term sustainability of forest resources. An example of the underlying dynamic would be the emergence of a significant number of Manjago compounds in a section of Gambian forest which formally belonged to Brikama, but which the alkalo (or village chief) of Kassakunda was responsible for overseeing. In 1968, the Manjagos became sufficiently numerous in the forest to secure the right to participate in the selection of an alkalo at Nyofelleh, provoking a bitter dispute.[14] In cases like this, the expansion of settlement was thought to come at the expense of the forest. In the Gambia, where a policy of encouraging demographic growth continued unabated, there was particular concern about the environmental consequences.

As was true in other domains, government policies evolved in parallel, but with no effort to produce an integrated forestry policy. The common thread was an attempt to regulate access to the forests and the production of charcoal, whilst promoting sustainable woodlands for community use. Hence, the second five-year-plan (1981-86) in the Gambia envisaged the creation of village woodlots that would create a sustainable energy source (Republic of Gambia 1984: 2-10). This followed a ban on the production of charcoal in 1980 (Republic of Gambia 1984: 1-3). Richard Schroeder (1999) has pointed to some of the tensions that arose out of the gendered nature of access to community resources and the shifting nature of donor priorities. In particular, he has traced the history of the rise and fall of market gardening, which received its ideological thrust from the Women in Development movement. It emerges from Schroeder's account that the promotion of alternative crops produced by women (e.g. shallots, cabbage, and capsicum), and supported by the donors, was closely related to the stimulus of the *lumo* or cross-border markets that were a particular feature of the north bank (Schroeder 1999:

[14] Commissioner, Western Division, Brikama, to Acting Permanent Secretary, Ministry for Local Government, Lands and Mines (18 November 1968), NAGB SEC 1/896 "Complaints and Petitions".

37). In other words, it was the trade into Senegal, as well as the demand in Banjul, that was driving innovation. The downfall of the initiative, Schroeder maintains, is attributable to a paradigm shift that downgraded the emphasis on food security and replaced it with a discourse of environmental sustainability in which the planting of more trees was identified as the over-riding priority.

In Senegal, the period immediately after independence was characterised by the imposition of tighter state controls over forest use. In 1965, the forestry service was given exclusive rights to manage forestry resources and further revisions were made to the Forest Code in 1974. Indicatively, the boundaries of the Niokolo Koba National Park were greatly expanded, displacing farming populations in the process (Bandiaky-Badji 2011: 182-183).[15] Hence 'bewildering' had become an active process at a time when the role of the state as the engine of development was being actively re-inscribed. The driver for change in the 1990s was the marriage of community-based resource management approaches and the pursuit of administrative decentralisation. In effect, control over many forest resources was formally vested in elected local councils in a way that was supposed to enhance a sense of local ownership. But as Giorgio Blundo (2007: 72-78) has indicated, these reforms were in tension with the militarisation of the forestry service, which also managed to blunt the effects of the decentralisation reforms.

The outcomes in the Casamance were very different to what was promised. In April 1990, the village of Séléty hit the Senegalese news after an armed attack on the border post that left two Customs officers dead. The Senegalese press was quick to recall an earlier incident in 1917 when a radical marabout from the French Soudan, El Hadj Haidara, secreted himself in the forest at Kujube from where he launched an assault on the same Customs post – beheading the French officer in the process.[16] This second Séléty incident heralded the launch of the secessionist insurgency of the Mouvement des Forces Démocratiques de la Casamance (MFDC), which has continued in fit and starts down to the present day. The irony is that the push for secession came about not when the Casamance was largely forgotten about in Dakar, but precisely when it began to be more closely integrated into Senegal. The many Jola who migrated to Dakar felt their sense of marginalisation from the Wolof mainstream, but as importantly it was the newly allotted role for the Casamance in national development planning that raised suspicions about a hidden agenda. Although the *National Domain Law* had been introduced in 1964, it had never been implemented in the Casamance. Its operationalisation

[15] The expanded park was three times the size of its colonial counterpart.

[16] "Attaque du poste du douane de Selety: de la barbarie premeditée", *Le Soleil*, 25 April 1990.

at this juncture seemed to presage a land-grab by northerners, eager to acquire land for farming and tourist development. Hence, the attempt to push community-based resource management – in the shape of a new participatory forestry code in 1993 and decentralisation reforms in 1996 – fell on stony ground.

A number of commentators have pointed to the discursive terrain on which the war has been fought (Marut 1994; Marut 2000; Gasser 2002). It has been pointed out that the culture of the Jola, and in particular the centrality of the sacred forests, became central to the construction of the exotic 'other' which framed the perceptions of northern Senegalese – for whom trees were quite literally few and far between – and provided the pitch for tourism. Conversely, the discourse of the MFDC inverted this stock of images and used them to make the case for a Casamance that was culturally distinct from, and necessarily at odds with, the rest of Senegal. The main challenges to the French had always emanated from the forests and the mangroves, and this pattern was repeated after 1990. The fact that the MFDC was able to make use of forest spaces and border zones tended to reinforce a strong sense of the historicity of resistance to an alien state. The pattern of the low-intensity war connects with two of the themes that this paper has sought to address. On the one hand, it relates to a much deeper history of mobility. The violence did not lead to full-scale refugee flows, but more typically, people moved across the border into the Gambia where they re-joined kinsmen and others who had previously shared a place of residence. For example, the border town of Darsilami in the Kombos was already home to long-term migrants from the Casamance and Guinea-Bissau who readily received others seeking to avoid the insecurity across the border. Whenever the violence subsided, a certain proportion of those who had crossed over returned to the Casamance.

On the other hand, the insurgency became closely bound up with contestation surrounding resource management. As the region became more insecure, the forest guards withdrew from areas that were not the established centres for charcoal production and in effect, the state presence became confined to the main towns – leaving the rural areas to the MFDC. In part because the latter did not have the luxury of wealthy backers, it functioned in a highly decentralised manner while its fighters essentially lived off the land. The MFDC insurgency came to depend to a considerable extent on the raiding of forest resources, from which the fighters took their cut. In the early 1990s, the MFDC had already split between the Front Nord, which signed an agreement with the Senegalese government, and the Front Sud, which continued to fight on. In the areas close to the Gambia border, the MFDC fighters respected a ceasefire with the Senegalese army and continued to subsist by virtue of a combination of a trade in wood and charcoal and whatever they could extract from surrounding villagers. Martin Evans (2003: 9) has provided a detailed analysis based on information gleaned from carpenters in the Casamance, most of whom acquired their timber from illicit sources. He identified an MFDC sawmill at Diakaye, located between Bignona and the Gambia, which drew on wood from the forests in the Diouloulou (Narang) and Sindian districts (ibid.: 9-10). Proximity to the Kombos meant that it was relatively easy to dispose of wood across the border at a profitable rate of return. Given that state control of forest resources had never been regarded as legitimate, and given also that the administrative structures enjoyed little local support, raiding nature's cupboard was not necessarily seen as illegitimate. The fact that the trade in timber was also actively carried out by members of the Senegalese army probably also played a part. What was distinctly unpopular was the predatory character of the MFDC occupation. Although the insurgency went into abeyance for some years, it has recently threatened to return. A report from 2011 alleged that lorry loads of lumber have been making their way into the Gambia in a way that has benefited the rebels, the local population and the Gambian government.[17]

5 Conclusion: Straddling, Serialism, and Suture

In this paper, I have set out to achieve two things. First of all, I have sought to account for the reasons why colonial governments and their independent successors have found it so difficult to countenance the sharing of resources across their common boundary. I have also considered some of the consequences of a zero-sum approach to resource management. Secondly, I have sought to explore the ways in which borderlanders managed to negate the effort to create a relatively hard border. There are three particular forms assumed by trans-boundary resource use over the past century: straddling, serialism, and suture. In the first case, borderlanders attempted to pursue their livelihoods across and through the border. Although some examples of shared access do exist, such as the exchange of farming rights between Darsilami and Touba, governments have not been in favour of such arrangements for the simple reason that it blurs a line that they would like to retain in sharp relief. Serialism refers to the practice of people moving on from one locality to the next, making use of the opportunities that may arise as they progress. The drift of the Manjago across the Casamance and into the Kombos would be an example of this. This has generally been encouraged by government actions that have imposed relatively few impediments to human flows. Suture sits somewhere

[17] "Illegal loggers profit from conflict in Senegal's Casamance", http://www.illegal-logging.info/content/illegal-loggers-profit-conflict-senegals-casamance.

in between straddling and serialism: In this case, the protagonists have migrated, but in such a way as to multiply their number of possible claims. Hence, farming in one country and keeping cattle and relatives in another is a way of keeping the options open. The case of Sécou with which I began, is an early example. This has not been greatly to the liking of governments, but it has been difficult to monitor in the context of highly fluid population movements.

By way of an epilogue, it may well be that the Senegalese and Gambian governments will break with more than a century of habit. With the departure of Yahya Jammeh from office in 2017, the chances are better than ever that substantive progress will be made. In addition, it has been reported that the Gambian forestry service has offered to place its expertise at the disposal of its counterpart in the Casamance.[18] If any of this comes to pass, it would undoubtedly represent progress, but it also amounts to catching up with what borderlanders have been doing for decades: namely using resources in a joined-up way.

Primary Materials

Centre des Archives d'Outre-Mer (CAOM), Aix-en-Provence.
Gambia National Archives (NAGB), Banjul.
Senegal National Archives (SNA), Dakar.

[18] http://www.illegal-logging.info/content/gambia-cu-introduces-new-initiative-tackle-illegal-logging-and-deforestation.

“Stop the Sahara!” Combatting Climate Change and Desertification in the Niger-Nigeria Borderlands, with Wildlife Lessons from the Negev

William Miles

1 Introduction

In the lead-up to Nigeria’s national elections in mid-1983, candidates for office travelled to Daura emirate, in the far north of the country, to stump for themselves and their parties. Daura lies along the border with Niger Republic, and as such shares the same harsh Sahelian climate and fragile topography subject to desertification, drought, and periodic famine. Sahel, Arabic for “edge,” refers to the southern band of semi-habitable, transitional land between the water scarce Sahara Desert and the more agriculturally viable (but still water sensitive) savanna to the Sahel’s South.

As a coastal nation deriving most of its revenues from oil exploitation in the country’s southern Delta region, Nigeria does not identify as a Saharan state (such as its near eponymous neighbour, Niger, whose Human Development Index ranking is consistently the lowest in West Africa). The desert, the Sahara, is viewed as alien, threatening, encroaching. And so, speaking in the local Hausa language used on both sides of the border, the warm-up speaker for the candidate of the National People’s Party vowed that, if elected, his party would build a wall of trees along the border with Niger Republic to prevent the Sahara Desert from entering Daura (Miles 1989: 329) (in length, the entire border is two short of 1.500 kilometres).

In the thirty years following this eco-extravagant campaign pledge, no such plan to stop the Sahara from invading Nigeria has been put into effect. But, there has been growing recognition on the part of local academics and scientists that climate change is indeed aggravating the tenuous environment of the Nigerian-Nigérien frontier, and that action needs to be taken lest the borderland – already blighted by the disappearance of various species of wildlife – continue its downward spiral. Action is taking the form not of wall or fence but grassroots research and development projects. The purpose of this chapter is to investigate the state of such environmental action research, the cultural role of endangered and/or extinct wildlife, and the possibility of species reintroduction using a Middle Eastern example. Throughout, the transboundary implications of wildlife sustainability and movement frame the discussion.

2 An Ecologically Fragile Borderland

The topographical zone, which has become the borderland between Nigeria and Niger, has long been subject to period drought and famine. Watts (1983) has taken a long-term perspective that includes pre-colonial and early colonial instances of what he calls the "silent violence" of acute water and food scarcities. During fieldwork on both sides of the Nigerian-Nigérien boundary in the early 1980s, the present author catalogued the famines that informants personally recalled (using them, for instance, to calculate their own age) (Miles 1994: 39-41). The earliest such one was Kakalaba (identified by Abraham (1958) as "the Great Famine of 1913-14") during which villagers survived on fig trees without fruit, weeds, grass burrs, a resin-yielding shrub, and of course flour gruel. They also went to the mounds constructed by black ants and which contained individual grains that the ants carried there. The latest of the great famines in living memory was Mai-Amaro, so named because groundnuts were the only regular source of sustenance. Interestingly, the Sahelian droughts of the early-1970s (Kakuduba) and mid-1980s (Takakabwa) are remembered more benignly because food aid (local and international) averted death by starvation.

The early 1990s saw the publication of A.I. Asiwaju's and Barkindo's edited volume (1993) on trans-border co-operation spanning the Nigeria-Niger boundary. Several of the contributions focused on the geographical and environmental dimensions of the cross-border phenomenon. Iren (1993: 33-36), for example, contrasts physical similarity (geological, climatic, morpho-structural, hydrological) with economic distinctiveness (cereals, salt, livestock out of Niger to Nigeria; other cereals and manufactured goods crossing Nigeria into Niger). Iliya (1993: 37) emphasises the shared "physiographic characteristics" of the trans-border region, such as the shared Inter-Tropical Discontinuity (ITD) zone, and "the need to stop or limit the rate at which the Sahara Desert is encroaching" into the shared borderland (43). Odihi (1993: 169-177) chronicles drought-induced cross-border mobility and the concomitant need for pro-active disaster mitigation planning for those environmental refugees taking refuge in Nigeria. Saulawa zeroes in on the Katsina and Maradi administrative divisions of Nigeria and Niger, respectively, particularly as relates to drought and livestock. "From all indications," he states in diplomatic litotes (understatement), "it could not be said problems relating to animal husbandry have received sufficient attention in Nigeria and Niger Republic" (Saulawa 1993: 224). Many of the Asiwaju and Barkindo volume contributions (1993) draw on the decades-long drylands research in Northern Nigeria of Michael Mortimore (1967; 1989; 1998; 2005). Continuing research into northern Nigerian drought and desertification, with attendant policy implications, have taken such expressions as Medugu, Majid and Choji (2008). On the Nigérien (Francophone) side, Crombé and Jézéquel (2009) emphasise the multiplicity of sources that bring about famine in a rain-scarce context.

In recent decades, the theoretical frame for studying ecological fragility and disaster in the Nigeria-Niger borderlands has evolved from what one could call the Three Devastating Ds – deforestation, desertification, and drought – to the paradigms of climate change and global warming. The perils of life in the borderlands are no longer conceived as resulting from natural periodic fluctuation of rainfall aggravated by local overexploitation of the land by a demographically growing population that itself pits grazing for livestock against decreasingly productive cropland. Even the 'remote' borderlands of Nigeria-Niger are now understood to be part of a much broader planetary shift to more extreme weather patterns as a result of manmade changes to the atmosphere fueled by industrialisation and related high-consumption economic patterns of developed nations. Significantly, local populations themselves are attributing the local environmental changes, including that of the climate, to human activity (Ishaya/ Abaje 2008). That perspective applies specifically to biodiversity, which rural Hausa populations strive to prevent even in the absence of a formally formulated paradigm (Etkin 2002).

It is in this context that an Interdisciplinary Research Team on Climate Change for the northern zone of Nigeria, headed by Professor of Geography Emmanuel Oladipo, has been established at Ahmadu Bello University in Zaria. Arising out of the National Climate Change Support Group (or NCCSP) linking the Federal Ministry of Environment with Nigerian universities, in addition to furthering academic research a major goal of the research team is to raise local awareness about the existence and sources of climate change. A cross-border component has been to tease out differential local environmental response patterns emanating from the superimposed boundary separating erstwhile undivided villages (subject of Miles 1994). Preliminary results indicate greater density of trees, and overall environmental sensitivity, on the Nigérien side of the border in comparison with the Nigerian (Abdulkarim 2011).

3 Bilateral and Multilateral Actions at Addressing Environmental Stress and Climatic Change

Concomitant with academic efforts in the Nigerian-Nigérien borderlands to understand and respond to environmental stress (increasingly understood to be aggravated by climate change) have been inter-governmental actions. Eleven years after both countries' independence in 1960, the Nigeria-Niger Joint Commission (NNJC) was established in 1971 for the purpose of harmonising relations between the bordering states. NNJC operates by rotating chairmanship and a secretariat based in Niamey, capital of Niger. In 1984, its deliberations focused on food production, irrigation, and water resources.

The extent to which survival in these borderlands is vulnerable to variation in seasonal rainfall cannot be sufficiently stressed. Dry grain farming constitutes the single most important economic activity in this mostly rural eco-zone. A single, annual rainy season (*damuna*, in Hausa) that is expected to begin in May/June and last for approximately four months is the sine qua non for the sustainability of human life. For sure, erratic rainfall patterns have long punctuated the history of precipitation in Hausaland, including what became the Nigerian-Nigérien borderlands; Hill (1972: 312) chronicled this phenomenon for one such rural Hausa community decades ago. But now that manmade weather change patterns are believed to affect rainfall globally, the impact on chronically water sensitive areas is all the more critical. Lake, river and watershed areas have similarly been areas of government concern.

It is in this vein that in 1980 Nigeria and Niger entered into an agreement designed to foster "equitable sharing in the development, conservation and use of their common water resources." Known as the Maiduguri convention (named for the northeastern Nigerian city where the pact was hammered out), Nigeria and Niger bind themselves to share information with each other through the NNJC for informational and decision-making purposes. The pact recognises the extent to which "orderly management of scarce water resources" is key to development on both sides of the border and the maintenance of good bilateral relations. It also stipulates an array of factors that determine equity in water use allocation.

International resources have also been marshaled. The United Nations Environment Programme – Global Environment Facility has funded an eight-year, two-phase programme known as Integrated Ecosystem Management (hereafter IEM) in the Transboundary Areas between Nigeria and Niger. Phase I, beginning in 2006, focused on strengthening legal and institutional frameworks for IEM bilateral collaboration and pilot demonstration in the transboundary catchments of the two nations. Phase two, concluded in 2014, aimed to put into motion management strategies for sharing of natural resources. In both phases, improving both rural livelihoods and conserving the ecosystem has been an overarching objective. Measures to achieve this goal include water resource management, land use sustainability, and regional cooperation. In a nutshell, "[d]esertification control, conservation of biodiversity and poverty alleviation are priorities in the transboundary zone, where the threat is perceived to be the degradation of natural resources, the deterioration of productive capital and the weakening of local economies through the destruction of vegetal resources, a loss of farmland, food and income, decreasing yields owing to erosion, and a lack of alternative livelihoods" (UNEP n.d.: 8).

IEM is not Nigeria's only project dealing with drought and desertification; problems which have been at the top of the ecological agenda of Niger, most of whose territory is solidly implanted within the Sahara. The paper referenced earlier by Medugu, Majid, and Choji critiques several of these programmes, including the Nigeria-Niger Trans-boundary Ecosystem Management Project. Overall, they find several common weaknesses affecting the implementation of these projects. The first is a centralising tendency and the attendant top-down management. Second is an inconsistency of government policies. Third is a general neglect of indigenous knowledge. Fourth is the use of inappropriate technology, and fifth is inadequate raising of environmental consciousness among the rural poor. With regards to the borderlands in particular, we can say that it is impoverished villagers and herders who both bear the brunt of lack of natural resource conservation and contribute the most to it.

4 Wildlife Extinction and Models of Reintroduction

Although the terms "biodiversity" and "wildlife" often make their way into the academic literature and related reports, Nigeria is hardly a primary destination for the serious safari traveller. Game reserves in Nigeria, according to Anadu (1987: 213) "are little more than paper reserves," lacking infrastructure and poacher protection. Indeed, unlike Serengeti in Tanzania or Masai-Mara in Kenya, at time of writing the world knows of a Nigerian reserve (Sambisa) because that is where over two hundred girls kidnapped by Boko Haram in the first half of 2014 were being hidden.

Not only is "big game" lacking in borderland reserves in Nigeria's Sahel: Non-human mammals are increasingly scarce. This is striking not only for ecological reasons but for cultural ones as well. Rattray (1913), in his two-volume collection on Hausa culture and folklore, devotes an entire thematic section (the others be-

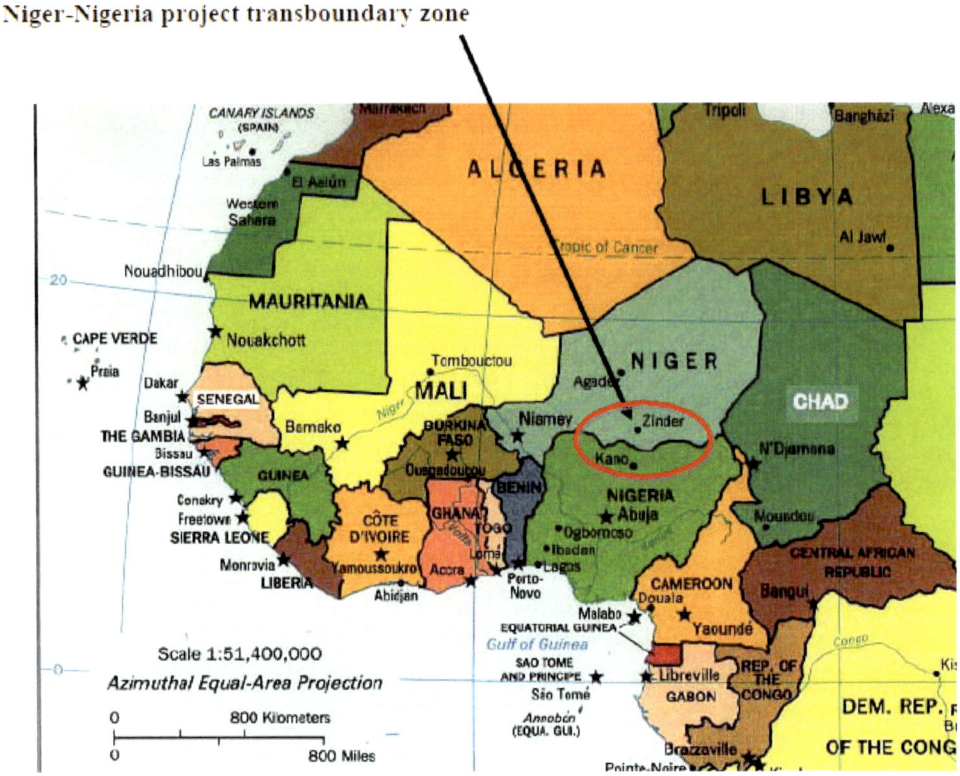

Figure 3: Niger-Nigeria Project Transboundary Zone

ing tales, customs, arts, and proverbs) to "animal stories". They include the lion, leopard, hippo and elephant – none of which survives in the Hausa bush.

In his collection of five hundred Hausa proverbs, Kirk-Greene (1966) includes over a dozen that invoke species that are now extinct in the region, the most prominent one being the hyena. Examples include:

- "A hyena and a dog cannot live together."
- "As soon as he sees his home a dog will abuse a hyena, but never abroad in the forest."
- "If the hyena had any medicine to cure diarrhea, it would have cured itself."

Similarly, folktale collections from Niger (Coppé/ Garba 1984; Glew/ Babalé 1993; Pucheu 1982) invoke large mammals (lions, hyenas, elephants) that virtually no Hausa denizen of the Niger-Nigeria borderlands has ever seen with her or his own eyes. In short, a major fount for imparting indigenous culture, wisdom, and morality has disappeared from the life experience and horizon of even the most rural of Hausa borderlanders. Can one envision a modest reintroduction of species in this zoologically denuded dryland that, in addition to the cultural revival, would have political (qua trans-border cooperative) and economic (qua tourist-based foreign exchange) benefits?

5 The Hai-Bar Example of the Arava

In Biblical times, the kingdom of Edom covered one hundred square miles, ranging from the southern tip of the Dead Sea to the Gulf of Aqaba. An arid and stony desert, the mountains and plateaus of ancient Edom lie in present-day Jordan and Israel. The portion lying in Israel is known as the Arava, a lesser known drylands topography than the Negev Desert which covers approximately half of Israel's entire land surface. Climatic, hydrological and ecological conditions of the Negev and Arava resemble more the Sahara and the Sahel than they do the central and northern regions of Israel. The biogeographic zone names are even more evocative of the African parallel: "Saharo-Arabian" for the Negev, "Sudanese" for the Arava.

In the early 1950s Israel's first prime minister, David Ben-Gurion, established a committee to identify the location of all flora and fauna mentioned in the Old Testament. Larger animals had long since disappeared from the Arava, a combination of gradual ecological change and rapid firearm hunting first introduced in the nineteenth century. In 1968, twelve square miles were set aside for the Hai-Bar Nature Reserve of the Yotvata region with the bio-cultural aim of reintroducing and acclimatising species that had become extinct to the Arava. The acacia tree is a recognisable feature of the Hai-Bar reserve and as such is evocative of the Niger-Nigeria borderland landscape.

Six species have been reintroduced from Hai-Bar, with two of them (the onygar and the Arabian [white] oryx) already being released into nature outside of Hai-Bar itself. Experiments are continuing for the release of ostriches. The release of one species introduced at Hai-Bar with a particular connection to sub-Saharan Africa is the Somali wild ass, a herd of which (eight males, four females) was purchased and flown in from Ethiopia in 1972 (1972 was also the year in which the Arabian oryx was hunted into extinction in the wild; the Arabian oryx became extinct in Arabia itself in the late 1930s). In addition to the primary aim of preserving an individual species, release of the Arabian oryx has had an additional, and unforeseen, beneficial effect in terms of restoration of the ecosystem through their dissemination of ingested acacia seeds (Polak et al. 2014). Such restorative

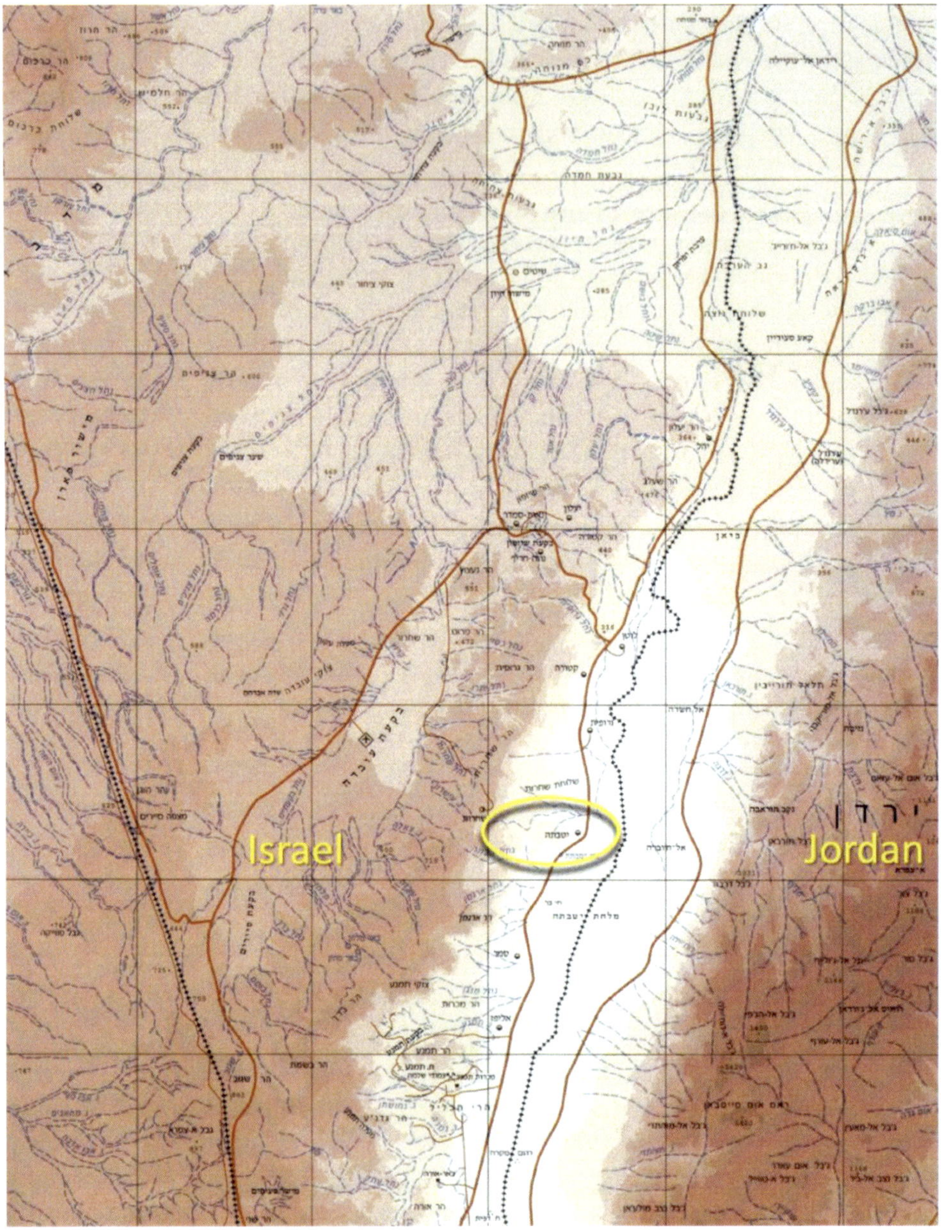

Figure 4: Hai-Bar Nature Reserve in Arava

properties of species restoration may very well have similar benefits for the overly cultivated and deforested Sahelian borderlands of Nigeria-Niger.

The addax, brought to Hai-Bar in 1969 from Chad, represents a reverse case of Israeli-African species preservation. Hunting had rendered the addax extinct in the Sahara, and bringing examples to Israel enhanced prospects for species survival. Not mentioned in the Old Testament (and therefore not to be reintroduced into the general Israeli landscape), the addax is nevertheless bred at Hai-Bar. Another Saharo-Sahelian nation benefitting from the species restoration programme in Hai-Bar is Senegal, which has received eight Saharan oryx from there.[1]

Out of the framework of Transboundary Protected Areas and Transfrontier Conservation Areas, advanced by the World Conservation Union, has risen the notion of peace parks (Ali 2007: 1-2). Peace parks (also referred to as Transboundary Protected Areas, or TPAs) take as their point of departure the view that environmental challenges confronting bordering nations, including natural resource scarcity (an increasing threat from climate change), can be a stimulus for conflict resolution, not only conflict *per se*. Worldwide, there are approximately 200 such areas. Even when the goals and approaches are asymmetric (as in the case of Niger, Benin, and Burkina Faso, partners in the Park W savanna), peace parks can work. The creation of a peace park between Nigeria and Niger, using the controlled reintroduction of previously endemic wildlife, would be in line with what Barkindo (1993) has recommended: Using border region development as an impetus for trans-border cooperation. Given the lack of successful dryland examples of peace parks and species reintroduction in the Sahel, Israel and Hai-Bar serve as potential model and/or partner for such an endeavour.[2] And even where contemporary political conditions render peace parks unrealistic in the immediate future, "optimistic planning" in borderlands – such as Yaar-Waisel (2018) documents for Israel with respect to some of her immediate neighbours – makes eminent sense.

1 Additionally, two Arabian oryx from Hai-Bar have been relocated to a zoo in Johannesburg (personal communication from Yehoshua Shkedy of the Israel Nature and Parks Authority).

2 Further north, at the confluence of the Jordan and Yarmouk Rivers south of the Sea of Galilee, a cross-border Jordan River Peace Park is being developed between Israel and Jordan. Emanating from the Camp David Accords of 1994, and advanced by a Memorandum of Understanding signed in 2008 between Israeli mayors (of Bet Shean and the Jordan Valley Regional Council) and their Jordanian counterpart (in North Shuneh), this peace park aims to rehabilitate the lower Jordan River while providing opportunities for income diversity in the tourism and agricultural sectors. Restoring riverine biodiversity to the area is one of the major aims of the project, as well as creating a bird sanctuary (*New York Times* 2008; Friends of the Earth Middle East information sheet; Ya'ari 2014).

6 Conclusion: International Politics, Public Administration, and Hyena Tails

To some, given the sensitive regional and international political context, invoking the Jewish State as a potential model for biodiversity restoration and game reserve construction in the mostly Muslim borderlands of Nigeria-Niger may sound problematic. But, it is precisely because of the unlikeliness of the model that it should be examined. Two reasons in particular shore up this perspective.

The first has to deal with the trans-border reality with which conservationists in the desert region of the Arava need to contend. "Movement ecology" (not to be confused with the "ecology movement") emphasises the need for species to range throughout their ecological niche, unimpeded by political or national borders (see Nathan 2008 and the rest of the special issue in which that overview appears). Thus, in the case of the oryx reintroduced from Hai-Bar, "[t]he greatest concern was the narrowness of the Negev in these areas ~ 20 – 50 km in terms of proximity to international borders" (Saltz 2008: 186). Long-range, cross-border movement of ungulates, like the oryx, typically occurs shortly after release (Saltz, personal communication), a reason for proactive dialogue with bordering country authorities. Dealing with conservation counterparts in neighbouring countries whose governments conserve at best a cold peace with Israel is not easy. Yet even here, in this politically-fraught region, when rare and endangered injured Egyptian vultures tagged in Israel have crossed into neighbouring states there have been instances of quiet cooperation to protect and return them (Hatzofe 2014).[3]

The second justification for the Hai-Bar model invokes longstanding development cooperation between the Jewish and various African, including Muslim-populated, states (see Decalo 1998; Frank 1988; Miles 2014; *Israel and Africa* 2006, passim). Such development cooperation also occurs largely under the radar, and is inevitably subject to ebbs and flows emanating from the wider Arab-Israeli conflict. That said, Israeli ties to West Africa have been longstanding and are sufficiently positive at the current time to envision the kind of trans-border environmental assistance, based on the controlled reintroduction of disappeared species into a trans-boundary drylands peace park or game reserve, that is being suggested here.

From an international relations theory, one might invoke functionalism: working on common problems that transcend narrow political differences in a way that

[3] Internal security measures can also cause a threat to endangered species: oryx have died after entangling themselves in the fallen white parachutes of IDF military flares, to which they are inexplicably attracted (Saltz 2008: 187).

fosters international cooperation and peace. From a public administration perspective, it is universally acknowledged that, within the problem-solving cycle, the implementation phase is generally more difficult than the problem identification one. Without the benefit of social science theory, but with the benefit of keen observation of erstwhile wildlife, the Hausa have been saying as much for many years: "It is not changing into a hyena that is difficult, but getting the tail" (i.e. it is easy enough to begin a thing, but harder to complete it). Now that the bioclimatic, environmental, agricultural, and economic problems defining the Nigerian-Nigérien borderlands are better defined, and the interrelationship among them better understood, it is time "to get the tail," using all knowledge, and experience, available on the planet.

Image 33: Ju/'hoansi San before Sunday service.

Image 34: A Ghanzi supermarket, Botswana.

Image 35: Healing dance in Djxohkoe.

Image 36: Justice Manxiweni Zikhali in Mabibi.

Image 37: Thandi Shabalala, iSimangaliso.

Image 38: Warrior procession.

Image 39: Elmont Mkhonto, Kosi Bay.

Image 40: InDuna during Umthayi Festival.

Image 41: Tembe Elephant Park.

Image 42: Puros Conservancy, Kunene Region.

Image 43: Tembe Elephant Park.

Image 44: Pilanesberg National Park, South Africa.

Image 45: Cheetah in Phinda Private Game Reserve.

Image 46: Madikwe Game Reserve.

Image 47: Madikwe Game Reserve.

Image 48: Sabi Sabi Private Game Reserve.

Image 49: Lioness with cubs.

Image 50: Mkhuze Game Reserve, iSimangaliso.

Image 51: Madikwe Game Reserve.

Image 52: Sabi Sabi, Greater Kruger.

Image 53: The big yawn.

Image 54: Londolozi Private Game Reserve.

Image 55: Sabi Sabi, Greater Kruger.

Image 56: Londolozi, Greater Kruger.

Image 57: Madikwe Game Reserve.

Image 58: Tembe Elephant Park.

Image 59: iSimangaliso Wetland Park.

Image 60: Tembe Elephant Park.

Image 61: N≠aisa N!ani, Doupos.

Part III

iSimangaliso Wetland Park: South Africa's New Governance Model of Conservation and Development

Communities, Conventions, and Conservation: The Spectrum of Participation and Power

Jennifer Kelleher

1 Introduction

The conservation of nature is generally deemed a laudable pursuit, a practical and moral necessity to protect the planet from the excesses of the Anthropocene (Crutzen 2010). The global efforts to address these issues are generally thought of as beginning in 1972 with the United Nations Conference on the Human Environment or Stockholm Convention, which was followed by the creation of several international conventions on flora and fauna, most notably the Convention on Biological Diversity (Convention on Biological Diversity, Rio de Janeiro, Brazil, 1992). This prompted an increase in the number of protected areas once national state parties became signatories. Protected areas are the cornerstone of nature conservation and are geographically delineated spaces set aside for the protection of biodiversity – the variety of living things on earth. However, they face a vast number of external threats including encroachment by adjacent land-use, extractive industries, and pressures from increased local population growth, land grabbing, lack of connectivity corridors, poaching, and a lack of resources. Despite the fact that robust nature conservation laws exist at international, regional, and national scales, the corresponding quality of global biodiversity continues to deteriorate, and mixed performance results question their effectiveness (Thomas/ Gillingham 2015).

The legal systems designed to implement nature conservation have multiple layers. Indeed, nature conservation law and practice is a Russian doll of sorts, a tale within a tale, within a tale. Its outward exterior begins with the story of the practical, moral, and commendable necessity of creating protected areas to mitigate biodiversity loss on Earth. Running through this history is the powerful current of the international environmental ethic, a unified, universalised response to a global problem. The ethic is based on the construction of an abstract international environment, guided by eco-centric principles.

Beyond this narrative of a global need for conservation, we reveal another layer that describes the long history of national statutory conservation law and protected areas as a means of regulating and restricting the consumptive use of biodiversity-rich areas. Indeed, it was in the colonies that conservationist thinking and protected areas first emerged as a state practice (Grove 1987: 21; 1995: 40), and in Africa where nature conservation law first appeared as a supra-national legal tool.

These early laws carried occidental ideas of nature that came to shape the norms underlying nature conservation. As a result, the African landscape was reimagined with nature and people as dichotomous concepts, drawing lines across landscapes, delineating those inside and those outside. These colonial roots of conservation infused certain elements of power, control and hegemony into conservation practices. The grundnorm of state-led conservation anticipates government intervention into land use in the interest of the public good. This intervention was concretised into statutory rules on land use and top down positive law as a means of carrying this out.

Peeling back one more layer, we reveal yet another hidden tale of how these particular ideas and related practices changed the way land, and the natural resources therein, were regulated, protected, and used. This contributed to the destruction of indigenous and local systems of land tenure, the displacement and impoverishment of pastoralist and hunter-gatherer communities, the consequent extinguishing of customary laws, cultural practices, traditional ways of life, and the loss of vernacular environmental knowledge (UNCHR Rapporteur 2017, online; IWGIA African Commission, adopted by the African Commission on Human and Peoples' Rights 2005, online). The concepts 'protected area' and 'conserving biodiversity' thus become loaded terms that carry with them particular definitions of nature as well as the undermining of the power and participation of local communities and their forms of knowledge. The coloniality of conservation law then, can be expanded to mean the intervention and influence of conservation law and policy into four key motifs: law, control over land, ethics/values, and knowledge.

Since 2003, and through various avenues, a shift in the conventional conservation paradigm has emerged that ushers in a more inclusive and participatory approach for local communities. Since many global biodiversity hotspots are located in developing countries, there is a twofold challenge. The conservation imperative often collides with an urgent need for poverty alleviation and socio-economic progress. The new conservation paradigm, therefore, entails a delicate balancing of goals, to not only conserve biodiversity but to do so by embracing the inclusion of local, often vulnerable, communities. Amongst these new conservation approaches is the rights based approach (hereafter RBA; Greiber et al. 2008: 1). The RBA asserts that the conservation of land and resources cannot begin without identifying the rights of local peoples at each stage of protected area establishment, management, and governance, including tenure and procedural rights. Yet, the RBA is neither a simple nor a linear solution toward inclusive conservation because the coloniality of law and its interventions into the four key motifs are tangibly, temporally, and conceptually pervasive.

This chapter will argue that nature conservation law displays enduring key characteristics, which can be referred to as the coloniality of nature conservation law, discernable by examining its historical phases. This is exacerbated by a problem of scales, the global environmental ethic which advocates for the increased implementation of statutory conservation law and its hallmark of protected areas, to the smallest unit of analysis, the local landscape, that of a modern protected area and its buffer zone. The latter will be presented through a case study, in iSimangaliso Wetland Park, which covers one of the oldest protected sites in Africa, and which has been on the UNESCO natural heritage site list since 1999. On the occasion of its 20-year anniversary, it is timely to examine some of the challenges involved.

2 The Coloniality of Conservation Law and the Illuminations of History

When problematising conventions and communities, the illuminations of history ought to be considered. By tracing a line back, a revealing history emerges: Firstly, on the international level, and the cultivation of a strong, international, environmental ethic which will later reach into the most local soils. Secondly, on the state level, and the government led conservation laws that created norms and regulations. Pulling these strands together, it becomes therefore important to problematise the four key motifs: law, control over land, ethics/values, and knowledge. It is not however, the intention of the paper to argue against the rule of law in conservation nor conservation itself, but rather to obtain a better understanding of it by analysing it as a powerful, political weapon, a Western cultural artefact, and the very Western reimagining of the African landscape in this instance, that cements its status and dominance, particularly on the international plane.

2.1 Positive law, its Products, and Institutions

The period known as the wave of 'New Imperialism' between 1870 right up to World War I, was a significant period for the proliferation of international conservation. This period began when a number of European colonial powers aggressively acquired overseas lands on the African continent, and in the process also transformed the political and natural landscape (Hertslet 1894: 1). Lands acquired on the African continent were quickly delineated into marked boundaries between white-owned areas and African communal areas. Conservation began to be considered as a solution when widespread land degradation began to occur. Mining took a toll, hunting led directly to the decimation of large game (Carruthers 2013: 16; Beinart/ Coates 1995: 80) as did epidemics of disease affecting large scale pastoralism, which led to programmes of the widespread, intentional killing of cattle and game (Perissinotto et al. 2013: 2). The 1872 Yellowstone model exported from the USA, prompted by the overexploitation of animal and plant species compounded by the romanticism of wilderness was deemed a suitable model of nature preservation and conservation.

It was in 1900 when a group of seven European countries decided to draw up the first pan-African conservation instrument, the 1900 *Convention for the Preservation of Wild Animals, Birds and Fish in Africa* (hereafter London Convention). No African groups were present at the deliberations. The preamble for the London Convention reads that it was intended to "prevent the uncontrolled massacre and to ensure the conservation of diverse wild animal species in their African possessions which are useful to man or inoffensive" (London Convention 1900: preamble). The substantive provisions of the draft text stated that certain animals deemed useful, rare or endangered were to be protected. However, certain species were deemed as pest species allowing for a justified culling if need be. Crucially, in its Article II (5), it suggested the creation of reserves. It standardised the practices of separating man from nature, traditional peoples from traditional hunting grounds and imposed 'schedules' of limited, licensed hunting conditions. This coincided with the banning of the sale of firearms to Black Africans. Article III of the 1900 convention permitted eradication programmes as long as they were "desirable for important administrative reasons" allowing for the lawful killing of lions, elephants, buffalo, and other large game (Perissinotto et al. 2013: 2).

In 1933, a second attempt at an international conservation treaty was made and this time it was enacted. The 1933 *Convention Relative to the Preservation of Fauna and Flora in their Natural State* (hereafter 1933 *London Convention*) was adopted on the 3rd of November 1933 and entered into force on the 14th of January 1936. The convention extended from its predecessor in a number of important ways. It extended the scope and geographical reach of the convention (Article 1) and now included precious flora, making illegal the collection of certain types of flora. It created the legal basis for the creation of delineated protected areas in the form of national parks and nature reserves (Article 2). The text of the convention bequeaths on the relevant public bodies the administrative powers and the "control of all white or native settlements in national parks with a view to ensuring that as little disturbance as possible is occasioned to the natural flora and fauna" (Article 4). Any lawful killing of an animal, regarded as trophies (denoting any animal, dead or alive – Article 9.8) in the text, are subjected to export prohibition and licensing fees, thus bringing the lawful killing of fauna under strict conditions to those with firearms and the ability to purchase licenses, again, bestowing on authorities the power to confiscate any trophies that are produced without a certificate of same. Under Article 10, specific methods of killing are prohibited, such as "the use of poisoned weapons, the use of nets [...] or enclosures, dazzling lights or flares" (Article 10.2. (a)-(c)). Further, the convention used the Annex system to list Class A and Class B species of plants and animals.

These conventions are important for three reasons. Firstly, they created the blueprint for nature conservation that persists today, both at the national and the international level. This blueprint, containing gazettes, schedules of restricted flora and fauna, and the concept of delineated geographical areas for protection continued to the 1968 *African Convention on the Conservation of Nature and Natural Resources* and beyond to the five major international biodiversity conventions protecting: wetlands (*Convention on Wetlands of International Importance especially as Waterfowl Habitat*, Ramsar, Iran, 1971), world heritage in 1972 (the *World Heritage Convention*), trade in endangered species and their products (*U.N. Convention on International Trade in Endangered Species of Wild Fauna and Flora* 1973), migratory species of wild animals in 1983 (*Convention on the Conservation of Migratory Species of Wild Animals*, 1983) and biodiversity (*Convention on Biological Diversity*, Rio de Janeiro, Brazil, 1992). Secondly, the conservation intervention became a state-led or supra-state enterprise, as opposed to something that is simply part of smaller-scale social organisation and practices.

Although never formally ratified, the *London Convention* heralded the creation of the first formal international legal normative framework constructed by state governments at the turn of the century. Positivism, the legal doctrine underpinning colonialism, now came to justify nature conservation on the international stage, by protecting nature from those ill-equipped to do so. And as Norgaard notes, it also bestowed a unique kind of social authority on the enlightened to do so (Norgaard 1994: 61). It legitimised the dominance of positivism. Thirdly, this supra-state approach requires large-scale, international institutional arrangements that led directly to the destruction or discouragement of institutional arrangements at smaller to medium scales (Ostrom 1998: 150). Further, these global networks of influence bind states to those institutions, designating local conservation actors as citizens of a distant metropole.

2.2 Control Over Land

Article II (5) of the 1900 convention suggested the creation of reserves, which the 1933 convention created the legal basis for in its Article 2 and the requirement of delineated protected areas in the form of national parks and nature reserves. This was the model of protected area first conceived of in post-industrial societies, and it stemmed from the United Kingdom. There, crown land was kept for the elite and for hunting small and large game found in the English countryside (Wilkinson 2003: 2). This was an idea to be transported from metropole to colony and was erroneous in its inception. Post-industrial societies, such as the United Kingdom, can be characterised by larger urban populations, increasingly large-scale industries, strong land tenure systems and the promotion of protected areas, as snow-globes where human activity is restricted to limited, recreational activities. Conversely, pre-industrial societies, where colonial metropoles cast their attention, are characterised by smaller urban populations, mostly small-scale subsistence agriculture or those living nomadic lifestyles, absent land tenure systems (in the sense of property law), and natural areas of wilderness, with megafauna and endemic flora flourishing. The landscapes in which this model of protected area was conceived were landscapes with high amounts of rainfall and low populations of endemic carnivores, exported to vast arid landscapes with high populations of carnivores. By designating these places as protected areas, the species and habitats were categorised as fragile, thus creating human-free landscapes where animals and plant life could thrive.

In practice, people were displaced from the land or disallowed from accessing natural resources, and laws set in place did not recognise any kind of participation in decision making or management at the local level. These developments occurred across Southern Africa in the late nineteenth century and early twentieth century (World Bank 1994; Kumleben Board of Investigation Report 1998: 42; Chatty/ Colchester 2002: 2; Nustad 2015: 26). This resulted in the forcible displacement and expulsion of many (UNCHR Rapporteur 2017, online; IWGIA African Commission, adopted by the African Commission on Human and Peoples' Rights 2005, online). These structural inequalities were further exacerbated in South Africa during apartheid by racially discriminatory laws and policy, particularly in land legislation. Protected areas by now were known as recreational spaces for the privileged elite (Paterson in Lausche 2011: 7), and also as a way for European powers to protect nature and natural resources by restricting and disempowering Africans under the guise of resource protection.

2.3 The Superiority of Knowledge and Ethics

Around the time of the deliberations of the 1900 Convention, external environmental factors such as drastic droughts and soil erosion contributed to the rise of scientific inquiry into the connection between human activities and environmental change (Grove 1989). These changes in the natural landscape were systematically surveyed through scientific collections of plants species, reptiles, mammals, birds, spiders, and fish (Bruton/ Cooper 1980: 432). The scientific credibility of Humboldtian science (Humboldt 1997, translated by Otté), ideas about the origins of diversity of life, namely speciesism (Darwin 1859: 1), the importation of Western ideologies regarding the scientific study of plants and animals to the colony such as German physician and botanist Pappe in 1854, and the European reimagining of the African landscape as an aesthetic object cemented concepts of the rigorous quantification and classification of nature and its subsequent part of a total ecosystem. This reimagining coincided with the rise of conservation societies in the United Kingdom such as The Royal Geographical Society in 1826 and The Royal Society for the Protection of Birds in 1891 to promote extensive exploration of Britain's extensive foreign possessions (Brotton 2012: 337*)*. Then, with the legitimisation and universalisation of veterinary medicine, zoology, and biology as disciplines and the increase in amateur conservationists, a new language emerged that introduced concepts such as biological diversity, preservation of ecosystems, conservation, and so on. These developments led to the acceptance of conservation as a viable pursuit in the region and a means to protect colonial biodiversity as a colonial possession. Rational scientific enquiry was its justification.

This scientific basis is inextricably linked to the rise of a certain environmental ethic. Aldo Leopold wrote "A thing is right when it tends to preserve the integrity, stability, and beauty of the biotic community. It is wrong when it tends otherwise" (Leopold 1949 in Wilkinson 2002: 227). This reliance on objective, rational science as a justification for nature conservation remains today with an open-ended intergovernmental scientific advisory body known as the Subsidiary Body on Scientific, Technical and Technological Advice, which provides the Conference of the Parties with assessments of the status of biological diversity and of the types of measures taken in accordance with the provisions of the convention. The inclusion of traditional knowledge in 8(j) of the *Convention on Biological Diversity* marks a great stride forward in this regard (8(j) Subject to its national legislation to respect, preserve, and maintain knowledge, innovations, and practices of indigenous and local communities embodying traditional lifestyles relevant for the conservation and sustainable use of biological diversity, to promote their wider application with the approval and involvement of the holders of such knowledge, innovations, and practices, and to encourage the equitable sharing of the benefits arising from the utilisation of such knowledge, innovations, and practices). Yet, it remains at the fringes of conservation practices, an appendage to consider, instead of being incorporated more generally and centrally.

Another key point in the environmental ethic is to note the difference between two kinds of anthropocentric ethics for the conservation of nature. Conservation is usually devised in the best interest of people and their health, evident from the preamble of many international environmental policies and the onus on future generations (*Stockholm Declaration* 1972; *World Charter for Nature* 1982; *World Commission on Environment and Development* 1987; *World Heritage Convention* 1972; *Convention on Biological Diversity* 1992). However, a second anthropocentric exists, one that is more holistic, stemming from the starting point that humans are connected to all aspects of the natural world (Matthews 1988). It is this second ethic that deserves further attention as it goes to the heart of conservation practices in many non-Western societies. In its Preamble, the *Convention on Biological Diversity* (CBD) recognises both schools of thought. The states' parties pronounce themselves to be "Conscious of the intrinsic value of biological diversity and of the ecological, genetic, social, economic, scientific, educational, cultural, recreational and aesthetic values of biological diversity and its components; [and] Conscious also of the importance of biological diversity for evolution and for maintaining life sustaining systems of the biosphere" (CBD 1992: preamble)

3 Decolonising Conservation: The Work Thus Far

Decolonising conservation law therefore speaks to the issues of participation, power, and understanding conflicting values. It should address power and authority, laws, land rights and use, knowledge systems, and local values.

3.1 Changing the Narrative

The process began during the period post World War II, when a general recognition of human rights united states in an international declaration of respect for human life as well as recognising the special rights of indigenous peoples and traditional communities. The *Universal Declaration on Human Rights* in 1948 was followed, some decades later, by the *International Covenant on Economic, Social and Cultural Rights* (1966), the *African Charter on Human Rights and People's Rights* (1981), and the *ILO Convention No.169 Concerning Indigenous and*

Tribal Peoples in Independent Countries (1989), each affirming that what their namesakes suggest. The more recent *United Nations Declaration on the Rights of Indigenous Peoples* (2007) expresses rights of special consideration for indigenous peoples (cf. Zips-Mairitsch 2013).

Within the international conventions themselves, special wording addresses the use of resources. The *African Convention on the Conservation of Nature and Natural Resources* 1968 called for the rational utilisation of resources (Article XIII), the *Ramsar Convention on Wetlands of International Importance* 1971 (Ramsar) called for "wise use" (Articles 2, 3, and 6), the *World Heritage Convention* called for natural heritage to be given "a function in the life of a community" (Article 5), and the *Convention on Biological Diversity* contained Article 10 with regard to sustainable use of resources with an emphasis on the use of traditional knowledge (Article 8j). Since 2003, and through various avenues, a shift in the conventional conservation paradigm has emerged that ushers in an approach that is more inclusive and participatory for local communities (Sanderson/ Bird 1998: 441; Philipps 2003: 8; CBD ecosystem approach 2003; Grazia Borrini et al. 2013: 13; Lausche 2011: 1; Greiber et al. 2009: 1).

The *Durban Accord* generated from the Vth *IUCN World Parks Congress* and the *World Conservation Congress* coupled these with invigorated approaches to biodiversity protection as seen in the *Aichi Targets 2020*, particularly Aichi Target 14: "By 2020, ecosystems that provide essential services, including services related to water, and contribute to health, livelihoods and well-being, are restored and safeguarded, taking into account the needs of women, indigenous and local communities, and the poor and vulnerable." Sets of case studies appeared of traditional peoples living in or near to protected areas (Beltran 2000: 19), as did a series of *Guidelines for Applying Protected Areas Management Categories* (Dudley 2008: 26) that identified four protected areas governance types: governance by government, private governance, shared governance, and governance by indigenous peoples and local communities. This last category has been interpreted as meaning where "the management authority and responsibility rest with indigenous peoples and/or local communities through various forms of legal, formal or informal, institutions and rules." Expanding on this governance option, the Community-Based Natural Resource Management approach has placed an onus on conservation of local resources, too, by devolving authority for ecosystem management to the local community level, "thereby empowering communities to manage their own resources without permanently damaging, depleting or degrading them" (Fabricius/ Collins 2007: 84). Much work has yet to be done. However, new and innovative kinds of governance structures and systems (Borrini et al.

2013: 29.), community-based authority and responsibility over natural resources to achieve ancillary conservation, and other effective conservation measures, especially with regard to the territories and areas conserved by indigenous peoples and local communities, have emerged.

3.2 The RBA and the Call for Conservation with Justice

This work to change the language and concepts around conservation has been 'strengthened from within' by the concept of conservation with justice and the RBA (Greiber et al. 2008: 1), the approach that asserts that the conservation of land and resources cannot begin without identifying the rights of local peoples at each stage of protected area establishment including addressing issues of tenure and procedural rights. The RBA can be understood as the incorporation of rights, norms, standards, and principles into policy, planning, implementation, and outcomes assessment to help ensure that conservation practice respects rights and their further realisation (Campese et al. 2009: 9). A 'stepwise' RBA is recommended by the IUCN publication "Conservation with Justice" (2009), which identifies the rights of local peoples at each stage of protected area establishment (Greiber et al. 2008: 23), the methodology and analysis of which we will now turn to. This step-wise approach advocates for a situation analysis: identifying scientific and economic circumstances, the policies, and relevant institutional and legal frameworks; identifying all stakeholders and rights holders; identifying applicable legal duties, rights, and claims; identifying negative impacts of the protected area; ensuring that free, prior, and informed consent is obtained; and ensuring full and meaningful participation (ibid.). It is to this methodology that we now turn. Thereby, we hope to uncover any critical linkages between nature conservation, peoples' rights, and their livelihoods.

4 iSimangaliso Wetland Park: Case in Point and the Spectrum of Inclusion

The IWP became South Africa's first World Heritage Site in 1999 (*The World Heritage Convention Act* (Act 49) of 1999) due to meeting three of the ten UNESCO criteria, namely outstanding examples of ecological processes (criteria vvii), superlative natural phenomena and scenic beauty (criteria ix), and exceptional biodiversity and threatened species (criteria x). An enormous space. It is 192 km long and covers 229.737 ha of land area and 102.598 ha of marine area, and contains an astonishing array of valuable biota. Comprising five ecosystems: marine, 25.000

year old coastal dune forest, wetlands, swamp forest, and grasslands, the area enjoys high species diversity in plants and birds and marine life. Some 2.505 plant species, 1.258 fish species and 526 bird species live in IWP (IWPA 2016, online). The park is also a critical habitat for five species of turtles including breeding leatherback turtles and for the single largest populations of hippos and crocodiles in South Africa, amongst other species. There are also 105 'Red Data' species (The IUCN Red Data List records the risk of extinction for thousands of species globally; IUCN 2017, online). It is also a fragile landscape. There are 3 major lake systems in the park, and the lake estuarine system, around St Lucia, the small village at the southern end of the park, is a constantly changing ecosystem with brackish water, testing the resilience of the animals and plants within the ecosystem. Natural challenges facing the region are periods of drought (South Africa overall is a water-scarce country) which affects the fragile ecosystems.

The iSimangaliso Wetland Park Authority (hereafter IWPA) is the protected area manager and has management authority over the area obliging them to take effective and active measures for the protection, conservation, and presentation of the cultural and natural heritage of the park (World Heritage Act 13 (2) 1999). Previously known as the Greater St Lucia Wetland Park Authority, the name change was effected by Government Notice 438 of 11 May 2007, an authority pursuant to section 9 of the *World Heritage Convention Act*, 1999. The KwaZulu-Natal Nature Conservation Board (hereafter Ezemvelo), established under section 4 of the *KwaZulu-Natal Nature Conservation Management Act*, 1997, was appointed conservation park manager. The park is subject to a raft of statutes and regulations meaning that entrance to, residence in, and any development, construction, and farming is prohibited without written permission as is the damage and removal of plants, vegetation, and any degradation of the environment (iSimangaliso Wetlands Park Authority and Others v Mthembu and Another (3188/2010) [2010] ZAKZDHC 29 (15 July 2010)). One of the key objectives of the IWP and the IWPA is to benefit the community through job creation, equity sharing, and capacity building (Govender 02.06.2016, interview).

4.1 People's Active Substantive Rights

4.1.1 Land and Tenure

"iSimangaliso's story is a story of restitution", so states Andrew Zaloumis, former CEO of IWPA (Zaloumis 2015, interview). Indeed, the park consolidated sixteen different land management regimes and other protected areas when it came into effect. The protected areas were: False Bay Park (1944); Sodwana Bay National

Park (1950); Kosi Bay Nature Reserve (1950); Sodwana State Forest (1956); Eastern Shores State Forest (1956); Cape Vidal State Forest (1956); Nyalazi State Forest (1956); Maphelane Nature Reserve (1986); Coastal Forest Reserve (1992); Lake Sibaya Fresh Water Reserve (1994); St Lucia Marine Protected Area (2000); and Maputaland Marine Protected Area (2000). The IWP is divided into three sections, A, B, and C, to identify and work together with communities and their land claims, see figure 5.

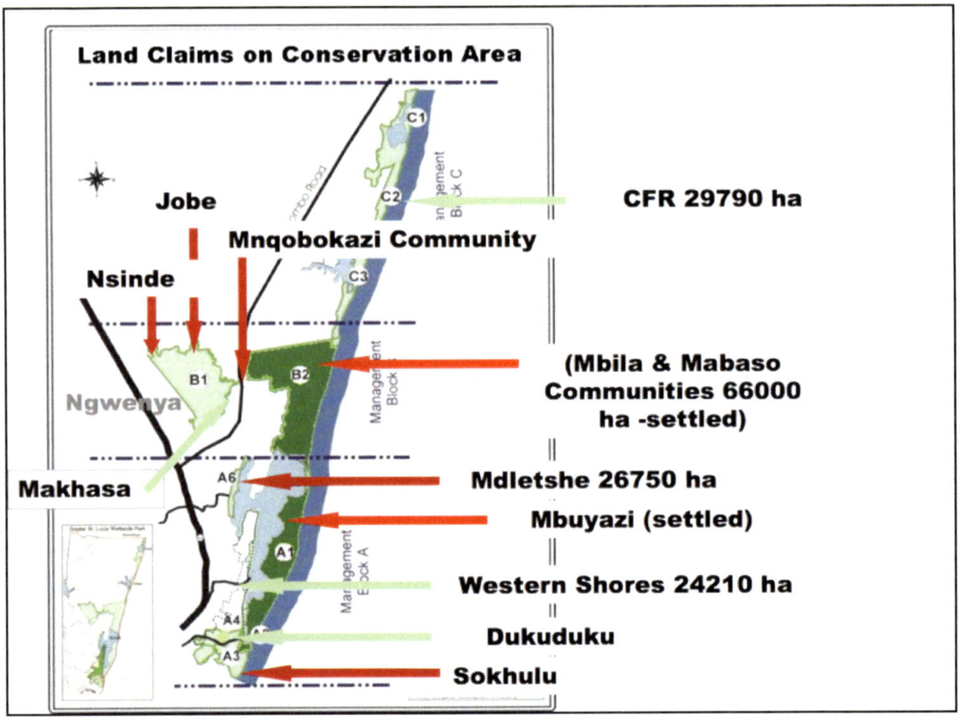

Figure 5: Land Claims on Conservation Area in IWP (IWPA 2016)

Two key components of this land reform programme are land tenure reform, particularly the move to recognise informal and communal land rights (Communal Property Association Act (28 of 1996), the Interim Protected of Informal Land Rights Act (31 of 1996), and Restitution of Land Rights Act (22 of 1994)), and land restitution, whereby those persons previously dispossessed of land for political reasons are enabled to reclaim such land (Restitution of Land Rights Act (22 of 1994)). South Africa has developed several novel land governance options to cope with contested land (Paterson 2011: 162) and the settled land claim communities illustrate one such option. In IWP, once communities receive title they enter into a mandatory partnership of 'conservation in perpetuity'. The strategy of the IWPA then has been to either pursue conservation in perpetuity or to use financial incentives to ask land claimants to relinquish their occupation, access and use rights. The *Bhangazi Settlement Agreement* (Department of Land Affairs and the Community of the Former St Lucia Eastern Shores/ Bhangazi Beneficial Occupants and Their District Descendants Deed of Settlement in terms of Section 14(3) read with Section 42D of the Restitution of Land Rights Act no. 22 of 1994, dated 24 September 1999) illustrates this option: The community relinquished the physical occupation of their land (after winning a land claim which recognised their forcible removal in 1976) with financial compensation. The land ownership option in IWP appears to be a non-owner, non-manager, mandatory partnership. The community is the owner of the land in title with no rights of occupation, access, or use, and the responsibility to manage the land lies with the IWPA, details of same are contained within management agreements that are drawn up between the parties. This substantive and 'active' right then is rendered toothless, against an agenda of heritage conservation. Further, there is the feeling that many communities entered into such agreements without understanding the gravity of the situation: "Because you see, when you are poor, you don't think about your property, you just think... about getting the money" (anonymous waiter and trained nature guide 08.06.2016, interview).

The land claims themselves tend to be lengthy affairs, complicated by 'new' and 'old' families both laying claim to ancestral lands thereby 'diluting' and frustrating the assertion of ancestral land (Lugagu 10.06.2016, interview). Dukuduku South situated in A3 of the above map, is an area that is divided into three parts. One part is a community that currently waits for their claim to the land on which they reside as ancestral land to be determined by the Land Claims court (Dukuduku Community v Regional Land Claims Commissioner: KwaZulu-Natal and another (LCC30/02) [2003] ZALCC 14 (30 May 2003)). They are suspended in a no-man's land, and have been for 13 years, whereby they do not belong to the nearby Dukuduku Khula village community, which is under a co-management agreement between their tribal authority and IWPA. This suspension has alienated them from their neighbours, yet offers a fascinating glimpse into land-use on small holdings in a protected area.

In a map drawn by an inhabitant living in Dukuduku South, he describes his neighbourhood as the 'dark side' (anonymous waiter and trained nature guide 08.06.2016, interview). It is called such as many houses do not have electricity. There is no access to clean drinking water within close proximity and no interaction with the tribal authority of Dukuduku. He describes alienation and fragmentation of families and communities, into those who settle with IWPA and those who don't. The 'dark side' shows scope for the fertile growth of various types of fruits, vegetables, and grazing which local people depend on for food and income. He explains the local economy: "My mom she is a farmer. So from when I started school, she was growing, you know, banana, grenadine, sweet potato, white potato, she planted those things and when it was ready to eat, she would take it and bring it to Mtuba Mtuba and sell it, so then I had shoes for school, she did this until I finished school" (waiter and trained nature guide 08.06.2016, interview).

Another inhabitant explains: "This area is very, very fertile. If you want to cultivate crops, you can cultivate crops, anything you want to do with the land, you can do… people cultivate banana and amadumbe, something like sweet potato… There are plenty of people in Dukuduku who are not employed, because there are no companies around this area, they only work for restaurants or hotels … This is why people are upset. If iSimangaliso took this area they would suffer. Because people sell their crops in town, like avocado, oranges and all the good stuff from the soil" (Ncube 03.06.2016, interview). The same inhabitants both identified 'roundhouses' on the land, which are spiritual places for local people, places to connect to their ancestry. A loss of land would, therefore, not only take their chosen method of sustenance away from them but also an important cultural and spiritual site.

Lastly, the land issue is a real example of the problem of competing ethics and values. Former CEO Andrew Zaloumis describes how "romantic notions of a return to the land also challenge the existence of protected areas like iSimangaliso" (Zaloumis 2015, interview). Yet, he taps into the romanticism linked to re-wilding a landscape as justification for its raison d'etre, saying that "Monbiot captures the issue of conserving our environment when he says rewilding brings back hope and inspiration, succour for the soul." (ibid.). This duality illustrates the very crux of global values versus local values, succour for the soul of mankind and not the local inhabitant. Local 'romantic' notions on ancestral homes are deemed naïve and rank second over romantic notions of a constructed wild and pristine landscape. This means that what should be the strongest of rights, namely tenure, is rendered weak, obsolete even.

4.1.2 Access to Natural Resources

The *South African Bill of Rights* addresses this right in its Chapter 2, section 24. The *National Environmental Management: Protected Areas Act* (Protected Areas

Act) 2003 specifically directs that its implementation must take place in partnership with the people and should allow provision for communal access and use rights (National Environmental Management: Protected Areas Act (57 of 2003) Section 3(b)). It allows the IWPA to negotiate agreements with a community and issue permits/licenses to it to enable the community to undertake commercial developments/activities in the protected area, to access, use, and share natural resources situated in the protected area, and to share in the benefits derived from such activities (section 5). According to the IWPA, the ongoing sustainable resource-use that is currently allowed involves grazing and harvesting rushes, reeds, ilala, and isikhonkho (Govender 02.06.2016, interview), and it "showcases cultural heritage, provides resources for traditional practices as well as subsistence." Referred generally to the "People and Parks" programme, in the words of one local it attempts to: "incorporate sustainable utilisation through conservation" (nature guide 08.06.2016, interview; security officer in Sodwana Bay 11.06.2016, interview). The IWPA allow 3.000 women to collect incema reeds every year in May (Govender 02.06.2016, interview) and ilala reeds, which are used for making hats, baskets, and mats for home use and sale. They also allow subsistence fishing in the estuary: "Some families, like further north in Kosi Bay, they've got fish crawls, which they herd fish into... And that has been going for hundreds of years. The conservation authorities are not stopping that but they are controlling it" (nature guide 08.06.2016, interview).

There are two kinds of natural resources in the park: Firstly, there are those wild resources that seem in plentiful supply. One nature guide states that "you could live forever in that park... the buffalo thorns have got berries, you can make coffee from the berries. It is ridiculous, the list is endless. We have got rock fig trees on the northern section of the park. You can eat the reeds, they have good nutritional value. A lot of the grasses have a small bulb at the bottom that is also very healthy to eat. And then the insects, any insect you can basically eat... there are also earthworms, there is anything... " (tour guide at Heritage Tours 07.06.2016, interview). And indeed, interviews with locals have indicated that they wish to be able to access wild fruit, firewood, medicinal plants, grasses, reeds, fish, and small game (Dukuduku South Community Land Claims Board member 03.06.2016, interview; waiter and trained nature guide 08.06.2016, interview; sangoma in Mabibi beach 02.06.2016, interview).

Secondly, the soil itself, which is extremely fertile to provide for cultivation. The issue has in the past been about securing funding to identify sustainable harvesting methods that do not damage or interfere with the fragile soil. Where community conservation officers have worked together with people, it appears to work: "Because research indicated that the harvesting of the ilala palm is sustainable, because they only take the leaves. And then they leave it to grow. So, we are not that much worried about over exploitation because it has proven itself to be sustainable, the way they harvest" (intern at IWPA 10.06.2016, interview). Sustainable cultivation has worked in the past, and as the local farmers in the "dark side" show, it works there, too. A small growers' scheme, initiated by IWPA, unfortunately lost funding from the Department of the Environment and Tourism (Govender 02.06.2016, interview). They were a short-lived success of "about 40 functioning gardens. People have planted mainly vegetables such as cabbage, spinach, tomatoes, beans, onions, and peri-peri. These are mainly for home consumption" (iSimangaliso Wetland News 2009, online).

The access to resources is generally prohibited. The Bhangazi community also lamented lack of access to land, trees, water, animals, birds, medicinal plants, ncema, and reed grasses at Lake Bhangazi under their management agreement. Where it is allowed it is tightly controlled (the income reed gathering did not take place in 2016 for example due to the extended drought period. Catch from the sea and the lake is also controlled and monitored by Ezemvelo, and fishermen are subjected to paid licenses and bag size limits (Lugagu 10.06.2016, interview). Monitoring of the take of natural resources is carried out by private security companies contracted by iSimangaliso and the police force (anonymous Ezemvelo staff member 09.06.2016, interview; Lugagu 10.06.2016, interview). However, it was conceded by several people that the restrictions do contribute to the problems of snaring and poaching (honorary Ezemvelo officer 09.06.2016, interview), two challenges which the authorities in IWP face. In an area as economically disadvantaged as northern KwaZulu-Natal with high unemployment levels, poverty often drives local people to predatory practices. The IWP is located within the uMhanyakhude District Municipality with an unemployment rate of around 43% in a population of 625,846 (South African census 2016, online). And indeed, there are reports of snaring around St Lucia and of people setting gill nets in the lake at night, which is prohibited (anonymous honorary Ezemvelo officer 09.06.2016, interview).

This means that nature conservation causes two problems. Firstly, it means that all natural resource use is seen as criminal activity that doesn't differentiate between the economic backgrounds of people. Adams notes how this renders "hunters into poachers, wood-cutters into law-breakers, and farmers into the enemies of conservation" (Adams 2004: 35). As one local St Lucia nature guide explains: "There are two types of poachers. There is the park poacher, who poaches to keep his family alive. Then you get the commercial poachers, so they will take meat orders in the community, they will select 20 to 30 animals and then sell them. Subsistence poaching is not the problem, because they take what they need. It is the commercial poachers. However, and this is the second problem, the presence of uniformed anti-poaching officers and Ezemvelo staff creates a climate of fear and, subsistence poachers receive the same force as commercial poachers, which increases the marginalisation of the impoverished and promotes painful and recent memories of segregation: "because at the moment, in some places, if you see a uniform, they know, that ... you will get arrested, you will get thrown in the back of the car, because you are poaching. Because that is the anti-poaching unit. It is not necessarily the image that the parks board portrays, but it is the image that the anti-poaching unit portrays" (anonymous nature guide 08.06.2016, interview).

Again, we see a collision of values. The flagship animal of the park, the white and even rarer black rhino are in great danger (UNESCO 2003, online). The nature guide goes on to explain: "At the moment, if you are dealing with rhino poaching, it is all armed with AK-47s, you are not going to ask someone 'are you here to set snares or are you poaching the rhino', you are going to address it with the maximum force. To keep yourself alive. They are fighting a full-scale war against rhino-poaching. We are losing a rhino every 8 hours [in South Africa]" (anonymous nature guide 08.06.2016, interview). An intern at IWPA expands on this consequence: "To them, conservation is just apartheid. That is the main issue, because to them, they don't understand why you care about plants and animals more than our survival as people" (Lugagu 10.06.2016, interview).

Access to resources may prove to be a key solution to alleviate poverty in communities, however, there seems to be a general mistrust of local people as genuine custodians of the park: "When something starts working too well, you are going to start getting a thing called greed. Where what they are getting is not enough anymore and that is where you are going to have to draw the line. This is how much you are getting and that's it" (anonymous nature guide 08.06.2016, interview). Further, "[People] would never be able to do it in a sustainable way. There are too many people. The park, I can promise you, if they do open the park for people to use resources, the park would be shut down in a week, guaranteed. The exception is the Bhangazi ladies gathering the grasses and reeds. But using other things, it is basically treated the same as rhino poaching. It is not allowed to be done, but it still gets done. Once people feel like they can get money from something, they will come at night, they will come whenever they can, if they can steal it, they will steal it. Sustainable use could actually be a win-win for everyone here, but a small few ruin it" (anonymous tour guide at Heritage Tours 07.06.2016, interview).

Any interference is seen as contravening the international values that are crucial to the world heritage site status. The principal values are to ensure that the combination of fluvial, marine and Aeolian processes, initiated in the early Pleistocene, are ongoing, there is significant diversity of African biota, including vivid natural spectacles such as nesting turtles, maintain the shifting salinity, and that the area remains geographically diverse with superlative vistas (UNESCO 2003, online). As mentioned before, the wetland soil is fragile, and tour guides and scientists interviewed both heavily pressed upon the constantly changing soil conditions as a threat to the landscape, the status of the heritage site even (nature guide 08.06.2016, interview; honorary Ezemvelo officer 09.06.2016, interview; Ezemvelo staff member 09.06.2016, interview), which can be retracted by UNESCO. This is linked directly to international conservation bodies: "Your estuaries are very, very important. They are the most sensitive ecological area that you can have, [particularly] the estuary mouth. Because there's a lot of fish species in the ocean, that use estuaries as nurseries. Now, because estuaries are so sensitive, it has become a very big controversial issue with a lot of conservancy organisations, conservation bodies, and Greenpeace and so forth" (nature guide 08.06.2016, interview). It seems imperative that IWPA identify vulnerable families, differentiate between subsistence poachers and commercial poachers, identify fertile soil for small grower schemes and secure funding for sustainable use and cultivation as a genuine way forward. Otherwise the 'active' substantive right of the use of natural resources as enshrined in section 24 of the Bill of Rights is obsolete.

4.2 People's Active Procedural Rights

Procedural rights also play a key role in the development of a RBA to conservation, since they are essential for supporting as well as ensuring the actual implementation of and compliance with substantive rights. The most pressing right for inclusion appears to be that of public participation. South Africans enjoy a right to participate, indeed the Constitutional Assembly Public Participation Programme was created to involve South African people to participate in the writing of the Constitution, to create "A People's Government, A People's Voice" (Parliament of the Republic of South Africa 2001, online). However, as one St Lucia resident remarked: "We have the greatest Constitution in the world, but they are not using it" (anonymous honorary Ezemvelo officer 09.06.2016, interview).

4.2.1 Public Participation

The *Protected Areas Act* seeks to provide for public participation and cooperative governance in the establishment and management of protected areas. Since this only came into effect four years after the park was already created, it is not possible to apply this retroactively to the establishment of IWP. In Chapter 10 of the Constitution however, public administration bodies are required to "respond to people's needs and encourage the public to participate in policy-making." Further, "public administration must be accountable' and 'transparency must be fostered by providing the public with timely, accessible, and accurate information" (Chapter 10, Section 195 (1) (e)). There is no indication from interviews that there had been community level workshops, meetings, or consultations before the proclamation of the park (Ncube 03.06.2016, interview; anonymous librarian in St Lucia 08.06.2016, interview; anonymous waiter and trained nature guide 08.06.2016, interview; Lugagu 10.06.2016, interview). The St Lucia Black Landowners Association complained that they were not consulted about the renaming of the site to IWP for example (Ncube 03.06.2016, interview).

According to Section 41(1) and (2), those protected area management plans should include procedures for public participation and should contain the implementation of Community-Based Natural Resource Management where appropriate. However, the development of local management capacity remains discretionary (Sections 41 (1) and (2) and 41 (3)). The *Bhangazi Settlement Agreement* (Department of Land Affairs and the Community of the Former St Lucia Eastern Shores/ Bhangazi Beneficial Occupants and their District Descendants Deed of Settlement in terms of Section 14(3) read with Section 42D of the Restitution of Land Rights Act No.22 of 1994, dated 24 September 1999), mentioned earlier, allows for participation through a *Memorandum of Understanding* (KwaZulu-Natal Nature Conservation Board/ Claimant Community Memorandum of Understanding 5 October 1999). The settlement states that the community should be represented in its dealings with IWPA and, therefore, also be a member of the community trust which sits on the IWPA's Board. However, as Paterson notes, this does not give the Bhangazi community any voice in the de facto management of the park (Paterson 2011: 264). Further, in an interview with community members, they state their frustration with the trust and the governance structure: "If God had given us and the members of the trust the key to heaven we would have been denied entrance into heaven by the members of the trust. We would rather have kept heaven for ourselves" (Linden 2007, interview). The financial compensation is not appropriate for the community who insists that having access to resources would improve their livelihoods, which have deteriorated greatly since the memorandum came into force (ibid.).

For those in Dukuduku, the communities participate in the park by attending meetings under the traditional authorities. There are notable problems with traditional leadership at the community level and a feeling of misrepresentation and poor traditional governance. One Dukuduku resident complains that: "And we don't have a say. He is the inDuna, if he says this is it, then this is it." Community meetings are sporadically planned, "[it is] now and then. It is not like there is a schedule." This makes it difficult for people to plan to attend: "On Sundays, he used to call the meetings. But now no. Now he just tells us a day before. Because if people want to go to these meetings, they need to make a plan. Some people need to work, and some people want to go to the church. But they rotate the meetings so it is hard for people" (anonymous waiter and trained nature guide 08.06.2016, interview). Any meetings are arranged through area managers of the IWPA, who, according to several of those interviewed, are rarely available and difficult to contact (Ncube 03.06.2016, interview; waiter and trained nature guide 08.06.2016, interview; Lugagu 10.06.2016, interview). There is evidence that when people's needs are discussed in an open and transparent way solutions come. Herbert Mthembu, a former member of the IWPA board, said that as part of one local conservation planning phase, the people concerned were interviewed and their needs discussed and this was incorporated into implementation of the project, "we've had a very good response from people because they were consulted" (iSimangaliso News 2016, online). This shows that when local values and needs are identified, discussed, and solutions found, it can indeed be a win-win situation for both the IWPA and the community.

4.2.2 Right to Information

The IWPA practices good governance in terms of affording people their right to information. Chapter 2, Section 32 affords everyone a right of access to information held by the government and information which is required for the exercise or protection of any constitutional right (Section 32). The *Promotion of Access to Information Act 2* of 2000 regulates access to information held by public bodies. It imposes strict obligations on these bodies to provide access to certain types of information held by them and prescribes detailed access procedures (Section 14-32). Every four years, the IWPA publishes their forthcoming management plan. The latest version is the IWPA 2016 Management Plan, which is available in English in the St Lucia library. However, more could be done to disseminate this information. According to the local librarian, there are no further materials or information from the IWPA despite the fact that "People are very, very, very interested in the park. They come to the library to ask about the park. But I don't have any materials from the park. I just have this [refers to the IWPA 2016 management plan]. They brought this in February but it is difficult to read, the language is technical and it is in English" (anonymous librarian in St Lucia 08.06.2016, interview). When one drives around the park, particularly at the entrance gates to beaches, and visits the offices of IWPA and Ezemvelo, large colourful posters in English inform the viewer about rare species, provincial regulations, laws, and other important information. This information is purely informative and is simplified. According to the intern of IWPA, "You cannot bombard people with acts . . . the Protected Areas Act regulations, they are simplified to notices when you enter the park. All those things are not allowed in terms of the Protected Areas Act but we must put it as a notice and write it in simple English" (Lugagu 10.06.2016, interview). One feels that it would be part of good governance again to begin a dialogue with communities that discusses information emanating from both sides.

4.2.3 The Use of Traditional Knowledge

A missed opportunity for further work is in traditional conservation and the incorporation of traditional knowledge and fostering of cultural practices. Andrew Zaloumis himself discusses his wish to embrace traditional conservation. He discussed his mentor, a (then) 75-year-old Mshwayisa who taught him the term *Umuzi*, which is a term to describe the unity of man and nature, "a view of conservation informed by 800 years of traditional practices." The IWPA intern mentioned community conservation officers who travel to the communities to discuss conservation methods. However, some from the communities interviewed said that they have had no contact with such officers although they would like to make contact (Lugagu 10.06.2016, interview). Herbert Mthembu, former member of the IWP board, described the need for conservation education and the work of small scale community workshops with local people to teach those to refrain from cutting down trees in the swamp forest. Yet, there seems no actual impetus to work with the community conservation officers. One thing that is particularly striking on gathering information from local people is the wealth of knowledge, varying from nature guides to older community members, to conservationists. There seems to be a vacuum for fusing together all of this knowledge and creating a compendium of knowledge that could be used for capacity building on both sides of the impasse.

However, as one nature guide said, there is a general mistrust of Zulu practices from a conservationist's point of view. Something that may be insurmountable: "There's been a couple of studies and it's completely useless. Absolutely useless. I mean there are some things that do work, like if you cut yourself, there are particular types of spider webs that will stop the bleeding. There are some things that do work. But not … a great deal of them. What we learn in bush school, knowledge of the animals and trees and that sort of thing is what I use mostly. Like what Lee Gutteridge is teaching" (anonymous tour guide at Heritage Tours 07.06.2016, interview). Any fostering of cultural activities appears to be carried out purely for ecotourism purposes as seen in the example of the Veyane Cultural village in Khula village (ibid.) based on the model of the Shakaland Zulu cultural village, a tourism resort that was originally the set of the movie Shaka Zulu. Local residents admit that the culture is "made up" (sangoma in Mabibi beach 02.06.2016, interview) and part of a spectacle showcasing traditional ways of life. Local medical healers and sangomas supplement their income through performances for tourists and crafts made with the financial support of IWP, intended for a high-end market (sangoma in Mabibi beach 02.06.2016, interview; Govender 02.06.2016, interview). Since the world heritage site is a UNESCO site, perhaps more attention should be paid to the UNESCO mission statement: "People must rely on the power of intelligence to innovate, expand their horizons and sustain the hope of a new humanism. UNESCO exists to bring this creative intelligence to life; for it is in the minds of men and women that the defences of peace and the conditions for sustainable development must be built" (UNESCO 2016, online).

4.2.4 People as Passive Benefactors

However, rights must be recognised progressively and this may not happen overnight. As aforementioned, the goals of the IWP and the IWPA are to benefit the community through job creation, equity sharing, and capacity building (Govender 02.06.2016, interview). So, the 'benefits' and equitable partnerships model has arisen, one that gives benefits that range from concrete jobs, to financial income, and limited resource-use towards 'softer' benefits such as education and awareness programmes. With this in mind, the inclusion of people can be seen along a spectrum of power and participation (figure 6).

The IWPA has realised these goals progressively with successful and innovative programmes. Capacity building can be thought of in three spheres of activity: developing vocational skills, tapping into traditional knowledge, and fostering the cultural activities of a given region. Regarding vocational skills, the

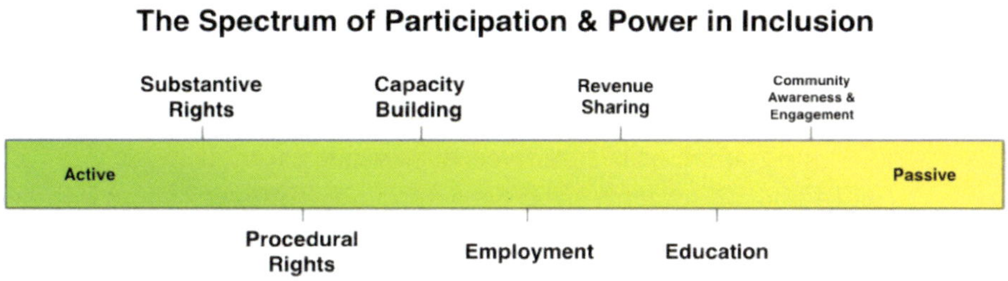

Figure 6: Spectrum of Power and Participation in People's Inclusion

Rural Enterprise Programme 2015/16 supported 94 small to medium enterprises: businesses in catering, events management, tuck-shops, construction, fashion design, and hair salons. A total of 6.8 million South African Rand was given out in 88 sub-grants. Further, programmes in entrepreneurship, tourism skills, and craft programmes have resulted in employment for local communities. An entrepreneur programme currently mentors and guides 80 existing entrepreneurs with plans to expand to take in 30 more. A tourism skills development course has trained 41 people in hospitality, 21 as assistant chefs, and 53 in the national qualification in tour guiding. Of these, 80% have found employment. A craft programme was supporting 360 crafters in development of products and linking their products to the high-end market, whilst an art programme was supporting 50 more in the same way. Empowerment education programmes allow young people in the area to educate themselves at a lower cost in tourism skills, which they pay for themselves. One local trainee describes how it encouraged him to work and save to afford the course: "I paid for this course myself, I worked for 3 months and kept the money, it was 3.700 Rand to do this course. I only earn 1.500 a month so for 3 months, I didn't buy anything at home just save, save, save" (waiter and trained nature guide 08.06.2016, interview).

According to the IWPA, in 2015/16, 1,547 temporary jobs were achieved and 15 permanent ones in alien plant cleaning, infrastructure, maintenance, and facilities management (Govender 02.06.2016, interview). The roads in IWP are maintained by Aqua Transport & Plant Hire (Pty) Ltd which provides jobs in road maintenance. Tourism is by far the largest provider of employment in the region and ecotourism is a central tenet of the IWP strategy. This has been successful in providing a limited number of jobs to households where breadwinners were needed (Dukuduku South Community Land Claims Board member 03.06.2016, interview; receptionist at uMkhuze Game Reserve 04.06.2016, interview; intern at IWPA 10.06.2016, interview). There are also several education programmes that offer training that can lead to jobs through IWPA. The Environmental Monitor programme trained 30 environmental monitors who will work at key ranger stations over the next three years from 2016 (Govender 02.06.2016, interview). A higher education programme was conceived for "creating tomorrow's CEO's and managers" (ibid.) and 77 students have been supported in total. There is a bursary programme and an internship programme, which host thirteen interns at the offices of IWPA, two of which have received permanent jobs. Nine interns have received one year contracts. This is especially important for an area where unemployment is high. Challenges remain however, with many locals angered by the fact that not all jobs go to local people (Dukuduku South Community Land Claims Board member 03.06.2016, interview; waiter and trained nature guide 08.06.2016, interview; intern at IWPA 10.06.2016, interview). Further 27.7% of the economically active population portrayed have been described in a government report as "discouraged work seekers" (UKDM 2014, online). This harsh reality was also mentioned by several locals, who see the high numbers of those receiving government welfare as a thoroughly negative factor frustrating progress in the region (tour guide at Heritage Tours 07.06.2016, interview; nature guide 08.06.2016, interview; honorary Ezemvelo officer 09.06.2016, interview).

Under the beneficiation agreement, the community sees a financial gain in the form of a community levy placed on ticket sales, an amount of 5 South African Rand is given to a community trust fund from each ticket sold. This trust is managed by traditional authorities and is directed toward community-based projects. In Khula village in Dukuduku for example, a health clinic providing free health care, a crèche, and a primary school were built (inDuna of Khula village 01.06.2016, interview). The *Bhangazi Settlement Agreement* also provides for a similar mechanism. However, challenges remain in the form of poor governance, lack of transparency, and actions which have not identified locals' needs. One Dukuduku resident complained: "We don't see the money, we just see the action, because we do not see how much money has gone into the account this month. He won't say 'this is the amount of money that we have', he would just call a meeting and say 'Ok guys we are going to build a crèche here.' He doesn't ask anybody what they think" (waiter and trained nature guide 08.06.2016, interview). Several community members were unable to identify positive changes that were made regarding the levy nor how it had been used (Dukuduku South Community Land Claims Board member 03.06.2016, interview; tour guide at Heritage Tours 07.06.2016, interview; waiter and trained nature guide 08.06.2016, interview; honorary Ezemvelo officer 09.06.2016, interview; intern at IWPA 10.06.2016, interview). Again, the principles of good governance, accountability, and transparency need to be implemented in line with Chapter 10 Section 195(1)(e) of the Constitution.

Education can be seen as a longer-term benefit with the goal of educating a new generation about the global value of conservation. As part of their environmental education and awareness programmes, the IWPA have held 25 hosted trips with 400 learners and 1.010 school field-trips, with ambitious plans to conduct further activities in the same vein for 2.000 learners. There are community awareness events held, six over 2015/16 and six more planned for the next year (Govender 02.06.2016, interview). These 'softer' benefits are a great initiative and of utmost importance for younger citizens in the area. The education centres around teach about a 'sense of place', which the Leon Commission identified as a key value when considering the denial of a mining license in the area (IWP 2016, online). Yet, one wonders if the education and awareness programmes could not be extended beyond art competitions and community events, and, rather, more geared toward learning about basic soil use, traditional knowledge, and sustainable cultivation techniques. It has been identified that this is sorely needed in at least one community: "They ... came to educate the children from school ... But they didn't come to tell people what they can do. I remember last year, I asked them to educate the people about how to save the wet area, where they can cultivate, where they cannot cultivate, which trees they can cut, which trees they must leave. But we are still waiting for them to come. Last year in March I asked, but they haven't come" (Dukuduku South Community Land Claims Board member 03.06.2016, interview).

5 Conclusion

By choosing a governance model that marries development and conservation, the IWPA is spearheading change that attempts to address the delicate balancing of goals mentioned in the introduction. It can be concluded that the RBA has been partially implemented in IWP and it certainly theoretically adheres to the rights that are enshrined in the post 1994 South Africa Constitution. The danger is, however, that the RBA is homogeneous and not heterogeneous. To the author, the RBA should be about asserting agency in a way that reflects the needs of the communities, and there should be an intelligent recognition of what that means. It has been shown that local people are positioned along a "spectrum of power and participation". Yet, sadly, the seemingly most active rights, the ones that offer the most potential for participation, are rendered positively inactive, through complex land management schemes that place conservation practices over local peoples' rights to tenure. The spectrum shows that local communities are seen as *stakeholders* not *rights holders*. Their interests, requirements, and wishes are seen contextually, alongside the myriad of other stakeholders in the region. Of course, rights must be recognised progressively, this is a slow process in a place which still bears the trauma of apartheid and sees abject poverty. The equitable approach offers a bridge towards that realisation. The equitable approach, however, requires good governance as a key component and considers community cooperation of the utmost importance. In order to move beyond the mistrust generated in IWP amongst people, it is essential to begin with transparent local governance structures and a needs-based approach, supplemented by the identification of local knowledge and values. This approach should not only identify the rights of people but should also identify *their* needs according to *them*. Despite their obligations under international human rights law, South Africa does not recognise the legal status of local communities nor their rights to their lands, territories, and resources. The different local groups should be identified as sub-communities who are not a singular homogenised unit.

To return to the concept of the coloniality of conservation law and the interventions into the four themes, namely law, control over land, ethics/values, and knowledge, these motifs provide ways forward. By recognising the self-determination of any local groups that hold a particular connection to a body of resources within the park, true and meaningful changes can be made to the cultural dominance of positive law, land use, international ethics, and occidental knowledge. The four motifs could be used as anchors from which to explore counter-hegemonic approaches: law by allowing for the study and practice of traditional laws and conservation practices; control over land by exploring sustainable land use methods, such as harvesting and cultivation, as a real solution by identifying locations and possibilities for growing food in small grower zones with UNESCO funding for the small growers schemes; ethics and knowledge by identifying local ethical approaches and value-driven activities and by developing a compendium of traditional knowledge that can be taught and used in conjunction with conventional scientists and researchers working in the park. This could be done in partnership with Ezemvelo and possible international partners, such as external third level education institutes. Then, perhaps, can the *World Heritage Convention*, in its own words, truly have "a function in the life of a community" (WHC, Article 5).

The Nature of Conservation: An Inquiry into the Practices of In- and Exclusion of Local Communities in the Management and Benefits of iSimangaliso Wetland Park

Christian Sterkl

1 Introduction

Nature and wildlife conservation are without a doubt some of the most pressing issues of our time. The perpetual destruction of 'natural resources' and consequently the eradication of different species of wildlife and biodiversity, that accompany the current extractive mode of production, call for a worldwide strategy to try and save as many of these endangered ecosystems as possible from the seemingly ever-expanding destructive forces that are the modern capitalist system. The rise of such organisations as the World Wildlife Fund, Greenpeace, International Union for the Conservation of Nature (IUCN), and the like are owed largely to the need to defend human and animal life as well as the planet itself from profit-hungry corporations trying to minimise their costs while maximising their profits, thereby externalising the cost of the destruction of the environment. It is left to governments and private organisations to deal with the problems resulting from such practices. Governments react to this mostly by implementing fines and pollution taxes to keep big corporations in check.

Another means to save 'the environment' and wildlife from falling victim to unsustainable practices is the setting-aside of large tracts of land for the sole purpose of creating a pristine habitat for animals and plant life. Such areas have been put aside in many countries around the world in the last two centuries. Simple enough, the common observer would comment, but in reality, it proves much more complicated: Setting aside potentially productive land for seemingly unproductive uses clashes with the idea of (exponential) economic growth in a capitalist world system. Every nation, no matter under which political leadership, depends by reason of state on economic growth to sustain its very existence. So, the notion of wildlife conservation seemingly for the sake of 'saving nature' has to be questioned and analysed in these problematic terms to begin with. Furthermore, one has to take a close look at the history of protected area nature conservation in order to understand its practices today. For centuries now, vital land has been declared 'protected', which consequently bares the questions: Protected from whom and for what purpose?

The objective of this paper is to delve deeper into the challenges of nature conservation within a neoliberal capitalist system and to highlight what the mainstream discourse of nature conservation tends to hide, namely the potential effects of protected area nature conservation for the local inhabitants living in and around such conservatories. To this end, the paper will focus on iSimangaliso Wetland Park (or IWP), a national park in the north-eastern KwaZulu-Natal coastal region of South Africa which is proclaimed to combine nature conservation with social development through inclusive policies towards local people and adjacent communities.

The research presented in the following paper is a socio-economic exploration of iSimangaliso Wetland Park drawing on significant literary sources as well as empirical research carried out over several weeks in iSimangaliso Wetland Park in June of 2016. With the intention of better understanding and explaining how nature conservation influences human organisation in its immediate surroundings we set out to collect data on-site.

iSimangaliso Wetland Park makes for a perfect example in this regard because it markets itself as a new model of conservation that includes local people in its management and its profits. Thus, the question arises whether the wetland park stands the test in terms of land reformation, land claim politics, democratic values concerning decision-making processes, and social transformation in line with the big promises made by the African National Congress (hereafter ANC), the first democratically elected governing party of the New South Africa after roughly 350 years of colonial and apartheid rule. This paper examines social justice and benefits surrounding the wetland park and will consequently try to deconstruct and present the power relations in the field of state operated nature conservation and its effects on local communities.

The key objective is thus to provide insight into the complex social and institutional structure of the wetland park with the intent to answer the following research question: Can social transformation and development – as promised by the ANC – be achieved through the inclusive policy and benefit system, as applied by the state-operated iSimangaliso Wetland Park management, within an inherently unjust system?

This paper will show that nature conservation is quite the controversial subject, rife with all kinds of contradictions. It will analyse the benefits to and effect on the local communities tied into the wetland park and ask the questions, whether this is an adequate approach to nature conservation, and if it is compatible with the need to protect and empower the formerly disadvantaged communities of South Africa. Furthermore, it is important to look at alternative strategies that would allow for the prospect of social empowerment, transformation, and consequently justice. One of the strategies important in understanding institutionalised social change is Black Economic Empowerment (hereafter BEE). It is the largest governmental social strategy to scale that has economic empowerment of formerly disadvantaged communities and individuals as its prime goal.

Other forms of democratic decision-making processes are also important to social transformation. In this regard, one has to analyse the inclusion of local community members in important decision-making processes in terms of development and management strategies. Concerning iSimangaliso Wetland Park this means a close examination of its management board and the opinions of the local people with regard to their inclusion in its processes and procedures. Still, it is important to keep in mind that nature conservation with all its benefits and drawbacks must – for a holistic understanding of the topic – be viewed within larger systems such as the nation state or even a neoliberal world market. That is why this paper will provide insight into the local as well as global politics that shape(d) social reality in South Africa today. On the one hand, this means analysing South Africa's transformation from apartheid rule into a democracy, and on the other, understanding how neoliberal market logic influences nature conservation. But before delving into the specifics, the following section will provide a short overview of the history of nature conservation in Southern Africa and its inherent problems.

2 Historical Approach to Conservation in South Africa

To fully grasp the problems surrounding nature and wildlife conservation in South Africa and consequently the challenges the iSimangaliso Wetland Park faces, it is important to understand the historical events and developments that shaped today's conservation policies. To study the history of nature conservation in the modern sense, one has to look to 19th century North America for clues, where in 1872 the famous Yellowstone National Park was conceived. For the purpose of bringing tourists, investment, and infrastructure to the then undeveloped West of the United States, the Yellowstone region was advertised as a natural wonder of unparalleled beauty – pristine and unspoiled by man. The fact that the land was inhabited and used for subsistence by local people for centuries or millennia remains mostly ignored or forgotten (Adams/ McShane 1996: xvi; King 2009: 3) as the indigenous communities were relocated to designated Indian reservations.

The idea of a necessity for conservation in Africa started shortly after the first expeditions into the more or less undiscovered interior of the 'dark continent'. While the African coastlines were easily accessible by ships, and loading resources, including slaves, was efficient, the interior was largely avoided due to its treacherous attributes. Wild animals and barbaric warrior tribes, claim Adams and McShane (1996: 9 pp.), were feared and avoided. For these reasons expeditions to the interior didn't start until the late 19th century and were of little interest to merchants or the colonising powers. In search of sponsors and to raise public interest in funding their highly expensive journeys to uncover the mysteries of inland Africa, adventure-seeking expeditioners began to create fantastic stories and images about this region. Stories of never before seen natural wonders, magnificent landscapes, and exotic animals came to light during these times. "They communicated their impressions to an eager audience in Europe, and the language that they used helped create the myth of wild Africa" (Adams/ McShane 1996: 8).

Just as the Yellowstone National Park, the 'myth of wild Africa' and its untamed, unspoiled wilderness was seeded in the minds of Europeans and Americans at a time where nature was starting to be romanticised by the upper classes and scholars due to the rise of the industrial cities, the mechanisation of life in general, and the acknowledged ill effects of state-capitalism (ibid.: 6 pp.). Creating a protected 'untouched' nature sanctuary made financial sense because of the newly discovered value of so called 'original nature'. The romantic movement of the late 18th and early 19th centuries gave rise to the idea of the intrinsic 'value of nature'. The fact that people didn't fit into this image of 'original nature' is owed to the division between nature and culture – or nature and humans – that was established in early modernity and has since been perpetuated in the minds of 'western people' (Nustad 2015: 17 pp.).

In line with these developments, it was the big scale hunting trips of the Victorian elite that gave rise to the idea and need to preserve wild animals from extinction. While game reserves were established to keep enough animals alive for Europeans to hunt, colonial game laws forbade local people to kill their traditional food sources hence damaging their entire culture and wildlife heritage (Adams/ McShane 1996: 29). Furthermore, because the killing of wild animals was now limited to Whites, the villagers living in close proximity of these protected areas, faced harsh punishments for defending themselves and their crop against protected animals. Hunting was outlawed in many cases and strictly forbidden in protected wildlife areas: The original hunters, whose survival depended on these animals, became poachers "by the stroke of a pen', legally to be 'shot on sight" (Adams/ McShane 1996: 229, 234). In effect, national parks are areas protected by the government against its own people in order to keep them attractive to outsiders thereby maintaining the nature/culture divide (Zips-Mairitsch 2013).

3 Political and Economic Environment

Nature conservation today is, as we have seen, a product of the romantic notions of Europeans and Americans derived from the beginning of the industrial revolution over two centuries ago, coupled with the practice of land appropriation for European purposes worldwide. "What started as violent racialized dispossession of African property and personhood in the context of colonial rule [...] continues to starkly influence affairs and relations to this day: conservation continues to produce the aesthetics, symbols, and fables of white privilege" (Hughes, cited in Büscher 2013: 11).

Or, as Robert Nelson states in his paper "Environmental Colonialism: Saving Africa from Africans":

> "The greatest current efforts to 'save' Africa are associated with contemporary environmentalism. The results have not been as devastating as the experience of slavery, yet they have often served Western interests and goals much more than the interests of ordinary Africans. In some cases, local populations have been displaced and impoverished in order to create national parks and to serve other conservation objectives. Under the banner of saving the African environment, Africans in the last half century have been subjected to a new form of 'environmental colonialism."' (2003: 1, online)

Although, in the last three decades, with rise and popularity of the idea of 'sustainable development', there have been multiple efforts to include people in nature conservation. However, the benefits are often outweighed by the drawbacks to the majority of the communities (King 2007: 208 pp.; 2009: 3). To understand this lack of support for the impoverished rural communities by the South African government, it is crucial to reflect on the general 'failure' of the ANC to achieve the social transformation it initially envisioned after the end of the apartheid regime. To this end it pays to consider Marvin Harris' concept of 'cultural materialism' (1980). This research strategy brings to light underlying political and economic infrastructures that can be used to determine power relations within a social system that will be utilised to hinder social change in order to keep a powerful elite in its preferred position.

In the context of South Africa this is a highly important point to be further analysed in order to understand why the proposed and desired social change – or straight up socialist revolution, as Nelson Mandela and his fellow ANC members proclaimed (Law 2010: 317) – didn't pan out. The underlying infrastructure and powerful elite Harris talks about, was made up of a white minority that held almost all the land and means of production in the apartheid regime and, consequently, was able to accumulate wealth through the exploitation of oppressed Black and 'coloured' members of South African society. The abolition of the apartheid regime in 1994 would have meant the end of this elite's oppressive reign if it wasn't for their ability to resist social change by means of economic strength and cunning.

3.1 Lost in Transformation

After the end of apartheid, the political atmosphere in South Africa was filled with socialist/communist rhetoric. While Mandela definitely used his position as head of state to try and make right the wrongs of apartheid, it is important to critically assess the extent to which he truly lived up to his reputation. To this end it is useful to examine the underlying structures and power relations that ended up tying his hands in terms of nationalising the "heights of the economy" (Kasrils 2013: 3, online) and redistributing land to all South Africans, making "land a citizen's right". Ronnie Kasrils, a long-time member of the ANC who left the party in 2012, states that Mandela and his economic staff didn't pull through with any kind of nationalisation of the economy or even the redistribution of wealth due to the fact that they were "impressed with what the private sector could do for the young nation's economy." This led them to a change in policy from "growth through redistribution" to "redistribution through growth" (ibid.). "Our initial optimism", writes Kasrils, "overlooked the tenacity of the international capitalist system. From 1991 to 1996 the battle for the ANC's soul got under way, and was eventually lost to corporate power: we were entrapped by the neoliberal economy – or, as some today cry out, we 'sold our people down the river'" (ibid.).

Stellenbosch economist Solomon Terreblanche, who has done half a century worth of research on poverty and structural injustice in South Africa, maintains that Mandela and his staff were threatened and extorted into maintaining private sector liberal market principles with threats of economic stagnation and decline if they were to socialise the economy (ibid. 2013, online). He writes about secret nightly meetings between Mandela and South African business mogul Harry Oppenheimer, who pressed for private sector expansion rather than redistribution of wealth: "Present were South Africa's mineral and energy leaders, the bosses of US and British companies with a presence in South Africa – and young ANC economists schooled in western economics. They were reporting to Mandela, and were either outwitted or frightened into submission by hints of the dire consequences for South Africa should an ANC government prevail with what were considered ruinous economic policies" (ibid.). They have succeeded, argues Terreblanche, since wealth, land, and crucial industry stayed in the hands of the white elite (ibid). Mandela's persuasion into liberal market ideology can also be found in Patrick Bond's work on the impact of IMF and World Bank influence on South African politics, where he writes that "Nelson Mandela was periodically fêted in Washington during the early and mid 1990s by World Bank and IMF leaders" (Bond 2003: 69).

Rather than change the countries' economic system as promised, Kasrils and Terreblanche state that the newly elected government sold out its people by adopting neoliberalism as the nation's recipe for economic growth and attracting foreign investment. This wasn't necessarily only by choice, but also because the New South Africa took on a 380 million dollar loan from the IMF on top of the already existing multi-billion dollar debt to the World Bank accumulated by the apartheid government, the National Party (ibid.: 68). Such loans always entail so called structural adjustment programmes, which serve as an insurance for the lenders to make sure the borrowing country is in line with the most profitable economic strategy – which, in this case, was state operated neoliberalism. "These conditions included not only items from the classic structural-adjustment menu (lower import tariffs, cuts in state spending, large cuts in public-sector wages, etc.)', writes Bond, 'but also informal but intense pressure by IMF managing director Michel Camdessus to reappoint both finance minister Derek Keys and Reserve Bank governor Chris Stals, the two main stalwarts of National Party neo-liberalism" (ibid.).

With regards to this IMF loan, Ronnie Kasrils stated:

> "All means to eradicate poverty, which was Mandela's and the ANC's sworn promise to the 'poorest of the poor', were lost in the process. Nationalisation of the mines and heights of the economy as envisaged by the Freedom charter was abandoned. The ANC accepted responsibility for a vast apartheid-era debt, which should have been cancelled. A wealth tax on the super-rich to fund developmental projects was set aside, and domestic and international corporations, enriched by apartheid, were excused from any financial reparations. Extremely tight budgetary obligations were instituted that would tie the hands of any future governments; obligations to implement a free-trade policy and abolish all forms of tariff protection in keeping with neo-liberal free trade fundamentals were accepted." (Kasrils 2013: 3, online)

Intended as a tool for rapid economic growth, implemented by the United States and Britain in order to catch up with post WWII France and Germany, neoliberal ideology holds that the role of the state be reduced to that of a 'watchdog', protecting private property rights (Büscher 2013: 12), and letting the economy be guided by laissez faire free market principles. In other words: Relieve the state from its obligation to protect its citizens against exploitative capitalist ventures for the sake of economic growth. With regard to social transformation and social justice, it is quite telling what the founder of neoliberal theory, Friedrich Hayek, had to say about such ideals: "The notion of social justice is totally useless in a capitalist economic system" (Hayek, cited in Pellar 2000, online).

The IMF's and World Bank's structural adjustment policies, with regard to South African social development, have been highly controversial, argues Bond: "By all accounts, World Bank projects were not aimed at furthering the causes of racial equality, economic justice and ecological sustainability but, on the contrary, promoted white-controlled infrastructure for the benefit of extractive, exploitative white economic interests and relatively wealthy white consumers" (ibid. 2003: 62). He further points out that "[t]he IMF/World Bank agenda has been – and continues to be – disastrous for South Africa, for it imposes eurocentric notions of development and modernity; downgrades democracy; serves transnational corporate and banking interests above all else; values people and nature less than (narrowly defined) economic growth; hurts women, disabled people and the vulnerable in society far more than other social sectors; amplifies an already exceptionally unequal distribution of wealth; and often leads to economic disaster, even on its own limited terms" (Bond 2003: 55).

The influence of the World Bank and the IMF on South African politics and policies show that social transformation, as envisioned by the ANC and the South African public, faced structural challenges from the outset. In Kasrils words, it was a "Faustian pact selling out South Africa's poorest" (Kasrils 2013: 1, online).

3.2 Neoliberal Nature Conservation

To analyse the benefit system of the state operated iSimangaliso Wetland Park, it is important to understand how neoliberal market logic is being used in the management of what researchers have termed 'Neoliberal Nature', or 'Nature^{TM}Inc.' (e.g. Büscher/ Dressler/ Fletcher 2014).

Bram Büscher (2013), who has done extensive research on 'neoliberal conservation' in South Africa, argues that in neoliberal capitalism, where the role of the state is limited to that of a watchdog over private property privilege and enterprise, conservation has to be framed in "neoliberalism's operational logic: competition and commodification" (ibid.: 12 pp.). The discourse about conservation is, in effect, not a political one, but one of advertising. His main point is "that in a neoliberal political economy tensions between material realities and reified representations are political opportunities that must be exploited to gain competitive advantage. [...] In order to gain legitimacy, credibility, and support in the conservation marketplace, actors must exploit the cracks between constructions and realities of complex and contradictory socio-ecological dynamics" (ibid.: 5).

If nature becomes a commodity and enters into a competitive value-system, it has to play by the rules of basic marketing. This leads us to the second point Büscher argues: The discourse about conservation is being upheld by consensus, antipolitics, and marketing, rather than based on facts, political debate, and scientific findings (ibid.: 18). Consensus is a necessity if you want to legitimise such grand protected areas as national parks. Yet, since there are so many contradictions surrounding their implementation the demand for consensus becomes greater. Here, Büscher names three political courses to "try and regain control over governance processes: actually creating consensus, making people believe there is consensus, or positing consensus as a discursive umbrella to forge through particular political agendas" (ibid.). The perception of consensus on the matter of nature conservation is vitally important to keep the agenda in motion unquestioned. And as Goldman and Papson observed:

> "In remarkable synchronicity, the sustainability crowd and the neoliberal development crowd have united to remake nature in the South, transforming vast areas of community-managed uncapitalized lands into transnationally regulated zones for commercial logging, pharmaceutical bio-prospecting, export oriented cash cropping, megafauna preservation and elite ecotourism." (2006: 9)

The second parameter of Büscher's analysis, antipolitics, means "the political way of doing away with politics", denying actual politics, which he defines as "the mediation and contestation of different interests and power struggles" (Büscher 2013: 20 pp.). This, as will be shown in the following section, is a problem found regarding the restrictive policies of the iSmangaliso Park Board towards local communities. Büscher further describes the four main forms of antipolitics used in the conservation discourse as "instrumental, amoral, moral, and aesthetic antipolitics" (ibid.: 21). Instrumental, meaning that all decisions "be made by technocratic experts and based on rational cost-benefit analyses" not taking "political resistance as serious, as this must stem from irrational ignorance" (ibid.). Amoral antipolitics means the "privatization of the public domain" as is inherent to neoliberalism, where people are conceived as utility-maximisers, acting solely on economic rationale. With moral antipolitics, claims Büscher, "material norms' replace 'procedural normative arrangements, thereby stifling the political debate", while in aesthetic antipolitics it is the replacement of words with "images, theater and drama" that harms the political process (ibid.).

Modern conservationism has to be portrayed in these antipolitical terms, says Büscher, as not to be challenged on the international conservation stage about the enormous contradictions it gives rise to. The truth would be less romantic since "[f]eeding the emotional needs of Europeans and Americans on the backs of the rural African poor is not a pretty sight" (Nelson 2003: 11, online). Instead, large parts of the world are sectioned off and remade to foster the fantasies of Western (and other) tourists. Nature conservation is offered up as an "easy consumption-based solution to complex socio-ecological problems" as Büscher et al. (2012: 18) put it in their "Synthesized Critique of Neoliberal Biodiversity Conservation". Collectively, we buy into the idea that environmental exploitation can be offset by nature conservancies. In fact, as Büscher et al. explain: "[S]uch trade-offs are portrayed as conservation success stories and benefit conservation NGOs, tour companies, local and national elites, and the agencies, foundations, and international financial institutions that fund them" (ibid.: 20).

So, as we move on to the case study of iSimangaliso Wetland Park it will be important to keep these broader neoliberal and (a)political processes and their direct impact on conservation initiatives in mind. As the research presented in this paper will demonstrate, the people connected to iSimangaliso Wetland Park are affected by exactly these market mechanisms. Büscher et al. write: "The peoples thereby affected become constrained to participate in and benefit from neoliberal conservation initiatives to the extent that they accept associated opportunities and compensation only in particular economic terms" (ibid.: 24).

As anthropologists Knut Nustad and Melissa Hansen, who have done extensive research on iSimangaliso Wetland Park, point out, significant problems stem from the idea of commodifying nature as well as neoliberal market principles as a managerial strategy. Nustad concludes: "The main problem is [. . .] that conservation goals are inherently contrary to capitalist expansion under neoliberalism" (Nustad 2015: 156). Hansen (2014: 34) sees this as especially problematic, since she holds that "neoliberal economic policies prevalent in South Africa – based upon the New Growth Path (NGP) framework – are doomed to failure in meeting the needs of the majority of the population." She argues that "neoliberal policies, when played out on the ground, are fundamentally harmful to poor people, diminishing human development, and ultimately exacerbating poverty. Measures to address poverty should directly target human development, if they are to be successful" (ibid.). Poverty alleviation cannot be achieved through neoliberal practices, according to Jo Littler, since "neoliberal capitalism relies on a disparity between rich and poor" (Littler, cited in Hansen 2011: 29).

4 iSimangaliso Wetland Park as a New Model of Conservation?

It is within the context of these inherent problems of nature conservation that the iSimangaliso Wetland Park has to be viewed. The 'official version' of discourse regarding the conservancy has it, that the inclusive management policies, namely the notion of a 'park for the people' (Scott et al. 2012: 4), and "benefits beyond boundaries" (iSimangaliso News & Info 2009), are beneficial to all stakeholders: Conservationists will have this 'biodiversity jewel' preserved, private sector business can invest in the development of tourist based infrastructure, which yields large amounts of revenue tax along with territorial control to the state, and brings general development and jobs to the impoverished region through ecotourism. In iSimangaliso's own words: "[O]ver the past ten years there has been a detailed and comprehensive process underway to protect, conserve and manage its resources for the benefit of all South Africans, in general, and, in particular, the communities living in and around the iSimangaliso Wetland Park" (ibid.).

At a first glance, this would fit nicely with the poverty-reduction, empowerment, and development strategies introduced by the post-apartheid government, the ANC. And while there are a number of strategies that include local people in the benefits of this world heritage site, critical studies and our own research on the topic reveal a different reality. Knut Nustad (2015) has identified some critical points that have resulted from the contradictions of what he calls 'conservation nature'. The argument is based on questioning the division of 'society' and 'nature' as two opposed realms. Nustad sees this division as stemming from the romantic turn in Europe around the time of the industrial revolution, where nature was turned into a productive asset on the one side (productive nature) and – due to its rapid disappearance for that same reason – into a commodity (consumption nature) on the other. This newly developed appreciation for nature by the educated upper (and later middle) classes led to the notion that pure nature had to be rid of any human inhabitation (ibid.: 17 pp.). Indigenous peoples living in such newly declared conservation areas had to be removed in order to – ironically – modify 'nature' in a way where it appeared yet unmodified and unspoiled by humans (ibid.).

This notion of apartness, Nustad argues, is what led to the unsustainable appropriation and hence destruction of nature in the first place (ibid.). How, he asks, can the same idea of 'humans apart from nature' – in this case nature without humans – be a legitimate solution to the problem? Especially since this question has to be asked in the context of a society that doesn't necessarily share these western romanticised notions about nature (ibid.: 21). In an interview with David Coplan, of Witwatersrand University in Johannesburg, he stated in this regard that "a lot of African people don't like wild animals and don't see what this big conservation thing is necessarily about" (Coplan 27.6.2016, interview). He then further elaborates:

> "I always tend to joke with my African friends about their general dislike for animals. They don't care for them. To us, we think a lion is from Disney Land, you know we jump out of the car and go and have our picture taken with the lion, but it's going to eat you. They are probably right about that. But you know modern time comes and people are getting more to understand it, including those who are not English speaking. They are beginning to see the logic of using live animals as a resource rather than pieces of them" (ibid.)

Or, as one guard of an entrance control gate to the natural beauty that is iSimangaliso Wetland Park put it: "The park is beautiful for you, but not for us."

Nustad argues that the 'fences and fines' approach to conservation has to be questioned as a whole. While the iSimangaliso management assures an inclusive policy towards local communities, conservation goals and sustaining local people's livelihood through access to natural resources and farm land inside and in close proximity to these (arbitrary) borders seem to be incompatible (Nustad 2015: 29).

The fact that iSimangaliso Wetland Park is sold as such an untouched wildlife sanctuary, automatically negates the presence of people living inside its borders in a way that would enable them to use their natural surroundings according to their subsistence necessities or even cultural means: "Conservation projects give priority to biodiversity conservation – often understood as protecting nature from the impact of people, indigenous or otherwise" (ibid.). iSimangaliso Wetland Park is no exception in this regard. While the official decree is a development trajectory based on ecotourism that integrates "the conservation of World Heritage with poverty alleviation and local economic development, through private ecotourism" (Hansen 2014: i), the parks management plan prioritises the conservation of nature. In fact, when we spoke to Nerosha Govender, manager of development and planning for iSimangaliso Wetland Park, she estimated that the allocation of their available resources is split 70 to 30 percent between nature conservation and socio-economic development.

Thus, the question of whether a profit-oriented establishment like iSimangaliso Wetland Park can meet its well-intentioned social obligations within the context of South Africa's poverty alleviation and empowerment programmes while at the same time catering to nature lovers' romantic desires for untouched nature – which is, after all, the engine that drives nature conservatories – remains. The following sections provide an in-depth analysis of the implementation and effects of the wetland park's empowerment and benefit stratagem.

4.1 Nature Conservation versus Subsistence in iSimangaliso Wetland Park

One of the key issues for the local people in and around iSimangaliso Wetland Park are the difficulties they face in attaining access to natural resources, such as game, fish, and trees used for building or traditional medicine. Under the Protected Areas Act the development of the land, construction on it, and farming of it are prohibited unless written consent is given (NEMA 2004: 42). However, even if such permits are obtained, they are always limited to very strict and specific terms, quantities, and times. This, understandably, angers local people, especially as they witness mostly white visitors to the park doing much more damage to the area (Nustad 2015: 29). When we spoke with our informants it was clear that the restrictive regulations enforced by the iSimangaliso Wetland Park Authority were not a welcome change:

> "For our people, if you don't get a chance to go to college or university there is still this belief that we own the environment. [. . .] But if you come and say 'Okay, you need to obtain a permit to fish', then you are perceived as someone who is restricting them to have access to natural resources. But these are not iSimangaliso rules, it is national legislation, but it was not enforced before. So, we are sent by the national government to enforce the law. Now that law is seen as iSimangaliso rules." (anonymous tour guide 08.06.2016, interview)

Today, most of iSimangaliso Wetland Park is fenced off and the access to its natural resources is regulated, be it through strict prohibition or under the guise of sustainability, as is the case, for instance, with the incema plant. This sought-after resource, used in the production of sleeping mats and the like, only grows inside iSimangaliso Wetland Park, as was explained to us:

> "So for such resources you cannot just say 'you can come and harvest whenever you want. [. . .] So what we do, we have open season for it, like once a year, they come and harvest. [. . .] So in that way they see that we are not saying 'no, we don't want you to use the resources', but we are saying 'let's use the resources, but in a sustainable manner'." (ibid.)

In what seems to be a perpetuation of the idea that Africa is in need of being saved from Africans, the concept of sustainability is being used against these communities.

From a business point of view, it is understandable that iSimangaliso Wetland Park, as a state operated for-profit ecotourism venture aiming at economic growth and development through private sector investment, has to assure maintenance of a 'product' tourists are willing to consume. If nature becomes a commodity and enters into a competitive value system, it has to play by the rules of basic marketing. In the case of iSimangaliso Wetland Park the product is a sustainable, healthy, and diverse ecosystem, making it glaringly obvious which interest groups and demands are being met by these regulations. Hansen challenges the concept of unaltered, uninhabited nature for conservation by pointing out that "[p]rotected areas, conventionally understood as those areas with a minimal human presence and a limited history of alteration can lead to the foreclosure of future land use options, with potentially significant economic opportunity costs, and substantial negative effects on local people. "There is a strong concern", she goes on to say, "that global efforts to maintain biodiversity are in conflict with those to reduce poverty" (Hansen 2014: 4). Or, as Nustad puts it, "empowerment, participation, ownership, and good governance" are nothing more than "empty catch-all phrases" (Nustad 2015: 165), which simply fit the new conservation paradigm of including people in nature conservation.

However, the human world will always find ways to encroach the natural world if they are divided along these extreme lines: "Nature, carefully carved out, fenced and policed, is subject to forces that insist on making it part of the social", effectively leading Nustad to question:

> "With what right do we continue to impose a separation of the natural and the social on rural landscapes? With what right do we restrict access to these areas to those who can afford to pay to enter them so that they can satisfy their yearnings for pure wilderness and untouched natures? With what right do we police and sometimes kill those who transgress the enactments?" (ibid. 2015: 153)

4.2 Nature Conservation and Dispossession in iSimangaliso Wetland Park

Nustad, who partook in many sessions and meetings with members of the affected communities for his research, witnessed great dissatisfaction among many of the members, who mainly perceive such "conservation policies [...] as unjustified interventions and unfunded restrictions on peoples' legitimate access to resources" (ibid.: 145). This dissatisfaction came up during our conversations with locals, as well. To those who rely on resources from the area, it is apparent that this enclosed conservancy is surrounded by an air of apartheid power relations:

"The main challenge is the way conservation was introduced in our country at large. Because we cannot ignore the fact that people were forcefully removed for conservation. [...] So now people feel that conservation only cares about trees, animals, it doesn't care about the survival of people. So that is the main issue, a sensitive topic to people. Especially in this area, because we are operating in an area where people were forcefully removed by the apartheid government for the sake of conservation. So now you need to make people understand that conservation is important. To them, conservation is just, it is apartheid." (Lugagu 10.06.2016, interview)

To these communities, Nustad affirms, "conservation is merely the latest incarnation of a long series of arguments used to justify their dispossession" (Nustad 2015: 146). This is especially devastating since by law most of the land in question (82% of the entire park) has been handed back to them in land restorations of formerly dispossessed people after the end of apartheid in 1994. While conducting our research it was recurrently confirmed that the relationships between all parties involved in land restoration within iSimangaliso Wetland Park were tense and communication limited, especially, as Nerosha Govender indicated to us, in the cases of those communities still inhabiting areas within park grounds and those communities who lived in and around the highly contested Dukuduku forest.

For over a century the Dukuduku area "has been characterised by forced removals, and by 1998, various governments had relocated people living in the Dukuduku forest area at least four times over the century for a diverse set of land use purposes" (Ngema 2009: 57 pp.). After the Restitution legislation passed in 1994 many of those dispossessed over the years saw an opportunity to reclaim their land. However, since filing an official restitution claim in the late 1990s, the inhabitants of the Dukuduku area have experienced continued persecution by a state that alleges the occupation of the Dukuduku forest is illegal (ibid.: 58). "But", as Siybane Ncube, a board member of the Dukuduku land claim committee, told us "the people refused [to leave] and they used to fight. The government sent soldiers and police and securities. But they failed to move the people" (Ncube 03.06.2016, interview). He explained that a ruling of the High Court of South Africa mandated the inclusion of the land claimants of the Dukuduku forest area in negotiations with iSimangaliso's Wetland Park Authority, who seek the conservation of this area to the dismay of the local communities:

"This area is very very fertile. [...] But the people of Dukuduku were crying because iSimangaliso wanted to fence all this area. [...] iSimangaliso wanted to take all this land but the people are not employed. There are plenty people in Dukuduku who are not employed because there are no companies around this area. [...] When iSimangaliso took this area they suffered. Because people sell their crops in town. [...] As for now, like I said, they still negotiate with the land commissioner, just to give us at least a piece of land where we can cultivate the crops. But we are still waiting that they give us a feedback." (ibid.)

When we spoke to Philip Mkhwanazi, the local inDuna of Khula village where some of the people from the Dukuduku forest were relocated to, he told us:

"People need this land. This area is always wet. You can plant anything: vegetables, African potatoes. Everything is growing. Even if you drive on the N2 [highway], if you look on this side, it's not the same like this. So people before were getting everything, they didn't have to go looking for a job, because they were getting everything here." (Mkhwanazi 01.06.2016, interview)

It is clear that access to land and property rights remain major issues in post-apartheid South Africa, whereby Nustad has noted that for those affected by dispossession in iSimangaliso Wetland Park "the main complaint was that people did not receive a right to the land itself." Rather they receive monetary compensation for their dispossessed land. "This', writes Nustad, 'deviates from the model now followed in cases involving conservation areas, where land tends to be restored to claimants, albeit without the accompanying right to occupancy" (Nustad 2015: 127).

With this model of compensation arises the problem of the complexities surrounding a simplistic understanding of communities. While members and representatives of iSimangaliso Wetland Park Authority argue for strict dealings with local traditional community leaders as representatives for entire communities, hoping to persuade a few persons with direct monetary benefits, a body of critique has arisen pointing to a long history of abuse of power and even violence amongst traditional leaders towards their subordinates (ibid.: 130 pp.). This frustration was shared by many locals and described to us as follows by Siybane Ncube: "We used to negotiate with iSimangaliso, [who promised] us different things but the problem is when they take the decision they were not including the land claim committee, they used to take the inDuna [traditional leader]" (Ncube 03.06.2016, interview). Upon further questioning of the community's relationship with the inDuna, Ncube explained:

"We don't have a relationship with the inDuna. Especially the land claimants. Because the inDuna doesn't care about the land, they only look for money. [...] There is no connection at all. They don't even want to see us, especially in the meetings. They don't want to talk to us, they don't want to listen to us. This is a problem." (ibid.)

Further problems arise due to the fact that the inhabitants of Dukuduku forest are made up of highly heterogeneous groups, not single communities. While some have proof of ancestors in the area, many others currently living there moved there in recent decades because of high fertility on the flood plains and were welcomed by the original inhabitants because they helped in the fight against government resettlement plans (Nustad 2015: 131 pp.). Rights to compensation and benefits becomes an issue of belonging to a specific community. Also, this model of governance is in stark contradiction to the newly established democratic values because it represents apartheid style indirect rule through a powerful minority (ibid.).

The reality for these communities affected by dispossession or fighting for land claims is what Hansen has described as a juxtaposition between "efforts to restore local land and resource rights against national and global interest in conservation" (Hansen 2014: 3). Adding to this equation the inherent power of the state and the subaltern status of the claimants, it becomes obvious that local interests and livelihoods have less political leverage to make their cases. Or, as Nerosha Govender described the issue, there is a wide scope of interest groups and not every point of view can be accommodated. This is why a key task of the iSimangaliso Wetland Park Authority is managing expectations both on the local and state level, all under the umbrella of international UNESCO conservation rules and guidelines.

4.3 Nature Conservation and Employment in iSimangaliso Wetland Park

Another recurring topic that was brought to our attention was that of employment, or rather the high levels of unemployment in the region. Socio-economic development is one of the key objectives of the iSimangaliso Wetland Park Authority, as Nerosha Govender told us. There are quite a few initiatives aimed at job creation, for instance through alien plant removal, infrastructure maintenance and establishment, and, of course, the tourism industry, and many programmes that focus on building entrepreneurial skill sets as well as educating people on nature conservation. However, when we spoke to many locals, they expressed discontent and anger about the type and amount of employment that seeps through:

> "When they [iSimangaliso] came here first they promised to employ the people, to take care of the locals, like helping them building schools and clinics and employ the people. But it did not happen. It doesn't happen. They only give us the contract to work one month a year. You can't do nothing with that." (Ncube 03.06.2016, interview)

Many of the jobs that iSimangalio Wetland Park provides are only temporary. They are needs based and as such not permanent employment opportunities that can provide a steady income: "I am working inside the park, but the problem is the contracts. We have one month left now. After that ends, my job ends", Ncube explained to us (ibid.).

Apart from these types of temporary employment contracts, the Ezemvelo rangers are a heavily represented profession in iSimangaliso Wetland Park. "There are a lot of security guards [...] in town" as a guide recounted. "I have seen a lot of Ezemvelo rangers in the iSimangaliso Park, in the anti-poaching unit" (anonymous tour guide 08.06.2016, interview). iSimangaliso Wetland Park Authority works with Ezemvelo KwaZulu-Natal Wildlife on the daily operations of the park's management and compliance. Phumlani Lugagu, an intern at iSimangaliso, explained their tasks to us as such: "Ezemvelo are contracted by iSimangaliso to carry out day to day conservation activities or enforcement. But within Ezemvelo there are officers called community conservation officers. So their job is to go out to communities and raise awareness" (Lugagu 10.06.2016, interview).

However, the presence of the Ezemvelo in the park is highly controversial among local people, as is the employment of private security personnel for the enforcement of park rules and regulations. In a conversation with the head of a security firm hired by iSimangaliso Wetland Park Authority he informed us that their role was to keep the locals in line and that conservation is the main priority. He perceived himself as a problem solver, explaining that anyone who acted against iSimangaliso's directives is removed from the grounds. His heavily armed task force, brought in from Durban to avoid local conflict of interest, acts by any means necessary to enforce conservation, which Nustad also described in his publication recounting the aftermath of an unarmed member of the Sokhulu community who was "shot and killed by a security company contracted to iSimangaliso while farming on the riverbed" (Nustad 2015: 150).

Other upsetting employment issues, as perceived by the local people, are the severe limitations set by the IWPA against small-scale community tourism development. Especially as tourism is considered the main driver of regional economic development, as Phillip Mkhwanazi, owner of Veyane Cultural Village and co-owner of Heritage Tours, commented: "In this area there is no factory. Our factory is tourism. There is no place where people can just go and work. Only people doing the crafts, doing the vegetables, or just go and work in the hotels" (Mkhwanazi 01.06.2016, interview).

Our findings are in line with those of Hansen, who discovered that there are numerous criminal and civil cases taken against local people trying to establish their own tourism developments on land that is owned by the iNgonyama Trust but falls under the Coastal Forest Reserve section of the IWP (Hansen 2014:

92). Upon asking two of the individuals involved in these undertakings, they told Hansen "that they believed they had gone through the necessary channels for authorisation – receiving the go-ahead from the local inDuna and the owners of the land, the iNgonyama Trust" (ibid.). The argument against individual tourism developments was the fear "that it [iSimangaliso] might lose its status as a World Heritage Site" (ibid.). This gives rise to the problematic notion held by locals that "iSimangaliso has stolen this area" (ibid.: 120). Anger arose amongst community members because of what they perceive as a twofold restriction on their livelihood: They are not allowed to develop their own tourist ventures, on the one side, and don't find enough work at the established tourist sites on the other (ibid.).

5 Co-Management and Socio-economic Welfare

Our research in and with local communities and people living in or in close proximity to iSimangaliso Wetland Park has led us to agree with Hansen who criticises the neoliberal, growth based development model that underlies iSimangaliso Wetland Park's mode of operation and sees its "measures to reflect more obviously the historical approach of the apartheid state, rather than that of a democratic developmental state" (Hansen 2014: 2). As this passage from an interview with a KwaDapha community member emphasises: "It's a new South Africa, but we are still living like in apartheid times. Nothing is happening, we are actually neglected. We are living in a World Heritage Site, but we are still neglected" (cited in Hansen 2014: 121).

iSimangaliso Wetland Park Authority, especially under the directive of former CEO Andrew Zaloumis, may have rid the area of its more obvious displays of apartheid, such as the boom gate restricted entrance to St Lucia that existed until 1999 where "black people if they came to St Lucia were stopped and their cars were searched" (Zaloumis 2016, interview). However, the outwardly portrayed inclusive policies by the IWPA suffice only for superficial means. For the local people, they effectively translate to "power relations that lead to their continued exclusion from access to resources, decision-making and co-management" (Hansen 2014: 144 pp.). As Hansen further elaborates, the "local people complain that the IWPA has developed its own plans in the area, without their consultation" (ibid.). "This', she argues, and I fully agree with her assessment 'is particularly problematic in contemporary South Africa, given the policy goal of redress for past racial inequalities" (ibid.: 4).

5.1 *"Benefits beyond Boundaries" in iSimangaliso Wetland Park*

This paper identifies the following benefits based on our own research conducted as well as literature published by iSimangaliso CEO, Andrew Zaloumis (2010), Diane Scott, Bronwyn James, and Nerosha Govender (2012), and anthropologist Melissa Hansen (2014):

- improved communication flows and cooperation between local and international (South Africa, Swaziland, Mozambique) communities and organisations in the iSimangaliso Wetland Park region
- improved regional infrastructure
- empowerment of local communities through education, skill building, and mentoring programmes
- bursaries to university students from communities within and adjacent to the IWP; specifically to pursue environmental studies and related disciplines
- employment opportunities, through short-term job creation
- establishment of trusts to fund community needs
- and establishment of mandatory equity partnerships (BEE)

These listed benefits have to be viewed with caution since many authors writing about Community-Cased Natural Resource Management (herafter CBNRM) and other empowerment and benefit schemes warn about their narrow effect range. As Ryan Hill, Yemi Katerere, and Sam Moyo state in their Critique of Transboundary Natural Resource Management in Southern Africa:

> "The nature of this 'community involvement' needs to be clearly articulated since such involvement could be limited to the extent to which local communities act as a labour pool to make protected areas and private property more productive. It is now evident that CBNRM needs to be capable of addressing local values, needs and interests; failure to do so undermines the potential of such initiatives. In order for communities to participate in [such] initiatives, the benefits of such initiatives must outweigh the costs from the community perspective." (Hill et al. 2001: 20)

Chellan and Kahn write with regard to iSimangaliso Wetland Park's "benefits beyond boundaries" approach:

> "In relation to whether local communities adjacent to the Park benefit from ecotourism, both Wild Life and Environment Society of South Africa (WESSA) and Ezemvelo-KZN Wildlife stated that there were limited benefits. The main benefits for local communities were identified as the selling of crafts which was significant only during peak tourism seasons. A concern with regards to ecotourism development was that the incremental increase in economic development may occur at the expense of the natural environment. Other concerns emerging from stakeholders who stated that a 'few get richer with very

little trickle down effects especially to poor communities' and as 'economic imperatives drive the industry the profit motive will dominate', respectively." (2008: 284)

This view can also be taken from Brian King's research on community benefit schemes in other locations in South Africa, where he argues more generally that "there is a growing disenchantment with community conservation within the academic and policy communities resulting from concerns that these initiatives are largely ineffective in meeting their ecological and social goals" (King 2007: 209). Elsewhere he states:

"In considering the histories of these models in Sub-Saharan Africa, I argue that conservation planners often prioritize economic and ecological factors over the political circumstances that influence the effectiveness of these approaches. The effectiveness of conservation in the 21st century will require a renewed engagement with research that demonstrates its political dimensions in order to ensure that the protection of biodiversity occurs in conjunction with meeting the social, cultural, and economic needs of people directly impacted by conservation planning." (King 2009: 11)

In his paper on CBNRM, King also underlines the importance of seeing communities as differentiated (ibid. 2007: 209 pp.). This was our experience, as well, while talking to a multitude of different people with different relations to iSimangaliso Wetland Park. Within communities surrounding protected nature areas, the views and perceptions about these vary from strong opposition amongst those who directly depend on the land and its resources for subsistence, to being favoured by those who are in positions of power and hence benefit directly from such enterprises. This emphasises the point made earlier about the attempt by iSimangaliso Wetland Park officials to deal with traditional leaders in an apartheid manner attempting to attain 'community agreement'.

Issues raised by researchers, such as those listed above, and based on our experiences and interviews with locals, this paper questions the proclaimed 'win-win' situations of protected area nature conservation. So far, it can be assessed that while iSimangaliso Wetland Park holds the reputation of being an establishment that combines nature conservation with community empowerment and sustainable development of an impoverished rural region, our research of the affected communities (not even including those communities whose land claims haven't been settled yet and, hence, see very little more in iSimangaliso than harsh restrictions on their freedoms and ways of life) shows that many are disillusioned with the forthcoming of promised benefits from ecotourism that would come with the inauguration of a nature reserve.

5.2 Black Economic Empowerment in iSimangaliso Wetland Park

One of the key concepts of iSimangaliso Wetland Park's benefit system that deserves a closer look is that of BEE. Considered the largest social empowerment strategy to scale, BEE emerged out of the post-apartheid political setting and has been implemented by the ANC government to ensure the integration of formerly disadvantaged people into the national economy. Describing the complexities of BEE would go beyond the scope of this paper, it shall suffice to give a short overview of this strategy and its often criticised shortcomings with regard to iSimangaliso Wetland Park.

The idea of BEE is that state legislature can achieve racial equity in business and ownership by threatening businesses into "the transfer of stakes in white-owned businesses to a new class of black investors" (The Economist 2013, online). Stakes have to be bought from the businesses, while the loans to do so would usually be supplied by banks or the businesses themselves.

Apart from the fact that BEE seems to have done very little in terms of helping the poor, it appears to have helped to create "a sliver of super-rich blacks", which does little more for the general poor public but ensure that wealth will stay in the hands of a now slightly "blackened" elite (Law 2010: 318). While it can't be denied that BEE has helped some people, as one of the few studies done on the extent of BEE benefits by Leila Patel and Lauren Graham (2012) shows, the problem of the lacking trickle-down effect remains: "While claims that only a small black elite has benefited enormously from BEE appear to be true, the base of BEE beneficiaries seems to be changing slowly. Employees of companies involved in these deals are the main beneficiaries, followed by women and a range of community, education and development trusts. Youth and people with disabilities benefit to a far lesser extent" (ibid. 2012: 205). "The new black bourgeoisie", writes Kate Law, "have so far been interested only in creating the most sybaritic lifestyles for themselves. This is further evidence that the ANC have prioritised black capitalism rather than non-racial socialism, as their liberation rhetoric had indicated" (Law 2010: 316). Especially since so far this has been true for people with close affiliation to the ANC itself, which leads many critics to call the BEE scheme a bad case of nepotism (ibid.: 314).

The entire scheme and failing of BEE to achieve "structural change in the lives of the poor" (ibid.: 316) and to create business equity, makes more sense if viewed from a different perspective. The Economist reports: "The original idea for BEE actually came from white business leaders. Though some genuinely wanted to make the system a bit fairer, most saw it as a good way to ward off any attempt at nationalisation by the new black government. In that sense BEE has been a roaring success. Whites still hold the bulk of the country's wealth" (The Economist 2009, online). Law (2010: 317) states in this regard that "the National Party were prioritizing the creation of a black proto-capitalist supportive class in an attempt to 'reform' the apartheid system to ensure its continuation."

This was a theme we encountered repeatedly during our research. In St Lucia, and arguably in most other areas of the wetland park, 95 percent of businesses are still white owned and run, as Nerosha Govender told us. Hansen, even goes a step beyond, citing iSimangaliso Wetland Park officials who accuse "white partners of hijacking the development process for their own ends, and to the detriment of the local community" (Hansen 2014: 121).

Moreover, the highly commended mandated equity partnerships and community trusts that aim at aiding the historically disadvantaged communities of the area lose their value amidst frequent displays of corruption. The trusts, according to a safari operator, "are supposed to give back to the community, through the inDuna. But", he adds, "I doubt it does. It is very, very corrupt, it is ridiculous" (anonymous tour guide 08.06.2016, interview,). When we asked Phumlani Lugagu about this problem he explained that the money in the community trust is at the sole discretion of the traditional leadership which is not held accountable for where the money is subsequently channelled into. He stated "iSimangaliso pays the trust but we don't have the power as the authorities to go back and check 'what did you do with the money that you got?'" (Lugagu 10.06.2016, interview).

Along the same lines, the BEE-backed partnership policy proved to be less mandatory as our sources confirmed:

> "Here, you don't have to have a black partner, but your business will do a lot better if you do. Because you get government funding as well. And then you get the BEE ranking, and when you get a higher ranking, you can tender for things, that a completely white company cannot tender for at all." (anonymous tour guide 08.06.2016, interview)

6 Conclusion

While a legitimate case can be made for environmental protection in the form of nature conservation, the reality of fencing off large stretches of land in the name of shielding ecosystems from detrimental human intervention has given rise to a whole new set of highly politicised problems.

As we have seen, the establishment and preservation of such nature conservancies in South Africa is not only rooted in a history of dispossession and exclusion, but continues to carry an aftertaste of apartheid power relations, where access to land is a privilege reserved for those with influence and money. Still, the past three decades have seen a major change in South Africa's approach to nature conservation brought on by critique of 'conservation fortresses', especially in a new democratic South Africa, where social equity and land reform play a significant role in the nation's policies. Here, nature conservation for ecotourism cannot afford to be viewed in a light of apartheid-style land appropriation.

In this setting, iSimangaliso Wetland Park has been trying to accommodate strategies for social change and community empowerment. Through their "benefits beyond boundaries" action plan, the iSimangaliso Wetland Park Authority strives to include local people and communities in the decision-making processes and socio-economic payouts of the wetland park. However, as Nerosha Govender put it, participation does not necessarily mean consensus. With so many different interests represented and in view of the high levels of corruption, it is no wonder iSimangaliso Wetland Park officials reiterate the need to manage expectations of the world heritage site. Despite their efforts they, too, are subject to the underlying economic structures that make up the base of every social system and thereby influence every branch of the same. With neoliberalism as the adopted strategy for economic growth, it comes as no surprise that state operated iSimangaliso Wetland Park is managed along the same profit-oriented free market principles, much "to the detriment of the local community" (Hansen 2014: 121).

So, while there is evidence of job creation, entrepreneurial enterprise, community empowerment, and sustainable resource management, the impact is, in fact, much smaller than one is led to believe and primarily serves iSimangaliso's interests of self-preservation. By their own account, iSimangaliso Wetland Park Authority lean heavily on the side of nature with 70 percent of their resource allocation going towards the conservation of the world heritage site, leaving only 30 percent for local socioeconomic development. The justification for this prioritisation lies in the South African state's general growth based development plans that regard iSimangaliso Wetland Park as an economic asset and driver of regional economic growth, as Nerosha Govender explained. Thus, as stated above, if the product is a sustainable, healthy, and diverse ecosystem, then it is clear which interests and demands are being met by iSimangaliso Wetland Park's management objectives. In effect, if iSimangaliso Wetland Park truly wanted to alleviate poverty and empower the poor rural communities of the region their management would need to change its focus from a growth based, neoliberal mode of operation to one that is specifically tailored to the needs of local individuals, beyond the scope of what is state enforced.

To answer the proposed research question more directly, the evidence put forward in this paper conveys that even though the new model of conservation adapted by iSimangaliso Wetland Park includes and benefits local communities to a certain extent, the principal land use option is to attract investment for ecotourist ventures that rely on iSimangaliso Wetland Park fulfilling tourists' expectations of a natural world heritage site: unspoiled nature absent of human existence. Effectively, this paper concludes that iSimangaliso Wetland Park policies do little in terms of pushing the agenda for real social transformation.

Traditional Leadership and Sustainable Development at the iSimangaliso Wetland Park: A Paradox?

Tibor Böhm

1 Introduction

The iSimangaliso Wetland Park was declared South Africa's first UNESCO World Heritage site in 1999. The Park in north-eastern KwaZulu-Natal is marketed as a prime example of a progressive and inclusive nature conservation approach characterised by the sustainable development of surrounding communities and eco-tourism.

Nature conservation in protected areas and national parks has been repeatedly criticised for being exclusive to local populations, even leading to their forceful removal. This is due to formerly popular conservationist stances which promote that secluded areas of external 'nature' have to be protected from human influence. Recent approaches to nature conservation, as is the case in iSimangaliso, challenge these criticisms.

In May and June of 2016, a group of anthropological researchers from the University of Vienna visited the park and its surroundings. The aim was to inquire whether the promises of new 'sustainable' approaches to nature conservation were coming true. One of the main research interests was whether communities adjacent to the wetland park, whose members had previously been partly removed from the conservation area, were now able to benefit from its existence. In particular, as the uMkhanyakude district in which the park lies is one of the most impoverished regions of South Africa characterised by high rates of HIV/AIDS, unemployment, and a lack of basic infrastructure.

This paper focuses on a village close to the park's main town of St Lucia[1]. The village is ruled by the local *inDuna*, a so called traditional leader and sub-chief to the Zulu king Goodwill Zwelithini. Traditional authorities are recognised in the post-apartheid South African constitution and are especially prevalent in the former bantustans or homelands. Local customary leaders such as *izinDuna* (pl. of inDuna) are the representatives and heads of communities. Among others, they have the rights to distribute land or to manage community affairs. For the

[1] In order to protect our informants neither the name of the village nor the names of any individuals will be mentioned in this paper.

iSimangaliso Wetland Park, the izinDuna of the surrounding communities are important contact persons in the negotiations of conservation matters or allocations of benefits like job opportunities, community levies, etc. However, the roles of traditional authorities in post-apartheid South Africa are highly contested. Many scholars perceive them as undemocratic remnants of the times of colonialism and apartheid (cf. Ntsebeza 2008; Claassen 2014; Buthelezi/ Yeni 2016).

In this paper, I argue that the benefits of iSimangaliso Wetland Park are not equally shared by all members of the local communities. With the help of the park management and uplifting programmes, like Black Economic Empowerment (hereafter BEE), the local inDuna of this case study has become a very successful owner of tourist businesses. Yet, his community is only partly able to reap benefits from the wetland park and on a much lower scale. On a local level, I argue, the benefits of the park remain to be shared decidedly unequally while 'traditional' power relations are being continuously reinforced.

To introduce this topic, I will first give a short account of the history of contemporary iSimangaliso Wetland Park, in particular highlighting its legacy of conservation and dispossession. Afterwards I will present some findings of our research and discuss them by drawing on current South African debates about traditional leadership legislation.

2 The History of iSimangaliso Wetland Park

iSimangaliso Wetland Park stretches from the small holiday town St Lucia in the South along the coast up to Kosi Bay on the border to Mozambique. Its landscapes attract a great variety of mammals, birds, and other animals and constitute a unique ecosystem (iSimangaliso Wetland Park Authority 2011).

2.1 The Social Construction of Conservation Space

Protected areas like iSimangaliso Wetland Park are based on the idea of nature conservation. This idea suggests that it is necessary to single out certain areas in which flora and fauna, considered to be nature, should be protected from the influence of humans, who are not regarded as part of that nature but rather as something opposed to it, which we can call culture or society. Thus, the idea of nature conservation is based on a fundamental ontological and axiomatic distinction between nature and humans. This assumption might be so internalised that it could seem universal or, indeed, natural, which it isn't. The idea that nature and humanity are two fundamental opposites has very specific historical reasons which can be traced back to certain European developments. Many societies, however, don't distinguish between nature and humans. Instead, they see people as an inherent part of nature (West/ Igoe/ Brockington 2006).

The idea of a binary opposition between nature and people can be traced back to European enlightenment thinkers, most prominently to the writings of the French philosopher René Descartes who, in his writings, divided the world into antagonisms (Adams/ Hutton 2007; Scheper-Hughes/ Lock 1987). Although these Cartesian Dualisms were the foundation stone, the concept of nature vs. humans only fully developed with the emergence of the Industrial Revolution and capitalism from the late eighteenth century onwards. The accelerated destruction of natural environments through the new modes of production was followed, in turn, by an enhanced romanticisation of a nature seemingly "untouched" by humans (Adams/ McShane 1996: 6). Industrialisation led to a division of surrounding environments into landscapes of production, which were destroyed in the process of commodity fabrication, on the one hand, and landscapes of consumption, which should not be destroyed in order to be enjoyed as external assets, on the other. These landscapes of consumption were imagined as 'untouched' nature: nature without human beings, without any signs of production. Knut Nustad writes: "The idea of untouched nature can be traced back to fundamental changes in property relations that took place in Europe during the transition to capitalist forms of production" (Nustad 2015: 24).

Out of this ideal of pristine nature untouched by humans, the idea of nature conservation emerged, which, in turn, led to the formation of protected areas and national parks from the end of the nineteenth century onwards. All over the world areas were created in which the natural environment should be preserved from human influences (Adams/ Hutton 2007). People who actually lived in those areas were many times seen as a disturbance of the 'pure' nature and therefore often forcibly removed (Chatty/ Colchester 2002). Fences were erected to keep nature in and people out thereby making the ontological division between nature and people a reality. The binary opposition between nature and people also underlies the creation of iSimangaliso Wetland Park. As Nustad states: "An enactment of nature as the opposite of industrialisation as external to humans and an object of preservations also shaped St. Lucia" (Nustad 2015: 99).

2.2 History of Conservation

The area of the present-day park became a popular hunting ground during the second half of the nineteenth century. At the time, large parts of Southern Africa developed into target areas of big scale hunting trips of British Victorian elites. After the massive extinction of wild animals by these hunting parties, the first game preservation was established to save the remaining prey for future shoots (Adams/ McShane 1996). In the area which today is northern KwaZulu-Natal, however, things went a little differently. There, the hunting activities of the time were not sports hunting enacted by a colonial elite for pleasure but commercial hunting which supplied a global demand for animal goods, in particular ivory. This sort of hunting was conducted by white hunter-traders based in Port Natal (later Durban). By the end of the nineteenth century, the most desired hunting animals were close to extinction. The last elephant in the St Lucia area was shot in 1916.

At the end of the nineteenth century, in the year 1895, the region around St Lucia was declared an animal preservation area for the first time. It came to be known as the Cape St Lucia Game Preserve. Interestingly, these preserves, of which St Lucia was one in a row of many in Zululand, were at first not declared to save the remaining wild animals, but to protect farmers and their livestock by transferring these wild animals into the designated areas.

In the first half of the twentieth century, major changes took place in Zululand and in South Africa in general. Zululand gradually transformed from an area of hunting grounds to an area of productive fields for industrial agriculture, cattle farming, and forestry. This went hand in hand with the very large extinction of game which was perceived as the carrier of diseases threatening the livestock. Consequently, the Cape St Lucia Game Reserve was un-proclaimed in 1928 and subsequently made accessible for white farmers. Sugarcane production and forestry soon became the two major industries in the St Lucia area and remained so until the end of the 20th century (Nustad 2015). Nevertheless, a bird sanctuary was established in the area in 1927, and a nature reserve comprising Lake St. Lucia and its Eastern Shores was re-proclaimed in 1938.

In 1928, the all-white holiday town of St Lucia was established and became very popular, especially for fishermen, from the early 1930s onwards (Walker 2008). Conservational ideas continuously gained ground from the 1960s again. In 1966, government plans to build a dam on the nearby Hluhluwe river prompted the first environmentalist protests in the area. The plans were successfully halted and in 1977 the Eastern Shores of Lake St Lucia came under the protection of the Natal Parks Board and the Department of Forestry. In 1986, St Lucia was declared a wetland of international importance under the Ramsar Convention (Nustad 2015). Nevertheless, in the late 1980s the government enforced plans to mine the dunes of St Lucia for titanium and other precious metals. These plans in favour of multinational mining companies prompted an unexpected nationwide resistance. Environmentalist groups from the whole country campaigned against the government's plans. As Walker writes:

> "[T]his Campaign for St. Lucia grew rapidly into the largest and ultimately most successful environmental campaign yet seen in South Africa, overseeing an effective media campaign, collecting thousands of signatures for a national petition, and lobbying Parliament." (Walker 2008: 121)

The government responded to the protests by commissioning an Environmental Impact Assessment to investigate the effects of mining on the natural environment. The final Environmental Impact Report was in favour of a touristic use of the area rather than mining. After the fundamental political change to democracy in 1994 the newly elected ANC government finally decided in 1996 against mining and for the proclamation of a new wetland park which should bring benefits for the whole region (Walker 2008). Finally, the Greater St Lucia Wetland Park was established in 1999 and in the same year listed by the UNESCO as South Africa's first World Heritage Site (UNESCO 2016). The park was renamed iSimangaliso Wetland Park in 2007 – *iSimangaliso* meaning "miracle" or "wonder" in Zulu (iSimangaliso Wetland Park Authority 2016).

2.3 History of Dispossession

The history of the area was also characterised by large scale forceful removals of local people from their land. From the 1950s onwards, dispossession of land for various reasons was prevalent in the region that is now the park. Until the 1980s, around 1,200 households were forced off their land. Cherryl Walker focused her research on these dispossessions, especially of the Bhangazi community, whose members were living on the Eastern Shores of Lake St Lucia. People were forcefully moved from there in three different phases. The first phase started in 1956 after the establishment of the Cape Vidal Forest Reserve. The Department of Forestry announced that from then on only people who worked for the reserve were allowed to settle in the area. The second phase of dispossession was due to the growing concerns of nature conservationists in the region. The government had appointed the Kriel Commission which released a report in 1966 recommending the enlargement of the existing conservation zone highlighting the unique environmental conditions of the land. Local inhabitants were seen as a disturbance to that undertaking and it was advised to remove them from their homes. The third phase was due to South Africa's growing political isolation. The government identified the border region to Mozambique as an area of high military importance and established a missile testing range on the Western Shores of Lake St. Lucia in 1968, which led to the forceful removal of more than 3,000 former inhabitants. By 1974 the last remaining families were removed from their homes on the Eastern Shores (Walker 2008).

Yet, with the massive political changes in South Africa in the early 1990s, issues of land dispossession of local people gained greater importance. This also held true for the St Lucia area and the increasing number of claims for land restitution. As Walker states:

> "The seismic shifts in the political terrain that followed the release of Nelson Mandela from prison impacted profoundly on the future of Lake St. Lucia. As the space for mobilization and debate was flung open, new opportunities were created not only for land claimants but also for the environmental lobby groups dedicated to the protection of the significant natural resources of the area." (ibid.: 121)

After the election of the ANC for government and its decision against mining and for the establishment of a wetland park, the settlement of land claims was an important goal. Walker who acted as Land Commissioner for the claim of the Bhangazi community on the Eastern Shores describes this case in detail (2008). In the end that claim was settled by monetary compensation payments to eligible community members or their heirs. Resettlement in their ancestral locations was declined, not least because this would have counteracted the social construction of nature conservation spaces as areas without people. It was argued that in the long-term the benefits of a wetland park would affect more people than the resettlement of a few families.

2.4 Sustainable Development and Ecotourism

The newly established wetland park was based on the ideas of sustainable development ecotourism, which should bring economic growth for the whole region. Thus, the contradiction between conservation and local inhabitants was increasingly scrutinised. Therefore, the progressive conservation model of the park tries to bridge the gap between "conservation without humans" and sustainable community development. This new approach put emphasis on the social impact of nature conservation developed from the 1970s onwards and was supported by global actors such as the IUCN (International Union for Conservation of Nature and Natural Resources, NGO), UNESCO, the World Bank, etc. As Adams and Hutton state:

"By the 1980s, the whole conservation paradigm had changed to feature social inclusion rather than exclusion [...] On paper at least, the needs of local people were firmly on the conservation planning agenda. Community-based approaches dominated debate about conservation strategies in the rural developing world in the last two decades of the twentieth century [...] 'People and park' projects were developed in many countries, although many involved simply a repackaging of existing approaches." (Adams/ Hutton 2007: 150 pp.)

While Adams and Hutton draw a very positive picture of this new paradigm which seems to resolve all contradictions concerning the social aspects of nature conservation, it has also become increasingly criticised. West et al. argue that ecotourism, often seen as a key to more inclusive conservation approaches, often does not deliver the expected results:

"[E]cotourism often causes conflict and changes in land-use rights [...], fails to deliver promises of community-level benefits [...], actually damages environments [...], and has myriad other social impacts [...]. Indeed, many argue repeatedly that ecotourism is neither ecologically nor socially beneficial (...), yet it persists as a strategy for conservation and development." (West/ Igoe/ Brockington 2006: 262)

Progressive sustainable development approaches to conservation offering inclusion of local people sometimes resemble emerging neoliberal conservation models that promise 'win-win' situations which should solve the nature/society divide based on market logic. It is claimed that local communities could benefit from protected areas through job opportunities, professional trainings, etc.

Scholars, such as Bram Büscher, indeed posit that mainstream conservation is an integral part of neoliberal capitalism rather than an independent discourse drawing on the economic ideas of neoliberalism (Büscher 2013). Büscher and Fletcher go as far as to view conservation as a new mode of capitalist accumulation, which serves to deny the negative environmental impacts of the capitalist mode of production (Büscher/ Fletcher 2015). Referring to Büscher, Nustad argues that even the academic discourse on conservation drifts increasingly in the direction of neoliberal ideology. He states that:

"[T]his was expressed in the adoption of market terms such as "ecological services" and "ecological economics", but also more subtly in the implicit assumption that all conflicts surrounding conservation could be accommodated within "win-win" solutions, and the use of (empty) catch-all phrases such as empowerment, participation, ownership and good governance." (Nustad 2015: 165)

Whether one agrees with Büscher or not, it should be emphasised that win-win discourses mask the way in which conservation goals are inherently contradictory to capitalist production and expansion under neo-liberalism. In fact, nature conservation is being outsourced – destruction in one place is supposed to be balanced by the protection of another.

iSimangaliso Wetland Park is marketed as such a 'win-win' situation capable of overcoming the mutually exclusive division between nature and people by offering business opportunities to the local communities. The park is advertised as a "park for the people" and is said to have created "a successful conservation model that also offered tangible benefits to poverty stricken communities in and around the area" (Espley 2015, online). In the Africa Geographic Magazine, it is claimed that:

> "[T]he development of infrastructure in the park is creating employment, and land claimants are empowered to co-manage the area, while the iSimangaliso Authority enables community members to develop skills in hospitality and guiding so that they can prosper in the local tourism industry." (ibid.)

One of the key questions of our empirical research was whether these promises hold true. We were inquiring whether iSimangalison Wetland Park's sustainable development and ecotourism approach is able to solve the societal contradictions of protected area management. This question shall be discussed in the next chapter where some of our research findings will be presented.

3 The Role of 'Traditional' Leadership

Our research was conducted in a rural community outside St Lucia, the touristic centre of iSimangaliso Wetland Park. In apartheid times (and even a couple of years after) St Lucia was an all-white tourist town to which Black and 'coloured' people were only allowed entrance for work. Until today, business owners and tourists in St Lucia continue to be predominantly white while the workers remain predominantly Black and are recruited from the adjacent communities. The park management aims to change this situation and offers activity concessions inside the park only to tour operators whose businesses conform to BEE legislation (iSimangaliso Wetland Park Authority 2011).

BEE is an affirmative action business policy launched by the ANC government that privileges formerly disadvantaged population groups such as Black, 'coloured', Indian, or Chinese people. Under the BEE framework, companies are at least partly owned by 'Black' people (including other formerly disadvantaged groups) (Marcus 2007; Zips 2008). The BEE programme has been heavily criticised from various stances. It is argued that the affirmative action approach enforces unequal racialised recruitment the other way around. Rather than providing equal education opportunities for everybody, BEE forces businesses to hire people with regards to their skin colour instead of their qualifications. Another major criticism is that BEE has not led to an uplifting of previously marginalised majorities but rather to the creation of a small Black elite (Law 2010; Tangri/ Southall 2008).

The inDuna in the community close to St Lucia where our research was based was one of the beneficiaries of iSimangaliso's compliance with BEE. Over the years he has built his own tourist enterprise in the community – a Zulu cultural village which also offers food and accommodation. In this cultural village, which imitates the structures of a traditional Zulu community, tourists can stay overnight in round huts and experience shows exhibiting 'traditional' Zulu culture. This encompasses music, dances, or the visit of a traditional healer – a *sangoma*. The marketing of traditional Zulu culture through staged authenticity (Comaroff/ Comaroff 2009) is a very successful business and attracts many visitors from St Lucia.

The inDuna also runs a successful tourist boat business in a BEE collaboration with a white entrepreneur from St Lucia. They have two boats on which they offer tours on the St Lucia Estuary. Their collaboration is beneficial for both parties. While the inDuna profits from large investments, for his white business partner BEE is the only possibility to get concessions from the park in order to operate tours inside of it.

Yet, the inDuna is not only a successful business man. He also has a very powerful role in his community. The South African Constitution of 1996 recognises the institution of traditional leadership. The existence of chieftaincy had long been fought by the ANC before it came to power. Supposedly 'traditional' leadership was in fact a form of indirect rule, first by colonial powers and later by the apartheid government (Ranger 1997). The latter secluded certain areas from South Africa, which they called bantustans and later homelands. These economically highly underdeveloped areas, like KwaZulu, the Transkei, and others, served as separated living space for Black people and labour reservoirs for the apartheid economy. So called traditional authorities who collaborated with the apartheid regime ruled in the bantustans while their people had no rights to land. The perceived 'traditionality' of these institutions has been repeatedly criticised:

"The view that chiefs held ultimate power and authority in African societies has progressively been shown to be erroneous: it is the internalisation of late nineteenth century writings about African societies as "tribes" with chiefs as all-powerful sovereigns at the apex. This reading of African societies was part of colonial processes of indirect rule in which British authorities sought to rule African societies through gaining control of chiefs and making them do their bidding while maintaining the veneer of leaving the Africans to be ruled in their own historic ways. This kind of control of chiefs greatly intensified under apartheid, leading to chiefs largely losing legitimacy in Bantustans as they became instruments of the apartheid government, often imposed by the state because they would support its policies and actions, with no downward accountability to their people." (Buthelezi/ Yeni 2016: 4)

Nevertheless, the ANC changed its negative stance towards traditional authorities. Over time, the party had developed more and more into an urban organisation and decided to ally with chiefs in order to gain more influence in rural areas and secure the votes of the countryside.

Since the establishment of the new constitution, important legislation has been passed that enforces the control of traditional authorities of former bantustan areas and thereby perpetuates apartheid legacies. As Ntsebeza argues: "the ANC-led government has given powers to traditional authorities on basically the same lines as its predecessor, the apartheid state" (Ntsebeza 2008: 238 pp.). This holds especially true in the administration and allocation of land as well as in the representation of communities.

This is also the case in the area around St Lucia. The inDuna has the power of distributing the land to members of his community. If a resident of his village wants to build a house the inDuna may allocate a piece of land to him or her and demand a fee for it. Furthermore, the inDuna is an important representative for the community, not least in dealings with the iSimangaliso Wetland Park. He has the power to delegate jobs offered by the park to people in his community. As he, himself, states in an interview with us:

"I'm talking on behalf of other inDunas. We have an agreement with iSimangaliso, that if there are job opportunities, they must bring these opportunities to us, to see how many people they need and then we are going to see who these people are that are going to get the job opportunities at iSimangaliso." (anonymous inDuna 01.06.2016, interview)

In a poverty struck district like uMkhanyakude this capacity alone would make him a very powerful man. Yet, for the state and iSimangaliso in particular he serves another important function. He also constitutes an institution of unofficial law enforcement. For instance, if people from his community break into the park in order to hunt or collect resources he will punish them for their offences. As he puts it:

"People used to cut the fence because they need (sic!) to steal the animals. The securities are armed and the people are also armed. I said: 'no, if you catch somebody, don't shoot them or take them to the court, just phone me, I'm going to charge them'. Because they know if I charge them it's tighter than jail because I'm going to take cows from him and also chase him away if he continues." (ibid.)

This quotation emphatically demonstrates the inDuna's coercive power and his important role for the wetland park as a ruler of his community. The inhabitants of the area are fully aware of his authority as the following statement of a villager underlines:

"He's the one who communicates us all here. He's the umbrella of us. He runs the place. If you want to stay there you give him the money and he gives you a place to make your home. [. . .] He's got the power to remove you. [. . .] He's the one who can determine what to do around here. It's his area around. So are you able to oppose him? No. You are not going to oppose him. [. . .] Once you speak the truth you are going to be killed. Because you are suspicious you must move away." (anonymous villager 02.06.2016, interview)

The same villager, like many other people of his village, is unemployed. He does not have the family ties to the inDuna or the money for bribery to be allocated a job. People from the village who are able to find work in the tourism industry of St Lucia as cleaning ladies, waiters, gardeners, etc. are, for the most part, paid poorly for long working hours. Nevertheless, our interviewee confirmed that he would take any possible job that was offered to him. He stated: "I'm suffering like never before. [. . .] I would take any job. Just to put something for my kids on the table, just to survive" (ibid.).

While the majority of people living in the adjacent communities are not able to gain substantial benefits from the wetland park it seems to be no coincidence that the inDuna does. Considering the overarching national situation, Buthelezi and Yeni argue that "conservative customary authorities have been loudly clamouring for power claiming to speak on behalf of communities, but evacuating the very people from decision-making processes for their own financial gain" (Buthelezi/Yeni 2016: 2). This also seems to hold true in our case.

Yet, the situation close to St Lucia does not seem to be a singular case or an exception but rather the rule. Melissa Hansen who has conducted extensive field work in the most northern part of iSimangaliso, particularly in a community inside the park close to Kosi Bay called KwaDapha, describes similar instances:

"[O]nly certain men had access to the privileged domain of negotiation with the state by virtue of their claim to be traditionally sanctioned representatives of local people. Often they used these negotiations to further their own private political and economic interests. For example, in 2011 I spoke with a young entrepreneur and relative of the king, who managed a tourist camp at the entrance to the Kosi Bay mouth, together with a white partner. The camp was well frequented and advertised. Permits to enter the Coastal Forest Reserve section at the Kosi Bay estuary were sold exclusively at this camp. The young man recounted a recent instance when he had been invited to attend a high-level event with the president of Mozambique. The opportunities available for him in promoting his business seemed greatly at odds with the way in which commercial tourism initiatives are treated at KwaDapha." (Hansen 2014: 50)

The cooperation between parks like iSimangaliso and traditional authorities should be thoroughly scrutinised. It is convenient for the management of parks to work with traditional leaders who act as representatives of their communities. However, in doing so authoritarian power relations in communities remain unchanged and unchallenged which undermines the rights and possibilities for a major part of the people living there. Borrowing from Aninka Claasens we can call such cooperation as in iSimangaliso 'power-sharing deals' between government bodies and local actors:

"In the context of the former bantustans, power-sharing deals include the state, traditional leaders, and politically connected business people who have amassed substantial wealth as beneficiaries of the 'Black Economic Empowerment' (BEE) quotas required by the post-apartheid government." (Claasens 2014: 769)

In our case the two latter groups involved in those deals are even merging. Claasens heavily criticises the legislation which manifests the power of so called traditional authorities by arguing that "recourse to 'timeless custom' serves to disguise the ways in which resources and power are being concentrated in the hands of a small elite, at the expense of the poorest South Africans" (ibid.: 777).

4 Conclusion

iSimangaliso Wetland Park has made creditable efforts to provide sustainable development opportunities to land claimants and surrounding communities. Yet, one can argue that the results of redressing past injustices show a rather imbalanced outcome. A majority of white entrepreneurs in St Lucia and elsewhere continues to run most of the profitable businesses. The jobs which are created for the rural Black population are predominantly in low income sectors. Only few individuals of rural communities are able to substantially benefit from the park and become successful entrepreneurs themselves. These individuals benefit from measures like BEE and/or from being a traditional authority. This leads to the development of a small Black elite while the Black rural majority remains in poverty. Of course, this is a nation-wide phenomenon and not restricted to the area of iSimangaliso. Furthermore, this is the outcome of a capitalist economy, a fact that puts the whole concept of sustainable development into question. However, that is not the central topic in this article.

Nevertheless, if iSimangaliso and other parks want to achieve empowerment and participation of the underprivileged rural population by creating various kinds of opportunities, they should thoroughly question their cooperation with traditional authorities. By taking for granted the representation of communities by customary leaders, parks like iSimangaliso are strengthening highly unequal power relations in the surrounding areas. Rather than being traditional these hierarchical, authoritarian, and undemocratic power relations are remnants of colonial and apartheid eras. This situation not only demands a call for action and policy change on the level of park management, like in iSimangaliso, but also necessitates alterations on a national legislative level. As Mbongiseni Buthelezi and Stha Yeni highlight in their paper for the Council for the Advancement of the South African Constitution:

> "In policy and legislation, government continues to work with problematic assumptions that traditional leaders are generally benign people who consult and engage openly with the inhabitants of the areas they lead in a way that is democratic and inclusive of women, men and youth. However, the few examples described in this paper show that this is not the case. Worrying power dynamics are always at play: traditional leaders tend to make decisions on their own when there are business opportunities, and in cases where they get confronted by those they claim to represent, they use coercion. There is an urgent need to restart the process of moving towards a more just South Africa." (Buthelezi/ Yeni 2016: 14 pp.)

Even if there are positive examples of participatory traditional leadership these seem to be rather the exception than the rule, and neither iSimangaliso nor the South African government should just assume their universality. Regarding customary authorities, both the management policy of protected areas as well as the national legislation require urgent change and action.

iSimangaliso Wetland Park: A Nexus of Conflicting Interest

Patrick Cassidy

1 The Challenge of Transforming a National Park in a Post-Apartheid Context

Since its inception as a UNESCO World Heritage Park in 1999, iSimangaliso Wetland Park (or IWP) has vowed to be a space of sustainable ecological development and conservation, whilst simultaneously providing local people with jobs, opportunities, and the financial means to alleviate the poverty in the area. This approach has been heralded as a new model of transformation because of the way it utilises local people to make the land both profitable to themselves, and environmentally sustainable. Undeniably, attention across the world is becoming more fixed on changes in the environment; record levels of extreme weather conditions are being recorded monthly, with a growing demand internationally for spaces to be protected for wildlife. IWP has had many successes regarding 'rewilding' the space it occupies, but the second objective it aims for – the alleviation of poverty amongst local people – is being challenged by a growing number of scholars and activists. This paper will examine some of the critical voices talking about iSimangaliso but will also contextualise the area by examining the historical roots of the park and some of the bureaucratic and governance systems it interacts with to understand some of the decisions that are being made by the park authorities. A lot of the critical work aimed at the park attaches a lot of blame to the actions of the leaders. This paper will utilise the voice of the park as well to formulate a rounded understanding of the situation.

2 History of the Park

It is important to understand that IWP has a fabled and important place in South Africa's recent history, playing a crucial role in restoring a national affinity with nature conservation. It encompasses many of the noble and great aims that the country has sought to attain and its existence has been enabled by many of important figures in South African politics and the anti-apartheid resistance. Its story aims to intertwine and illustrate all of what is admired and revered about the new 'rainbow nation'. Endorsed by Nelson Mandela after apartheid was defeated, the park was created at the expense of corporate interests vying for natural resource extraction. This was presented as evidence of a new wave of political strength and typified the desire to protect, conserve, and build new hope and beginnings for South Africa. Article 24 of South Africa's Constitution (Act 108 of 1996) states that everyone has the right to an environment that is not harmful to their health or well-being and to have the environment protected, for the benefit of present and future generations.

The story of South Africa, a deeply racist and divided society that has sought to find peace and reconciliation, mirrors in many ways the story of IWP. It, too, has a hugely destructive past. Many people were kicked off the land and persecuted. Where South Africa can draw inspiration from the figures of Nelson Mandela and Archbishop Desmond Tutu as saviours, the IWP can draw upon their victory over the mining companies in the 1990s and the many grassroots activists who played huge roles in achieving that victory. International natural resource extraction companies wanted to go in and drill the land which would have been ecologically destructive and symbolically catastrophic. A groundswell of activists, citizens, and public figures petitioned the government to protect the land. They succeeded and so the recent history of the park is intertwined with social and environmental activism.

The former CEO of IWP, Andrew Zaloumis, is one such activist from that time. In an interview with Manuela Zips-Mairitsch and Werner Zips, he describes himself as a former "long-haired" anti-apartheid activist (Zaloumis 2014, interview). He has now become embedded in the management and governance of the park. He states that the park has a "nasty history" but he immediately links the park to the release of Mandela which makes it a "very special park". It is seen as a symbol, a "peace park". With a background in development rights and an ability to speak articulately and passionately about the park, he makes a case for the park as a space for change. Situated in the second poorest region in the country, the park is viewed as an "opportunity" not only for jobs and to recognise those who have been discriminated in the past, but also the "views, ideas and opinions" of people who live there. He makes central the desires of locals as a strategy to make the park work. He also stresses that the park is "unique" and "original", as a major aspect of being an UNESCO site is that originality is a key asset. This gives an indication of one of the stresses or pressures weighing on the management team: To remain an UNESCO site by retaining that sense of originality.

In an acceptance speech delivered in 2015 for the WWF Living Planet Award, Zaloumis made an impassioned speech about the importance of the park. As he was bestowed with a global conservation seal of respectability and approval, he tied together the history of both the country and the park. He described it as a "symbolic landscape" to view the backdrop of conflict that has shaped the country. He makes the point that British colonial exploits left little room for conservation, seeing the land as a valuable commodity from which they could extract massive benefits, which resulted in "the decimation of game, the destruction of swamp forest, the drying up of lakes, the expansion of conservation-incompatible land uses such as military bases" (Zaloumis 2015, speech). On top of this, he acknowledges how the "apartheid regime carried out forced removals of local populations to expand commercial plantations and establish a missile testing ground" (ibid.). Faced with this history, the piecing together of the park was fraught with difficulties and conflicts. He also remarks how the mining companies wanted to tear apart the region. The economic aspects of the park are touched upon by Zaloumis when he says:

> "In truth, however, iSimangaliso will always be a work in progress as our society changes and economies shift. The already limited livelihood choices available to iSimangaliso's 640,000 people will become fewer as economies tighten, unsustainable practices continue and the impacts of climate change begin to be felt. The prognosis is not good, not just for iSimangaliso, but for the globe if our natural resources continue to remain 'economically invisible'." (ibid.)

Zaloumis can be viewed as a mouthpiece for the proponents of the park but he does draw attention to the same issues that many critics of South African policy do as well. He is aware that the wider financial issues both in the country and globally will hit IWP and the people who can, or should, benefit from it. In his interview with Zips-Mairitsch and Zips, he provides a very clear view of the priority of the park. He claims that it offers benefits to people but these are "limited, if you want to retain it as a park" (Zaloumis 2014, interview). Understanding that these benefits are limited means that there must be compromises or choices made to decide where these benefits are enjoyed. In this case, as stated by Zaloumis himself, the focus is on conservation. These compromises should be understood in their correct context: as 'hard-choices' that determine what is valued or preserved. Both McShane et al. (2010) and Dahlberg and Burlando (2009) discuss these 'trade-offs' and the importance of transparent discussions regarding their implementation. Either conservation-for-all or conservation with economic development (for some) will be prioritised, and an honest discussion about this allows us to have a clearer picture of what is happening in IWP.

Zaloumis, a former hard-core liberal who has devoted his career to studying and attempting to represent the voices of the marginalised now holds power in a region where change can be affected. His use of language is important because although he speaks with great eloquence about the complexities facing the impoverished people, the park itself is very much run on a business model. He described to Zips-Mairitsch and Zips how the park is no longer a "start-up organisation" but is now internationally recognised. It is forced to "adapt" and keep "innovating" to stay relevant at a global level (Zaloumis 2014, interview). The examples that the park has chosen to look towards are other business models. These are predicated on free-market principles where offering opportunities to private sector actors are the norm. This is the logic and it makes complete sense for a business. However, for a park that is championed as the new model for combining conservation and economic development there is an obvious contradiction if the local people do not see these same benefits.

The 'rewilding' of key areas is a crucial aspect of CEO Andrew Zaloumis' larger plans for the park. Bringing back the 'big five' and other historically important animals to the area speaks to the importance that the park romanticises. In October 2016, a new pride of lions was reintroduced to the park as well as wild dogs. Zaloumis stated the importance of such projects:

> "This historic introduction brings iSimangaliso closer to achieving its conservation vision, the full restoration of eco-systems functioning, and the re-establishment of the migratory patterns of historically occurring animal populations – from the top of the Lebombo Mountains to the sea – as they occurred in the times of Shaka and before fencing fragmented the landscape and constrained animal movements. It is a reversal of the historic decimation of game for apartheid military bases, commercial plantations and other agriculture." (SABC News 2016, online)

This prioritisation placed on environmental sustainability will be important later when we assess the balance between the dual aims stated by IWP.

For advocates of the park, there is a very clear narrative running alongside it. The country was emerging from a disastrous history. Hope hung heavily in the air. Foreign investors sucking the natural resources of the country dry were pushed back through the force of activists and popular public opinion as well as the advocacy of the symbol of hope, Nelson Mandela. In a speech marking the reintroduction of elephants to the park in 2002, Mandela showed his admiration and love for the park when he stated that:

"iSimangaliso Wetland Park must be the only place on the globe where the oldest land mammal and the world's biggest terrestrial mammal share an ecosystem with the world's oldest fish and the world's biggest marine mammal." (South Africa Net n.d., online)

The park was forged from the ruins of racism and violence. It was a huge victory and it continues to hold massive symbolic value internationally. Its recognition as a global conservation player offers management opportunities to promote it and open it up for tourism in a way that are difficult to conceptualise happening otherwise given the realities of international discourse. Moreover, it is stunningly beautiful. The diversity of life in the park is almost incomparable and it is rightly sustained.

These are some of the reasons why the park has been shaped by protectionist policies, even if economic logic has dictated who gets access. It is worth bearing this in mind because the people working in the park hold it sacred as a place of real change and hope. The people closest to the park are themselves pawns to the financial markets and forces that ultimately decide upon the governance structures and their views are equally as important to understand. Zaloumis' deliberations, whether to be taken at face value or not, speak to the 'realities' of the park. Charged with protecting the land, they face opposition from wider political and economic forces. From his speeches and interviews he has conducted, it seems clear that he does not consider the park to be 'winning', rather it is protecting the natural resources and attempting to educate children on the importance of the environment. Both are to be commended, but the fact remains that there are impoverished people being marginalised and it is here where the contradiction of the official aims of the park confuse the issue.

3 Trade-offs

A problem that arises when attempting to achieve these dual aims is that there is an eventual need to prioritise one aim over another. The problem of these trade-offs is exacerbated by the ways that IWP interacts with different bodies that examine and manage the area. I will draw upon a few documents to show how there is a 'laissez-faire' attitude to the social work of the park, and a more intense spotlight shone onto the ecological side of their work.

3.1 Corporate Charter

The park can be examined as a product of business strategy by reading the corporate charter released in 2015 (iSimangaliso Corporate Charter 2011-2015, online). It is a compilation of statistics and goals couched in neo-liberal jargon. It describes the aims of the park in the same way that UNESCO would as an attempt to "preserve and protect the park" as well as "empower historically disadvantaged adjacent communities". However, it also describes the park as a "product" and the aim of the iSimangaliso Wetland Park Authority (hereafter IWPA) is to "create an appropriate business environment and reduce risk for tourism." It includes uplifting impoverished people from their circumstances but it is within a framework of creating opportunities for wealthy businesses. Furthermore, the way that the park can influence policies is touched upon:

> "iSimangaliso's approach is to strategically influence critical areas through lobbying, alignment with Government's key goals and programmes, and ensuring the delivery of economic benefits and empowerment where challenges are beyond its sphere of control." (ibid.)

This delivery of economic benefits sounds fantastic but it is being distributed to those who have the clout to back the lobbying in the first place. There is no doubt that the park has an obligation to react and interact with the realities of modern-day politics and economics, however, the issue is that the adoption of this policy is not seeing a Machiavellian-like means-to-an-end for the poorest in the region. Zaloumis spoke about the "limited" benefits available from the park and this is clear when reading the "modus operandi" of the park. The aims are:

- To run a "lean, cost-efficient system"
- To maintain "a minimum and appropriate number of full time staff" to fulfil a very particular set of jobs predicated on Western-style instruments of power and governance
- The "outsourcing" of all "specialist professional services" and most "non-core operational services". This is not focusing on including local people in this job market.

The charter is written in much the same way that you would expect to see from a corporation existing in any business sphere. There are graphs and numbers detailing the value of the land and the revenue costs of employees. There is a breakdown of the yearly percentage of workers. It also mentions the international actors it is in constant discussion with. This makes economic logic and helps to sustain a business model which allows 'growth' in the park. This growth and business model is predicated on the ability of the park to continue to produce profits and attract investors. These investors have no financial reason to improve the lives of the local communities. Based on purely economic principles and statistics, as shown by this charter, there are solid reasons for continuing with the management of the park in this way. The problem, which has been raised by researchers on the ground, is the social impact it has on communities and workers in the region.

"iSimangaliso's role, with respect to tourism development, is to guide the development of the product, create an appropriate business environment and reduce risk for tourism" (ibid.: 2). The importance of this strategy depends on what perspective you choose to view it from. Members of the Dukuduku community that I spoke to would challenge the benefits they have seen from this strategy. They are currently in dispute with the park and have a land claim in progress. The so-called 'risk for tourism' is their potential dissidence or hostility towards the park because of the way they feel they are being treated. Another perspective was highlighted by a high-ranking security official we spoke to. Despite initially championing a peaceful approach to protesting communities, going as far as quoting His Holiness, the Dalai Lama, as well as drawing upon his many years of interaction with people in a security role, he quickly relented. When pressed on how Dukuduku should be dealt with, he ultimately exclaimed that they should be thrown "off the land". Seen as detrimental to 'development' in the area because of their reluctance to accept iSimangaliso's terms, his views show the mind-set of the private security that police the park and protect its interests. These nuanced, conflicting points of view are not contained in the corporate charter, nor are they visible in other institutional documents that track and record the park's operation.

Two other documents that illuminate the scale and complexity of governance in IWP are an IUCN World Heritage Outlook conservation assessment completed in January 2015 and a briefing conducted by Terri Castis, as acting CEO of IWP at a parliament meeting group on August 30 of 2016, where she laid out details of iSimangalio's land claimants' process.

3.2 IUCN World Heritage Outlook Report

The sheer scale of the management of the park becomes clear whilst reading this report. It is twenty-seven pages long and details the key conservation issues as identified by the conservation assessment. This text-dense document does touch upon some social concerns, too. It uses a 'rating system' throughout that judges how 'effective' the park is at doing its job. It refers to the social issues facing people in and around the park with this statement:

> "The socio-political context is a challenge, however significant progress has been made to ensure participation in decision making and the resolution of land claims, as well as economic and other benefits for local communities." (IUCN 2015: 2)

This 'significant progress' really depends on what communities are assessed and what kind of information is gathered about them. The issue in the park, as Jackie Sunde and Moenieba Isaacs state about communities in Marine Protected Areas, is that: "to date, none of the parks has developed databases to monitor the impacts on the livelihoods of these communities" (Sunde/ Isaacs 2008: 14). This makes it difficult to believe that 'significant progress' has been made throughout communities and calls into question the criteria the World Heritage Outlook report utilised.

This sort of institutional requirement is just one of a myriad of responsibilities the park must fulfil to judging authorities. This is important to keep in mind when understanding that the park has conflicting and diverse opinions to answer to. Andrew Zaloumis pointed out that, to remain a UNESCO site, IWP must stay original. They are also obligated to fulfil these obligations and some of these authorities carry more power and are more important to pacify. The importance of keeping these authorities happy is understandable, as funding and power are retained by the park. However, how is the social impact on people's lives valued or judged in the area?

3.3 Land Claims Sharing Model: iSimangaliso Wetland Park Authority Briefing

At an environmental affairs committee meeting, chaired by Mr P. Mapulane of the ANC, on August 30, 2016, Terri Castis represented IWPA. South African National Parks (SANParks) were also present and both entities expanded on their sharing of biodiversity assets with communities and on their land claims sharing model. The minutes of the meeting recognised iSimangaliso as "an authority accountable for the government mandate" regarding settling land claims (SANParks/ IWPA 2016, minutes). This was a meeting between IWP and the government, and the aim of this meeting was to get an understanding of how the park intended to provide local people with opportunities and livelihood chances.

During the meeting, Castis presented how iSimangaliso recognises their preferred model of co-management agreements, noting that there is an equal emphasis between the claimants and IWPA with regard to conservation and economic opportunities. The claimants, so Castis, have the responsibility (1) to own and support conservation strategy, (2) to nominate board representatives, develop a local area plan, and an annual co-management plan, and (3) to understand tourism development and invest wisely on behalf of land owners. While they stand to benefit from (1) access to resource use, (2) representation on the board, and (3) profits from economic development opportunities from revenue and equity sharing, bursaries, cultural heritage programmes, tourism skills and contracts, and improved infrastructure, to name a few. (IWPA 2016: 10-12, online)

After, Castis provided an example of such a co-management agreement: The Thonga Beach Lodge, a revenue sharing equity partnership with tourism concessions (ibid.: 12). Castis also referred briefly to some of the challenges that exist in these agreements, particularly regarding the "payment of money under existing settlement agreements in question". The minutes note that there were some brief explanatory follow-up responses from Castis about some questions committee members had. However, in general, the report concludes that:

> "The Chairperson felt the Committee received, from the briefings, a sense of the role national parks were playing in the communities where they were located. The information received would be taken and at this point, the Committee was pleased with the role national parks were playing especially in the communities in which they were located. He liked the concept of a wildlife economy where communities and emerging entrepreneurs were able to participate." (SANParks/ IWPA 2016, minutes)

This briefing demonstrates the way that information about disputes is passed on from the authorities of the park to the governmental structure they answer to. It is relatively uncritical and does not highlight the same issues that have been reported by researchers on the ground in these areas. There is nowhere near the same level of scrutiny placed on the exact ways that local people's lives are being affected.

4 The Marginalised Communities

Despite the successes that IWP can point towards regarding the rewilding of the park, and some small steps towards co-management agreements, critical voices have emerged against the park in recent years. Melissa Hansen and Knut Nustad are two of the most prominent and important scholars, while Jackie Sunde and Moenieba Isaacs have also written critically about Marine Protected Areas (MPAs) in South Africa, including two in IWP. Despite the best intentions, goodwill gestures, and legislative measures put forward in South Africa in the last two decades, it remains true that "appeals to rights and entitlements that have moved the world forcefully have often tended to ignore the freedoms of particular groups" (Anand and Sen 2000: 2029). It is with these sentiments in mind that I examine some of the literature on the subject.

Nustad describes the land reform movement as occurring within a "nexus, where identities, social relations, rights and environments are intertwined" (Nustad 2011: 20). Attfield et al. make a similar observation, describing the mesh of different actors and relationships as "a complex triangular relationship between the concepts of land reform, sustainable livelihoods and sustainable development" (Attfield et al. 2002: 2). Hansen, meanwhile, argues that IWP has developed as a result of "national ambitions for the conservation of ecological World Heritage – and the recognition that arises out of that – as well as for regional and national modernisation and economic growth strategies" (Hansen 2014: 47). This emphasis that has been placed on modernisation and economic growth has been unevenly distributed. The very same key players in industries prior to the election of the ANC continue to reside in lofty positions of power. Thus, the 'real' trickle-down tends to reveal disparities in how the benefits end up getting distributed. Conserving and protecting areas is an "inherently political process, and the goals are often not achieved" (ibid.:159). The desire to appease different lobbyists and groups leads to preferential treatment at some point. As outlined by Hansen, in the case of the IWP, the inhabitants of these areas are most often the ones who have been excluded due to new management decisions:

> "The imposition of new rules of governance for conservation management in the IWP also constrains the economic and social development activities of – and opportunities for – local users and inhabitants." (ibid.: 49)

The ways that the traditional communities have been affected has been in effect since the proclamation of the IWP in 2000 when 'new rules for conservation management have been imposed upon local users and inhabitants' (ibid.) which has been the result of an instrumental approach that seeks to control and restrict access. The logic behind this strategy is that degradation of the environment is impossible to stop without imposing some restrictions. The conservation of the environment is clearly crucial because the effects of destructive human practices are becoming more visible with each passing month and there is an increasing urgency to protect. However, advocating conservation and adopting policies to follow this path should not exclude voices who have historically lived in those regions. Preserving the environment should not, and does not have to, come at the cost of maintaining status quo class and social systems.

The situation can be improved only by implementing conditions conducive to uplifting people from situations where their livelihoods have been stripped away from them. Attfield et al., writing about land reform in South Africa, describe how "without sustainable livelihoods, sustainable development could not as much as begin to be introduced into any society" (Attfield et al. 2011: 3). Knut Nustad offers a perspective of oppression regarding conservation discourse, arguing that "conservation is merely the latest incarnation of a long series of arguments used to justify" the dispossession of land from local communities (Nustad 2015: 146). The continuous practice of dispossessing the most vulnerable from their land and offering monetary compensation shows a disconnect between the authorities and these groups. Even when land claims are 'settled', the local groups do not receive ownership, but rather are permitted to live there and use the land. Castis' presentation at the environmental affairs committee meeting in August 2016 is an illustration of how there is a disconnect between the local community and the authorities in the park.

Hansen found that people are confronted by social and institutional barriers. She encountered a lot of dissidence throughout the interviews she conducted in the field. One of the community members remarked that "it's a new South Africa, but we are still living like in apartheid times" (Hansen 2014: 121). The implementation of regulations, fences, and permits fit into a grand narrative of taking back the environment so it can be protected. The people who are being pushed off the land and isolated from using it are kept in the dark, unheard of outside of international NGOs or activists pursuing deeper knowledge on the situation.

A.T. Nzama, writing from the Department of Recreation and Tourism at the University of Zululand, attempted to examine the nexus between sustainable livelihoods and ecological management. By speaking with local community members as well as workers for the local and regional authorities, Nzama attempted to ascertain what kind of understanding exists on the ground about the structural forces at play. There was a relative lack of knowledge about what authorities oversee in policy creation. Nzama acknowledges that "it is evident that there is still a need for more awareness programmes" that aim to reach out to community members (Nzama 2009: 40). The lack of consultation with occupants of land is a massive problem. Beyond not granting access to local communities to have a say in how resources and land are managed, it limits the understanding of local cultural practices and understandings too. Nustad acknowledges that there has been a history of traditional authorities deceiving their communities and benefitting at their expense (Nustad 2015: 130), which will be expanded on in the conclusion of this paper.

Hansen and Nustad concluded from examining the land issues in IWP that there is a wide-range of problems occurring at the same time which are contributing to the further marginalisation of people. The historical issues surrounding discriminatory policies have not been properly addressed and have bled into the new governance structures. This, combined with weak local and regional authorities, a confusing intersection of conflicting interest groups all out to achieve contradictory aims, and a neoliberal economic ideology underpinning business strategies and models is crushing the weakest sectors of the region by placing the restrictions on their rights and the burden of self-sufficiency without adequate support on their shoulders.

5 Conclusion

It must be understood that IWP is still relatively young. It has moved beyond infancy and is now in the difficult teenage years. It can point to many successes with regards to its rewilding and conservation programmes. Its formation in a post-apartheid state has brought many challenges; the hangover of distrust between person and authority based on decades and centuries of subjugation has carried over into relations between communities and the IWPA. Despite acknowledging these complex problems, there are clear shortcomings when it comes to the disparity between the aims and achievements claimed by the IWPA and the contested marginalisation felt by people on the ground. Different perspectives highlight how governance structures are seen in contradictory terms. The convoluted nature of the IWP answering to a global institution as well as national and local authorities complicates and confuses people both working and living in and on the fringes of the park. There is ample evidence to suggest that economic logic and ideological preferences are leading to certain actors in society receiving more benefits than others, and this has been a result of a continuation of policies in the country at large. IWP has spoken about trying to arrest this cycle but the reporting of excluded voices on the ground in the pursuit of bureaucratic arrangements with governance structures is testimony to the opposite occurring.

There is strong advocacy from the park towards a tourism-based approach to alleviating poverty. The successes in this regard are small and there are more and more cases emerging that show it is having the opposite effect for entire communities. Some of the strategies adopted have had successes, but each situation must be dealt with uniquely, accounting for the complexity of historical contexts in that area. Democracy arrived in the country over twenty years ago, but the wealthy class did not lose influence or power. Rich landowners and business people maintained their control and, based on free-market principles, have sought to enrich and improve upon their status. An ideological battle exists between those wanting to expose the park to as many profit-generating enterprises as possible and those who argue that this is counter-intuitive to promoting and maintaining inclusive development strategies for communities.

Case studies in the park continue to highlight that privileged actors are being presented with access, resources, and business opportunities while others are being systematically marginalised through either physical restriction, lack of access to opportunities and knowledge, or/and the creation and implementation of Western-style instruments of power that require people to apply for permits that they never receive or, in some cases, are completely ignored. It is understandable in these circumstances that local communities respond by flaunting these regulations. Their deep-seated distrust of authorities, who they perceive to be excluding them, has manifested itself in resistance, both physical and non-confrontational. For any measure of steps forward to become a reality there must be arduous, pain-staking work done to build trust and communication at the local levels of communities.

While there has been a lot of criticism towards Western-style governance supplanting local and traditional hierarchies, it has also been evident that some of these leaders are flawed and have not always included their communities in decisions and their benefits. Thus, looking to implement wide scale changes at a national or regional administrative level alone is not going to work. A challenge going forward for discourse around sustainable development and conservation has been highlighted through the case of IWP – there is no template or fixed strategy that will bring harmony and prosperity to places of disputed land ownership and displaced peoples. Promoting a park as a new and innovative model that can completely reshape the current environmental landscape appears to be a wonderful marketing strategy for attracting tourism and revenue but it is also misinformed and disingenuous with regards to the wider effects occurring within local communities in the area.

The trust and mutual respect between local communities and administrative bodies has been eroded, if it had ever been established in the first place, and is one of the key areas that needs to be addressed for participatory conservation to become a realistic aim. The studies that are grounded in fieldwork and grassroots activism strongly advocate for local people having a say in how the community manages resources and distributes wealth. The absence of understanding among people in communities studied about their supposed stake in lodges and tourist ventures shows that much work needs to be done regarding the alignment of the lofty aims on paper with real action on the ground. These difficult 'trade-offs' are demonstrably important for IWP because of the guidelines from international organisations that establish discourses and outline assessments, which the park must abide by. The IUCN report discussed in this paper shows the disparity between the environmental targets it strives for, versus the social impact the park has. This stark contrast is understandable within a report designed to predominantly examine the natural effects of human interaction on the park, even if it does contain a miniscule section on local populations. More revealing, however, are the interactions the park has with authority figures in the government who assess the ways the park is dealing with communities in and around the park. There is very little overview, and what does exist is more of a presentation than a critical dialogue. Setting aside any 'cynical' ideas about why the park places more emphasis on the development of environmental policies and far less on the involvement of communities in decision-making processes and opportunities, there clearly exist far more powerful incentives to direct attention towards ecological issues and not human ones.

The park was established at a time when positivity and aspiration for change were washing across the political spectrum in the country. The symbolic nature of the park has helped it to become a place that represents hope. The former CEO Andrew Zaloumis has been clear in his message that, while the park is establishing some fantastic projects and investing in the future, particularly by educating children, the park is not magically washing away the structural inequalities created over decades of apartheid, nor is it capable of uplifting over half a million people in the area from poverty. The problem lies not only with IWP but with the larger structures in place that it must answer to. The lack of oversight about what these co-management agreements mean to the local communities needs to be highlighted and challenged because research on the ground, in academic circles, has shown that there is a huge dearth of opportunities for those living in the area.

Exploring Local People's Agency in Community-Based Nature Conservation: Lessons Learned at the iSimangaliso Wetland Park

Georg Bergthaler

1 Introduction

Located in one of South Africa's poorest districts, the iSimangaliso Wetland Park (or IWP) encompasses an area stretching southwards from the north-western tip of the country at the border to Mozambique (Obura et al. 2012, online). Since the uMkhanyakude district was declared KwaZulu 'homeland' in 1977 under the apartheid regime, basic infrastructure and the delivery of social services – among them sanitation, health services, clean water, education, and housing – have not been set in place until very recently.

The town of St Lucia, today's touristic heart of the park, had been a stronghold of white supremacy since the late nineteenth century. The St. Lucia Hunting Grounds, which were established in the vicinity of today's park already in 1895, initially were a game reserve intended almost exclusively for entertainment and pleasure of colonial elites, trophy hunters, and self-styled 'sportsmen'. Successively, access became restricted to the locals (Nustad 2011: 95; van Damme/ Meskell 2009: 74).

When South Africa became a democracy in 1994 and the Greater St Lucia Wetland Park was proclaimed a World Heritage Site in 1999 (only later to be renamed to IWP in 2007), the socio-political situation started to shift in the area. The park was seen as a major driver of socio-economic development in the region. With the intention to break with the history of exclusion in nature conservation, land claimant communities, driven from their territories during apartheid, were included in the management of the park (Fabricius/ de Wet 2008: 143 pp.).

From late May to mid-June 2016 a team of post graduate anthropology students (to which I belonged) visited the IWP with the shared intention to explore how Community-Based Natural Resource Management (hereafter CBNRM) was implemented and experienced on the ground. Within the scope of our team's research objectives, the central aim of this paper is to identify and analyse the current status and participation of the local community in the management of iSimangaliso Wetland Park and in the ecotourism sector. As mentioned above, these factors are promoted as central economic drivers for local development by the iSimangaliso Wetland Park Authority (hereafter IWPA). The main objective is to find out how residential people perceive or feel about iSimangaliso and whether they are collectively empowered through the project. Consequently, the following two research questions have been framed to receive thorough attention by this paper:

(1) How and on which discursive and legal basis has involvement of locally residing communities been integrated in the planning and realisation of CBNRM at IWP?

(2) How successful or effective have the IWPA's strategies been in achieving local communities' political empowerment so far and what are major challenges faced in these respects at the moment?

The first section of this paper will briefly outline how political discourse concerning nature parks, which started in the 1980s, opened up to broader perspectives and – as a result – encouraged legislative measures internationally and nationally which created the framework for CBNRM. I will then also elaborate on socio-historical events, environmentalist ideas, developmental plans, and political decisions taken locally that had a strong impact on the park's current status. Further, special attention will be given to how the IWPA balances development and conservation interests by deploying concepts of co-management in governance and private equity-partnerships.

Thereafter I will focus on traditional fishing communities' livelihoods inside the park. In particular, economic opportunities and participatory governance structures set in place in the Kosi Bay area will be analysed in greater detail.

The final section will be dedicated to the discussion of CBNRM implications in iSimangaliso Wetland Park and critical concerns with regard to power relations between communities and the IWPA. In conclusion, I will answer my research questions on the basis of my previous argumentation.

2 A New Model for Nature Conservation: CBNRM in iSimangaliso Wetland Park

2.1 People and Parks: Political Discourse and Legal Incentives

Towards the end of the 20th century, the dominant conservational concept aimed at excluding people from demarcated areas for the protection of 'pristine wilderness'. This concept, prominently referred to as 'fortress conservation', became increasingly contested by critical scholarship. Critics emphasised the 'constructedness' of seemingly uninhabited 'wild' places by pointing out that indigenous and local communities had been deliberately expelled from many areas that had been set aside for conservation. In scholarly debate, the so called 'Yellowstone model' was scrutinised through the lens of effectiveness and social justification. Based on the weight of evidence provided in various studies the view prevailed that framing landscapes as natural or cultural and 'productive' or 'consumptive' rests on a dualistic worldview which ignores the fact that environment has been historically shaped by people for millennia. As a consequence, international pressure is increasingly put on nations and conservation agencies to shift towards more participatory, human-centred approaches (Adams 2003: 34; Agrawal/ Gibson 1999: 632; Sudnes 2013: 6, 19; Hughes/ Beinart 2007: 303; Nustad/ Sudnes 2013: 495; Zips-Mairitsch/ Zips 2007).

Already in 1982, the IUCN World National Parks Congress in Bali addressed that "people are part of nature" (Turner 2014: 294). In 1992, the United Nations Convention on Biological Diversity (hereafter CBD), a legally binding treaty which declares "1) the conservation of biological diversity, 2) the sustainable use of components of biological diversity, and 3) the fair and equitable sharing of the benefits arising out of the utilization of genetic resources" (Reimerson 2013: 999) as its main objectives, was signed by 193 States at the Earth Summit in Rio de Janeiro (Crane et al. 2009: 144). In its preamble, it explicitly recognises "the close and traditional dependence of many indigenous and local communities embodying traditional lifestyles on biological resources, and the desirability of sharing equitably benefits arising from the use of traditional knowledge, innovations and practices relevant to the conservation of biological diversity and the sustainable use of its components" (CBD 1992: preamble, online).

South Africa formally ratified the CBD in 1996, only shortly after the country's first democratic elections were held in 1994. In the following years, South Africa consecutively opened up for more collaborative approaches in the management of protected areas. The aim to join interests of conservation and socio-economic development becomes apparent in the newly re-framed South African Constitution. The Bill of Rights Section 24 states that: "Everyone has the right to an environment that is not harmful to their health or well-being; and to have the environment protected, for the benefit of present and future generations, through reasonable legislative and other measures that prevent pollution and ecological degradation; promote conservation; and secure ecologically sustainable development and use of natural resources while promoting justifiable economic and social development" (Parliament of the Republic of South Africa 1996, online).

In the National Environmental Management: Biodiversity Act 10 of 2004, the "fair and equitable sharing" of benefits among stakeholders is emphasised. The Protected Areas Act of 2003 promotes the "sustainable utilization of protected areas for the benefit of people" as well as "participation of local communities in the management of the protected areas, where appropriate" (Isaacs/ Sunde 2008: 8). In its fifth five-year obligatory report to the Convention on Biological Diversity, South Africa's focal person highlighted that the "People and Parks" programme addresses "issues at the interface between conservation and communities, in particular the realisation of tangible benefits by communities who were previously displaced to make way for the establishment of protected areas" (CBD 2014, online). In this context, iSimangaliso Wetland Park is referenced as a primary example for the successful implementation of co-management agreements and structures supporting socio-economic development and communities which live in or adjacent to the park.

iSimangaliso was declared South Africa's first World Heritage Site in 1999 and was considered an "asset of global significance" for the world, meeting three out of ten criteria established by the World Heritage Convention: The park was noted to be of "outstanding universal value" for its "(vii) superlative natural phenomena or natural beauty, (ix) ongoing biological and ecological processes and (x) biological diversity and threatened species" (Obura et al. 2012: 23 pp.). Additionally, the park contains four wetlands of international importance under the Ramsar Convention (Scott et al. 2012: 205). Almost simultaneously with iSimangaliso's listing as a World Heritage Site, the South African government adopted the World Heritage Convention Act. This measure was meant to ensure both the protection of values and principles of the World Heritage Convention and the alignment with the country's tourism and poverty alleviation strategies by creating jobs and entrepreneurial opportunities for local communities (Magi/ Nzama 2009: 97). The Act highlighted the necessity to involve "vulnerable and historically disadvantaged persons" in the management of the park by emphasising that "decisions must take into account the interests, needs and values of all interested and affected parties" (Hansen et al. 2014: 45).

Since iSimangaliso is both a terrestrial and a marine World Heritage Site, it is listed as a representative example for marine World Heritage Sites by the World Heritage Convention, which also acknowledges: "(T)he presence of people for thousands of years in the area [. . . who] today continue to have a rich relationship with the land", and further points out the need to deliver economic opportunities for "neighboring communities, without which the long term integrity of the property could be compromised" (Obura et al. 2012: 23).

2.2 Socio-historical Background of the Transnational Lubombo Area

Before the declaration as a World Heritage Site, the dunes along the park's coastlines were targeted by a multinational company for mining of titanium and other heavy metals in the late 1980s and early 1990s. However, the project was opposed by a strong environmentalist movement collecting half a million signatures – among them Nelson Mandela's, who was later elected South Africa's first democratic president. Thus, the issue attracted international attention.

As a result, an environmental impact assessment was undertaken by a state-appointed commission chaired by Justice Ramon Leon. The commission concluded in its final report to the cabinet that ecotourism would be a more sustainable land-use option than mining, the latter only providing employment for a limited time and comparatively few people (Chellan/ Khan 2008: 281 pp.; Hansen et al. 2014: 46 pp.). Thus, the new democratic government ruled against mining and for the protection of the areas, which it regarded as the more feasible economic growth strategy.

Originally, iSimangaliso was part of a much bigger project, the Lubombo Spatial Development Initiative (hereafter LSDI), a transnational project to upgrade infrastructure and internationally upscale a transfrontier area between Southern Mozambique, Northern KwaZulu-Natal in South Africa and Eastern Swaziland. The aim of this project was to end what Nelson Mandela famously called the "paradox of human misery amongst natural plenty". This is confirmed by the former CEO of the IWP, Andrew Zaloumis, who was project manager of the former Greater St Lucia Wetland Park (Zaloumis 11.11.2014, interview). In order to achieve their objectives, the LSDI strove to provide means to "generate economic growth by making maximum use of the inherent, but underutilized, potential of the area; to maximize private-sector involvement and create an attractive and stable climate for investors to operate in; and to maximize job creation by ensuring that the new industries being stimulated are competitive and have a long-term future in the region" (Hansen et al. 2013: 45). After its launch, the governmental development plan first sought to reduce the high levels of malaria, which was a common cause of death among local populations and hindered tourists from visiting the region. This was accomplished through an intensive spraying programme, almost ridding the South African region of LSDI completely of malaria. Secondly, access to the area was improved through infrastructural upgrades: The N2 highway from Durban to St Lucia was modernised and a new road was built from Hluhluwe to the Mozambique border. Thirdly, visas between the three participating countries were dropped (Zaloumis 11.11.2014, interview).

Due to the high tourism potential of the Lubombo region, another agreement for a Transfrontier Conservation and Resource Area (hereafter TFCA) was put into effect in 2000, shortly after the proclamation of the then Greater Wetland Park as a World Heritage Site. Thus, the area became one of five distinct TFCA Areas (Hansen et al. 2014: 46), linking the Mozambiquan Ponta do Ouro Marine Protected Area (MPA) to iSimangaliso's Kosi Bay MPA (Zaloumis 11.11.2014, interview).

The main objective of these measures was to "accelerate development, generate sustainable jobs and create conditions for the establishment of an internationally competitive tourism destination" (Moosa 2000 cited in Hansen et al. 2014: 46), as pointed out by the South African Minister of Environmental Affairs and Tourism at the time. As a consequence, the authorities endeavoured to develop ecologically sustainable tourism. Since the status as a World Heritage Site attracts international recognition, the prominence of the area has risen considerably: Not only as a 'not-to-be-missed' tourist attraction but also as a promising project location for raising international financial funding (such as from NGOs) and as an inviting environment for private investors. In order to secure and support this boost of entrepreneurial activity, one of the key goals of the park's management is to retain the World Heritage status by maintaining its high natural standards through sensitive conservation measures (Magi/ Nzama 2009: 97). Since it is a developmental agency as well, the iSimangaliso Wetland Park Authority is thus confronted with the challenge of linking strict conservation policies with the improvement of socio-economic conditions for the local people.

2.3 Land Rights, Co-Management, and Equity Partnerships

Initially, the sixteen different parcels of land which were consolidated (by also incorporating the space in between) under the proclamation of the park as a World Heritage Site were under land claim to one-hundred percent (Zaloumis 11.11.2014, interview). So far, nine of fourteen land claims have been settled (as of June 2016). However, the restitution of land to formerly forcibly resettled people creates problems for nature conservation since generally land ownership grants the right to use the land and harvest its resources. This is perceived as a potential threat to conservational interests by the IWPA; especially, if the World Heritage status, dependent on the ecological integrity of the park, is at stake. Former CEO Andrew Zaloumis presents the authority's solution, a proposal for a compromise: "People must get titles. It's non-negotiable. But the trick is, in the settlement, that you get the title, you don't come back and settle the land, but you enter a co-management agreement" (Zaloumis 11.11.2014, interview).

In case of successful land claims, this means that physical occupation of land does not take place. Rather, the title is only transferred to the respective communities under specific cooperative agreements, often granting them limited access to natural resources in the park and financial compensation through various benefit sharing arrangements (Hansen et al. 2015: 404). For instance, land right owners get a share from gate intakes, called "community levy" (collected for land claimants in a trust to be distributed among community members if their claim is successful) (Shabalala 05.12.2014, interview; Mkhwanazi 01.06.2016, interview). Also, they are mandatory BEE (Black Economic Empowerment) partners in private sector enterprises. As regards tourism activity-licenses, these are only issued to enterprises which are co-managed by the community that holds at least 70% of the shares. Furthermore, accommodation facilities have been established that provide equity shareholding for the community in the range of 20 to 61%. The high-class luxury establishment, Thonga Beach Lodge, and the Mabibi Community Campsite are prime examples of such establishments (Scott et al. 2012: 212). According to the local traditional authority, inDuna Issiah Mabibi Mdletshe, the community is presently still paying off the 6 million Rand funding with the incomes. However, in about 10 years profit is supposed to be generated through the Lodge that currently employs 38-40 locals (Mdletshe 16.02.2012, interview).

Such equity partnerships form an essential component of the IWPA's five-year Integrated Management Plan (hereafter IMP) which is set to deliver "benefits beyond boundaries" – the slogan promoting CBNRM as "a new model" for protected area management internationally – while conforming to strict environmental guidelines accorded to maintain world heritage standards (Magi/ Nzama 2009: 97; Scott et al. 2012: 216). According to Hansen et al., such state-led nature-based tourism initiatives trying to "integrate conservation and sustainable development in the context of free markets [. . .] are often conceptually geared at the ecological modernization paradigm, which is based on the theory that economic growth can be reconciled with ecological conservation, ideally bringing about so-called win-win situations" (Hansen et al. 2015: 401).

Critical scholars, however, question the supposed balance of interests of this approach by bringing forth empirical evidence from field studies where, in many cases, conservation clearly turned out to be the primary focus of co-management agreements rather than an effective "instrument for poverty alleviation". Such evidence has been submitted by Sunde and Isaacs (2008) in the context of marine protected areas, where they also refer to two examples in iSimangaliso Wetland Park.

For Hansen et al. (2014: 49), the focus on conservation as the primary concern of IWP, supposedly framing locally beneficial development only as a secondary priority, becomes already apparent in the park's official choice of words when it comes to its "develop to conserve" approach. Hansen et al. allege that this approach regards economic involvement of local people only as an unavoidable, compulsory compromise to guarantee the security of the park's natural bounty in favour of conservationists' interests. However, there are also different approaches: Thandi Shabalala, iSimangaliso's tourism and information coordinator, states that "this place [was suggested by the Leon commission to] be developed for ecotourism" (Shabalala 22.02.2012, interview) as a legitimate alternative for employment as opposed to mining. Furthermore, she highlights the facts that "tourism is helping our youth to learn, so they can benefit from this area [... and that] iSimangaliso itself has programmes that are educating and raising awareness in the communities." By emphasising these factors, Thandi Shabalala, reveals a broader perspective represented by the IWPA and creates a more nuanced and differentiated picture of the park's considerations inherent to their management concept.

As of 2014, "iSimangaliso has created 40,354 temporary jobs and 1,037 permanent jobs, has offered training to some 33,000 people in a wide range of skills, from art to hospitality, supported 67 young people through university [scholarships], and provided entrepreneurial support to 174 small businesses" (IWP 2016, online). Temporary jobs for members of communities adjacent to or inside the park include various rehabilitation programmes for flora (and fauna), reintroducing indigenous vegetation in some areas and cutting down alien plants in others as well as infrastructural projects such as building roads through the park, setting up fences and preparing tourism facilities. Training programmes are offered or supported by the park authority in hospitality, tourism and tour-guiding, handicrafts, various arts, acting drama, and business skills (Scott et al. 2012: 213 pp.).

However, what former CEO Andrew Zaloumis regards as most promising in terms of 'deep' empowerment are high education scholarships. Such scholarships are issued by iSimangaliso for students from local communities coming from an economically disadvantaged background. In the same vein, entrepreneurial mentoring programmes are designed to assist Black local entrepreneurs in the start-up phase of their businesses (Zaloumis 11.11.2014, interview). Zaloumis states proudly: "We have about fifty students currently at university [...]. There is a 98% passing rate [...] and these are kids from deep rural areas who don't have the same access to electricity, school books, extra lessons. And, they're coming back into the park and they are tomorrow's CEOs. [. . .] in May this year we had our first ten, eleven interns into a very small organization" (ibid.).

Zaloumis mentions Philip Mkhwanazi to be a good example of a successful entrepreneur; he is the inDuna or headman of Khula village, which is located in the Dukuduku forest at the park's Western border along the road to St Lucia. His community, previously led by his father, was forcefully removed from another section of the forest. According to him, Philip has not received higher education. Working first for iSimangaliso to remove alien plants in the forest and later as a taxi driver for workers, he raised money to slowly build up a cultural village, for which he also received direct financial support by the park authorities (Mkhwanazi 01.06.2016, interview). Today, it has become a working place for about 23 families, and every Saturday and Sunday Philip provides temporary jobs for young adults who attend educational instutitions throughout the week. Meanwhile, he also offers boat cruises in the estuary system of the park through a co-management partnership with Mandy Muir, a tour operator in St Lucia (ibid.). Philip, who regards iSimangaliso as a great economic driver in the region that grants a range of opportunities to small businesses and creates employment, heavily promotes the park in his community. Although, he also recognises: "Not everybody is going to get a job. Like here in Khula, 17,000 people plus minus, they are not gonna get a job with iSimangaliso. [. . .] So people that don't work for iSimangaliso, they are angry with iSimangaliso. Even though we tell them, iSimangalio – they employ people from areas along the Umfolozi River up to Kosi Bay" (ibid.). This fact is also acknowledged by CEO Andrew Zaloumis. Considering the approximately 620,000 people living in and around the park who legitimately have a right to benefit from the park on their ancestral lands, he states: "Yes, it [iSimangaliso] can deliver jobs, it can deliver benefits, but it's limited [. . . There is also] the need for other drivers in the region, whether it's industry, whether it's agriculture, [or] forestry" (Zaloumis 11.11.2014, interview).

3 Possibilities and Limitations of Economic Life inside iSimangaliso

3.1 Traditional Fish Trapping at Kosi Bay

Traditional fishing practices by communities living around the Kosi Bay lakes are estimated to have existed for up to seven hundred years in the area. Using traditional fish traps to catch fish is believed to have remained fundamentally unaltered for generations. The so-called kraals, heart shaped configurations of wooden fences placed in shallow waters along the shores of the Kosi lakes, direct fish towards grills or small baskets between one and two meters wide with a valve opening constructed in a way that fish can get in but (except for very small ones) cannot escape again. These kraals are traditionally inherited patrilineally from fathers to sons.

The fish, travelling upstream in the lakes and channels at night towards the estuary system's mouth which forms the connection to the ocean, get caught in the traps and are then usually speared by trap owners the next morning. According to marine scientist, R. Kyle, who has been studying fish populations in the lakes for about three decades: "[T]he surrounding area is very rural, with little formal employment, and the community is heavily dependent on natural resources for their basic needs of food, shelter, medicines and warmth" (Kyle 2013: 68).

In 1981, a cooperative monitoring process with residential community members was initiated because environmental managers from Ezemvelo KwaZulu-Natal Wildlife (hereafter Ezemvelo KZNW) were worried that potential conflicts between increasing numbers of recreational anglers and subsistence trappers could harm fish stocks. According to the results, an increase in catch numbers corresponding to an increase in traps that negatively impact sustainability levels of various fish species could only be detected in the last decade of the study (ibid.: 75).

As Kyle suggests, however, the major causes of the decline in fish were not, the increased number of traps – as new ones had to be built in less propitious areas since the better areas were already occupied by first trappers – but the use of modern materials and placement of traps inside formerly trap free channels. Nylon ropes and gum-poles reduce the gaps between the terminal baskets to such an extent that smaller, (and consequently) younger, immature fish could not easily escape the traps any longer.

Kyle as well as many locals and even some trappers themselves regard the recent economic improvements in the region and better access to marketplaces as the key drivers of this development. With sales going up, prices for fish went down. While historically fish trapping was only meant to supplement income for small trade or reciprocal gift exchange and primarily intended as a means to acquire vital proteins to satisfy basic nutritional needs, it has, in the last couple of years, become vehemently commercialised. This has raised criticism for instance with regard to trucks coming from Durban to transport tons of cheap fish back to markets in the city. Such concerns were voiced by a contracted boat driver who provides guided tours in two of the Kosi Bay lakes for tourists staying at the community-owned and managed Utshwayelo Lodge, thus affirming Kyle's argumentation (Kyle 2013: 74 pp.).

Furthermore, the new economic incentive has led to the abandonment of traditional constraints. Under the pressuring conditions of cut-throat market competition, many trappers sell fish of any size since the only thing that counts at the markets is the weight of the catch. Jeffery Tembe, a staff member and security employee at the Utshwayelo Lodge as well as owner of a few kraals (for subsistence purposes), stated: "People don't care about tomorrow." When asked about the overfishing, he added that some species have become extinct in the past or are now non-existent in the lakes due to such practices.

Following Kyle's recommendation for "management intervention [. . .] now required to reduce catches to levels that appear to be wise, sustainable and appropriate for this World Heritage Site, to the mutual benefit of local trappers and other fishers" (ibid.: 77), the iSimangaliso Park Authority has developed some measures in close collaboration with its contracted partner Ezemvelo KZNW, who is responsible for the day-to-day conservation business. iSimangalso thus profits from Ezemvelo KZNW's extensive and long-standing expertise and is able to focus primarily on innovation (Zaloumis 11.11.2014, interview; Lugago 10.06.2016, interview; Tunley 2009: 43). These measures intend to protect species and reduce fish catches to ecologically sustainable levels by constraining commercial activity.

There continues to be a "mixed tolerance for illegal fishing activities within the communities" (Tunley 2009: 138), since selling fish was already forbidden for fishers with subsistence permits in MPAs under the Marine Living Resources Act (MLRA Act 18 of 1998) which is overseen by the Marine and Coastal Management (hereafter MCM), a national conservation agency for MPAs contracted to work with Ezemvelo KZNW (Isaacs/Sunde 2008: 10 pp.). However, "growing support for conservation staff with some opposition that could be overcome through the involvement of communities" (Tunley 2009: 130) has been reported to funding agencies of iSimangaliso's MPAs such as the World Wildlife Fund for Nature (hereafter WWF). This statement was confirmed by one interviewee, Mduduzi Tembe, a 19-year-old fisher and kayak tour guide for visitors from the Utshwayelo Lodge, who spoke in high tones of iSimangaliso, saying that the project is a "good thing", educating people about sustainable harvesting (methods) and creating jobs for the future (Tembe 08.06.2016, interview).

Other means to raise awareness and to contribute to local capacity are, for instance, the adult environmental education programme for subsistence fishers and staff as well as the distribution of pamphlets in English and Zulu, including practical information about tide-times or MLRA regulations. Representatives from the IWPA also reported to WWF in 2009 that community meetings with fish-trappers, anglers and traditional harvesters from the communities take place once a month, although it remains unclear to which extent people actually and effectively participate in the decision-making concerning their activities and their existence inside the park's territory. Mduduzi Tembe mentioned that in the meeting in June 2016, it was decided by iSimangaliso that each household or family would be allowed to own and operate only two kraals in the future. According to him, the iSimangaliso authorities argued that this would be a necessary measure to prevent overexploitation of the local fish species (ibid.).

The majority of people in the area on both the South African and Mozambiquan side of the border are of Thonga descent. The communities, however, were divided with the establishment of the border into two chiefdoms, both under the rule of a royal family member of the Tembe clan (CBD report 2014, online), called inKosi, to whom the inDunas, appointed by the inKosi, are subordinate. The Utshwayelo Lodge, another example of an equity partnership between locals and the private sector, is "currently run and managed by Ken Whitfield and Enock Tembe in association with Chief Tembe and the community elected committee. [... It] provides an income to the community in the form of rental, profit share and job opportunities" (Utshwayelo Lodge 2011, online). In recent years, an influx of people from Zulu origin migrated to the area, this is also why new kraals are now distributed to all community members by the inKosi, including Zulu residents. With the rising demand on fish traps and increased restrictions from the park, people like Mduduzi, who inherited the kraal from his father, do not see any economic future in fishing: "I wanna do something that I can look better for myself because this one [fishing] is just to survive, you cannot depend on this for the rest of your life" (Tembe 08.06.2016, interview).

3.2 Legal and Socio-political Restrictions of Community Members' Livelihoods

Other empirical studies on iSimangaliso reveal similar confinements on resource use (for basic needs). This makes traditional economic activities increasingly unattractive, leading either to their diminution or the criminalisation of people who do not see or do not have alternative options to sustain their (families') lives other than to continue with illegalised practices.

Sunde and Isaacs found that members of the Mabibi community admitted to harvest and fish "beyond the legal limits and outside their subsistence permit conditions" (Sunde/ Isaacs 2008: 26) out of mere frustration about what they saw as insufficient numbers of fish to take out, as they are apparently limited to the same catch per day as recreational fishers. Further, they were not allowed to launch any vessels, not even non-motorised canoes from the shore in contrast to the local Thonga Beach Lodge, a partly community-run luxury accommodation, which has its own private access road to the beach. Consequently, desperation was shared among fishers who felt treated unjustly by Ezemvelo, whom they considered responsible for these inequalities. Sunde and Isaacs also highlight that community members were not aware of any benefits coming from the lodge or trainings offered by iSimangaliso. Apart from working at the lodge, the close-by Mabibi campsite, or for the (now discontinued) Coast Care Programme no alternative economic opportunities existed in the area (ibid.: 26 pp.).

Research in KwaDapha by Hansen et al. also showed that people felt very restricted in their ways of life, quoting a number of reasons. For one, the community was not allowed to build a primary school in the village, for it was regarded as ecologically irreconcilable by the IWPA (Hansen et al. 2013: 52). Further, they were prohibited from renovating a publicly desired new Methodist church, or even their houses, and from fishing in the lake St Lucia. With regard to their instrumental freedoms, Hansen et al. concluded that people did not feel as though they were taken seriously in their wishes, concerns, and plans. When local applicants intended to establish a four star diving lodge as an equity partnership with a private investor as their mandatory community partner, quite similar to the example of the Thonga Beach Lodge in Mabibi, their application faced heavy opposition by the IWPA who condemned the project, labelling it "ecological theft" (Hansen et al. 2013: 409).

Moreover, tribal authorities were identified by many scholars as highly ambiguous figures with regard to their roles as community representatives. Because the IWPA engages in negotiations on issues concerning the whole community through mostly small committees or tribal councils, internal hierarchies often block the flow of information, thereby potentially hindering benefits from "trickling down" (Hansen 2013: 408; Sunde/ Isaacs 2008: 27). It is up to the inKosis (Lugago 10.06.2016, interview) and / or inDunas (Mkhwanazi 01.06.2016, interview), who receive the subvention-cheques, to decide how to invest the money generated from the community-levy or other funds collected in so called community trusts. However, some community members complain about the lack of transparency in the distribution of revenues: "[W]here the money goes afterwards [the inDunas receive it], very few know", as was also stated by an intern working for the IWP authorities (Lugago 10.06.2016, interview). The legitimacy of traditional leaders is increasingly disputed within communities: Critical voices accuse the inDunas of acting only in and for their personal interest, or their inKosi of "not acting as a people's king" (Hansen 2013: 408). Land claimants at Dukuduku

South even completely reject their tribal authorities "because the traditional leaders want to sell the lands but [...] we want to keep land. If iSimangaliso wants to conserve, wants to use our land, we must be part of the negotiation", as put forward by the vice chair and board member of the Land Claimant Committee in Dukuduku South, Siybane Petros Ncube (Ncube 3.6.2016, interview).

4 Participatory Governance: A Pathway towards Local Communities' Empowerment?

In alignment with other studies about communities' livelihoods inside iSimangaliso Wetland Park, our research in the area brought the tensions between conservational and local people's interests to the fore. Although participatory governance structures, in cooperation with the park's authorities and through several entrepreneurial partnerships with private investors, have been partly set in place, a lack of information about individual and collective rights as well as ongoing beneficiary programmes and projects seems to limit many residents in their perspectives. This may be partially owed to collaborative agreements that were primarily negotiated with tribal authorities suspected by some to distribute incomes disproportionately. For many who depend on natural resources to sustain their (families') lives, restrictions have led to frustration about what they consider to be conservationists' attempts to criminalise their resource use by deeming their activities "over-extractive" (Isaacs/ Sunde 2008: 37).

Several interviewees (e.g. Zaloumis 11.11.2014, interview; Mkhwanazi 01.06.2016), among them an intern working for the IWPA, stated in reference to the history of racial segregation in South Africa that: "To [many local community members], conservation is just ... it is apartheid" (Lugago 10.06.2016, interview). Along the same lines, Hansen et al. speak of a "decrease of local people's entitlement to land and access to resources" through the implementation of what they define as "neoliberal" and market-based pseudo "win-win" mechanism, which they regard as a continued form of spatial, economic, and political separation (Hansen et al. 2015: 410).

In the context of securing the park's status as a World Heritage Site, the persistent notion among representatives of concerned agencies, such as the WHC, Ezemvelo KZNW, or the IWPA, is that communities need to be involved for the sake of conservation. There is a widely shared consensus that communities are otherwise exposed to internal or, as the case of unsustainable fishing in Kosi Bay has shown, external incentives that lead them to destroy or rob the natural resources in their surroundings for personal gains. As interpreted by IWPA's intern Phumlani Lugago: "getting that from the bible [. . .] people as homo sapiens [think they] own the environment, that they can do whatever they want with the environment, [that] they are the owners" (Lugago 10.06.2016, interview).

This notion of communities or people being exploitative of resources *by nature* has most famously been used by Hardin in his theory about the 'tragedy of the commons'. As published in an often-cited article from 1968, he suggested that people would always overuse resources that were freely accessible based on the capitalistic concept of "homo oeconomicus" which assumes that human beings act primarily for their personal benefit. Hardin argued that individuals strive in their own best interest to gain private profit first, therefore rendering them unable to effectively share common resources. Since, however, critical scholarship has discredited Hardin's theory by delivering numerous examples (e.g. Ostrom 1990) which prove that communities are capable of coordinating themselves to sustainably manage common resources through developing systems for mutual monitoring and institutions to set up and adjust norms and sanctions (Bergthaler 2015: 20 pp.). Thus, it is important to note at this point that communities are indeed able to self-manage their lands if given the necessary time to harmonise or sensitise with their environments and build up functioning societal structures out of such synergies. However, the prevalence of top down mechanisms in the governance structures of the IWPA – resembling an approach to counter a tragedy of the commons in iSimangaliso – are partly justified through the argument that many land claiming communities, for the most part removed from the site during what is often termed 'Grand Apartheid' between 1950 and 1970 (Nustad/ Sudnes 2013: 298) and now "come back as visitors", have lost their strong connection to and in-depth knowledge of the land, as explained by former CEO Zaloumis (Zaloumis 11.11.2014, interview).

Accompanying and assisting communities in processes of maintaining or re-establishing sustainable relationships to their lands is surely supportive of both the development of a high quality of life for local people of land claiming or land-owning communities, who either returned or never seized to live inside or around IWP, and the protection, preservation, and improvement of natural balance and bounty across the park's borders trans-regionally. The example of traditional fish-trapping at Kosi Bay proves that carefully mediated intervention is an appropriate way to prevent ecological damage or crises of resource scarcity. As mentioned above, this is necessary due to an increased market demand for fish, which leads to rising numbers of immigrant trappers settling in the communities and the use of newly introduced materials for resource harvest.

Various cooperative education programmes have been set up by the IWPA, Ezemvelo KZNW, and other environmental NGOs and governmental agencies. These programmes teach about the necessity of rules and regulations limiting, for instance, the outtake of fish and guaranteeing an ecologically sustainable extraction of resources (e.g. incema grass). Further, they recommend subsidised or otherwise facilitated and promoted alternative economic options for concerned or dependent people. Such programmes have been designed, implemented, and are continuously re-evaluated in accordance to the experience gained from different programmes' strengths and weaknesses, successes or failures.

Providing education and alternative livelihood options are key steps in helping people regain an ecologically sustainable relationship with local environments. These measures also correspond with conservation interests. Simultaneously, I would identify them as forming two of four pillars that enable local communities' sovereign empowerment, as described by Arun and Clark (1999). The third pillar is democratic involvement and representation of all interests of individuals or groups within communities, which need to be perceived as inherently heterogeneous rather than homogenous in their composition. Finally, the fourth pillar is the acknowledgement of communities as rights holders, not merely stakeholders and treating them accordingly. This means meeting and negotiating with them on an equal footing and gradually handing over more management responsibilities to them, for which they are compensated appropriately; especially if sensitive conservational issues are at stake.

In this context, I can only affirm Manuela Zips-Mairitsch' and Werner Zips' statement: "The object is that they [indigenous people] achieve a self-determined future, based on regained control over natural resources. [. . .] Community-based management arrangements including land restitution [. . .] are a step in the right direction, provided that they are combined with a democratization process based on communicative rationality, instead of partisan politics" (Zips/ Zips-Mairitisch 2007: 65 pp.). Empowering local people is also seen by CEO Zaloumis as a major goal that needs to be achieved to fulfil the park's vision of combining conservation with local development aimed at alleviating poverty through CBNRM.

As far as I could determine through in situ, literature, and desktop research, the IWPA shows increasing efforts to engage more qualitatively and democratically with individual members of communities (holding or claiming land rights) rather than continue to negotiate predominantly with tribal leaders, which runs the risk of fostering internal inequalities. For instance, through installing public forums or meetings for inter-communal exchange, through discussions concerning the park's management, and through the distribution of important information.

To conclude, I suppose that the success of CBNRM, which I regard as being rooted in communities' empowerment, will depend largely on whether locals will be conceptualised as passive beneficiaries or granted more space in the park's participatory management scheme as active agents in decision-making processes on central issues concerning their future economic survival as a collective. Instead of again dispelling residing populations from parks – as it has been done (violently) in the past – through strictly conservation-orientated prohibition-policies that make it impossible for people to live in the area, non-hierarchical collaborative management solutions could offer an eco-socially responsible alternative. This is achieved by addressing and including all social spheres and interest groups within a community as well as implementing functioning economic opportunity-structures.

5 Conclusion

In the last decades, the criticism of forced resettlement of indigenous populations for the preservation of natural spaces gave way to the formation of new subject positions being ascribed to indigenous peoples and local communities in the global discourse on conservation. This is accompanied by a number of legislative measures taken internationally and nationally. By these measures, indigenous and local populations have been formally acknowledged as rights holders of lands and natural resources. However, as can be seen in iSimangaliso that is often recited as a flagship for successful CBNRM, the implementation of policies that target the inclusion of local people in the management of protected areas reveals that land-entitled communities' agency is limited. In alignment with other studies undertaken in the area, our research in communities living inside and adjacent to the park has shown that benefits are very slow in 'trickling down' and are hardly or not at all perceived by some residents. Moreover, people often voiced resentment towards the park or conservation in general – sometimes even associating it with apartheid – because they feel heavily restricted in their everyday activities. One reason identified by scholars for the general lack of information among community members about conservation strategies and possible benefits from ecotourism and other income sources created by the park is the prevalent dominance of tribal leaders. The traditional ruling elite still posses the most power in the various Zulu and Thonga communities in and around the park, and make the majority of essential governmental decisions. They are often the ones first contacted by and with direct access to park authorities. This evokes a tendency that only the communities' headmen are the ones negotiating land rights and being handed over money from funds collected in community trusts primarily intended to finance local welfare projects from which the community is supposed to profit as a whole.

However, on the ground people do not recognise any or little financial benefits coming from the park or so-called equity partnerships with private investors. Although park legislation demands that locals are mandatory BEE-business partners in private enterprises, owning and managing at least half of it, it is, in many cases, only the inKosis, inDunas, or their families who are directly involved in such enterprises. Thus, in order to really engage local people in co-management mechanisms designed and installed primarily for the economic and social benefit of residents in order to alleviate poverty in the area, negotiations about central issues concerning all members of communities need to take place in democratic arenas. These need to be accessible to everyone to reach 'beyond boundaries' and thereby undermine the potential barrier of local elites.

First steps in such a direction have already been taken by the park's authorities: They encourage local empowerment through increased access to information about the park's policies, they offer a variety of educational programmes to re-establish sustainable methods of resource extraction in ecologically sensitive environments, and they discuss and consult about decisions (to be) made in regular open community meetings. However, it remains to be seen if the IWPA will continue to foster developments of community inclusion and will further help to expand indigenous peoples' and local communities' rights, responsibilities, and capabilities for them to successfully self-manage their lands in ecological ways and in accordance with conservation standards. Or if top down management, that harshly limits legitimate land rights holders' participation in the park's governance, will persist as the main strategy to guarantee the preservation of nature(s) in iSimangaliso.

"Weathering the Storms": Resilient Conservation for Making a "Park for the People" Work

Werner Zips and Manuela Zips-Mairitsch

"In today's world, with global warming and all the sustainability issues, for parks like this to be here for future generations, you actually need to increase resilience, both of nature and of people. Because only then you can start weathering the storms. Then you can see a possibility to adapt in the future and actually conserve." (Zaloumis 11.11.2014, interview)

1 Introduction

Nature conservation is 'naturally' highly susceptible to global political developments. With recent setbacks in the combat against climate change and for biodiversity protection, preservation efforts seem to be thrown into the eye of a hurricane. However, short-sighted politics are not the only threat. By reviewing literature on conservation and development achievements of *iSimangaliso Wetland Park* (IWP), it becomes evident why its former CEO Andrew Zaloumis frames the task of shaping a new model of a "park for the people" as a matter of "weathering the storms" (Andrew Zaloumis, in the interview cited above). Most of the authors echo the voices of local community members who are disillusioned by the delay of the proclaimed prospect of "benefits without boundaries". On these empirical grounds, the academic critique focuses on the presumed 'neoliberal agenda' behind the IWP conservation model. It makes the respective mode of governance, invented and applied by the *iSimangaliso Wetland Park Authority* (IWPA), the park's managing body, almost look like a remote outpost of the rogue financial market. This denunciation appears to fall in line with "a rapidly expanding literature on neoliberalism", which, in the words of James Ferguson (2009: 166), comes to the "unsurprising conclusion" that "neoliberalism is bad for poor and working people, therefore we must oppose it."

The negation and disdain of market-oriented 'neoliberal conservation' may be cited as yet another example of Ferguson's "the antis", alongside (inter alia) anti-globalisation, anti-privatisation, anti-imperialism, or even anti-capitalism. In our view, the efforts of IWP (and, in fact, other integrated conservation policies, as for instance the Namibian communal conservancies analysed in Part I) are thus too easily dismissed as either window-dressed expressions of the old model of conservation *against* local people or subtle new forms of continued marginalisation, exclusion, and dispossession. To a certain extent, five chapters on IWP in this book agree with the bottom line of the anti-neoliberal critique (regarding conservation) that more of the same (capitalist exploitation) cannot undo negative consequences caused in the past for the environment and the people living in, from, and with it. There is, of course, little to object to the insight attributed to Albert Einstein, that "we can not solve our problems with the same level of thinking that created them." But, are these perhaps self-ascribed "new models of integrated conservation" really on the same level of thinking? The comprehensive *Integrated Management Plan* 2017-2021 (iSimangaliso Wetland Park Authority 2016: 1) does not unequivocally support such a hasty conclusion. Rather, it emphasises that the high levels of poverty in the South African context necessitate an approach that optimises the economic potential of *World Heritage Sites* without compromising their natural and cultural integrity:

> "Indeed, in the current context of changing demographics and climate, growing inequalities, diminishing resources, and growing threats to heritage, there is a need to view conservation objectives, including those promoted by the World Heritage Convention, within a broader range of economic, social and environmental values and needs encompassed in the concept of sustainable development. In this regard, State Parties need to establish an appropriate balance between conservation, sustainability and development, so that World Heritage properties can be protected through appropriate activities contributing to the social and economic development, and the quality of life of communities." (ibid.)

However, an increasing number of academic critics, from the fields of environmental and developmental studies as well as political geography and social anthropology, consider such discourse hardly worth the paper it is written on, and refer to it as a predominantly semantic change from so-called "fence and fine conservation" (Büscher/ Whande 2007: 27) to exclusion in the name of "tangible benefits for all". Perhaps out of disillusionment with *Community-Based Natural Resource Management* (CBNRM) programmes' ability to contribute effectively to poverty alleviation and economic empowerment in many African locales, the promises of sustainability and other omnipresent universal remedies for the planet became suspect as discursive strategies to buy public and political consent, and, not least, funding. There are indeed solid grounds for questioning the sales talk of ready-made 'win-win' solutions marketed with the use of catch-all phrases, such as empowerment, participation, ownership, and good governance, as Nustad (2015: 165) sums up the commodification of conservation in South Africa (and beyond). Yet the questioning should not pre-empt the denunciation of all market-oriented conservation efforts as representing the global "triumph of neoliberalism" (Hansen 2014: 117).

2 Neoliberalism Against its Own Grain?

Apart from theoretical and methodological flaws in the equation of neoliberalism with conservation (referred to in the introduction of this volume), there are practical reasons, why, again borrowing from Ferguson (2009: 167), the critical questioning should not stop short by asking: "what are we against?" but pose the more difficult question: "what do we want?" The wish list for conservation generally includes empowerment, social justice, tangible benefits, democratic participation, rights-based and capabilities approaches, job-creation, poverty alleviation, and self-reliance (all without public spending, of course). Thus, the question, how such aims are achievable without market-oriented policies, needs to be answered. Otherwise, (any form of) conservation is from the outset tasked with the conundrum of squaring the circle.

The critique of (neoliberal) "Nature™ Inc." (Fletcher/ Dressler/ Büscher 2014) identifies the creation and marketing of any ecotourism product as the problem. It needs to be reasserted whether any assessment of negative or positive consequences for nature protection or restoration and for the affected local population depends on the actual 'product', i.e. the institutional arrangement and its implementation. Procedural considerations on the opinion- and will-formation involved in the agreement to create such a conservation product are of equal importance. In this view, the marketing and branding of "Nature™ Inc." may not prove the worst enemy. Whereas, if the imposition of new rules of governance for conservation management (e.g. in the IWP) allows for nothing else than the verdict of 'spatial domination', as Hansen (2014: 49, 119) suggests, then conservation management is simply and always the problem.[1] The question "what do we want?" is hence either obsolete or of lesser concern. Perhaps, the anti-conservation stance reveals an academic habitus of an anxiously critical and zealous political engagement for the poor (victims of the market), as Ferguson (2009: 167) notes in the overall context of a more reflexive than reflective "anti-neoliberalism":

> "Denunciatory analyses often treat government as the simple expression of power or domination – the implication apparently being that it is politically objectionable that people should be governed at all. But any realistic sort of progressive politics that would seek a

[1] This impression seems hardened by another quote from Hansen (ibid.: 118): "Attempts to control spatial patterns through the establishment of strict protected areas can be understood as an instance of spatial domination."

serious answer to the question "what do we want?" will have to involve an exploration of the contemporary possibilities for developing genuinely progressive arts of government."

Provided that the main aim of the critique is to define neoliberalism as the root of all evil, then any bona fide attempt to reconcile environmental protection with social justice and rural development will not only be discredited from the start but faced with an unsolvable predicament (cf. Adams 2004: 235-240). Conservation would always face the choice of dirtying its hands in order to avoid showing up with empty hands to the developmental governance table. Apart from that, an undifferentiated denouncement of 'neoliberal conservation' creates a tautology of the sort of "conservation is bad, because it is neoliberal, and neoliberalism is bad as such" and thereby tends to reduce conservation governance to a single logic. Neither the *Integrated Management Plan* (IWPA 2016) – if only on paper – nor its practical implementation so far offers much support for the assumption of a foremost and decidedly neoliberal master plan. On the analytical level, the ignorance of a polyvalent content of conservation, in order to win another round against the archenemy of neoliberalism, may hamper the critical value of the evaluation, as Ferguson (2009: 171) argues in the context of other social policies (particularly Basic Income Grants) in South Africa:

"[T]hat such an all-encompassing entity (of neoliberalism) can easily come to appear as a kind of gigantic, all-powerful first cause (as categories like "Modernity" or "Capitalism" have done before it) – that malevolent force that causes everything else to happen. This yields empty analysis (since to say that all our problems are caused by "neoliberalism" is really not to say much), and may also lead to an ineffectual politics – since all one can do with such a gigantic, malevolent "thing" as "neoliberalism" conceived in this way is to denounce it. (And *that*, the evidence suggests, doesn't seem to do much good)."[2]

In relation to the condemned neoliberal "Nature™ Inc." one may wonder: How could and should a governmental agency such as IWPA create benefits without marketing 'the nature'? This is not to deny that nature is indeed trademarked and

[2] It may be interesting to note that this reasoning leads Ferguson (ibid.) to consider a renunciation of the notion (of neoliberalism), which could find support in the consideration that the notion appears far too euphemistic right from the start. After all, there is not much 'neo' nor 'liberal' in the financial policies attributed to the crude ignorance of legitimate social interests and concerns of the vast majority of global citizens. Devoid of minimal standards of communicative rationality, what is usually referred to as "neoliberal economics" might simply be reframed as the irrational exploitation of nature, culture, animals, and humans alike. Although a critique of the empirical validity of the concept is far beyond the scope of this volume, we wish to emphasise that the concept 'neoliberal' appears problematic not only because of its unspecified use in the discourse on (inter alia) conservation, but also because of its inherently positive connotations that suggest a 'new' progressive state of 'freedom'.

to some extent marketed as a product, to be sure. But, the economic targets are visibly pursued against a refined backdrop of environmental and social interests. Within an overall economy of interests, the commercialisation and marketisation of nature appears, at least in this case, not as the blanket aim in itself and, indeed, not even as the prime course. Quite to the contrary, this perhaps (in the double sense) bewildering commodification of nature arguably bears much less resemblance to a hedge fund in its daily operations than to a NGO dedicated to and driven by the common good. It is, therefore, questionable to conceptualise the IWP as nothing more than a commercial business that (unrealistically) claims the potential to help drive the economic revival of a region that was systematically underdeveloped in the past, as Hansen (2014: 117) has it. We further doubt her conclusion that economic growth is represented by IWP as a cure for regional underdevelopment, much less *the* (sole) cure. This critical assessment turns the various challenges and dilemmas, openly acknowledged by IWPA (inter alia, in numerous passages throughout the *Integrated Management Plan* 2017-2021), into a double bind of asking for a timely and efficient deliverance of tangible benefits while proposing a commitment to non-commercial modes of governance. In contrast, a balanced evaluation of IWP's strategies may engage with its proposed means of playing the "neoliberal card" against the grain of the characteristics and rules of the (neoliberal) game (cf. Ferguson 2009: 174).

An appraisal of the *Integrated Management Plan* (IWPA 2016) reveals that its strategic drivers fit only vaguely to the broad seven-point definition of neoliberalism presented by Castree (2010b: 28), namely: the principal characteristics of privatisation, marketisation, state roll back or deregulation, market-friendly reregulation, use of market proxies in the residual governmental sector, the strong encouragement of 'flanking mechanisms' in civil society, and the creation of self-sufficient individuals and communities. That particular political initiatives and programmes borrow from the neoliberal bag of tricks, as they clearly do in the case of IWP, "doesn't mean that these political projects are in league with the ideological project of neoliberalism [. . .] – only that they appropriate certain characteristic neoliberal 'moves'." As Ferguson (2009: 174) further develops his argument: "These moves are recognizable enough to look 'neoliberal', but they can, I suggest, be used for quite different purposes than that term usually implies."[3]

Building on this perspective and personal observations (from 2011-2018) on the making (including the trademarking) of IWP as the intended "world class world heritage site", we believe that the IWPA appropriated such (neoliberal

[3] The text of the *Integrated Management Plan* bears ample evidence in this regard.

game) 'moves', as referred to above. In this sense, the management body hijacked neoliberal strategies for its own means rather than beeing abducted by 'neoliberalism'. Many programmes outlined in great detail (and with evident reference to neoliberal discursive elements) in the *Integrated Management Plan* and according practices of implementation would seem economically 'fruitless' or even counterproductive from a stringent neoliberal logic or rationality. However, the double agenda of simultaneous environmental protection as well as habitat and biodiversity upgrading and social as well as economic transformation has put to work a strong reliance on discursive elements readily identifiable as neoliberal. Let us, for instance, take the significant recourse of the IWPA to the concept of resilience, identified by Joseph (2013: 38) as a "neoliberal form of governmentality" whose "real aim" lies in removing barriers to open markets: "[T]he recent enthusiasm for the concept of resilience across a wide range of policy literature is the consequence of its fit with neoliberal discourse."

In the case of IWP, this may not necessarily be a sign of a governmental approach embedded in neoliberalism (cf. Joseph 2013: 52) but a (self)-motivating allusion to individual and communal responsibility for making the new conservation model work. Good governance in the interest of local empowerment – though never to be taken at face value – could potentially denote more than just a pretence.[4] The following passage from the *Integrated Management Plan* (IWPA 2016: 9) may provide some evidence for this interpretation:

> "For iSimangaliso, restoration and rewilding of the ecosystems means that communities can sustainably participate in the economic and social benefits from the Park. The ecological resilience of the Park will thus go hand–in–hand with more resilient livelihoods for people dependent on it."

3 Resilience as a Means to Face Historical Inequalities and Legal Pluralism

To combine social transformation with the defining objective of conservation (the double intentions of preservation and restoration) indeed requires a form of re-

[4] Although resilience may be used as a tool to discipline states, governments, and elites to the neoliberal free-market agenda, "[I]ts meaning varies depending on the place and the level where this occurs and the aims and objects of governance", as Joseph (2013: 52 pp.) reminds us. Within the debate of democratising conservation science and practice (cf. Salomon et al. 2018), the concept of resilience becomes increasingly linked to the extent of connectivity between social groups, in order to increase information sharing, the spread of new ideas and the promotion of trust and reciprocity.

silience perhaps even novel to "neoliberalism", in as much as it strives to pave the way for combating dependency. Notably, the relationship between social transformation (to a higher level of political self-determination and economic self-reliance) and conservation is still an uneasy one, as the latter was utilised as an important historical strategy to gain white control over vast tracts of land and thereafter retain spatial domination in South Africa. Historical inequalities are therefore among the major challenges and persistent obstacles that effect IWP. They owe their continuity to the monstrous distortion of a human society, legally made to live apart through the system of apartheid. The sheer abundance of legal pluralism, as precursively cited in the *Integrated Management Plan* (IWPA 2016: 133-147), creates a not even remotely comprehensible legal and institutional framework. Thus, the first democratic South African government was faced with the tremendous task of rewriting the entire national legal system without the possible recourse to earlier legislation predating the deliberate legal injustice system of apartheid.[5] Since laws fundamentally become embedded in all kinds of power structures, social and economic relationships, first and foremost in the relations to land, their mere legal revision does not automatically change the political conditions induced by their historical effectiveness. For instance, the traditional authorities (that Tibor Böhm discusses in his chapter) recreated through apartheid inventions, such as bantustans or homelands, were re-legitimised by post-apartheid governments to enhance local governance, communal empowerment, and a system of checks and balances. All this led to a "bewildering kaleidoscope" of a multi-legal field of conservation (cf. von Benda-Beckmann 2001: 129; Zips/ Weilenmann 2011: 22).

Internal contradictions between transnational conventions, international and regional agreements, South African legislation, provincial statutory provisions, customary law, NGO project law, and so forth contribute to a legal arena resembling a maze for governance.[6] A conflict of compliance cannot easily be re-

5 We are thinking here of a relatively fast-tracked return to a complete legislative system available for the post-Nazi governments in Austria and Germany (by declaring all legislation of the Nazi-regime invalid).

6 Legal pluralism is, of course, no exception but the rule, particularly in postcolonial states (of mind). The governance of legal pluralism in the post-apartheid state involves a challenge of developing new progressive arts of social policies that may employ "neoliberal tricks" without succumbing to an entire "neoliberal logic". According to Ferguson (2009: 182): "[...] they illustrate a process through which specific governmental devices and modes of reasoning that we have become used to associating with a very particular (and conservative) political agenda ("neoliberalism") may be in the process of being peeled away from that agenda, and put to very different uses." Cf. Zips/ Weilenmann (2011) for a general discussion of the governance of legal

solved where the constitution does not offer a clear determination of legal hierarchies. The *Integrated Management Plan 2017-2021* (IWPA 2016: 146) gives an overview of legal documents and policy instruments, while implicitly reminding its audience about the formidable task of compliance: "There are many such policies and it is not the intention of this IMP to list all the policies, regulations and other legal precepts with which the iSimangaliso Wetland Park Authority must comply." The legal pluralism and divergent political claims mirror these power relations. What is perhaps even more conspicuous in this regard is the IWPA's awareness of historical land dispossession and forced removals:

> "[T]he area has a long history of poverty, neglect and dispossession, stemming as far back as the creation of 'native reserves' during the colonial period, and later, the establishment of ethnic bantustans, or homelands by the Apartheid Government. These periods were attended by widespread and very significant loss of land, and the start of the migrant labour system, through which the absence of men, and their inability to contribute to economic development at home, forced poverty and stagnation upon rural areas. In efforts to consolidate the homelands of the former Apartheid State, the most recent forced population removals in what was then KwaZulu began in the 1960s, including those of large numbers of farm workers following the abolition of labour tenancy, and persisted up until as recently as 1983. During this period, much land was lost to conservation, military areas, and commercial forestry plantations. Significantly, given the population of KwaZulu–Natal, land allocation has led to small land holdings, and low income generation from agriculture. The acute land degradation in former homeland areas is partly a legacy of the country's Apartheid history, which saw the relocation of subsistence farmers to 'homeland' areas often characterised by low agricultural potential. The Surplus People Project estimates that in Natal between 1948 and 1982, 745,500 people had been removed from their land. As a result, individuals in many of iSimangaliso's neighbouring and land claimant communities are able to clearly recall the trauma of these events." (IWPA 2016: 17)

We quoted this passage of the *Integrated Management Plan* to mark the appreciation of a distinct historical context for conservation efforts in South Africa. This consciousness supports the claim to envisage the full complexity of the evolving IWP and contrasts a hasty reading of its neoliberal discourse as reflecting a mere commercial venture. In the following sections, we will present some additional views of its administrative staff as well as the voices of some directly affected community members to further stretch the angle chosen by the analysis in the preceding contributions. Our main aim is to provide some food for thought beyond the natural reflex of condemning the "neoliberalism we love to hate", as Ferguson (2009: 178) puts it in relation to other market-driven social policies: "They do

---

pluralism.

not permit the simple denunciations (Aha! Neoliberalism!) that have become so familiar a part of the politics of the "anti-", even as they clearly require us to turn a thoughtfully critical and skeptical eye toward their dangers and ambiguities" (Ferguson 2009: 181).

We agree with his view that any congruencies with neoliberal discourses, practices, and strategies should not automatically trigger a final reprobation of (conservation) strategies and practices. Some recent examples of integrated conservation policies do not just leave the key task of social transformation and economic empowerment 'to the market'. Instead, the *Integrated Management Plan* of IWP indicates the willingness of a state-founded conservation agency to shape the (local ecotourism) market as much as possible to serve an emerging agenda of conservation co-orchestrated with neighbouring communities[7]: "iSimangaliso's neighbouring communities are important stakeholders, especially the beneficiaries of land claims settlements on the iSimangaliso Wetland Park" (IWPA 2016: 72). One may wonder how the recognition of partly pending judicial decisions in the land restitution process may correspond with the presumably straightforward neoliberal agenda. Legally insecure property relations will hardly lure the private sector to invest time, energy, and capital under such uncertain circumstances. The explicit compliance with and corroboration of the guiding objective of correcting the legacy of apartheid venerated by the IWPA seems in contradiction to the critique of its selling out to the market. Thus, the agenda setting of IWP appears much less directed at the maximisation of profits and further commodification of nature and wildlife with the overall purpose of economic growth, than some critics make believe (cf. Hansen 2014: 121; Nustad 2015: 166).

Remarkably enough, the foregrounding of social transformation reveals a tension with the allegedly intended large-scale privatisation. Creating an investment-friendly environment usually depends on clarity, predictability, and stability of regulatory frameworks. The recognition of legal pluralism and plural land ownerships in a dynamic context of land restitution and legal transformation of apartheid property relations has obvious effects for the rule of law. From the perspective of private investors, the multifarious and highly dynamic legal field hardly embodies legal security as an important condition, if not a *conditio sine qua non*, for safe

7 Notwithstanding its usage of a neoliberal lingua referring to communities as 'stakeholder groups': "Since the inception of the iSimangaliso Wetland Park, significant resources and effort have been focused on the delivery of social and economic benefits to impoverished neighbouring communities, through various programs. However, unrealistic expectations of delivery and the potential for delivery of benefits pose a key risk for iSimangaliso, as does the difficulty of balancing interests within and between stakeholders groups" (IWPA 2016: 44).

investments. Conservatives and progressives may interpret the rule of law differently, but the function of legal security is its core value.[8] At least on paper, the IWP appears to have a sound awareness of the lasting effects of apartheid for the equitable distribution of benefits through tourism. The apartheid history of colonial conservation still constrains community participation in ecotourism.[9] It is of great importance that these and other constraints are explicitly recognised by IWP in its management plan. This includes an appreciation of negative local attitudes towards conservation and authorities due to people's historical loss of land and resources (IWPA 2016: 54; see also 44-54).

The *Integrated Management Plan* indicates that IWP's emphasis on empowerment and poverty alleviation is not mere 'green-washing' rhetoric spawned by sales talk that will eventually materialise the presumed project of neoliberal expansion. There is more evidence on paper that IWP sets the development agenda as a priority without selling it out to conservation interests and fact-based managerial imperatives under the guise of a green fig leaf (cf. Nustad 2015: 164). Its practical implementation will be discussed in the following chapters. However that may be, IWP's priorities are a far cry from the ideas and ideals of bare-knuckle neoliberal self-proclaimed 'conservationists', who, for instance, propose in all seriousness a derivative approach to endangered species conservation, namely "that governments issue modified derivative contracts to sell species' extinction risk to market investors and stakeholders" (Mandel/ Donlan/ Armstrong 2010: 44).[10]

In fact, published policy documents, such as the *Integrated Management Plan,* and numerous interviews with officials (cited in this paper) attest the historical awareness on the former apartheid utilisation of a conservation rhetoric. Its barely hidden agenda is recognised as a strategy to effectively bereave local communities of their land and restrict their resource access. Credibly, the conservation authority (IWPA) has demonstrated a sincere dedication to the decolonisation of nature, the

---

8 Nevertheless, the rule of law does not just provide legal protection to colonial property relations, as Murombedzi (2003: 135 pp.) seems to imply for the particular historical situation in Southern Africa. This legal concept rather emphasises the axiomatic principle of legal security in any constellation of power and law; it holds any person subject to the law, irrespective of their position as rulers, lawmakers, or judges. Legal anthropology has produced profuse evidence that the concept existed in pre-colonial African societies and may, thus, not be interpreted as an exclusive colonial invention (cf. Zips 2003; Hagan 1986).

9 Of course, reverberations of colonial conservation are not limited to the economic field but prevail on multi-level social and cultural relations to conservation areas. However, the unchanged ownership structure of businesses in St Lucia, the frontier town of *iSimangaliso Wetland Park*, is a major concern for transformation.

10 See also Büscher's (2014: 201 pp.) adequate critique of the hypercapitalist type of (what he coins "fictitious") conservation by its incorporation into the finance sector.

improvement of livelihoods, and the informed participation of those communities living in and adjacent to IWP. Obviously, this involves real life contradictions brought about by a divergence of interests vested in apartheid conservation as a sharpened form of colonial nature appropriation (Nustad 2015: 91-97; cf. Adams/Mulligan 2003: 42).

4 Decolonisation as Departure from the History of Colonial Conservation

The departure from the colonial conservation predecessors invokes a reversal from the material dispossession of indigenous and local communities to the economic utilisation of the very same natural landscapes and its flora and fauna (cf. Adams 2004: 214-225). Yet, to put 'development' first does not invariably mean to bring all fences down and to remove all restrictions or sanctions. A prudent – and perhaps unpopular or anti-populist – perspective on long-term prospects of conservation might reasonably discount a precipitate rescission from (all) former protective measures, however tempting that impulse may seem in the context of (post-)apartheid. Arguably, IWP went the most difficult way of even further consolidating the overall land mass to form a single unified protected area out of separate conservation tracts of land. But, the reconciliation of anthropocentric and ecocentric values through evolving joint management models with local communities is not a simple task. Especially, if these 'communities' are somewhat fictional and themselves just evolving out of a process of land claimants' associations, only in time developing into communal property associations. It is worth noting that such organisations further increase the legal pluralism and social complexities, not least because of their overlapping interference with traditional authorities and their subjects, who may or may not consider themselves a "local community" (cf. Nustad 2015: 125 pp.).

The attempted decolonisation of nature, howsoever well intended it may be, quickly hits the wall of conventional biodiversity conservation imperatives (Adams 2004: 207 pp.). If it ends there, it will inevitably be faced with the uncomfortable choice of either returning actual land possession to local communities, whose legitimate rights may be internally contested (as in the case of consecutive waves of removals)[11], or risking (the blame of) a recolonisation of nature through a contractual agreement, which acknowledges (limited) property rights without

[11] The contested Dukuduku forest in IWP is such an example, as analysed by Christian Sterkl and Jennifer Kelleher in this volume; see also the comprehensive empirical study of Nustad (2015: 121-139).

transferring physical possession (Magome/ Murombedzi 2003: 131).[12] The first option comes with the additional obstacle that local communities are hardly prepared for the complex tasks of protected areas management, while the second one may easily show off the symbolic capital of legitimation by international conservation standards. It is revealing to study the preliminary answers of IWPA to these difficult questions. Not only do they show a clear recognition of limitations to the ecotourism approach but they also emphasise that democratisation, economic development, empowerment, and so forth belong to the legal and political sphere of primary governmental institutions as such. They remind those critics overestimating the transformational power of integrated conservation that its agencies only exercise managerial power:

> "While iSimangaliso is an important economic driver for the region, it is not the economic panacea of common perception. Many people, particularly land claimants and neighbouring communities, have high expectations of the economic opportunities that the Park will generate. Such expectations of a natural asset and of the tourism sector are unrealistic. iSimangaliso is committed to fulfilling its development mandate but cannot singly resolve regional economic issues, including the alleviation of widespread poverty. Multi-level interventions which address the historical under-development of the region are still required." (IWPA 2016: 42)

In our view, the undertone of management guidelines and target definitions of IWPA, as publicised in the *Integrated Management Plan,* display little affinity to the "neoliberal peace parks discourse of harmony between conservation, development, and capitalism" that some academic critics generally associate with the "holy grail" of tourism within contemporary projects of (transfrontier) conservation (Büscher 2013: 59). While skepticism towards the grand vision of peace parks seems indispensable the actual evidence on the impact of tourism and the extent to which local residents are conceived as partners not subjects of incentive-driven conservation should determine any assessment, and not a general sentiment of distrust (Adams 2004: 213).[13] We agree with van der Duim et al. (2015: 9) that the polarisation between an instrumental view of an incentive-driven conservation policy as rational problem solving and the critical view of its neoliberal usurpation have blocked the way for a more insightful analysis of how novel institutional arrangements address the tourism-conservation-development nexus. It always de-

12 See Jennifer Kelleher on this problematic choice, in this volume.

13 However, as Adams (2004: 210) remarks, impact assessments have often been carried out by the very people who have run the project, and exaggerate the presumed successes of wildlife tourism operations. This opens up a vast field for discourse-critical analysis on the procedural participatory quality of particular projects.

pends on the mundane, real-world negotiations and consented policies to answer the question, if market-oriented conservation does more good than bad in the social arena of a particular empirical context. Realistic appraisals of the historical injustice and the precolonial human history in the area, as exemplified by the following interview with former CEO of IWP, Andrew Zaloumis, may serve as a first hint in this regard. They contextualise the need for a people-centred approach to tackle the colonial legacy of what eventually became iSimangaliso:

> "Before IWP became a World Heritage Site, all this wasn't one park. It was sixteen separate parcels of land, which were hundred percent under land claim and it had very recent forced removals. The apartheid state had developed military missiles in one part of iSimangaliso, so it was really a place with a fairly nasty history. And yet it's because of that history that the government saw the need to both recognise iSimangaliso as a natural wonder and also as a peace park, a park that can actually deliver benefits to the second poorest area in South Africa. People have lived here for thousands of years and they've shaped the park. There's no part of iSimangaliso that hasn't had people living in it at one stage over the last several thousand years and actively shaping it. The wonderful grasslands you see, with hundreds of different species, are there because of farming people. In the days of King Shaka, there was forge-welding and steel-making in the area. It has a very deep human history. That's why for us, as iSimangaliso, it's all about people-centred conservation. You cannot do conservation without people and especially here. Although, it's very complex. We have fourteen amakhosi or traditional chiefs around us. We have many municipalities. We have 620.000 people and we are the second poorest area in South Africa, with some of the greatest development backlogs." (Zaloumis 11.11.2014, interview)

In line with this footing by its CEO, the *Integrated Management Plan* affords a high level of transparency for the park's manifold missions: Besides its overall foundation in the protection, conservation, preservation, and presentation of World Heritage values, the document places a strong emphasis on local economic development and declares the means of accountable implementation. A careful study of the 172 pages strong guidelines of the IMP reveals the delicate footing of conservation in post-apartheid South Africa as a highly contested social space. A quarter century after the dawning of democracy, the Black majority's reservoirs of patience for a profound socio-economic transformation draw to a close. This observation is not confined to conservation policies but perhaps more rampant in the context of nature and wildlife protection. Disappointed communities and individuals, cut off from benefits held out in prospect for too long, are tempted to comparisons to the olden days (of apartheid), as our research team got to hear more than once (and referred to in their papers). After all, the material means of exclusion, in the form of fencing off local populations' access, are even more acute in conservation *zones* (with their discursive match to the historicity of zoning off Black people) than in other social spaces. The spatial segregation of people and animals in game reserves is prone to the old historicities of differentiation and privileging. It mostly excluded people who were historically pushed off their lands or denied admission on the sole grounds of racial categorisations (cf. Nustad 2015: 25-32).

In this (post)colonial context, the usual branding catchphrases, such as 'primordial wilderness' or 'untouched nature', sound totally different to the imaginations of wealthy urban ecotourists and dispossessed local communities. If the natural beauty hidden from the original inhabitants of the land is turned into a commodity still consumable only by a few, the disadvantaged majority can legitimately expect a share of the revenues (ibid.: 78-91). Decolonisation efforts are measured by local stakeholders against the usual allures of ecotourism marketing of a biblical Eden and paradise on earth. They only become credible for those concerned if their participation in development policies is not viewed as a top-down affair (cf. Sullivan 2006: 117; 128). The *Integrated Management Plan* - and the IWPA responsible for its final formulation – pays attention to a meaningful ex-ante participatory approach. In concrete terms, this means that the 'community-based' conservation policy, as a key target, is not restrained by goals that have been externally imposed by the conservation body or superior state agencies (cf. Nustad 2015: 31 pp.). The management plan envisages the participatory approach (we will turn to in the next chapter) as the paramount pathway to strike a balance between the interests of conservation, ecotourism, development, and (Black) economic empowerment:

"The transformation and empowerment strategy provides an overview of iSimangaliso's beneficiation programmes, including those concerned with economic transformation and job creation, community-based natural resource use, capacity building, training and equitable access. It also includes the strategies for participation in planning, such as Local Area Plans, and decision-making, such as co-management agreements; and environmental education and awareness programmes. iSimangaliso also implements the iSimangaliso People and Parks Programme, which focuses on co-management, community public private partnerships, land reform, conservation, and strengthening and expansion of the Protected areas network." (IWPA 2016: 119)

5 The Participatory Approach – a Pathway to Decolonisation?

Decolonisation, in the context of conservation, must arguably start with a participatory process of renaming. This highly contested debate in South Africa focuses on the colonising frameworks and relationships expressed in the naming of the land. Renaming aims at a fundamental reconciliation process healing the alienated relationship of colonised people with the land occupied by the colonisers. Like so many other colonial conservation areas, and of course most names of places in South Africa, the former *Greater St Lucia Wetlands Park* expressed the dynamic of assimilation, as Plumwood (2003: 67) stressed on a general level of colonial naming: "The land is defined in terms of colonial relationships that exhibit Eurocentricity and nostalgia for the European homeland. Such naming practices refuse to relate to the land in its own terms, denying it the role of narrative subject in the stories that stand behind its name."

Apart from its Portuguese origins, the name St Lucia refers to a Christian saint and reflects paradigmatically the global colonial naming practices. Thus, the fact that it is homonymous with other 'overseas possessions', such as the Caribbean island Saint Lucia, is not coincidental at all. It invariably leads to confusions, even more so because the Caribbean namesake hosts yet another UNESCO *World Heritage Site*. The renaming to the Zulu word iSimangaliso, which means "miracle" or "miraculous", qualified not only as a suitable signifier of the land's natural beauty but also because of its reference to the history of the Zulu land and its African inhabitants (Zaloumis 11.11.2014, interview). What is even more important here is the consultation process that led to the name selection:

> "The stakeholders, which are the neighbours of the park, the schools, the residents and some NGOs were consulted in that process and they submitted names, which they thought would be appropriate names for this park and iSimangaliso was chosen. I can tell you why iSimangaliso was chosen: it was seen as the best name to actually describe this park for what it is. iSimangaliso means "miracles" and relates to a story from long ago, when King Shaka died in 1828 and his personal assistant uJeqe fled to the Thonga land to avoid being buried with him. He instantly fell in love with this beauty, and reported to have seen miracles and wonders of the flatlands and the wetlands of this area, and from there comes the Zulu saying that is still used today: 'If you have seen miracles, you must have seen, what uJeqe saw in the Thongaland'. Literally translated it says: 'Ubone isimanga esabonwa uJeqe kwelama Thonga'." (Shabalala 22.02.2012, interview)

Renaming as a prerequisite for decolonisation potentially reaches beyond the symbolic realm of 'historical healing' if it is procedurally translated into a transfer of ownership on the basis of cultural cooperation and convergence. Until the restructuring of iSimangaliso, St Lucia – the town and by extension the nature reserve in its surroundings – was a centre of 'Afrikanerdom'[14], and perhaps still is under the surface. To its white majority population, the allusion to Black (Zulu and Thonga) history may have felt like a threat to their legal status and cultural supremacy but

[14] A self-identification of the white Boer immigrants that conspicuously omitted indigenous or 'African' territorial sovereignty, land rights, and cultural integrity.

was, in the end, ambiguously acceptable because of the expected value of the new trademark for World Heritage tourism. Our evaluation of narrative interviews and informal conversations with the predominantly white landowners in St Lucia indicate a broad range of attitudes from frustration, anger, to sheer enthusiasm for the social transformation as envisioned by the IWPA.[15] But clearly, there is a widely shared awareness, that "things have indeed changed" quite drastically. This local sense of the 'winds of change' attests to the appraisal that there is more at work than "(empty) catch-all phrases such as empowerment, participation, ownership, and good governance" (Nustad 2015: 165).

The *Integrated Management Plan* for 2017-2021 (IWPA 2016) refers to the concept of participatory integration of the previously disadvantaged and disenfranchised racialised communities already in its title. Apart from declaring an overall aim, it provides a detailed framework of guidelines for its conceptual idea of 'integrated management'. It dedicates an entire chapter to this overall aim (IWPA 2016: 78-132). This final chapter 5 of the document spells out its policies for co-management, transformation, and empowerment inter alia through the *Land Claims Framework*, the *Tourism Concessioning Policy*, and the *Public Participation Strategy*. When land claims are finally settled by the *Regional Land Claims Commission*, the IWPA and the successful land claimants are supposed to enter into a co-management agreement, which includes a benefit package of economic training and job opportunities, equity partnerships in tourism facilities, rights of access, use of natural resources, and the establishment of an education trust to educate land claimant youth (ibid.: 120). Income from tourism has grown tremendously since the establishment of the park authority, whose concession policy for new tourism activities prescribes obligatory empowerment criteria (ibid.: 66, 121).[16] The public participation strategy, based on informing and consulting stakeholders via a structured process, both proactively and responsively is given much space in the management plan but lacks a rights-based institutionalisation of procedural steps in the forefront of decision-making (ibid.: 123-129). A full-

---

15 See Sieder (2014) on the praxeological interpretation of narrative interviews.

16 However, exact figures for the growth are currently unavailable. Some other tourism-related figures are given in the IWP 2017/18 *Annual Performance Plan*: 84 percent increase in tourism from 2000-2011, which makes up for 0.06 percent of South Africa's tourism GDP or 6.8 percent of the KwaZulu-Natal tourism GDP; tourism creates 8.000 direct jobs with an expenditure of 1.219 million Rand per annum. Five wholly community-owned tourism licenses for fishing charter, estuary cruises and turtle tours have been granted as well as concessions for four community-owned lodges (IWP 2017a: 10; IWPA 2016: 21). In absolute figures, the *Annual Performance Plan* for 2018/19 aims to increase revenue collection for the park from commercial sources from Rand 17.4 million to Rand 20.7 million (IWPA/ SANBI 2018: 1).

fledged local democratisation process, however, perhaps demands too much from a conservation agency, and depends on institutionalised structures of local governance.

Certainly, actions speak louder than words (as Jennifer Kelleher analyses in her contribution), but for a management plan with a future dimension, it is advisable to accredit a bit of time to oversee its actual implementation merits. The publicised document, available on the IWP website, will in time function as a procedural parameter for the critical reconstruction of actual consultation in the processes of opinion- and will-formation and decision-making. Against this background, the current leadership entities of IWPA will be held accountable, first and foremost by the local communities themselves. According to Thandi Shabalala, the tourism and information coordinator of IWPA, iSimangaliso has learned its lesson from the unilateral, top-down conservation of the past (22.02.2012, interview):

> "It is very important that we acknowledge that in the past conservation was not brought or introduced to people as it should have been. Because it was just taking care of the environment outside of the people, but you can't really do that without people. It's people, who brought the bad impact into our environment and it is people, who must come in and fix that. We need people to work with us. People own the area, they own the land and they will have to be responsible for looking after the environment and ensuring that it is kept and protected for the generations to come. So, the communities are not just left out there to see these changes happening around them, but they are very much involved. For all the developments that happen in the area, the communities are brought in during discussions and we hear their views and they are part of the whole process. That's the main thing for us to ensure their empowerment. They are considered in all the plans that are made for this area, because it's theirs."[17]

On a comparative level to other conservation authorities within South Africa and beyond, it is remarkable that the IWPA supports the land reform process in theory and practice. Settling land claims is given first priority. This precondition for legal security of ownership became associated with the close nexus of natural and economic resilience, as Andrew Zaloumis consistently reiterated:

[17] This position was underscored by the following interview passage from Andrew Zaloumis (11.11.2014, interview): "Without people conservation cannot prevail. And iSimangaliso offers a huge opportunity in this regard, not just for jobs, not just for recognition of people, but also for people's original views, their thoughts, their origins, where they came from. We've really got three pillars. The one pillar is obviously the hard conservation, the bird diversity, the number of animals. The other one is really landscape and the beauty of it. And, the third is people." Once more, this mission statement may serve as a parameter to measure the actual implementation of ex-ante participation.

"We were the first park in South Africa to say people must get titles. It's non-negotiable. Nelson Mandela, who was very instrumental in this park being here today, wrote a very famous speech which was about closing circles in his life. He talked about restitution, both restitution of nature and restitution of people. Our whole drive has therefore been two-fold: To improve iSimangaliso's World Heritage values, its natural resilience, by taking out the plantations, bringing back the wetlands, bringing back game that was here in the time before colonial people were here, that got shot up by hunters. And, in doing that, creating jobs, creating empowerment, improving tourism and recognising the rights of people." (Zaloumis 11.11.2014, interview)

This dedication entered the key written document for the future management parameter of a participatory approach premised on an equity partnership. It thus at least envisions a 'community-based' approach that does not settle with development impositions thought best *for* a community but aspires to create procedures of decision-making *with* communities. Aware of the risk of academic naiveté, we merely suggest here to apply a procedural (and comparative) approach for future assessments of shortcomings, failures, and progress in this regard. From the perspective of a critical discourse ethic, management guidelines submit a tangible framework geared towards the realisation of an informed consent on the basis of fact-based persuasive arguments:

"On-going consultation and dialogue with our co-management partners and other community stakeholders is vitally important. Guided by this IMP, the Authority will implement strategies enabling stakeholders to participate meaningfully in the Park's rewilding, and will continue to prioritise the maintenance of effective relationships with iSimangaliso's neighbours. Experience shows that the time and effort put into creating and maintaining clear channels of communication is an essential investment in conservation." (IWP 1917: 10)

The intended restoration of biodiversity through the eradication of alien plants and the rewilding of meta-fauna species (such as elephants), as the prime conservation target, therefore becomes, in principle, linked to the procedural aim of participation.[18] It is worth noting that some of these animal species had become extinct before the British colonialists proclaimed the *Cape St Lucia Game Preserve* in 1895, not least as a pretext for the forced removals of the Thonga people from the area (McCracken 2008: 121 pp.; see also Nustad 2015: 78-83). In order to 'turn

[18] Particularly the rewilding of elephants requires a long-term wildlife management vision. When confined to fenced in conservation zones, elephants have a high reproduction rate, even under mediocre environmental conditions. The elephant population in the reclaimed Madikwe wilderness has reached a number of over 900 within less than three decades. They now constitute 43 percent of the herbivore biomass in the reserve (Madikwe Game Reserve 2019).

the table' to a developmental approach of conservation, ecological policies need to be intertwined with economic empowerment and environmental education. These two associated imperatives took the shape of the rural enterprise programme and the environmental education programme (which will be the subjects of the following two chapters). In the words of Thandi Shabalala (22.02.2012, interview), there are three main ingredients for iSimangaliso, namely nature conservation, rural development, and environmental education:

> "Our mandate is to see that the communities living around here, receive economic opportunities for rural development. Since this was a region with so much poverty, nature conservation cannot be targeted mainly to just care for the nature, but we need to make people out there aware why we have to value and protect this environment. This means to ensure that everyone is educated as much as possible in all these fields."

6 The Rural Enterprise Programme

The model of nature conservation intricately linked to tourism is often scrutinized for benefitting "those [overwhelmingly white] market leaders much more than [the poor] local people" (Büscher 2013: 59) and for creating a form of indentured labour through precarious, temporary, and low-paid jobs (Dowie 2009: xxvi). In contrast to this tendency, our personal experiences with ecotourism facilities in South Africa (and the neighbouring countries of Namibia and Botswana) support a more balanced view in this empirical context. Numerous encounters with members of formerly disadvantaged groups in middle management and even leadership positions in the *Greater Kruger National Park* and its adjacent private tourism enterprises as well as in various other private game reserves from Madikwe to Phinda, to Kwandwe and other community conservation areas, such as the Tembe Elephant Park in KwaZulu-Natal, provide sufficient evidence that the empowerment commitments of most businesses might not be mere rhetoric.[19] iSimangaliso undertakes a vanguard role in this regard as a quasi-state institution. Through the *Rural Enterprise Programme,* it provides sub-grants and technical assistance

[19] Although, such a statement requires some reservation for general management positions, which are still occupied by the former privileged (white) elite or (equally white) expatriates. However, there are already some notable exceptions in this regard, as for instance Sphamandla Shabalala, the GM of Rhino Post, the only private lodge in *Hluhluwe-uMfolozi Game Reserve*, whom we first met as assistant manager of *Thanda Private Game Reserve* in KwaZulu-Natal (in 2012). The tourism ventures of Tembe Elephant Park, for instance, employ almost exclusively local community members, including their management and head rangers. In our view, it is precisely the lamentable outcome of market-based solutions in conservation (criticised by Dowie 2009: xxv) that ask for vital (empirical) alternatives.

for start-ups and existing small-scale businesses. The latest 2016 figures of 215 small businesses that have received mentoring and support may, of course, appear quite modest in relation to the 55.547 temporary jobs created so far, besides the over 1.000 permanent jobs (Africa 2017; IWP 2017a).[20] Yet, the transformation of Black entrepreneurship set in motion through the facilitation of local community members forming their own companies should not be underrated. The number of 80 start-ups (until 2016 with a projected steady growth) is indeed considerable, even though its comparative evaluation depends on the chosen frame (see IWP 2013; IWP 2018a; IWP/ SANBI 2018).

We are conscious of the fact that the very same figures may be used for an alternative reading or even an inverse conclusion (i.e. the continued dependence of the majority). But in the context of almost exclusive white entrepreneurship of various tourism enterprises in the town of St Lucia, the ground-breaking function of the rural enterprise programme may in time evolve to transfer a much bigger share of the considerable stakes involved in the iSimangaliso tourism development initiative to the formerly disadvantaged communities. According to Mandisa Nkosi, the Community Liaison Officer and intern of *iSimangaliso Higher Education Access Programme*[21], IWPA proactively engages the communities through workshops held in community locations, for consultations about entrepreneurial ideas, facilitating grants, and the necessary application procedures. The introduction of ambitious crafts projects responsible for the training of some 3.000 crafters, artists, and tour guides so far, catapulted the producers to the top of the value chain (Nkosi 06.11.2014, interview), not least due to the foundation and construction of a craft shop. It is centrally located at the jetty, where large tour buses park and the boat cruises on the famous estuary take off. While craft artisans and local craft traders were located on the lowest level of the value chain before, at the mercy of intermediaries and shop or market space owners, this best-stocked craft shop in the area now gives them access to fixed fair prices (in consultation with iSimangaliso staff). It is managed by local community members and further promoted by a permanent arts exhibition at the same location. The

---

20 The figures are stated by the *iSimangaliso Wetland Park Performance Plan* (IWP 2017a) and updated by the South African *Minister of Environmental Affairs*, Dr. Bomo Edna Molewa, at the time of Andrew Zaloumis' retirement from office in September 2017. The *Integrated Management Plan* (2016) states 178 enterprises who have participated in the programme, of which 71 enterprises have received grants to the value of R 6.350.134. A mid-term 2016 announcement by IWP states 187 beneficiaries and 80 grants to the value of R 7.8 million, which shows a steady increase from the start-up phase of the programme in 2010 (IWP 2016).

21 Mandisa Nkosi is herself a beneficiary of the tertiary education bursary programme, which has afforded university studies for 87 students until 2017 (Africa 2017).

crafts programme is but one of the key instruments complementing the rural enterprise programme, which is perhaps best characterised by Zakithi Mngomezulu, its technical officer (10.11.2014, interview):

"I manage the entrepreneurship programme that trains new and existing business people in the area. We look at businesses that are conservation compatible, which means that they are in line with iSimangaliso's main aims, which is conservation and development. We have a range of businesses that we are currently supporting: from people offering catering to businesses that are directly tourism or conservation related. Entrepreneurs such as tour operators, guides for birding and fishing boat charters and an even wider range of different businesses receive support on request. We look at businesses local community members are currently engaged in, and we train them to upscale or improve their businesses. There are people who own tuck shops, which are convenient community-owned shops where you can go to buy your groceries. We also have people who organise events. Our programme is structured in such a way, that we have technical training in class rooms firstly, that people need to attend. It is an eighteen months training programme, which teaches the basics of business management and financial management, how to keep your sales and income going, as well as marketing your business and expert personal development. And secondly, once you have completed the class room training we go out to do site visits, to look at how the businesses are run in their particular context, what the challenges are and how iSimangaliso can assist them."

It is indeed a broad range of enterprises, ranging from small shops and offices for IT solutions, to fashion design, or even hair salons (see IWP 2013 for further details). We interviewed a number of IWPA-funded entrepreneurs between 2012 and 2016, for instance Bongiwe Khambule, who was assisted with the opening of a container hair salon in Kosi Bay. With the help of this small enterprise, she manages to support herself and her family (05.12.2014, interview; see the film Zips/ Zips-Mairitsch 2016). The founder of the company *Zulubirding & Ecotours*, Themba Mthembu, exemplifies how a convincing business idea can be turned into a viable micro-enterprise. His life story is particularly interesting as he, according to his own words, started out as a subsistence hunter in his youth. He became interested in the cultural tour guide courses offered by iSimangaliso to the communities adjacent to the park. During this course, he took the chance to prove his ecological knowledge on the local fauna and flora, particularly on the birdlife and received an endorsement from the iSimangaliso environmental education programme for schools. After further studies at the *Southern African Wildlife College*, supported with an iSimangaliso grant, and various assessments of his progress, he received another grant from the enterprise programme for his ecotourism start-up, specialised on birding. Now on the brink of expanding his business with employees, Mthembu's views on iSimangaliso should be taken into account, at least for a balanced preliminary assessment of the rural development programmes but perhaps also for a better understanding of how the various programmes are designed to complement each other:

> "I see iSimangaliso as a conservation body, whose priorities are to make sure that communities neighbouring the park are integrated and benefit from any positive changes. So that they can feel being part of it. If people are not part of it, eventually it is not going to work well. I think that's one challenge for us to make sure that all conservation activities involve the communities at large. What they have done for me was to enlist me in their environmental education programmes. A lot is done in terms of environmental education, for instance we visit local schools, local communities, train and educate locals about the importance of the environment." (Mthembu 13.11. 2014, interview)

Nature guide training programmes, particularly specialist ornithology courses, have become extremely expensive in South Africa because of the huge international demand for wildlife-related knowledge (and, indeed, the promise of related adventures). The admission of local community members to free education programmes is, therefore, essential to enabling their access into a competitive business sector. Coming back to the question of alleged 'indentured tourism labour' (Dowie 2009: xxvi; cf. Büscher 2013: 59), funding necessary start-up investments is extremely important. Zakithi Mngomezulu (10.11.2014, interview) offers insight on how the IWPA accomplishes this with fairly limited funds at its disposal:

> "Our funding is not in terms of giving you cash, but you apply for what your business requires. If you are in construction you can apply for various materials or equipment that you need. Let's take the example of Themba Mthembu: he has applied for binoculars for his business, which is important to find the birds, when he takes tourists on a guided walk. He also applied for company registration, as well for marketing and branding materials, like brochures and flyers, and some office equipment and furniture. Tourists need to know your office and expect an environment that is appealing to them. After that we do provide constant mentoring to offer sustainable assistance."

At the time of writing, we are looking at close to one hundred of such individual cases of grant-assisted entrepreneurs and about 200 entrepreneurs who received training and general support. It depends on the economic criteria to assess the relative success of the initiative.[22] Once more, in relation to 620.000 people living in the area and hoping for opportunities this may appear very little, as IWPA staff members such as Nerosha Govender made quite clear to us. But their openly shared concerns about the limited impact of the rural enterprise pro-

22 This assessment is beyond the capacities of research presented in this book. Further inquiries into the performance potential of such programmes are highly desirable for any comparative evaluation of macro-economic objectives.

grammes should not be mistaken for self-accusations but rather taken as appeals to national, international, and transnational funding agencies. If these interventions depend on returns from local tourism, the effects for poverty alleviation will be of very limited scale. It is somewhat ironic that conservation bodies, such as IWPA, are blamed almost exclusively for the shortcomings of community development. With these reflections, we also want to encourage a shift of critique on conservation. The accusations of empowerment lip-service and mere developmental rhetoric might reasonably become redirected to those powerful and wealthy states, and agencies who talk a great deal about poverty alleviation but actually do much less than the – give or take – 30 staff members of IWPA. In this light, singular individual cases, such as the catering enterprise of Mary Baines, in our view, implicate a call for more engagement, which iSimangaliso – or any other conservation body or private enterprise – can hardly achieve alone:

"I became one of the trainees out of 60. We were trained for twelve months, how to start a business, how to make profit, how to manage that business, and how to grow the business. After the twelve months, about half of us were selected and given starting equipment. I received equipment for catering, worth approximately 20.000 Rand. Then I joined another training of tour guiding. The nature tour guiding enabled me to join the Environmental Education, which takes schools for instance to Sodwana Bay. In the process they do mentoring, where they come to your business place to see how they can sort out problems. I was able to get my business card, to make flyers and to register my business legally. So, I am now running a business, which is doing very well. Whatever problems I came across, I would go to my mentor, the facilitator, to explain what I am experiencing and how they might help me. They connected us with other business people that we needed for the networking. For somebody like me from a rural area, there are few opportunities, in fact we absolutely have nothing. It's only unfortunate that we are so many who are all looking to iSimangaliso. Now I'm able to take care of my children. That is something they had given me, which is priceless and nobody else could have given me that. They have given me and my kids a future." (Baines 22.12.2012, interview)

A final example of an entrepreneur, who has evolved into some sort of local player in the tourism market, is Phillip Mkhwanazi. He is the inDuna of Khula village and founder of the Veyane cultural village, started in 1997. The Zulu-styled cultural village modelled on the *Shakaland Zulu Cultural Village* in Eshowe, hosts a bed and breakfast unit of a 'neo-traditional', hut-like guesthouse that offers local food and regular as well as specially arranged cultural programmes. Before he got involved in the enterprise programme, Phillip Mkhwanazi was a small contractor for the alien plant removal programme of iSimangaliso Wetland Park. His economic success with his cultural village as an "Ethnicity, Inc." enterprise and as an empowerment partner in a variety of other businesses (e.g. a boat cruise company) has earned him quite a bit of rivalry and political opposition in his community (as elaborated by Christian Sterkl, Tibor Böhm, and Georg Bergthaler in this volume). His position as a traditional authority of Khula village has brought him in even closer contact to IWPA, which is supposed to consult and cooperate with traditional authorities. Phillip Mkhwanazi is no exception to other traditional authorities in the region (and beyond) investing their symbolic, cultural, and social capital into viable business partnerships. The inescapable conflict of interests has been referred to in various interviews with local community members, many of whom complain about a presumed nepotistic bias of the inDuna in the allocation of jobs in the cultural village and inequality of benefit sharing. Depending on the angle of observation, his life story has, nevertheless, a lot to tell. For himself it is "a dream come true", as he explains in the following interview (09.11.2014):

"Unfortunately, I could not attend better schooling. For a long time, I had no job. Then I became a taxi driver. Imagine, the person who was driving local taxis is now the owner of the boat cruise and the owner of the Veyane cultural village. My life has changed and you know one day I will take my children to the sort of school, where they can learn better English than me. Tomorrow I'm going to Australia for the World Park Congress. I'm sponsored by iSimangaliso Wetland Park to attend this world summit to represent our community and the communities who are neighbours of iSimangaliso Wetland Park. And also, the small businesses trained by iSimangaliso Wetland Park. To me, this means the dreams are coming true, because my wish was to go overseas one day. I'm very happy and I'm very excited about that special occasion to be there for our country."

Obviously, there are two sides to this coin and many more perspectives on each side. These reflect the divergence of interests and the larger societal struggles concerning the reallocation of vital resources in a dynamic situation of political change. There is fierce intra-community and inter-community competition for new opportunities cropping up from the rapid rise of tourism within IWP (highlighted by all previous contributors to this volume). It is fairly unsurprising that IWPA would receive criticism for their allocation of grants, contracts, and even co-management agreements after settled land claims.[23] In order to avoid these cir-

[23] Andrew Zaloumis (11.11.2014, interview) elaborates on internal negotiations and disputes after a land claim settlement and, thus, provides further evidence on the divergence of interests within a 'community': "Settling a land claim is not an easy thing. Even when it is finally settled, people don't always agree and they change allegiances and you get break away groups. That's the reality anywhere. The youth normally are keen on a claim being settled with the park because of their interest to participate in tourism. But the older people aspire very often the physical possession of their land, to herd their cattle and to adhere to their traditional way of life. For them it is a yearning to try and get back what was lost. That's a generational issue, it's an age-gap-issue. But increasingly there is a swing, where the youth want to come back to their land as visitors in

cumstances, IWPA would have to abstain from any involvement in development of enterprises or at least avoid sustained relationships with its beneficiaries. But the preferential procurement of grants, funding, and mandates to reliable long-term partners does not necessarily indicate favouritism or even nepotism. Otherwise, erstwhile beneficiaries would have to be excluded from further support. Understandably, this is not a viable option for IWPA since empowerment and sustainable growth of supported business models are specified aims:

> "For us, entrepreneurship is different from small businesses. An entrepreneur is a person who has the ability to do business. It doesn't matter what kind of business. We don't lecture them, and we don't teach them in this regard. It is a mentorship programme. When we started, we couldn't find any local Black entrepreneurs around this park involved in tourism. The programme may be small, but it's growing and, for me, that's very important. People can see the success. It matters that people working at iSimangaliso don't come from a pure conservation background. IWPA, therefore, is a development conservation organisation. So, it's conservation-centred and it's people-centred." (Zaloumis 11.11.2014, interview)

Arguably, it is the success of IWPA in making a change that upsets stakeholders who feel overlooked, marginalised, or threatened by the social transformation and *Black Economic Empowerment* (BEE) agenda. It is in this context that the 'neoliberal' reference to resilience should be adequately interpreted (IWPA 2016: 10, 42). In the milieu of St Lucia, the gateway white frontier town to the recreated wilderness of IWP, this emphasis on resilience appears even more understandable. Empowerment, especially *Black Economic Empowerment* (BEE) and social transformation, is perceived by its predominantly white population as an implicit threat to their livelihoods based on ecotourism or even as a menace of future dispossession and eviction. Most of such statements happen off records, since BEE is considered a prerequisite for an appropriate business etiquette in the new democratic South Africa. A rights-based approach is regarded as indispensable to change the business practices of the formerly exclusive white business community of St Lucia (and beyond). Their complaints about the 'sudden' introduction of myriads of new laws and regulations from the *Broad-Based Black Economic Empowerment Act* (2003) to labour laws and conservation regulations reflect their previous 'ownership' of law, which produced attitudes of living above the law.[24]

the context of tourism."

[24] Concessionaires running private enterprises in the IWP are constantly monitored with respect to their compliance with park regulations, as an interview with Leigh-Ann Morrison (27.03.2012), the owner of the single private lodge within the Western Shores section of IWP, underlines: "As concessionaires with IWPA, we work under the iSimangaliso Wetland Park rules and regulations

In this context, the institutional stress on the rule of law tends to unleash a deeper process of decolonisation. The empowerment strategy in line with the system of business concessions within the park's boundaries is meant to complement the legal sphere of social transformation:

> "When we put out tenders for lodges, one doesn't just evaluate them on terms of the revenues expected to come to the park, but rather the shareholding of local people. There are criteria around empowerment for job allocations and trainings, where local people actually set off on a career path. The idea is: when you come back to the lodge in ten years' time, maybe the manager is going to be local, maybe the deputy accountant will be local. I can tell you in terms of iSimangaliso's overall spending that about 73% of our spending goes to local Black Economic Empowerment." (Zaloumis 11.11.2014, interview)

Alongside the programmes for BEE, iSimangaliso continues to implement environmental education programmes to contribute towards community empowerment. School awards and environmental education programmes provide free access to the park for young learners. A bursary programme enables local students to pursue conservation and tourism-related subjects at the tertiary level (IWPA 2016: 9). These two levels of environmental education are intertwined by the creation of internships and employment opportunities for tertiary education beneficiaries of the free access programme for schools. All school visits to the park are guided tours, often organised and carried out in participation with former bursary students. iSimangaliso has been on the forefront of taking up this important measure of empowerment through knowledge transmission and growing awareness for environmental concerns. Other state-run conservation areas (e.g. the Kruger National Park) are slowly picking up on this initiative.[25]

7 Environmental Education

As mentioned above, the *Integrated Management Plan* for 2017-2021 (and its precursor) and the *Environmental Education Programmes* stipulate the provision of free access to the park for provincial schools on application and on a regular ba-

and it is all pretty much a very organised system. There are high standards we have to maintain, which is important for a park of this size."

25 These programmes constitute national policies of social transformation related to environmental awareness and protection. According to the *Kruger National Park Management Plan* for 2018-2028, such efforts are envisaged for the future decade with a total budget of 0.22 percent of the entire expenditure: "A dedicated Youth Education and Development Programme will be implemented to raise awareness about conservation and build the capacity of young people to implement effective local programmes that will contribute to biodiversity management and job creation" (South African National Parks 2018: 153, 199).

sis – a *novum* for conservation sites (iSimangaliso Wetland Park Authority 2016: 9). At present, it is planned to increase the equitable access from 4.500 to 5.000 students per year (IWPA/ SANBI 2018: 2).[26] All other South African schools qualify for a discounted ticket price access into the park.[27] Having had the chance to join a number of these school visits with different age groups, we are inclined to highlight the importance of the IWP's educational programme. In the social environment of post-apartheid South Africa, this leg of the environmental education programme points the way to inclusive conservation measures. It signifies a fundamental break from apartheid concepts of conservation, which resulted consistently in the alienation of local communities from the nature they used to live in and with. Through these policies and legal distinctions, different groups of people were not only separated from each other but the majority was also forcefully detached from the most beautiful natural sceneries and disconnected from nature and wild animals. Furthermore, they were also kept 'apart' from knowledge transmission of nature and conservationist concerns. This is the main target of the second leg of the environmental programme, as elucidated by Nerosha Govendor, iSimangaliso's Senior Research Manager (until August 2018):

> "Our bursary programme, the most important programme in my view, supports kids from rural areas to go to universities and technikons to get diplomas and degrees in conservation and tourism. Some of them have come back to iSimangaliso Authority to work as interns and some have found permanent employment within our organisation. This allows the people and communities to see the effect of how a World Heritage Site can yield benefits to communities. When these graduates go back to their communities to become facilitators of environmental awareness, this has a huge impact, because they will relate the issues differently, from a community perspective. It also conveys the powerful message that their own kids are conserving the park. When we go out to do workshops with the communities for environmental awareness raising, the communities start to see the benefits in these kids. This is very tangible, because they can do these workshops differently, since they've grown up in these places. It was very interesting for us too, because the programme was all about them learning from us, but actually we have learned more from them." (Govender 10.06.2016, interview)

[26] This shall be implemented in cooperation with the *South African National Biodiversity Institute* (SANBI), established in 2004 in terms of the *National Environmental Management: Biodiversity Act* (Act No 10 of 2004).

[27] Thandi Shabalala (22.02.2012, interview) sketches the intentions for these school visits: "We encourage very much that schools come to the park, where we organise qualified guides, like myself, to accompany them and share the information in the park during game drives, on different locations like the Eastern Shores, the Western Shores, Sodwana Bay, or Kosi Bay. We inform them why we have to conserve and why we have to look after our environment."

A close reading of the interviews with the (former) leadership of IWPA aids to evaluate the strategies of the concept of "people-centred resilience". Its idea of social resilience complements the emphasis on ecological resilience often referenced in biological considerations of conservation (cf. Adams 2004: 239). There is no way that an organisation of some thirty regular staff members could withstand the potential pressure of 620.000 people living in and adjacent to IWP. Without their tolerance, adherence, and at least partial support conservation is doomed to fail. How a bursary programme for roughly 100 tertiary education students can make a meaningful difference may be concluded from another interview passage of former CEO, Andrew Zaloumis. In the same vein as Nerosha Govender, he stated:

"Increasingly more and more people are seeing the value of the park. On New Year's Day, for example, we have 80.000 to 90.000 people from the local communities coming to the beaches. There are different levels of empowerment. For me personally, one of the most exciting programmes is the higher education programme. It means a form of 'deep empowerment'. These kids from around the park very often come from disadvantaged communities. Their parents can't afford fees for university. When we get them into university – there are about 50 students currently in university – they're passing astonishingly well. The pass rate is 98 percent. Your average pass rate in South Africa at university is around 36 percent. And these are kids from deep rural areas who don't have the same access to electricity, school books, extra lessons. When they're coming back into the park, they will be tomorrow's CEOs. We're excited, because in May this year we took our first eleven interns into a very small organisation. They are all from the area and they have all got degrees. I often go to big community meetings, sometimes there are a thousand school children gathering there and the Premier of the province is present to speak about jobs and careers. When they ask me to speak, I merely introduce the young person who's from that place, got a degree and came back to work with the park. And, suddenly you see the thousand learners, absolutely listening and watching. Afterwards, when they queue up to enquire more, that queue of the local graduate is always the longest, that's a big success."[28] (Zaloumis 11.11.2014, interview)

All these individual and small-scale success stories raise the issue of whether sufficient progress is made in social development. Strikingly, the IWPA has consistently maintained that their impact is much too small, as the interviews indicate.

[28] Mandisa Nkosi, the Community Liaison Officer and intern for the iSimangaliso *Higher Education Access Programme*, is one of these first eleven students, who enrolled in the inauguration programme: "The budget covers the accommodation, the education fees and many other things. I took the opportunity, applied for the programme, became accepted, and right now I'm an intern. IWPA covered my education for the three years duration" (06.11.2014, interview). See also IWP (2018b) on the *Higher Education Programme*.

The responsible staff members convincingly regret the small scale and highly selective measures at their hands to make a meaningful change to rural development in the form of economic and educational empowerment. Among IWPA’s leadership, the widely shared conviction persists that all success of nature conservation depends on the consent of local communities to the park and that this is based on the satisfaction with material and immaterial benefits from commercial ventures and knowledge transmission, or at least realistic future expectations thereof. However, there is shared agreement as well that current possible allocation of financial and human resources does not allow a (much) greater impact. Social scientists, including our research team of social anthropologists, tend to marginalise the resources necessary to cover assigned costs of environmental protection, surveillance, and biodiversity restoration. The latter sets the stage for the projected transfrontier initiative, which we want to focus on in the final chapter prior to our conclusion.

8 Biodiversity Restoration and Future Transfrontier Perspectives

It should not be underestimated what it means to effectively monitor a coastline of over 220 kilometres, almost nine percent of South Africa’s coastline, with the help of the provincial conservation agency *Ezemvelo KZN Wildlife*. ‘Working for the Coast’ is the descriptive title of the Department of Environmental Affairs’ *Expanded Public Works Programme*, which the iSimangaliso Authority is responsible for implementing in line with the *Integrated Coastal Management Act* 28 of 2008. Its main aim is to ensure that the coastal environment is conserved, protected, and sustainably enhanced. Reading between the lines, the massive amount of responsibilities can be taken from a statement of Luvuyo Mlilo, the Chief Director of the *National Department of Environment’s Environmental Protection and Infrastructure Programmes* (quoted in IWP 2017b):

> “The main vision of ‘Working for the Coast’ is a healthy and sustainable coastal environment that is equitably maintained and preserved for current and future generations. Categories of projects implemented under this programme include: Improvement of access to and along the coast, cleaning of the coast, maintenance of visitor facilities, removal of illegal and abandoned structures, removal of invasive alien vegetation, rehabilitation of degraded areas – such as dunes and estuaries – and monitoring of compliance.”

The same newsletter on the iSimangaliso website informs about the tremendous challenge the implementation of this project poses. According to the legal entrustment, the IWPA functions as the auditing agency for the preservation of an unpolluted coastline. This nearly impossible task, considering the global situation of marine pollution, has been outsourced to a 'cleaning and greening' company, which provides permanent employment for 96 previously disadvantaged women and men from neighbouring communities. Their assignment consists of patrolling and cleaning the entire coastal zone on a permanent basis. Although patrol crews bag all beach litter and transport it away for disposal twice a week, the ever-increasing marine plastic pollution of the sea has presented an overpowering foe in recent years.[29] As Andrew Zaloumis notes: "We can do a massive clean-up and the next day a strong prevailing wind or tide can line the whole coast with rubbish again. It is always going to be a challenge, while those who produce this waste do not take responsibility for it" (IWP 2017b).

Compared to this regular task of Sisyphean dimension, the restoration of biodiversity through the reintroduction of animal species, historically abundant in the region, is one of the salient improvements of the past two decades. It goes hand in hand with the restoration of the habitat and large tracts of what now constitutes iSimangaliso, which has been degraded in particular through large-scale commercial forestry. The reintroduction of species once endemic in the area is well worth noting, particularly in view of the fact that it is so often passed over by anthropocentric social scientists. Yet, this endeavour deserves special attention, not only for its successes in the struggle against species extinction but also for its holistic vision of potentially integrating the requirements of wildlife with the needs of local people, the economy, and tourism (Colston 2003: 263).[30] According to its former CEO, regional awareness campaigns and procurement of tangible benefits for adjacent communities to iSimangaliso are prerequisites for efficient protection and reintroduction measures:

"We have developed some of the biggest populations of rhinos in South Africa. In fact, we reintroduced all the historically occurring species back into the park. They were shot out by hunters over the years. The last major hunting operation, what they called 'big-game extermination campaign', was in 1943, when they shot 17.000 wildebeest, because it was thought that the animals were spreading a cattle disease, called ngana. Since iSimangaliso is listed as World Heritage Site, we found at least one new species every year, at a time

[29] It is noteworthy that South Africa is currently expanding its network of coastal protection by 20 new *Marine Protected Areas*. This was approved by Cabinet on 24 October 2018. iSimangaliso's new CEO, Sibusiso Bukhosini, appointed in September 2018, welcomed this increase of ocean protection by approximately 50.000 km^2 (IWP 2018c; see also SANBI 2018). To which extent national environmental policies may halt global marine pollution remains to be seen.

[30] Cf. Pimm et al. (2014) on the alarming rates of extinction; cf. Felbab-Brown (2017) on the extinction market and potential control measures.

when the world is experiencing about a thousand extinctions of species per year and that's a conservative estimate." (Zaloumis 11.11.2014, interview)[31]

While most of the reintroduced species, such as elephants and lions, thrive very well in their new terrain, the rhino population is afflicted by a massive onslaught, triggered by the high demand for rhino horn (inter alia for fictitious medicinal purposes) in various Asian countries. In response, the *iSimangaliso Wetland Park Authority* and *Ezemvelo KZN Wildlife* had little choice but to take a pro-active step in deterring poachers from targeting rhinos in the *World Heritage Site*. They implemented a rhino de-horning programme throughout the Western Shores section of the park. Although this is not considered a guarantee against poaching, it effectively reduces the pressure on a particular area, though perhaps to the detriment of other regions where poachers see better chances of success. For conservationists, this means a devastating measure, moreover at high costs, as it requires veterinary expertise and expensive equipment, such as helicopters. The highly ambivalent solution, born out of desperation, risks causing harm or even death to individual animals in order to safeguard their survival as a species. Sizo Sibiya, the park's Organisational Director, describes the emotional and material costs of the endeavour (10.6.2016, interview):

"Dehorning the rhino, for a conservationist it's something we do with a bleeding heart. It will inevitably change the behaviour of this animal and we are depriving this animal of the only tool it can use to help raise its offspring. It's like cutting human limbs off. We have dehorned them, but we still need to wait and see if it actually helps in reducing rhino-poaching. We understand from lessons of other countries, such as Namibia and Zimbabwe, that the animals were still poached. Therefore, it is essential to combine the dehorning with strict law enforcement and economic upliftment. We also need to spread awareness that the rhinos are dehorned. Because we understand that sometimes poachers who track an animal for a day or two, only to find it dehorned, might kill it for the actual fact that it is dehorned. We face a situation where we believe that poverty has pushed people into being exploited by those who have money, but do not risk getting arrested. We want people to understand that they can only sell crafts to tourists, as long as they come. If we don't have rhinos anymore, that opportunity will be gone."

The *Integrated Management Plan* for 2017-2021 reviews poaching in critical tension with the high levels of poverty in the uMkhanyakude region as a whole and the areas neighbouring the park in particular. It refrains from anti-poaching efforts that are overtly dependent on strict law enforcement, which has been criticised as paramilitary interventions within unilateral protection regimes. Rather, it puts

31 The historical campaign referred to in the interview worked in both ways: it eradicated the ngana disease, spread by the tsetse fly, and most of the wildlife with it (cf. Clarke 2017).

special emphasis on the creation of conservation awareness as a precondition for armed environmental protection within the park's borders. The neighbouring rural areas include some of the most impoverished communities in South Africa, where many households rely extensively on natural resources from iSimangaliso for survival, for example harvest of reeds and fruit, agriculture, and fishing. The policy document refers to the depletion and degradation of natural resources in communal areas, which has reportedly led to increasing pressure on the resources within the park (IWPA 2016: 35).

Other challenges for the restoration plans are equally discussed in some detail; first and foremost, the successful reopening of the estuary mouth after 50 years of partial separation (for the purpose of sugarcane plantations) of the uMfolozi River. In the last years, the Lake St Lucia water system has been re-connected to the estuary, returning its major source of fresh water and re-establishing the dynamic natural processes governing the opening and closing of the estuary mouth (IWPA 2016: 9, 12, 38 pp.). There is but one important aspect, on which the policy document and the interviews remain quite silent and vague, i.e. the projected transfrontier conservation area with Mozambique. The *Integrated Management Plan* (IWPA 2016: 61) has only this to say: "iSimangaliso will continue to support the establishment of one of South Africa's five Transfrontier Conservation Areas (TFCAs), viz. the Ponto do Oura – Kosi Bay TFCA (Mozambique/SouthAfrica)."

In an interview (11.11.2014), the former project manager for the TFCA, Andrew Zaloumis, avoided the sensitive issue of bilateral environmental conservation between South Africa and Mozambique with some fairly general remarks:

> "IWP at this point represents the South African part of the projected transfrontier park that is supposed to encompass southern Mozambique, northern KwaZulu-Natal and eastern Swaziland. When iSimangaliso has been established it was part of this much bigger project, called Spatial Development Initiative in South Africa. It was launched by presidents and kings. The governments looked at this area and saw the huge potential and immense natural resource space in the poverty-stricken area. At the time Nelson Mandela called it the 'paradox of human misery amongst plenty', natural plenty, that is. Out of the Lubombo SDI emerged iSimangaliso, but the first thing the governments tackled was the malaria prevention project."

It is a matter of speculation why little progress has been achieved for the planned TFCA.[32] In any case, such agreements belong to the sphere of multi-lateral inter-

[32] According to the Peace Parks Foundation (2018), the iSimangaliso Wetland Park Authority, the management of the Ponta do Ouro Partial Marine Reserve, and Peace Parks Foundation entered into an agreement in August 2015 to conduct a multi-sectoral study: "The aim of this study, which will encompass the coastal areas of Mozambique and South Africa in the Ponta do Ouro-

national agreements and their subsequent implementation by national legislation. They are, therefore, beyond the immediate scope of agencies such as IWPA.

9 Conclusion

It has almost become a countertrend in developmental studies to bemoan the elusive hopes and failings of community-based conservation projects (especially in Southern Africa). Their major setback is seen in bringing forth sustainable transformation to the integrated benefit of both nature and humans (cf. Büscher 2013: 38 pp.). For Nustad, the very source for these prevalent failures in conservation practices (including *Community-Based Natural Resource Management* programmes) lies in the preconceived dichotomies of nature and culture. In his convincing conclusion, this duality leads to a corresponding neglect of thinking in relational terms: "Instead of assuming an a priori distinction between the natural and the social, the material and the cultural, or humans and animals for that matter, the task must be to develop analytical frameworks that examine divisions empirically rather than starting out with them as analytical givens" (Nustad 2015: 53 pp.).

Strict protection measures are critically questioned for their reproduction of the "myth of wild Africa" (Adams/ McShane 1996), which arguably has a white racist bottom line. In the 'natural wild Africa', envisioned as a borderless space, the primordial landscapes reserved for wild animals conform to the legal legitimation of a fictitious African terra nullius, purportedly free for (historical) European occupation (cf. Adams 2003: 20). Today's elites, according to this critique of a racialised mode of conservation, seek to conserve large tracts of lands for themselves and their own commercial purposes under the pretext of nature conservation and protection of biodiversity. Nature conservation in Africa has thus come under the academic suspicion of protecting the land against a rapidly growing African population encroaching on a presumably pristine nature. The sheer abundance of well-established land claims on protected areas based on legal provisions for land restitution proves, in the eyes of some critics, the fallacy of Eurocentric visions claiming to save Africans from themselves (Büscher 2013: 73).

With this contribution, we sought to infer that this might be the case in some instances but that the general assumption of a racial bias attached to conservation regulations may overshoot the mark. The IWP and its central hub, the town of St Lucia, provide a comparative example for an impartial protective regime. In

Kosi Bay TFCA, is to assess the impact and threats posed by large development projects in the TFCA."

the years of apartheid, it was the ruling white elite that treated the natural environment like their private gardens. The exclusive access to the massive coastline, for instance, through beach driving with buggies and fairly uncontrolled excessive utilisation of resources became one of the first targets of protective measures at the dawn of democracy. Therefore, the purported colonial and racial agenda of nature conservation as predominantly protecting Africa from (Black) Africans can hardly be verified through empirical evidence in this case. Eurocentric stereotypes of wild Africa are, in our view, much less held by conservationists but rather by the old elite (of South Africa) and, perhaps, some international tourists. St Lucia palpably offers a constant involuntary parody of the white myths of discovery. Traffic in this iSimangaliso frontier town shows an abundance of over-equipped 4 x 4 vehicles signalling the 'adventure' of an expedition into a park offering almost fully tarred roads and even a filling station. Individual, mostly white, South African 'explorers' stack provisions from the Spar supermarket, as if setting out for the discovery of the source of the Nile in the days of Livingstone, only to land on the amplified and fully equipped campsite at Cape Vidal, some 36 kilometres from the entrance gate on the Eastern Shores. When then some of them ignore huge billboards warning against feeding the wild animals, while watching rugby on TV with a satellite dish attached to their kitchen trailer, one obtains yet another reason for protective measures against ignorant humans of any provenance.[33]

Critical arguments against these and other colonial legacies attached to the myth of 'unspoilt Africa' should not mislead to construct an inherently racist neoliberal conservation agenda set out to protect Africa from (only Black) Africans for the benefit of the rich and the white. Nature can be exploited and degraded in terms of biodiversity values by people of any colour, ethnicity, or class. The well-established decline of many flora and fauna species, the incremental habitat loss, the marine pollution, and so forth are unfortunately no myths. Of course, there are complex causes behind these dramatic developments. Therefore, critical conservation studies within social and natural science should focus on careful investigations of the entire spectrum of harmful practices and their structural reasons. We believe, on the grounds of the empirical examples dealt with in this volume, that a priori condemnation of all market incentives does little to inspire novel institutional arrangements of integrated conservation based on all kinds of different partnerships (van der Duim et al. 2015: 13). The IWP gives an instructive example on how 'neoliberal modes of governance' use commodification and marketing

[33] We refer to these personal observations to underline the inescapable impressions of inequalities and social differentiation our research group encountered. These personal experiences, endorsed by many interviews with local residents, accentuated the critical framework of the research.

strategies of nature for a credible conservationist struggle open to the participation and integration of all directly affected sectors of society. Not to be mistaken, it is useful to deconstruct the hypocritical ingratiation of a 'pristine African wilderness', wherever it occurs. But, the pure promotion of natural sites – for instance iSimangaliso's "ten jewels" – needs to be analysed in terms of its social targets. The mere identification of an emerging market as infected by the abhorred disease of "Nature™ Inc." does not contribute much to a solution for the integration of development (based on self-determination) and conservation.

The more difficult question of "what do we want?" (Ferguson 2009: 167) portends to an analysis of successes, shortcomings, and failures. It further enquires which actors within an overall economy of interests could improve their performance in which regard. If key aims are defined as poverty alleviation, economic empowerment, self-reliance, local democratisation, and participation in the entire decision-making process to achieve social transformation, then the alarmism, fatalism, and sheer defeatism predominating the current literature on 'neoliberal conservation' will not suffice.

The focus of this critique appears to start from the wrong end: the incentive- or market-oriented field of contemporary conservation. Against this framing, we argue that economic interests alone present an insufficient overall indicator for the neoliberalisation of nature. In our view, it rather depends on the actual institutional arrangement and the procedures undertaken to come to binding decisions in this regard.[34] This approach pays special attention to the very agency of local actors who have achieved some successes in forcing themselves into the mainstream of market-conscious conservation in various locales of Southern Africa. Their political actions tend to disappear behind the current general critique of 'neoliberal conservation'; sacrificed on the altar of a neo-Marxist orthodoxy. On the critical parameter of a procedural or discourse-ethical approach, by contrast, the focus shifts to all concerned and affected stakeholders. First of all, local people – the so-called 'communities' – are recognised as possible co-designers of conservation aims, means, and policy implementations. Furthermore, this theoretical approach based on empirical reconstructive investigation questions their decision-making power in determining the distribution of eventual economic and social benefits. This chapter, therefore, suggests shifting the focus to the field of (discursive) power, the actual procedures of participation and inclusive leader-

[34] Such institutional arrangements have been broadly defined "as a set of organizational forms, policies, rules, practices and cultural norms designed and deployed to govern a group of actors towards the attainment of a particular objective" (van der Duim et al. 2015: 3).

ship, as well as the institutional set-up at work in the implementation process of the conservation-development-tourism nexus.

However, the papers on iSimangaliso in Part III of this volume seem to agree that many local people interviewed during the 2016 research in the field have felt little or no benefits so far. Of course, this has to be viewed in relation to the 620.000 people living in the area, who are considered potential beneficiaries of IWP. Obviously, a realistic perspective has to concede the sheer disparity between expectations and viable prospects within a given time frame. In order to afford justice to the IWPA conservation efforts in empowerment one needs to pose the question, which other resource usages might have achieved a better performance and at what environmental costs. Nevertheless, the fact remains that the inauguration phase created high expectations of economic benefits that could not realistically be accomplished.

In terms of Ferguson's suggestion of "saying what we want", the overall consent of chapters in Part III emphasises that *iSimangaliso Wetland Park* perhaps stepped into the trap set by its own progressive optimism to ventilate a new model of integrated governance. In this sense, the first two decades of IWP give rise to an important warning against the sales talk discernible in a plethora of conservation-development-tourism ventures trying to sell a project to a highly differentiated and heterogeneous audience of politicians, traditional authorities, investors, developers, transnational environmental organisations, ecologists, conservationists, local people, and the general public.

The main agenda of our collective research was to provide an overview, an evaluation, and some food for thought on whether the proclaimed "benefits beyond boundaries" are at least partially realised for neighbouring communities, the stakeholder group most affected. Some papers implicitly or explicitly suggest a more modest approach of prospecting possible benefits for some stakeholders that can be realised in a reasonable time span. Therefore, it may be recommended, that expectations raised by such 'grand visions' of "benefits beyond boundaries" need to be defined in more concrete and realistic terms. Disappointment of local people, within the contextual history of apartheid conservation, may easily lead to frustration of surrounding communities. In turn, such sentiments hamper the positive and progressive intentions ventilated in policy documents. We also propose to increase transparency of procedural requirements for the formation of consensual, i.e. 'integrated' decisions. Institutionalised modes of decision-making based once more on procedural rights would certainly increase organisational accountability and local ownership, and thereby the social resilience of concrete measures (cf. Salomon et al. 2018).

Of course, democratisation from below falls within the legal sphere of national institutions and can only be supported by a conservation organisation. At this point in time, there appears to be a gap between the policy formulations and the actual processes of information, opinion- and will-formation and final decision-making in the IWP context (and, indeed, beyond). In other words, there is a well-defined public participation strategy embodied in the *Integrated Management Plan* for 2017-2021, which is reflected by a strong emphasis on participation throughout the entire text, but the actual legal procedures and other administrative prescriptions remain quite vague, as our empirical data suggest. Public discourses in community meetings seem to be organised mostly impromptu. There is obvious space for improvement in this regard. Nevertheless, it has to be conceded that the *Integrated Management Plan* of *iSimangaliso Wetland Park Authority* almost completely lacks common patterns of marketing lingua. It is, on the contrary, quite frank. Though bidding to strike a balance between the interests of conservation, ecotourism, development, and economic empowerment, conservation goals are prioritised:

> "However, notably, this balance is not an equal one: in order to ensure World Heritage values are not compromised, conservation objectives need to be foremost, with the emphasis on 'development for conservation'. In this context, economic empowerment and job creation, through appropriate tourism development, are necessary to achieve conservation goals. The purpose of the IMP is to guide this balance." (IWPA 2016: 1)

Such a clarity may paradoxically help local residents' understanding that they are taken seriously as stakeholders but their stakes may not yet be that high. The extraordinary achievements of IWP should not become sacrificed or diminished in relation to more ambitious requests of urgent economic and social transformation, as exigent they may indeed appear. In many regards, IWPA may justifiably assert substantial progress, especially given the relatively short time frame since its inauguration and the very limited financial and human resources at its disposal. These undeniable accomplishments include: foremost the integration of formerly unprotected areas, preservation and reintroduction of animal species, eradication of alien plants, biodiversity increase, and, on a symbolic level, ground-breaking efforts in environmental education. The IWP is no exception to other projects discussed in this volume, which have been reviewed as conservation efforts with great potential yet not without shortcomings, failures, or social deficits. *iSimangaliso Wetland Park* credibly made a promising depart from colonial conservation with its former exclusion of local and indigenous communities.

The literature on neoliberal conservation creates the impression that conservation closely linked to tourism should eventually be abandoned altogether. But what then? A return to mining, as prevented through the interference of the great late Nelson Mandela and civil society resistance before IWP was declared a UNESCO *World Heritage Site* (on the grounds of South Africa's government respective demand)? Or the approval of even more extensive pine and eucalyptus plantations, which have severe and well documented consequences of biodiversity degradation, not least the decline of groundwater reservoirs? Or an unregulated return of land to local populations with a laissez faire policy on protective provisions that potentially allows contingent decisions on resource use to gain the upper hand? None of these seem of great advantage, particularly to the very population that was kept from environmental education and was economically decapitated by apartheid. In all likelihood, a populist deviation from conservation interests would lead to a setback of successfully established environmental upgrading measures within IWP. These efforts were meticulously undertaken to minimise or even reverse negative impacts on the wetlands, which are highly sensitive to external factors from small-scale ones, such as farming, forestry, or mining, to large-scale factors, such as global marine pollution or climate change. Moreover, even a partial renunciation of evaluation mechanisms for the capable management of a vulnerable ecosystem might open the door to fierce internal competition and potential conflicts with other South Africans trying to cash in on emerging short-term economic possibilities created by a vacuum of monitoring and control.

In our view, social sciences have a considerable responsibility in this regard. Sweeping judgments of incentive-driven conservation may easily play into the hands of those who consider nature as a mere asset of exploitation and conservation regimes as obstacles for short-term material gains. This appears even more acute in recent years, after more and more global (and oval) offices of power have been re-occupied by politicians who put anything and everything first, but nature. Instead, a critical social science review of integrated conservation efforts could augment the pressure on national and international agencies to enhance the democratic institutionalisation of conservation bodies and their co-management partners. Naïve? Perhaps, but at least more constructive in helping to answer the question "what do we want"?

The discourse-critical approach marks a departure from the redundant repetition of a 'conservation guilt' for global (neoliberal and other ill-conceived) developments that affect and determine conservation. To abstain from generalised accusations against conservationists as agents of neoliberalism appears less a matter of fairness than a commitment to avoid an inversion of perpetrator and victim, which has nowadays become so common in the global assault on critical voices and media. Many ardent conservationists on the ground struggle with tempo-centric politics narrowed to short-term gains, insufficient funding, and, more often than not, ignorance for rational concerns. The *iSimangaliso Wetland Park* has enjoyed broad support but remains no exception as the park is understaffed and lacks the material resources necessary for greater impacts in the social sphere. Still, its small management team has evolved, just as the park has moved on from struggles based on passion and resilience to the establishment of novel institutional arrangements. Their key intention is to set rural development and empowerment as priorities. Arguably, during its two decades of existence, the foundation for IWP to become an acknowledged model of integrated conservation-development has been successfully laid. There are few international examples with a comparative record of fast-tracking conservation and development in parallel, as IWP's former CEO asserts:

> "I think iSimangaliso is a park in the making and it is a park that's been made after Nelson Mandela was released. So, for South Africa, it is a very special park. And, like any organisation, we've passed the start-up phase, where we were boxing above our weight. We are now recognised, we have won a number of national and international awards for the work we do. But, we're now in a position where we're having to manage a big park, it's increasing, it's growing. iSimangaliso will not be the same tomorrow. We are hoping, that increasingly more and more people around the park will actually come on board in support. Not everyone around the park supports the park, at all. They can't be expected to." (Zaloumis 11.11.2014, interview)

IWP and its governing body credibly face the history of colonial conservation in its most extreme expression of apartheid. However, statements such as the one cited above spread the conditional optimism it takes to win support. Critical social science investigations may be viewed as contributions to achieve the kind of "Vital Alternatives", that even critics of current so-called 'neoliberal' conservation practices seem to evoke (cf. Dressler/ Büscher/ Fletcher 2014: 250 pp.). Far from proposing an exculpation for the devastating policies referred to with the notion of 'neoliberalism' and its legalist entrenchments, this praxeological reading of IWP and its governance framework aspired to go beyond judging 'neoliberalism' as an evil essence or uniform automatism. Instead we suggest exploring the field of specific governmental techniques (and rhetoric), as Ferguson insinuated (2009: 183).

The findings presented here seem to support this author's (ibid.) key hypothesis of polyvalent neoliberal mechanisms of governance: "We may be surprised to find that some of them can be repurposed, and put to work in the service of political projects very different from those usually associated with this word." This chapter sought to make yet another modest contribution in this respect, in a similar manner to the other papers assembled in the volume. African borderlands, 'bewildered' with wild animals, may indeed under specific procedural conditions evolve as revitalised "theatres of opportunity" (Nugent/ Ajiwasu 1996), and thus become less bewildering for its human inhabitants (and perhaps critical analysts).

References

Abdulkarim, Binta (2011): Journey to Latitude 13° Without a Map (unpublished field-notes).

Aborne – The African Borderlands Research Network (2018): http://www.aborne.org/

Adam, Rachelle (2012): *Nature, Colonialism and Conservation Organisations: How international law became the response to the biodiversity crisis*. Doctoral Dissertation, Hebrew University of Jerusalem.

Adam, Rachelle (2014): *Elephant Treaties: The Colonial legacy of the Biodiversity Crisis*. Hanover/ London: University Press of New England.

Adams, Adrian/ So, Jaabe (1996): *A Claim to Land by the River: A Household in Senegal, 1720-1994*. Oxford: Oxford University Press.

Adams, Jonathan S./ McShane, Thomas O. (1996): T*he Myth of Wild Africa: Conservation Without Illusion*. Berkeley: University of California Press.

Adams, William M./ Mulligan, Martin (2003): Introduction. In: Adams, William M./ Mulligan, Martin (eds.), *Decolonizing Nature. Strategies for Conservation in a Post-Colonial Era*. London: Earthscan Publications Ltd, pp. 1-15.

Adams, William M. (2003): Nature and the Colonial Mind. In: Adams, William M./ Mulligan, Martin (eds.), *Decolonizing Nature. Strategies for Conservation in a Post-Colonial Era*. London: Earthscan Publications Ltd, pp. 51-79.

Adams, William M. (2004): *Against Extinction. The Story of Conservation*. London: Earthscan.

Adams, William/ Hutton, Jon (2007): People, parks and poverty: Political ecology and biodiversity conservation. In: *Conservation and Society*, 5(2), pp. 147-183.

Africa, Tamaryn (2017): Andrew Zaloumis steps down as iSimangaliso's Wetland Park CEO. In: *Business Report*, 4.9.2017. https://www.iol.co.za/business-report/andrew-zaloumis-steps-down-as-isimangaliso-wetland-park-ceo-11070235

African Union Border Programme (2017) (AUBP) – Uniting and integrating Africa through peaceful, open and prosperous borders. http://www.peaceau.org/en/page/27-au-border-programme-aubp

Agrawal, Arun/ Gibson, Clark C. (1999): Enchantment and Disenchantment: The Role of Community in Natural Resource Conservation. In: *World Development*, 27(4), pp. 629-649.

Aicken, Michelle/ Ryan, Chris (2005): *Indigenous Tourism*. London: Routledge.

Akuupa Uusiku, M. (2011): *The formation of 'National Culture' in post-apartheid Namibia: a focus on state sponsored cultural festivals in Kavango Region*. Doctoral Dissertation, University of the Western Cape.

Alam, Undala (2012): Co-operating internationally over water: studying l'espace OMVS. In: *Journal of Modern African Studies,* 50(2), pp. 175-199.

Alden Wiley, Liz (2003): *Governance and Land Relations: A Review of Decentralisation of Land Administration and Management in Africa.* London: International Institute for Environment and Development.

Ali, Saleem H. (ed.) (2007): *Peace Parks. Conservation and Conflict Resolution.* Cambridge: Massachusetts Institute of Technology.

Alivizatou, Marilena (2011): Intangible Heritage and the Performance of Identity. In: Jackson, Anthony/ Kidd, Jenny (eds.), *Performing Heritage.* Manchester: Manchester University Press, pp. 82-93.

Anadu, Pius A. (1987): Wildlife Conservation in Nigeria: Problems and Strategies. In: *The Environmentalist*, 7(3), pp. 211-220.

Anand, Sudhir/ Sen, Amartya (2000): Human Development and Economic Sustainability. In: *World Development,* 28(12), pp. 2029-2049.

Angula, Hilma M./ Hill, Greg Stuart / Ward, David/ Tatongo, Greenwald/ Diggle, Richard N./ Naidoo, Robin (2018): Local Perceptions of Trophy Hunting on Communal Lands in Namibia. In: *Biological Conservation*, 218, pp. 26-31.

Apeldoorn, G. Jan van (1981): *Perspectives on Drought and Famine in Nigeria.* London: George Allen & Unwin.

Arthur, Kwame Boafo/ Gyimah-Boadi, E. (2006): Africa's Evolving Relations with Israel. In: *Israel and Africa.* Assessing the Past, Envisioning the Future. American Jewish Committee and Tel Aviv University, pp. 26-33.

Asiwaju, Anthony I./ Barkindo, Bawuro M. (eds.) (1993): *The Nigeria-Niger Transborder Co-operation.* Lagos: Malthouse.

Ax, Christina/ Brimnes, Niels/ Jensen, Niklas Thode/ Oslund, Karen (eds.) (2011): *Cultivating the Colonies: Colonial States and Their Environmental Legacies.* Ohio University Press.

Bandiaky-Badji, Solange (2011): Gender equity in Senegal's forest governance history: why policy and representation matter. In: *International Forestry Review,* 13(2), pp. 172-194.

Barkindo, Bawuro M. (1993): Border Region Development as Impetus for Transborder Cooperation and Integration in Africa: The Nigerian Experience. In: *Journal of Borderlands Studies*, 8(1), pp. 21-38.

Barnabas, Shade/ Finlay, Kate (2012): Shifting Representations of the Bushmen. In: Tomaselli, Keyan G. (ed.), *Cultural Tourism and Identity. Rethinking Indigeneity.* Leiden: Koninklijke Brill NV, pp. 71-84.

Barry, Boubacar (1998) *Senegambia and the Atlantic Slave Trade.* Cambridge: Cambridge University Press.

Barry, Boubacar (2012): *The Kingdom of Waalo: Senegal Before the* Conquest. New York: Diasporic Africa Press.

Barth, Fredrik (ed.) (1969): *Ethnic Groups and Boundaries: The Social Organization of Culture and Difference.* Bergen: Universitetsforlaget.

Begbie-Clench, Benjamin (2015): *Illegal Grazing in Nyae Nyae Conservancy: Assessment and Recommendations*. Windhoek: Nyae Nyae Development Foundation of Namibia and Legal Assistance Centre.

Beinart, Williams/ Coates, Peter (1995): *Environment and History, The Taming of Nature in the USA and South Africa*. Routledge.

Beinart, Williams/ Hughes, Lotte (2009): *Environment and Empire, Oxford History of the British Empire Companion*. Oxford: Oxford University Press.

Beker, Avi (2006): Tikun Olam in Africa. In: American Jewish Committee (ed.), *Israel and Africa. Assessing the Past, Envisioning the Future.* Tel Aviv: Tel Aviv University, pp. 34-42.

Benda-Beckmann, Franz von (2001): On the reproduction of law: Micro and macro in the time-space geography of law. In: Fikentscher, Wolfgang (ed.), *Begegnung und Konflikt – eine kulturanthropologische Bestandsaufnahme*. München: Verlag der Bayerischen Akademie der Wissenschaften, pp. 119-131.

Bergthaler, Georg (2015): *Die Sharing Economy – Hebel zur sozio-ökonomischen Transformation? Eine theoretische Abhandlung über das gesellschaftliche und ökologische Potential gemeinnütziger Organisationsstrukturen*. Bachelor Thesis, University of Vienna 2015.

Bergthaler, Georg (2016): *The Historical Development of Nature Conservation and Protected Areas in South Africa: An Analysis Based on the Example of the iSimangaliso Wetland Park in KwaZulu-Natal*. Term Paper, University of Vienna.

Biesele, Megan/ Barclay, Steve (2001): Ju/'hoan Women's Tracking Knowledge and Its Contribution to Their Husband's Hunting Success. In: *African Study Monographs*, supplementary issue 26, pp. 67-84.

Biesele, Megan/ Hitchcock, Robert K. (2011): *The Ju/'hoan San of Nyae Nyae and Namibian Independence: Development, Democracy, and Indigenous Voices in Southern Africa*. New York and Oxford: Berghahn Books.

Binter, Julia (2014): Vermittler zwischen Vergangenheit, Gegenwart und Zukunft. Ethnographische Museen im Spannungsfeld von Orten der Repräsentation und 'glokalen' Kontaktzonen. In: Wernhart, Karl R. / Zips, Werner (eds.), *Ethnohistorie. Rekonstruktion, Kulturkritik und Repräsentation – Eine Einführung*. Vienna: Promedia, pp. 80-100.

Blundo, Giorgio (2014): Seeing like a State Agent: The Ethnography of Reform in Senegal's Forestry Services. In: Bierschenk, Thomas/ Olivier de Sardan, Jean-Pierre (eds.), *States at Work: Dynamics of African Bureaucracies*. Leiden: Brill, pp. 70-112.

Bodley, John H. (2015): *Victims of Progress*. Sixth Edition. Lanham: AltaMira Press.

Bolaane, Maitseo (2001): Fear of the Marginalized Minorities: The Khwai Community Determining their Boundary in the Okavango, Botswana through a Deed of Trust. In: Barnard, Alan/ Kenrick, Justin (eds.), *Africa's Indigenous Peoples: 'First Peoples' or 'Marginalized Minorities'?* Edinburgh: University of Edinburgh, Centre of African Studies, pp. 145-171.

Bolaane, Maitseo (2013): Chiefs, Hunters, and San in the Creation of the Moremi Game Reserve, Okavango Delta: Multiracial Interactions and Initiatives, 1956-1979. In: *Senri Ethnological Studies*, 83. Osaka: National Museum of Ethnology.

Bolaane, Maitseo (2014): San Cross-Border Cultural Heritage and Identity in Botswana, Namibia and South Africa. In: *African Study Monographs*, 35(1), pp. 41-64.

Bollig, Michael (2003): Between Welfare and Bureaucratic Domination: The San of Ghanzi and Kgalagadi Districts. In: Hohmann, Thekla (ed.), *San and the State. Contesting Land, Development, Identity, and Representation*. Cologne: Rüdiger Köppe Verlag, pp. 281-324.

Bond, Patrick (2003): *Against Global Apartheid. South Africa meets the World Bank, IMF and International Finance*. London/ New York: Zed Books Ltd.

Bourdieu, Pierre (1977): *Outline of a Theory of Practice*. Cambridge: Cambridge University Press.

Bourdieu, Pierre (1982): *Die feinen Unterschiede. Kritik der gesellschaftlichen Urteilskraft*. Frankfurt am Main: Suhrkamp.

Bourdieu, Pierre/ Wacquant, Loic J. D. (1992): *An Invitation to Reflexive Sociology*. Cambridge: Polity Press.

Brockington, Dan (2002): *Fortress Conservation: The Preservation of the Mkomazi Game Reserve, Tanzania*. Bloomington: Indiana University Press.

Brockington, Dan/ Igoe, James (2006): Eviction for Conservation: a Global Overview. In: *Conservation and Soiety*, 4(3), pp. 424-470.

Brockington, Dan/ Duffy, Rosaleen/ Igoe, James (2008): *Nature Unbound: Conservation, Capitalism and the Future in Protected Areas*. London: Earthscan.

Brockington, Dan/ Duffy, Rosaleen (eds.) (2011): *Capitalism and Conservation*. Chichester: Wiley-Blackwell.

Brownlie, Ian (ed.) (1979): *African Boundaries: A Legal and Diplomatic Encyclopaedia*. London & Berkeley: C. Hurst & University of California Press.

Bruton, M.N./ Cooper, K.H. (eds.) (2013): *Studies on the Ecology of Maputaland*. Rhodes University and The Natal Branch of the Wildlife Society of South Africa.

Bunten, Alexis Celeste (2008): Sharing Culture or Selling out? Developing the Commodified Persona in the Heritage Industry. In: *American Ethnologist*, 35(3), pp. 380-395.

Burg, Lisette van der (2013): *Commoditization of the Ju/'hoansi Culture: Destroying Authenticity or Revitalizing Tradition? A Study on the Impacts of Cultural Tourism on the Ju/'hoansi San in the Nyae Nyae Conservancy, Namibia*. Master Thesis, University of Leiden.

Büscher, Bram/ Whande, Webster (2007): Whims of the Winds of the Time? Emerging Trends in Biodiversity Conservation and Protected Area Management. In: *Conservation and Society*, 5(1), pp. 22-43.

Büscher, Bram (2012): 'Nature™Inc.: Changes and Continuities in Neoliberal Conservation and Market-based Environmental Policy'. In: *Development and Change Forum 2012*, 43(1). The Hague, pp. 53-78.

Büscher, Bram/ Sullivan, Sian / Neves, Katja/ Igoe, James / Brockington, Dan (2012): Towards a Synthesized Critique of Neoliberal Biodiversity Conservation. In: *Capitalism Nature Socialism*, 23(2), pp. 4-30.

Büscher, Bram (2013): *Transforming the Frontier. Peace Parks and the Politics of Neoliberal Conservation in Southern Africa*. Durham and London: Duke University Press.

Büscher, Bram/ Dressler, Wolfram/ Fletcher, Robert (eds.) (2014): *Nature™ Inc. Environmental Conservation in the Neoliberal Age*. Tucson: University of Arizona Press.

Büscher, Bram (2014): Nature on the Move I: The Value and Circulation of Liquid Nature and the Emergence of Fictitious Conservation. In: Büscher, Bram/ Dressler, Wolfram/ Fletcher, Robert (eds.), *Nature™ Inc. Environmental Conservation in the Neoliberal Age*. Tucson: The University of Arizona Press, pp. 183-204.

Büscher, Bram/ Fletcher, Robert (2015): Accumulation by Conservation. In: *New Political Economy*, 20(2), pp. 273-298.

Büscher, Bram/ Fletcher, Robert (2015): Accumulation by Conservation. In: *New Political Economy*, 20(2), pp. 273-298.

Buthelezi, Mbongiseni/ Yeni, Stha (2016): *Traditional Leadership in Democratic South Africa: Pitfalls and Prospects*. Paper prepared for the Council for the Advancement of the South African Constitution, Nelson Mandela Foundation and Hanns Seidel Foundation.

Butler, Richard/ Hinch, Thomas (eds.) (1996): *Tourism and Indigenous Peoples*. London: International Thompson Business Press and New York: Routledge.

Butler, Richard/ Hinch, Thomas (2007): Conclusion. In: Butler, Richard/ Hinch, Thomas (eds.), *Tourism and Indigenous Peoples: Issues and Implications*. Oxford: Butterworth-Heinemann, pp. 319-332.

Cadena, Marisol de la/ Starn, Orin (eds.) (2007): *Indigenous Experience Today*. Oxford and New York: Berg.

Campbell, Alec/ Robbins, Lawrence H. / Taylor, Michael (eds.) (2010): *Tsodilo Hills: Copper Bracelet of the Kalahari*. East Lansing: Michigan State University Press and Gaborone: Botswana Society.

Campese, Jessica/ Sunderland, Terry/ Greiber, Thomas/ Oviedo, Gonzalo (eds.) (2009): *Rights-based approaches. Exploring issues and opportunities for conservation*. Bogor, Indonesia: Center for International Forestry Research (CIFOR) and The International Union for Conservation of Nature (IUCN).

Cassidy, Lin/ Good, Ken / Mazonde, Isaac/ Rivers, Roberta (2001): *An Assessment of the Status of the San in Botswana*. Windhoek, Namibia: Legal Assistance Center.

Castree, Noel (2010a): Neoliberalism and the Biophysical Environment: What 'Neoliberalism' is, and What Difference Nature Makes to it. In: *Geography Compass*, 4(12), 1725–1733, 10.1111/j.1749-8198.2010.00405

Castree, Noel (2010b): Neoliberalism and the Biophysical Environment: A synthesis and evaluation of the research. In: *Environment and Society: Advances in Research*, 1(1), pp. 5-45.

CBD (1992): Preamble to the Convention. https://www.cbd.int/convention/articles/default.shtml?a=cbd-00

CBD (2014): South Africa's Fifth National Report to the Convention on Biological Diversity. https://www.cbd.int/doc/world/za/za-nr-05-en.pdf

CBD (2014): Global Biodiversity Outlook 4. https://www.cbd.int/gbo4/

Chatty, Dawn/ Colchester, Marcus (2002): *Conservation and Mobile Indigenous Peoples. Displacement, Forced Settlement and Sustainable Development*. Oxford/ New York: Berghahn Books.

Chazan, Naomi (2006): Israel and Africa: Challenges for a New Era. In: American Jewish Committee (ed.), *Israel and Africa. Assessing the Past, Envisioning the Future*. Tel Aviv: Tel Aviv University, pp. 1-15.

Chellan, Noel/ Khan, Sultan (2008): Contesting Ecotourism Development in the iSimangaliso Wetland Park in KwaZulu-Natal. In: *Alternation*, 15(1), pp. 268-289.

Christie, Iain/ Fernandes, Encida/ Messerlie, Hannah/ Twining-Ward, Louise (2014): *Tourism in Africa: Harnessing Tourism for Growth and Improved Livelihoods*. Washington, D.C.: The World Bank.

Claassens, Aninka (2014): Denying Ownership and Equal Citizenship: Continuities in the State's Use of Law and 'Custom', 1913 – 2003. In: *Journal of Southern African Studies*, 40(4), pp. 761-779.

Clarke, James (2017): *Overkill. The race to save Africa's wildlife*. Cape Town: Struik Nature.

Cohen, Erik (1988): Authenticity and Commoditization in Tourism. In: *Annals of Tourism Research*, 15(3), pp. 371-386.

Collett, David (1989): Pastoralists and wildlife: image and reality in Kenya Massailand. In: Anderson, David/ Grove, Richard H. (eds.), *Conservation in Africa: People, Policies and Practice*. Cambridge: Cambridge University Press, pp. 129-148.

Colston, Adrian (2003): Beyond preservation: The challenge of ecological restoration. In: Adams, William M./ Mulligan, Martin (eds.), *Decolonizing Nature. Strategies for Conservation in a Post-Colonial Era*. London: Earthscan Publications Ltd, pp. 247-267.

Comaroff, John L./ Comaroff, Jean (2009): *Ethnicity, Inc*. Chicago/ London: University of Chicago Press.

Coppé, Claudie/ Garba, Adamou (1984): *Contes du Niger*. Paris: Fernand Nathan.

Couzens, Edward (2003): The influence of English poaching laws on South African poaching laws. In: *Fundamina: A Journal of Legal History*, 3(9), pp. 62-72.

Craig, Donna/ Davis, Michael (2005): Ethical Relationships for Biodiversity Research and Sharing with Indigenous Peoples. In: *Macquarie Journal of International and Comparative Environmental Law 2005*, 2, pp. 31-74.

Crane, Wendy/ Sandwith, Trevor/ McGregor, Eleanor/ Younge, Amanda, (2009): Where conservation and community coincide: a human rights approach to conservation and development in the Cape Floristic Region, South Africa. In: Campese, Jessica/ Sunderland, Terry/ Greiber, Thomas/ Oviedo, Gonzalo (eds.), *Rights-based approaches: Exploring Issues and Opportunities for Conservation*. Bogor: Indonesia, pp. 141-162.

Crick, Malcolm (1989): Representations of International Tourism in the Social Sciences: Sun, Sex, Sights, Savings, and Servility. In: *Annual Review of Anthropology*, 18, pp. 307344.

Crombé, Xavero/ Jézéquel, Jean-Hervé (2009): *A Not-So Natural Disaster. Niger 2005*. New York: Columbia University Press.

Crutzen, Paul J. (2010): Anthropocene man. In: *Nature*, 467(7317), p. S10.

Cultural Heritage (n.d.): http://www.culturalheritage.cc/

Cumming, David H.M. (2008*): Planning and Priorities for the Kavango-Zambezi Transfrontier Conservation Area*. Report to Conservation International, Washington D.C.

Curtin, Phillip (1975): *Economic Change in Precolonial Africa: Senegambia in the Era of the Slave Trade*. Madison: University of Wisconsin Press.

Dahlberg, A. C./ Burlando, C. (2009): Addressing trade-offs: experiences from conservation and development initiatives in the Mkuze wetlands, South Africa. In: *Ecology and Society*, 14 (2), article 37.

Damme, Masuku van/ Meskell, Lynn (2009): Producing Conservation and Community in South Africa. In: *Ethics, Place and Environment*, 12(1), pp. 69-89.

DeGeorges, Paul Andre/ Reilly, Brian Kevin (2009): The Realities of Community Based Natural Resource Management and Biodiversity Conservation in Sub-Saharan Africa. In: *Sustainability*, 1, pp. 734-788.

Decalo, Samue (1998): *Israel and Africa. Forty Years, 1956-1996*. Gainesville: Florida Atlantic Press.

Denker, Helge (2011). *Living with Wildlife – the story of Namibia's communal conservancies*. Windhoek: NACSO.

Desmet, Ellen (2011): *Indigenous Rights Entwined with Nature Conservation*. Cambridge: Intersentia.

Dieckmann, Ute (2007): *Hai//om in the Etosha Region: A History of Colonial Settlement, Ethnicity, and Nature Conservation*. Basel: Basler Afrika Bibliographien.

Dieckmann, Ute/ Thiem, Maarit / Hays, Jennifer (2014): A Brief Profile of the San in Namibia and the San Development Initiatives. In: Dieckmann, Ute/ Thiem, Maarit/ Dirkx, Erik /Hays, Jennifer (eds.), *'Scraping the Pot': San in Namibia Two Decades after Independence*. Windhoek: Legal Assistance Centre and Desert Research Foundation of Namibia, pp. 29-36.

Divon, Haim (2006): MASHAV in Africa: the Israeli Government's Development Cooperation Program. In: *Israel and Africa. Assessing the Past, Envisioning the Future. American Jewish Committee and Tel Aviv University*, pp. 16-25.

Dobler, Gregor (2009): Oshikango: the dynamics of growth and regulation in a Northern Namibian boom town. In: *Journal of Southern African Studies*, 35(1), pp. 115-131.

Doolittle, Amity A. (2007): Fortress Conservation. In: Robbins, Paul (ed.), *Encyclopedia of Environment and Society*. Los Angeles et al.: Sage Publications, pp. 704-705.

Dowie, Mark (2009): *Conservation Refugees. The Hundred-Year Conflict between Global Conservation and Native Peoples*. Cambridge, London: MIT Press.

Dowson, Thomas (1991): *Rock Engravings of Southern Africa*. Johannesburg: Witwatersrand University Press.

Dudley' Nigel (ed.) (2008): *Guidelines for Applying Protected Areas Management Categories.* Switzerland: IUCN.

Duffy, Rosaleen (2002): *A Trip Too Far: Ecotourism, Politics, and Exploitation.* London: Earthscan.

Duncan, Carol (1995): *Civilizing Rituals: Inside Public Art Museums.* London/ New York: Routledge.

Dutton, Denis (2003): *Authenticity in Art.* http://www.denisdutton.com/authenticity.htm

Dressler, Wolfram/ Büscher, Bram/ Fletcher, Robert (2014): Conclusion. The Limits of Nature™ Inc. and the Search for Vital Alternatives. In: Büscher, Bram/ Dressler, Wolfram/ Fletcher, Robert (eds.), *Nature™ Inc. Environmental Conservation in the Neoliberal Age.* Tucson: The University of Arizona Press, pp. 246-253.

Duim, René van der/ Lamers, Machiel/ Wijk, Jakomijn van (2015): Novel Institutional Arrangements for Tourism, Conservation and Development in Eastern and Southern Africa. In: Duim van der, René/ Lamers, Machiel/ Wijk, Jakomijn van (eds.), *Institutional Arrangements for Conservation, Development, and Tourism in Eastern and Southern Africa: A Dynamic Perspective.* Dordrecht: Springer, pp. 1-16.

Economic Community of West African States (ECOWAS) (n.d.). *Vision 2020.* http://www.ecowas.int/about-ecowas/vision-2020/

Economic Community of West African States (ECOWAS) (2015). *Revised Treaty* (Abuja, Nigeria). http://www.ecowas.int/wp-content/uploads/2015/01/Revised-treaty.pdf

Eicher, Joanne Bubolz/ Roach-Higgins, Mary Ellen (1979): The Language of Personal Adornment. In: Cordwell, Justin M./ Schwarz, Ronald (eds.), *The Fabrics of Culture. The Anthropology of Clothing and Adornment.* The Hague/ Paris/ New York: Mouton Publishers, pp. 7-21.

Eicher, Joanne Bubolz/ Roach-Higgins, Mary Ellen (1992): Definition and Classification of Dress: Implications for Analysis of Gender Roles. In: Barnes, Ruth/ Eicher, Joanne B. (eds.), *Dress and Gender. Making and Meaning.* Oxford/ New York: Berg, pp. 8-28.

Eicher, Joanne B. (1995): Introduction: Dress as Expression of Ethnic Identity. In: Eicher, Joanne B. (ed.), *Dress and Ethnicity.* Oxford: Berg, pp. 1-5.

Espley, Simon (2015): iSimangaliso. Park for the People. In: *Africa Geographic Magazine,* 71. http://magazine.africageographic.com/weekly/issue-71/isimangaliso-wetland-park-kwazulu-natal/

Etkin, Nina L (2002): Local Knowledge of Biotic Diversity and Its Conservation in Rural Hausaland, Northern Nigeria. In: *Economic Botany,* 56(1), pp. 73-88.

Fabricius, Christo/ Wet, Chris de (2008): The Influence of Forced Removals and Land Restitution on Conservation in South Africa. In: Chatty, Dawn/ Colchester, Marcus (eds.), *Conservation and Mobile Indigenous Peoples. Displacement, Forced Settlement and Sustainable Development.* Oxford: Berghahn Books, pp. 142-157.

Felbab-Brown, Vanda (2017): *The Extinction Market: Wildlife Trafficking and How to Counter it.* Oxford: Oxford University Press.

Ferguson, James (1990): *The Anti-Politics Machine: "Development," Depoliticization, and Bureaucratic Power in Lesotho.* Cambridge: Cambridge University Press.

Ferguson, James (2009): The Use of Neoliberalism. In: *Antipode,* 41(1): pp. 166-184.

Fillitz, Thomas/ Saris, A. Jamie (eds.) (2013): *Debating Authenticity. Concepts of Modernity in Anthropological Perspective*. New York: Berghahn.

Fillitz, Thomas/ Saris, A. Jamie (2013): Introduction: Authenticity Aujourdhui. In: Fillitz, Thomas/ Saris, A. Jamie (eds.), *Debating Authenticity. Concepts of Modernity in Anthropological Perspective*. New York: Berghahn, pp. 1-24.

Fletcher, Robert/ Dressler, Wolfram/ Büscher, Bram (2014): The New Frontiers of Environmental Conservation. In: Büscher, Bram/ Dressler, Wolfram/ Fletcher, Robert (eds.), *Nature™ Inc. Environmental Conservation in the Neoliberal Age*.Tucson: The University of Arizona Press, pp. 3-21.

Fletcher, Campbell/ Pforr, Christof/ Brueckner, Martin (2016): Actors Influencing Indigenous engagement in tourism development: an international perspective. In: *Journal of Sustainable Tourism*, DOI: 10.1080/09669582.2016.1173045

Ford, Lucy H. (2003): Challenging Global Environmental Governance: Social Movement Agency and Global Civil Society. In: *Global Environmental Politics*, 3(2), pp. 120-134.

Foucault, Michel (1986): Of Other Spaces: Utopias and Heterotopias. In: *Diacritics*, 16(1), pp. 22-27.

Frank, Lawrence P. (1988): Israel and Africa: the Era of Tachlis. In: *The Journal of Modern African Studies*, 26, pp. 151-155.

Frederiks, Martha T. (2003): *We Have Toiled All Night: Christianity in the Gambia*. Zoetermeer: Uitgeveriz Boekencentrum.

Fried, Eli (2006): Soft Power and Israel's Policy of Development Cooperation. In: *Israel and Africa. Assessing the Past, Envisioning the Future*. American Jewish Committee and Tel Aviv University, pp. 43-55.

Gargallo, Eduard (2015): Conservancies and Contested Lands: The Case of Namibia's Communal Conservancies. In: *Journal of Contemporary African Studies*, 33(2), pp. 213-231.

Garland, Elizabeth (1994): *Tourism Development in Eastern Bushmanland: Final Report*. Windhoek, Namibia: Nyae Nyae Development Foundation of Namibia.

Garland, Elizabeth (1999): Developing Bushmen: Building Civil(ized) Society in the Kalahari and Beyond. In: Comaroff, John L. / Comaroff, Jean (eds.), *Civil Society and the Political Imagination in Africa: Critical Perspectives*. Chicago: University of Chicago Press, pp. 72-103.

Garland, Elizabeth/ Gordon, Robert J. (1999): The Authentic (In)Authentic: Bushman Anthro-Tourism. In: *Visual Anthropology*, 12(2), pp. 267-287.

Garner, Kerri (2012): *CBNRM in Botswana: The Failure of CBNRM for the Indigenous San, the Village of XaiXai, and the Wildlife of Botswana*. MSc. Thesis, Rural Planning and Development, University of Guelph, Canada.

Gasser, Geneviève (2002): 'Manger ou s'en Aller': Que Veulent les Opposants Armés Casamançais? In: Diop, Momar-Coumba (ed.), *Le Sénégal contemporain*. Paris: Karthala.

Giraudo, Rachel Faye (2011): *Intangible Heritage and Tourism Development at the Tsodilo World Heritage Site.* PhD Dissertation, University of California, Berkeley, California.

Glew, Robert S./ Babalé, Chaibou (1993): *Hausa Folktales from Niger*. Athens, Ohio: Ohio University Monographs in International Studies. Africa Series, no. 63.

Goffman, Erving (1959): *The Presentation of Self in Everyday Life*. New York: Doubleday.

Goldman, Robert/ Papson, Stephen (2006): Capital's brandscapes. In: *Journal of Consumer Culture*, 6(3), pp. 327-353.

Goodwin, Harold (2007): Indigenous Tourism and Poverty Reduction. In: Butler, Richard/ Hinch, Thomas (eds.), *Tourism and Indigenous Peoples: Issues and Implications*. Oxford: Butterworth-Heinemann, pp. 84-94.

Greiber, Thomas/ Janki, Melinda/ Orellana, Marco/ Savaresi, Annalisa/ Shelton, Dinah (2008): *Conservation with Justice: A Rights Based Approach*. IUCN Environmental Law and Policy Paper No. 71.

Griffiths, Ieuan (1994): Maps, Boundaries, Ambiguity and Change in the Gambia. In: Stone, Jeffrey (ed.), *Maps and Africa: Proceedings of a Colloquium at the University of Aberdeen*. Aberdeen: Aberdeen University African Studies Group.

Grove Richard H. (1987): Early Themes in African Conservation: The Cape in the Nineteenth Century. In: Anderson, David/ Grove, Richard H. (eds.), *Conservation in Africa; People, Policies and Practice*. Cambridge: Cambridge University Press, pp. 21-39.

Grove, Richard H. (1993): Conserving Eden: The (European) East-India Companies and their Environmental Policies on St. Helena, Mauritius and in Western India, 1660 to 1854. In: *Comparative Studies in Society and History*, 35(2), p. 318.

Grove, Richard H. (1995): *Green Imperialism: Colonial Expansion, Tropical Island Edens, and the Origins of Environmentalism, 1600-1800*. Cambridge: Cambridge University Press.

Guenther, Mathias (1999): *Tricksters and Trancers. Bushman Religion and Society*. Bloomington: Indiana University Press.

Guenther, Mathias (2002): Ethno-Tourism and the Bushmen. In: Stewart, Henry/ Barnard, Alan/ Omura, Keichi (eds.), *Self- and Other-Images of Hunter-Gatherers*. Senri Ethnological Studies No. 60. Osaka, Japan: National Museum of Ethnology, pp. 47-64.

Habermas, Jürgen (1996), *Between Facts and Norms. Contributions to a Discourse Theory of Law and Democracy*. Cambridge, Massachusetts: MIT Press.

Hagan, George P. (1986): The Rule of Law in Asante: A Traditional Akan State. In: *Presence Africaine*, University of Ghana, pp. 194-208.

Hall, C. Michael/ Gossing, Stefan/ Scott, Daniel (eds.) (2015): *The Routledge Handbook of Tourism and Sustainability*. New York: Routledge.

Hall, Gillette/ Patrinos, Harry Anthony (eds.) (2012): *Indigenous Peoples, Poverty, and Development*. Cambridge: Cambridge University Press.

Hanks, John/ Myburgh, Werner (2015): The Evolution and Progression of Transfrontier Conservation Areas in the Southern African Development Community. In: Duim,

René van der/ Lamers, Machiel/ Wijk, Jakomijn van (eds.), *Institutional Arrangements for Conservation, Development, and Tourism in Eastern and Southern Africa: A Dynamic Perspective*. Dordrecht: Springer, pp. 157-189.

Hansen, Melissa (2014): *Struggles over Conservation Space. Social Justice in the iSimangaliso Wetland Park, South Africa*. Doctoral Dissertation, Lund University Sweden.

Hansen, Melissa/ Ramasar, Vasna/ Buchanan, Kent (2014): *Localising global environmental governance norms: Implications for justice*. Research Gate, Open Source.

Hansen, Melissa/ Faran, Turaj/ O'Byrne, David (2015): The Best Laid Plans: Using the Capability Approach to Assess Neoliberal Conservation in South Africa – The Case of the iSimangaliso Wetland Park. In: *Jounal of Environment & Development*, 24(4), pp. 395-417.

Haratsebe, Manwa/ Moswete, Naomo/ Saarinen, Jarkko (eds.) (2016): *Cultural Tourism in Southern Africa*. Bristol, United Kingdom: Channel View Publications.

Hardin, Garrett (1968): The Tragedy of the Commons. In: *Science*, 162(3859), pp. 1243-1248.

Harding, Alan (2007): Taking City Regions Seriously? Response to Debate on 'City-Regions: New Geographies of Governance, Democracy and Social Reproduction'. In: *International Journal of Urban and Regional Research*, 31(2), pp. 443-458.

Harris, Marvin (1980): *Cultural Materialism*. New York: Vintage Books.

Hasselskog, Malin/ Schierenbeck, Isabell (2017): The Ownership Paradox: Community and Change. In: *Forum for Development Studies*, 44(3), pp. 323-333.

Henschel, Philipp/ Hunter, Luke (2014): The dire conservation status of lions in West and Central Africa. In: *Current Conservation*, 8(4), pp. 20-23.

Henschel, Philipp/ Coad, Lauren/ Burton, Cole/ Chataigner, Beatrice/ Dunn, Andrew/ Mac Donald, David/ Saidu, Yohanna Saidu/ Hunter, Luke (2014): *The Lion in West Africa Is Critically Endangered*. PLoS ONE 9(1): e83500. Doi:10.1371/journal.pone.0083500. http://journals.plos.org/plosone/article?id=10.1371/journal.pone.0083500

Hertslet, Edward (1909): *The Map of Africa By Treaty*. London: H.M.S.O.

Higgins-Desbiolles, Freya/ Powys-Whyte, Khyle (2015): Tourism and Human Rights. In: Hall, C. Michael/ Gossing, Stefan/ Scott, Daniel (eds.), *The Routledge Handbook of Tourism and Sustainability*. New York: Routledge, pp. 105-116.

Hill, Polly (1992): *Rural Hausa. A Village and a Setting*. Cambridge: Cambridge University Press.

Hill, Ryan/ Katerere, Yemi/ Moyo, Sam (2001): *A Critique of Transboundary Natural Resource Management in Southern Africa*. IUCN-ROSA Series on Transboundary Natural Resource Management. https://portals.iucn.org/library/efiles/documents/2001-046-1.pdf

Hitchcock, Robert K./ Brandenburgh, Rodney L. (1990): Tourism: Conservation, and Culture in the Kalahari Desert, Botswana. In: *Cultural Survival Quarterly*, 14(2), pp. 20-24.

Hitchcock, Robert K. (1991): Tourism and Sustainable Development among Remote Area Populations in Botswana. In: Pfotenhauer, Linda (ed.), *Tourism in Botswana*. Gaborone, Botswana: The Botswana Society, pp. 154-167.

Hitchcock, Robert K (1996), Subsistence Hunting and Special Game Licenses in Botswana. In: *Botswana Notes and Records*, 28, pp. 55-64.

Hitchcock, Robert K. (1997): Cultural, Economic, and Environmental Impacts of Tourism among Kalahari Bushmen. In: Chambers, Erve (ed.), *Tourism and Culture: An Applied Perspective*. Albany, New York: State University of New York Press, pp. 93-128.

Hitchcock, Robert K./ Biesele, Megan (2002): Controlling Their Destiny: Ju/'hoansi of Nyae Nyae. In: *Cultural Survival Quarterly*, 26(1), pp. 13-15.

Hitchcock, Robert K. (2012): Refugees, Resettlement, and Land and Resource Conflicts: The Politics of Identity among !Xun and Khwe San of Northeastern Namibia. In: *African Study Monographs*, 33(2), pp. 73-132.

Hitchcock, Robert K./ Sapignoli, Maria/ Main, Mike/ Babchuk, Wayne A. (2015): The Politics and Economics of Community-Based Natural Resource Management in /Xai/Xai, Ngamiland, Botswana. In: *African Study Monographs*, 36(4), pp. 211-260.

Hitchcock, Robert K. (2015a): *Improving the Viability and Sustainability of the Nyae Nyae Conservancy and the N≠a Jaqna Conservancy: A Mid-Term Evaluation of an NNDFN/Brot für die Welt Project in Namibia*. Windhoek: Nyae Nyae Development Foundation of Namibia and Berlin: Brot für die Welt.

Hitchcock, Robert K. (2015b): Authenticity, Identity, and Humanity: The Hai//om San and the State of Namibia. In: *Anthropological Forum: A Journal of Social Anthropology and Comparative Sociology*, 25(3), pp. 262-284.

Hitchcock, Robert K./ Sapignoli, Maria/ Main, Mike/ Babchuk, Wayne A. (2016): Botswana. In: Vinding, Diana/ Mikkelsen, Caecilie (eds.), *The Indigenous World 2016*. Copenhagen: International Work Group for Indigenous Affairs (IWGIA), pp. 439-447.

Hitchcock, Robert K./ Babchuk, Wayne A. (2016): *San Traditional Authorities, Communal Conservancies, Conflicts, and Leadership in Namibia*. Paper presented in a symposium entitled 'Evidence, Legitimacy, and Inequality in Indigenous Rights Spokespersonship', Nick Barber and Anne-Elise Keen, organizers and chairs. 115th annual meetings of the American Anthropological Association (AAA), Minneapolis, Minnesota, November 16-20, 2016.

Hitchcock, Robert K. (2017a): *Cross Cultural Analysis of Subsistence Hunters among African Foragers*. Paper presented at the 46th annual Society for Cross Cultural Research (SCCR) meetings, New Orleans, Louisiana, March 1-4, 2016.

Hitchcock, Robert K. (2017b): *Sustainability, Socioecology, and Resilience: Communal Conservancies and the Impacts of Development in North Eastern Namibia*. Paper presented at the 2017 INSAKA International Symposium, University of Namibia, Windhoek, Namibia, 19-22 June 2017.

Hodge, Joseph (2011): Colonial Experts, Developmental and Environmental Doctrines, and the Legacies of Late British Colonialism. In: Ax, Christina/ Brimnes, Niels/

Jensen, Niklas Thode/ Oslund, Karen (eds.), *Cultivating the Colonies: Colonial States and Their Environmental Legacies*. Ohio University Press, pp. 300-326.

Hohmann, Thekla (2003): 'We Are Looking for Life. We Are Looking for the Conservancy.' Namibian Conservancies, Nature Conservation, and Rural Development: The N/a Jaqna Conservancy. In: Hohmann, Thekla (ed.), *San and the State, Contesting Land, Development, Identity, and Representation*. Cologne: Rüdiger Köppe Verlag, pp. 205-223.

Hoon, Parakh (2014): Elephants are like our diamonds: Recentralizing community-based natural resource management in Botswana 1996-2012. In: *African Studies Quarterly*, 15(1), pp. 55-70.

Horton, Bernhard (2014): *My Forever Heartache: Four Years of Discovery with the Kalahari Bushmen*. Gaborone: Black Crake Books.

Hunters Living Museum (2018): *The "Little Hunter's Museum" of the Ju/'hoansi-San*. http://www.lcfn.info/juhoansi/home

Igoe, James/ Sullivan, Sian/ Brockington, Dan (2009): Problematising Neoliberal Biodiversity Conservation: Displaced Knowledge and Disobedient Knowledge. In: *Current Conservation*, 3(3), pp. 4-7.

Igoe, James (2010): The Spectacle of Nature in the Global Economy of Appearances. Anthropological Engagements with the Spectacular Mediations of Transnational Conservation. In: *Critique of Anthropology*, 30(3), pp. 375-397.

Iliya, M.A. (1993): The Geographical Imperatives of Transborder Co-Operation. In: Asiwaju, Anthony I./ Barkindo, Bawuro M. (eds.), *The Nigeria-Niger Transborder Cooperation*. Lagos: Malthouse, pp. 37-46.

Integrated Rural Development and Nature Conservation (2011): *Lessons from the Field: Community-based Natural Resource Management (CBNRM): IRDNC's Experience in Namibia*. Windhoek: Integrated Rural Development and Nature Conservation.

Iren, Wright (1993): Impératifs Géographiques de la Coopération Transfrontalière. In: Asiwaju, Anthony I./ Barkindo, Bawuro M. (eds.), *The Nigeria-Niger Transborder Co-operation*. Lagos: Malthouse, pp. 33-36.

IRIN News (2004): *Rural poverty is a condition not a culture: Mogae*. http://www.irinnews.org/fr/node/217035

Ishaya, S./ Abaje, I.B. (2008): Indigenous Peoples Perception on Climate Change and Adaptation Strategies in Jema'a Local Government Area of Kaduna State, Nigeria. In: *Journal of Geography and Regional Planning*, 1(8), 138-143.

iSimangaliso (n.d.): *iSimangaliso Opens Latest Visitor Destination Western Shores*. http://isimangaliso.com/newsflash/isimangaliso-opens-latest-visitor-destination-western-shores/

iSimangaliso (n.d.): *Twelfth Consecutive Unqualified Audit for iSimangaliso*. http://isimangaliso.com/newsflash/twelfth-consecutive-unqualified-audit-for-isimangaliso/

iSimangaliso (n.d.): *iSimangaliso Corporate Charter, 2011 – 2015*. http://pmg-assets.s3-website-eu-west-1.amazonaws.com/docs/2010/100310isimangaliso-strat1.pdf iSimangaliso News and Info (2009): *What happened to the iSimangaliso Wetland Park?* https://isimangalisonews.wordpress.com/2009/10/05/what-happened-to-the-isimangalisowetland-park-imp/

iSimangaliso Wetland News (2009): *Protecting Wetlands Through Wise Productions.* https://isimangalisonews.wordpress.com/category/good-news/

iSimangaliso Wetland Park Authority (2011): *iSimangaliso Wetland Park Integrated Management Plan (2011 – 2016).* http://isimangaliso.com/product-category/integrated-management-plan/

iSimangaliso Wetland Park (2013): *Annual Report. Self Made. The passion and pride of iSimangaliso entrepreneurs.* IWPA.

iSimangalio (2015): *Park for the People.* Africa Geographic Magazine Issue 7. http://magazine.africageographic.com/weekly/issue-71/isimangaliso-wetland-park-kwazulunatal/

iSimangaliso (2016): *iSimangaliso Authority.* http://isimangaliso.com/development/isimangaliso-authority/

iSimangaliso Wetland Park (2016): *It's About People.* Newsflash, 25.06.2016. https://isimangaliso.com/newsflash/isimangaliso-its-about-people/

iSimangaliso Wetland Park Authority (2016): *Land Claims Framework.* http://pmg-assets.s3-website-eu-west-1.amazonaws.com/160830andClaimsSettlementFramework.pdf

iSimangaliso Wetland Park Authority (2016): *Welcome to South Africa's first World Heritage Site.* www.isimangaliso.com

iSimangaliso Wetland Park Authority (2016): *iSimangaliso Wetland Park Integrated Management Plan (2017 – 2021).* http://isimangaliso.com/product-category/integrated-management-plan/

iSimangaliso Wetland Park (2017): *Portfolio and Select Committees 2017/18 Annual Performance Plan, March 2017.* https://isimangaliso.com/product/isimangaliso-wetland-park-authority-annual-performance-plan-2018-19/

iSimangaliso Wetland Park (2017): *Caring for the Coast.* Newsflash, 06.02.2017. https://isimangaliso.com/newsflash/isimangaliso-caring-for-the-coast/

iSimangaliso Wetland Park (2018): *Empowerment Programmes.* https://isimangaliso.com/pending/development/empowerment-programmes/

iSimangaliso Wetland Park (2018): *iSimangaliso Higher Education Access Programme.* https://isimangaliso.com/isimangaliso-higher-education-access-programme/

iSimangaliso Wetland Park (2018): *iSimangaliso's marine protecton set to expand as South Africa announces new Marine Protected Area Network.* Newsflash, 25.06.2016. https://isimangaliso.com/newsflash/isimangalisos-marine-protection-set-to-expand-as-south-africa-announces-new-marine-protected-area-network/

iSimangaliso Wetland Park Authority (IWPA)/ South African National Biodiversity Institute (SANBI) (2018): *iSimangaliso Wetland Park Authority & SANBI 2018/19 Annual Performance Plans*, 28 March 2018. https://pmg.org.za/committee-meeting/26079/

IUCN (n.d.): *Red List.* http://www.iucnredlist.org

IWGIA African Commission (2005): *Report of the African Commission's Working Group of Experts on Indigenous Populations/Communities*. https://www.iwgia.org/images/publications//African_Commission_book.pdf

Jackson, Anthony (2011): Engaging the Audience: Negotiating Performance in the Museum. In: Jackson, Anthony/ Kidd, Jenny (eds.), *Performing Heritage*. Manchester: Manchester University Press, pp. 11-25.

Jackson, Anthony/ Kidd, Jenny (2011): Introduction. In: Jackson, Anthony/ Kidd, Jenny (eds.), *Performing Heritage*. Manchester: Manchester University Press, pp. 1-8.

Jacobsohn, Margaret (1990): *Himba: Nomads of Namibia*. Cape Town: Struik Publishers.

Johnston, Alison M. (2006): *Is the Sacred for Sale? Tourism and Indigenous Peoples*. London and Sterling, VA: Earthscan.

Jones, Brian (2010): The Evolution of Namibia's Conservancies. In: Nelson, Fred (ed.), *Community Rights, Conservation, and Contested Land: The Politics of Natural Resource Governance in Africa*. London: Earthscan, pp. 106-120.

Jones, Brian T.B./ Diggle, Richard W./ Thouless, Chris (2015): From Exploitation to Ownership: Wildlife Based Tourism and Communal Conservancies in Namibia. In: Duim, René van der/ Lamers, Machiel/ Wijk, Jakomijn van (eds.), *Institutional Arrangements for Conservation, Development, and Tourism in Eastern and Southern Africa: A Dynamic Perspective*. Dordrecht: Springer, pp. 17-35.

Joseph, Jonathan (2013): Resilience as embedded neoliberalism: a governmentality approach. In: *Resilience*, (1)1, pp. 38-52.

Ju/'hoansi Living Museum (2018): *The Living Museum of the Ju/'hoansi-San*. http://www.lcfn.info/hunters

Kalahari Peoples Network (n.d.). http://www.kalaharipeoples.net/article.php?i=60

Kale, Steinar/ Brinkmann, Svend (2009): *Interviews Learning the Craft of Qualitative Research Interviewing*. Thousand Oaks: Sage Publications Inc.

Kasrils, Ronnie (2013): How the ANC's Faustian pact sold out South Africa's poorest. In: *The Guardian*. http://www.theguardian.com/commentisfree/2013/jun/24/anc-faustian-pact-mandela-fatal-error

Katz, Richard (1982): *Boiling Energy: Community Healing among the Kalahari !Kung*. Cambridge and London: Harvard University Press.

Keali'Inohomoku, Joann W. (1979): You Dance What You Wear, and You Wear Your Cultural Values. In: Cordwell, Justin M./ Schwarz, Ronald (eds.), *The Fabrics of Culture. The Anthropology of Clothing and Adornment*. UK: Mount Publishers, pp. 77-83.

Kearney, A. (2009): Intangible cultural heritage. Global awareness and local interest. In: Smith, L./ Akagawa, N. (eds.), *Intangible Heritage*. London/ New York: Routledge. pp. 209-225.

Keeney, Bradford (2010): *The Bushman Way of Tracking God. The Original Spirituality of the Kalahari People*. New York: Atria Books.

Keeney, Bradford (2013): Reentry into First Creation. A Contextual Frame for the Ju/'hoan Bushman Performance of Puberty Rites, Storytelling, and Healing Dance. In: *Journal of Anthropological Research*, 69, pp. 65-86.

Keitumetse, Susan/ Nthoi, Olivia (2009): Investigating the Impact of World Heritage Tourism on the Intangible Heritage of a Community, Tsodilo Hills World Heritage Site, Botswana. In: *International Journal of Intangible Heritage*, 4, pp. 144-150.

Kidd, Jenny (2011): Performing the Knowing Archive: Heritage Performance and Authenticity. In: *International Journal of Heritage Studies*, 17(1), pp. 22-35.

King, Brian (2007): Conservation and community in the new South Africa: A case study of the Mahushe Shongwe Game Reserve. In: *Geoforum*, 38, pp. 207-219.

King, Brian (2009): Conservation Geographies in Sub-Saharan Africa: The Politics of National Parks, Community Conservation and Peace Parks. In: *Geography Compass*, 3, pp. 1-14.

Kirshenblatt-Gimblett, Barbara (1998): *Destination Culture: Tourism, Museums, and Heritage*. Berkeley: University of California Press.

Kirshenblatt-Gimblett, B. (2004): Intangible Heritage as Metacultural Production. In: *Museum International*, 56(1-2), pp. 52-65.

Koot, Stasja P. (2013): Dwelling in Tourism: Power and Myth amongst Bushmen in Southern Africa. *African Studies Collection.* Volume 54. Leiden: African Studies Centre.

Koot, Stasja (2015): White Namibians in Tourism and the Politics of Belonging through Bushmen. In: *Anthropology Southern Africa*, 38(1-2), pp. 4-15.

Koot, Stasja/ Beek, Wouter van (2017): Ju/'hoansi lodging in a Namibian Conservancy: CBNRM, tourism and increasing domination. In: *Conservation and Society*, 15(2), pp. 136-146.

Kopytoff, Igor (ed.) (1987): *The African Frontier: The Reproduction of Traditional African Societies*. Bloomington: Indiana University Press.

Korom, Frank J. (2013): The Anthropology of Performance: An Introduction. In: Korom, Frank J. (ed.), *The Anthropology of Performance. A Reader*. Hoboken, NJ: John Wiley & Sons, Inc., pp. 1-8.

Kosi Bay (2011): *Utshwayelo Lodge*. http://www.kosimouth.co.za

Kreps, Christina (2009): Indigenous curation, museums, and intangible cultural heritage. In: Smith, Laurajane/ Akagawa, Natsuko (eds.): *Intangible Heritage*. London/ New York: Routledge, pp. 193-208.

Kuper, Adam (2003): The Return of the Native, *Current Anthropology,* 44(3), pp. 389-402.

Kyle, R. (2013): Thirty years of monitoring traditional fish trap catches at Kosi Bay, KwaZulu-Natal, South Africa, and management implications. In: *African Journal of Marine Science*, 35(1), pp. 67-78.

Lausche, Barbara (2011) *Guidelines for Protected Areas Legislation IUCN Environmental Policy and Law Paper* No. 81.

Law, Kate (2010): The Wild West World of BEE: Black Economic Empowerment Reviewed. In: *Safundi*, 11(3), pp. 313-323.

Layton, Robert/ Wallace, Gillian (2006): Is Culture a Commodity? In: Layton, Robert/ Wallace, Gillian (eds.), *The Ethics of Archaeology. Philosophical Perspectives on Archaeological Practice*. Cambridge: Cambridge University Press, pp. 46-68.

Lee, Richard B. (2016): 'In the Bush the Food is Free': The Ju/'hoansi of Tsumkwe in the 21st Century. In: Codding, Brian F./ Kramer, Karen L. (eds.), *Why Forage? Twenty First Century Hunting and Gathering.* Santa Fe, School for Advanced Research Press and Albuquerque: University of New Mexico Press, pp. 61-87.

Lennox, Corinne/ Short, Damien (eds.) (2016): *Handbook of Indigenous Peoples' Rights.* London and New York: Routledge.

Lepecki, A. (2010): The Body as Archive: Will to Re-Enact and the Afterlives of Dances. In: *Dance Research Journal*, 42(2), pp. 28-48.

Lewis, Lowell J. (2013): *The Anthropology of Cultural Performance.* US: Palgrave Macmillan.

Liebenberg, Louis (1990): *The Art of Tracking: The Origin of Science.* Cape Town: David Philip Publishers.

Liebenberg, Louis (1992): *A Concise Guide to the Animal Tracks of Southern Africa.* Cape Town, South Africa: Creda Press.

Liebenberg, Louis (2006): Persistence Hunting by Modern Hunter Gatherers. In: *Current Anthropology*, 47(6), pp. 1017-1025.

Lindsey, P. A./ Havemann, C. P./ Lines, R. M./ Price, A. E./ Retief, T. A./ Rhebergen, T./ Waal, C. van der/ Romanach, S. S. (2013): Benefits of wildlife-based land uses on private lands in Namibia and limitations affecting their development. In: *Oryx*, 48, pp. 41-53.

Littler, Jo (2011): What's wrong with ethical Consumption? In: Lewis, Tania/ Potter, Emily (eds.), *Ethical Consumption: A Critical Introduction.* New York: Routledge, pp. 27-39.

Living Cultural Foundation Namibia (n.d.): http://www.lcfn.info/

Loveridge, Andrew (2018): *Lion Hearted. The Life and Death of Cecil & the Future of Africa's Iconic Cats.* New York: Regan Arts.

MacCannell, Dean (1973): Staged Authenticity: Arrangements of Social Space in Tourist Settings. In: *American Journal of Sociology*, 79(3), pp. 589-603.

MacCannell, Dean (1999, orig. 1976): *The Tourist.* New York: Schocken.

MacKenzie, John M. (ed.) (1990): *Imperialism and the Natural World.* Manchester: Manchester University Press.

Madikwe Game Reserve (2019): *Madikwe's Big 5.* https://www.madikwegamereserve.co.za/big-5/

Magi, Lindisizwe/ Nzama, Thandi A. (2009): Tourism Strategies and Local Community Responses around the World Heritage Sites in KwaZulu-Natal. In: *South African Geographical Journal*, 91(2), pp. 94-102.

Magome, Hector/ Murombedzi, James (2003): Sharing South African National Parks: Community land and conservation in a democratic South Africa. In: Adams, William M./ Mulligan, Martin (eds.), *Decolonizing Nature. Strategies for Conservation in a Post-Colonial Era.* London: Earthscan Publications Ltd, pp. 108-134.

Maharaj, Rajendra/ Moonasar, Devanand/ Baltazar, Candrinho/ Kunene, Simon/ Morris, Natashia (2016): Sustaining control: lessons from the Lubombo spatial development initiative in Southern Africa. In: *Malaria Journal*, 15(1). DOI: 10.1186/s12936-016-1453-9

Mahoney, Florence K. Olamara (1963): *Government and Opinion in the Gambia, 1816-1901*. Unpublished PhD thesis, London University.

Mandel, James T./ Donlan, Josh C./ Armstrong, Jonathan (2010): A Derivative Approach to Endangered Species Conservation. In: *Frontiers in the Ecology and the Environment*, 8(1), pp. 44-49.

Marcus, Gill (ed.) (2007): *Visions of Black Economic Empowerment*. Auckland Park: Jacana Media.

Mark, Peter (1992): *The Wild Bull and the Sacred Forest: Form, Meaning and Change in Senegambian Initiation Masks*. Cambridge: Cambridge University Press.

Marshall, John/ Ritchie, Claire (1984): *Where Are the Ju/Wasi of Nyae Nyae? Changes in a Bushman Society: 19581981*. Communications No. 9, Center for African Area Studies, University of Cape Town. Cape Town: University of Cape Town.

Martin Evans (2003): *Ni Paix, Ni Guerre: The Political Economy of Low-Level Conflict in the Casamance*. HPG Background Paper. London: ODI.

Marut, Jean-Claude (1994): Le Dessous des Cartes Casamançaises: Une Approche Géopolitique du Conflit Casamançais'. In: Barbier-Wiesser, François George (ed.), *Comprendre la Casamance: chronique d'une intégration contrastée*. Paris: Karthala.

Marut, Jean-Claude (2002): Le Problème Casamançais: Est-il Soluble dans l'Etat-Nation? In: Diop, Momar-Coumba (ed.), *Le Sénégal contemporain*. Paris: Karthala.

Marut, Jean-Claude (2010): *Le conflit de Casamance: ce qui disent les armes*. Paris: Karthala.

Masilo-Rakgoasi, Rosinah (2002): *An Assessment of the Community-Based Natural Resource Management Approach and Its Impacts on the Basarwa: Case Study of Xaixai and Gudigwa Communities*. M.A. Thesis in Development Studies, University of Botswana, Gaborone, Botswana.

Massumi, Brian (2002): *Parables for the Virtual: Movement, Affect, Sensation (Post-Contemporary Interventions)*. Durham/ London: Duke University Press.

Massyn, Peter John (2007): *Tourism Assets and the Market: Evaluating Outcomes at Madikwe and Makuleke*. https://www.yumpu.com/en/document/view/48126916/evaluating-outcomes-at-madikwe-and-makuleke-by-peter-john-massyn

Mathau, Winston/ Namata, Kano/ Salami, Ayobami (2011): *Terminal Evaluation of the UNEP GEF* project *Integrated Ecosystem Management of Transboundary Areas between Nigeria and Niger (Phase I – Strengthening of Legal and Institutional Frameworks for Collaboration and Pilot Demonstration of IEM)*. United Nations Environment Programme, Evaluation Office.

Maude, Glyn/ Reading, Richard P. (2010): The Role of Ecotourism in Biodiveristy and Grassland Conservation in Botswana. In: *Great Plains Research: A Journal of Natural and Social Sciences*, 20 (Spring 2010), pp. 109-119.

Mbaiwa, Joseph E. (2003): The Socio-economic and Environmental Impacts of Tourism Development on the Okavango Delta, North-western Botswana. In: *Journal of Arid Environments*, 54(2), pp. 447-467.

Mbaiwa, Joseph E. (2004): The Success and Sustainability of Community-Based Natural Resource Management in the Okavango Delta, Botswana. In: *South African Geographical Journal*, 86 (1), pp. 44-53.

Mbaiwa, Joseph E. (2005): Enclave Tourism Development and Its Socio-Economic Impact on the Okavango Delta, Botswana. In: *Tourism Management*, 26(2), pp. 157-172.

Mbaiwa, Joseph E./ Mbaiwa, Onaletshepho I. (2006): The Effects of Veterinary Fences on Wildlife Populations in Okavango Delta, Botswana. In: *International Journal of Wilderness*, 12(3), pp. 17-23.

Mbaiwa, Joseph E. (2008): *Tourism Development, Rural Livelihoods, and Conservation in the Okavango Delta, Botswana*. PhD dissertation. Texas A&M University, College Station, Texas.

Mbaiwa, Joseph E./ Sakuze, Lolly K. (2009): Cultural Tourism and Livelihood diversification: The Case of Gcwihaba Caves and XaiXai Village in the Okavango Delta, Botswana. In: *Journal of Tourism and Cultural Change*, 7(1), pp. 61-75.

Mbaiwa, Joseph E. (2012): Hosts and Guests: Stereotypes and Myths of International Tourism in the Okavango Delta. In: Beek, Walter van/ Schmidt, Annette (eds.), *African Hosts and their Guests: Cultural Dynamics of Tourism*. London: James Currey, pp. 117-136.

Mbaiwa, Joseph E. (2016a): The Commodification of World Heritage Sites: The Case Study of Tsodilo Hills in Botswana. In: Haratsebe, Maria/ Moswete, Naomo/ Saarinen, Jarkko (eds.), *Cultural Tourism in Southern Africa*. Bristol, United Kingdom: Channel View Publications.

Mbaiwa, Joseph E. (2016b): Tourism Development, Dispossession, and Displacement of the Communities in the Okavango Delta, Botswana. In: Nepal, Sanjay/ Saarin, Jarkko (eds.), *Political Ecology of Tourism*. London: Routledge, pp. 193-206.

Mbaiwa, Joseph E. (2017): Effects of the safari hunting tourism ban on rural livelihoods and wildlife conservation in Northern Botswana. *South African Geographical Journal*, 100:1, 41-61. DOI: 10.1080/03736245.2017.1299639

Mboti, Nyasha (2017): 'Soetwyn': Visuality, Cultural Tourism, Desire Paths and the ≠Khomani. In: *Visual Anthropology*, 30(1), pp. 22-44

McAfee, Kathleen (1999): Selling nature to save it? Biodiversity and green developmentalism. In: *Environment and Planning D: Society and Space*, 17(2), pp. 133-154.

McCracken, Donal P. (2008): *Saving the Zululand Wilderness: An Early Struggle for Nature Conservation*. Auckland Park: Jacana Media.

McShane et al. (2010): Hard Choices: Making trade-offs between biodiversity conservation and human well-being. In: *Biological Conservation*, 144(2011), pp. 966-972.

Medugu, M./ Majid, Idris Nasiru Rafee/ Choji, I.D. (2008): A Comprehensive approach to drought and desertification in Nigeria. A brief evaluation of government policies. In: *Management of Environmental Quality: An International Journal*, 19(6), pp. 690-704.

Mendelsohn, John/ Jarvis, Alice/ Roberts, Carole/ Robertson, Tony (2009): *Atlas of Namibia: A Portrait of the Land and its People. 3rd edition*. Cape Town, South Africa: Sunbird Publishers.

Metcalfe, Simon (2003): *Impacts of Transboundary Protected Areas on Local Communities in Three Southern African Initiatives*. Paper presented at the 5th World Parks Congress, Durban, 12-13 September. http://www.tbpa.net/docs/WPCGovernance/SimonMetcalfe.pdf

Mickelson, Karen (1998): Rhetoric and Rage: Third world voices in international legal discourse. In: *Wisconsin International Law Journal,* 16(2), pp. 353-419.

Miescher, Giorgio (2012): *Namibia's Red Line: The History of a Veterinary and Settlement Border*. New York: Palgrave Macmillan.

Miles, William F.S. (1989): The Rally as Ritual. Dramaturgical Politics in Nigerian Hausaland. In: *Comparative Politics*, 21(3), pp. 323-338.

Miles, William F.S. (1994): *Hausaland Divided: Colonialism and Independence in Nigeria and Niger.* Ithaca: Cornell University Press.

Miles, William F.S. (2014): *Afro-Jewish Encounters from Timbuktu to the Indian Ocean and Beyond*. Princeton: Markus Wiener Publishers.

Milupi, Inonge/ Somers, Michael/ Ferguson, Willem (2017): A Review of Community-Based Natural Resource Management. In: *Applied Ecology and Environmental Research*, 15(4), pp. 1121-1143.

Minority Rights Group (2007): *Trouble in paradise: Tourism and indigenous land rights: together towards ethical solutions*. London: Minority Rights Group International.

Mook, Hubertus J. van/ Graessli, Max/ Monfrini, Henri/ Weisfelt, Hendrik (1964): *Report on the Alternatives for Association Between the Gambia and Senegal*. Appointed Under the United Nations Programme of Technical Assistance, Sessional Paper no. 13. Bathurst: Government Printer.

Mortimore, Michael (1967): Land and population pressure in the Kano Close-Settled Zone, Northern Nigeria. In: *The Advancement of Science,* 23, pp. 677-688.

Mortimore, Michael (1989). *Adapting to Drought. Farmers, Famines and Desertification in West Africa*. Cambridge: Cambridge University Press.

Mortimore, Michael (1998): *Roots in the African Dust. Sustaining the Sub-Saharan Drylands*. Cambridge: Cambridge University Press.

Mortimore, Michael (2005): Dryland Development. Success Stories from West Africa. In: *Environment*, 47(1), pp. 8-21.

Mosimane, Alfons Wahabe/ Silva, Julie A. (2015): Local Governance Institutions, CB-NRM, and Benefit-Sharing Systems in Namibian Conservancies. In: *Journal of Sustainable Development* 8(2), pp. 99-112.

Moswete, Naomi/ Lacey, Gary (2015): 'Women Cannot Lead': Empowering Women through Cultural Tourism in Botswana. In: *Journal of Sustainable Tourism*, 23(4), pp. 600-617.

Mountain, Alan (1990): *Paradise Under Pressure, St. Lucia, Kosi Bay, Sodwana, Lake Sibaya, Maputaland*. Halfway House, South Africa: Southern Book Publishers.

Mufune, Pempelani (2015): Community-Based Natural Resource Management (CB-NRM) and Sustainable Development in Namibia. In: *Journal of Land and Rural Studies*, 3, pp. 121-138.

Murombedzi, James (2003): Devolving the expropriation of nature: The 'devolution' of wildlife management in Southern Africa. In: Adams, William M./ Mulligan, Martin (eds.), *Decolonizing Nature. Strategies for Conservation in a Post-Colonial Era*. London: Earthscan Publications Ltd, pp. 135-151.

NACSO (Namibian Association of CBNRM Support Organisations) (2002): *Constitution of the Namibian Association of Community-based Natural Resource Management (CBNRM) Support Organisations* (NACSO). http://www.nacso.org.na/sites/default/files/NACSO_constitution.pdf

NACSO (Namibian Association of CBNRM Support Organisations) (2014): *The State of Community Conservation in Namibia: A Review of Communal Conservancies, Community Forests, and Other CBNRM Initiatives*. Windhoek: NACSO.

NACSO (Namibian Association of CBNRM Support Organisations) (2016): *The state of community conservation in Namibia – a review of communal conservancies, community forests and other CBNRM initiatives (2016 Annual Report)*. Windhoek: NACSO.

NACSO (Namibian Association of CBNRM Support Organisations) (2019): *Conservation and Conservancies Overview*. Windhoek: NACSO. http://www.nacso.org.na/conservation-and-conservancies

Naidoo, Robin/ Weaver, L. Chris/ Diggle, Richard W./ Matongo, Greenwell/ Stuart-Hill, Greg/ Thouless, Chris (2016): Complementary Benefits of Tourism and Hunting to Communal Conservancies in Namibia. In: *Conservation Biology*, 30(3), pp. 628-638.

Nas, Peter J. M. (2002): Masterpieces of Oral and Intangible Culture: Reflections on the UNESCO World Heritage List. In: *Current Anthropology*, 43(1), pp. 139-148.

Nathan, Ran (2008): An Emerging Movement Ecology Paradigm. *PNAS* (Proceedings of the National Academy of Sciences of the United States of America), special issue, 105(49), pp. 19050-19051.

Ndlovu, Joram/ Utete, Onward/ Kimaro, Mary Ellen (2014): Defying Extinction Through Conservation: Benefits of Black Rhino Tracking in the #Khoadi//Hôas Conservancy, Namibia. In: *Journal of Human Ecology*, 41(3), pp. 229-239.

Nelson, Fred (ed.) (2010): *Community Rights, Conservation & Contested Land. The Politics of Natural Resource Governance in Africa*. London. New York: Earthscan.

Nelson, Robert (2003): Environmental Colonialism: "Saving" Africa from Africans. In: *Independent Review*, 8(1). http://faculty.publicpolicy.umd.edu/sites/default/files/nelson/files/environmentalism_religion/ Environmental_Colonialism.pdf

New York Times (2008): *Plans for a Cross-Border Peace Park in the Mideast*. May 3.

Ngema, Nokuthula Dephney (2009): *The Development of Ecotourism in the Dukuduku Forest Reserve and Surrounding Settlements: Policy and Implementation*. Doctoral Dissertation, University of Zululand 2009.

Ntsebeza, Lungisile (2008): Chiefs and the ANC in South Africa: The Reconstruction of Tradition? In: Claassens, Aninka/ Cousins, Ben (ed.), *Land, Power & Custom: Controversies Generated by South Africa's Communal Land Rights Act*. Cape Town: UCT Press, pp. 238-260.

Nugent, Paul/ Ajiwasu, Anthony I. (eds.) (1996): *African Boundaries: Barriers, Conduits and Opportunities*. London: Pinter Publications.

Nugent, Paul/ Ajiwasu, Anthony I. (2010): The Paradox of African Boundaries. In: Nugent, Paul/ Ajiwasu, Anthony I. (eds.), *African Boundaries: Barriers, Conduits and Opportunities.* London: Pinter Publications.

Nugent, Paul (2019): *Boundaries, Communities and State-Making in the Senegambia and the Trans-Volta: The Centrality of the Margins.* Cambridge: Cambridge University Press.

Nustad, Knut G. (2011): Performing Natures and Land in the iSimangaliso Wetland Park, South Africa. In: *Ethnos*, 76(1), pp. 88-108.

Nustad, Knut G./ Sudnes, Frode (2013): The Nature of the Land: The Dukuduku Forest and the Mflozi Flats, KwaZulu-Natal. In: *The Journal of Modern African Studies*, 51(3), pp. 587-506.

Nustad, Knut G. (2015): *Creating Africas. Struggles over Nature, Conservation and Land.* London: Hurst & Company.

Nyae Nyae Development Foundation of Namibia (2017). https://www.nndfn.org/

Nyae Nyae Development Foundation of Namibia (2017): *San Conservancies urge the Minister of MET to visit and help address issues threatening their conservancies.* http://www.nndfn.org/san-conservancies-urge-the-minister-of-met-to-visit-and-help-address-issues-threatening-their-conservancies

Nzama, Thandi A. (2009): *The nexus between sustainable livelihoods and ecological management of the World Heritage Sites: lessons from iSimangaliso World Heritage Park, South Africa.* www.ajol.info/index.php/ijhss/article/download/62107/50146

Obura, David/ Church, Julie/ Gabrié, Catherine (2012): *Assessing Marine World Heritage from an Ecosystem Perspective: The Western Indian Ocean.* World Heritage Centre. United Nations Education, Science and Cultural Organization (UNESCO).

Odihi, John O. (1993): Nigeria-Niger Transborder Crossings During Environmental Crisis: Towards Planning for Disaster Mitigation. In: Asiwaju, Anthony I./ Barkindo, Bawuro M. (eds.), *The Nigeria-Niger Transborder Co-operation.* Lagos: Malthouse, pp. 169-177.

Odula, Tom (2018): *World's last male northern white rhino, Sudan, dies.* March 20, 2018. https://www.apnews.com/2de9d081adec407c9690b23544ab2e78

OECD (2009): *The Impact of Culture on Tourism.* Paris: The Organization of Economic Cooperation and Development (OECD).

Official Documents System of the UN (2017): https://documents-dds-ny.un.org/doc/UNDOC/GEN/G17/009/97/PDF/G1700997.pdf?OpenElement

≠Oma, Khao Moses/ Thoma, Axel (2002): Will Tourism Destroy San Cultures? In: *Cultural Survival Quarterly*, 26(1), pp 39-41.

Onishi, Norimitsu (2015): A Hunting Ban Saps a Village's Livelihood. In: *New York Times*, 12 September 2015, p. A6.

Ostrom, Elinor (1990): *Governing the Commons. The evolution of institutions for collective action.* Cambridge: Cambridge University Press.

Owens, Mark/ Owens, Delia (1980): The fences of death. In: *African Wildlife*, 34, pp. 25-27.

Owen-Smith, Garth (2010): An Arid Eden: A Personal Account of Conservation in the Kaokoveld. Johannesburg: Jonathan Ball Pulishers.

Packer, Craig (2015): *Lions in the Balance. Man-Eaters, Manes, and Men with Guns.* Chicago: The University of Chicago Press.

Pager, Harald (1993): The Rock Paintings of the Upper Brandberg. Volumes I, II, and III. Cologne: Heinrich Barth Institute.

Palumbo, Antonio/ Scott, Alan (2018): *Remaking Market Society: A Critique of Social Theory and Political Economy in Neoliberal Times.* Abingdon, New York: Routledge.

Pappe, Karl Wilhelm Ludwig (1854): *Silva Capensis, or Description of South African Forest-Trees, and Arborescent Shrubs, Used for Technical and Economical Purposes, by the Colonists of the Cape of Good Hope.* Cape Town: Van de Sandt de Villiers.

Patel, Leila/ Graham, Lauren (2012): How Broad-based is Broad-based Black Economic Empowerment? In: *Development Southern Africa*, 29(2), pp. 193-207.

Paterson Alexander (2011): *Bridging the Gap Between Conservation and Land Reform. Communally-Conserved Areas as a Tool for Managing South Africa's Natural Commons.* Doctoral Dissertation, University of Cape Town.

Paterson, Alexander (2011): Protected Areas: South Africa. In: Lausche, B. (ed.): *Guidelines for Protected Areas Legislation*, IUCN Environmental Policy and Law Paper No. 81.

Peace Parks Foundation (2018): *Lubombo Transfrontier Conservation and Resource Area.* http://www.peaceparks.org/story.php?pid=1006&mid=1065

Pellar, Brigitte (2000): *Neoliberalismus – Trendsetter gegen Gewerkschaftsbewegung und Sozialstaat.* http://www.arbeitwirtschaft.at/servlet/ContentServer?pagename=X03/Page/Index&n=X03_1.a_2000_03.a&cid=1206108339921

Perissinotto, Renzo/ Stretch, Derek D./ Taylor, Ricky H. (eds.) (2013): *Ecology and Conservation of Estuarine Ecosystems Lake St. Lucia as a Global Model.* Cambridge: Cambridge University Press.

Perkins, Jeremy S./ Ringrose, S. M. (1996): *Development Cooperations Objectives and the Beef Protocol: The Case of Botswana, a Study of Livestock/ Wildlife/ Tourism/ Degradation Linkages.* Gaborone: University of Botswana.

Perkins, Jeremy S./ Stuart-Hill, Greg/ Kgabung, B. (2002): The Impact of Cattle-keeping on the Wildlife, Vegetation, and Veld products. In: Sporton, Deborah/ Thomas, David S. G. (eds.), *Sustainable Livelihoods in the Kalahari Environments: A Contribution to Global Debates.* Oxford: Oxford University Press, pp. 67-90.

Pfotenhauer, Linda (ed.) (1991): *Tourism in Botswana.* Gaborone, Botswana: The Botswana Society.

Pimm, Stuart L./ Jenkins, Clinton N./ Abell, Robin/ Brooks, Thomas M./ Gittleman, John L./ Joppa, Lucas N./ Raven, Peter H./ Roberts, Callum M./ Sexton, Joseph O. (2014): The biodiversity of species and their rates of extinction, distribution, and protection. In: *Science*, 344(6187). DOI: 10.1126/science.1246752

Plumwood, Val (2003): Decolonizing Relationships with Nature. In: Adams, William M./ Mulligan, Martin (eds.), *Decolonizing Nature. Strategies for Conservation in a Post-Colonial Era.* London: Earthscan Publications Ltd, pp. 51-78.

Polak, T./ Gutterman, Y./ Hoffman, I./ Saltz, D. (2014): Redundancy in seed dispersal by three sympatric ungulates: a reintroduction perspective. In: *Animal Conservation*, 1-8. DOI: 10.111/acv.12122

Poteete, Amy (2009): Defining Political Community and Rights to Natural Resources in Botswana. In: *Development and Change*, 40(2), pp. 281-305.

Pucheu, Jacques (1982): *Contes haoussa du Niger*. Paris: Karthala.

Quick, Sarah (2012): "Frontstage" and "Backstage" in Heritage Performance: What Ethnography Reveals. In: *Canadian Theatre Review*, 151, pp. 24-29.

Ranger, Terence (1997): The Invention of Tradition in Colonial Africa. In: Horton, Robin/ Grinker, Richard R./ Lubkemann, Stephen C./ Steiner, Christopher B. (eds.), *Perspectives on Africa: A Reader in Culture, History, and Representation*. Oxford: Blackwell, pp. 211-235.

Rattray, R. Sutherland (1913): *Hausa Folk-Lore, Customs, Proverbs, Etc.* (two volumes). London: Clarendon Press.

Rehg, William (1996): *Translator's Introduction to Jürgen Habermas: Between Facts and Norms. Contributions to a Discourse Theory of Law and Democracy*. Cambridge, Massachusetts: MIT Press.

Reimerson, Elsa (2013): Between nature and culture: exploring space for indigenous agency in the Convention on Biological Diversity. In: *Environmental Politics*, 22(6), pp. 992-1009.

Ribot, Jesse C. (1993): Forestry policy and charcoal production in Senegal. In: *Energy Policy*, 21(5), pp. 559-585.

Rihoy, Liz/ Maguranyanga, Brian (2010): The Politics of Community-Based Resource Management in Botswana. In: Nelson, Fred (ed.), *Community Rights, Conservation, and Contested Lands: The Politics of Natural Resource Governance in Africa*. London/ Washington D.C.: Earthscan, pp. 55-78.

Rispel, Melanie/ Lendelvo, Selma (2016): The Utilization of Water Points by Wildlife Species in Nyae Nyae Conservancy, Namibia. In: *Environment and Natural Resources Research*, 6(4), pp. 91-103.

Ritterband, Salomé (2018): *Tracking Indigenous Heritage. Ju/'hoansi San Learning, Interpreting, and Staging Tradition for a Sustainable Future in Cultural Tourism in the Tsumkwe District of Namibia*. Berlin/ Vienna: LIT.

Robins, Steven (2001): NGOs, 'Bushmen' and Double Vision: The ≠khomani San Land Claim and the Cultural Politics of 'Conmmunity' and 'Development' in the Kalahari'. In: *Journal of Southern African Studies*, 27(4), pp. 833-853.

Rozemeijer, Nico (ed.) (2001): *Community-Based Tourism in Botswana: The SNV Experience in Three Community Tourism Projects*. Gaborone, Botswana: SNV (Netherlands Development Organization).

Rupoo, Connie (2016): Performance and the Economics of Cultural Festivals in Botswana: Cashing In or Selling Out? In: *Botswana Notes and Records*, 48, pp. 351-361.

Saarinen, Jarkko/ Moswete, Naomi/ Monare, Masego J. (2014): Cultural Tourism: New Opportunities for Diversifying the Tourism Industry in Botswana. In: Rogerson, C.

M./ Szymańska, D. (eds.), *Bulletin of Geography. Socio-economic Series 26*. Toruń: Nicolaus Copernicus University, pp. 7-18.

SABC News (2016): *iSimangaliso Wetland Park Welcomes New Lion Pride.* http://www.sabc.co.za/news/a/8174e8004ebff47b8fdbbf8984b1c843/isiMangaliso-Wetland-Park-welcomes-new-lion-pride-20162710

Salomon, Anne K./ Lertzman, Ken/ Brown, Kelly/ Wilson, Barbara K./ Secord, Dave/ McKechnie, Iain (2018): Democratizing conservation science and practice. In: *Ecology and Society*, 23(1), article 44.

Saltz, David (2008): Re-introduction of Arabian oryx into the Negev Desert, Israel. In: Soorae, Pritpal Singh (ed.), *Global Re-Introduction Perspectives. Re-introduction case-studies from around the globe*. Abu Dhabi: IUCN/SSC Re-introduction Specialist Group, pp. 185-187.

SANParks and IWPA (2016): *Committee meeting minutes*. https://pmg.org.za/committee-meeting/23156/?utm_source=homepage&utm_medium=meeting-card

Sapignoli, Maria (2015): Dispossession in the Age of Humanity: Human Rights, Citizenship, and Indigeneity in the Central Kalahari. In: *Anthropological Forum: A Journal of Social Anthropology and Comparative Sociology*, 25(3), pp. 285-305.

Sapignoli, Maria (2016): Indigenous Mobilization and Activism: The San, the Botswana State, and the International Community. In: Lennox, Corinne/ Short, Damien (eds.), *Handbook of Indigenous Peoples' Rights*. London/ New York: Routledge, pp. 268-281.

Saugestad, Sidsel (2001): *The Inconvenient Indigenous. Remote Area Development in Botswana, Donor assistance, and the First People of the Kalahari*. Uppsala: The Nordic Africa Institute.

Saulawa, A. A. (1993): Drought, Animal Husbandry, Impact and the State in Katsina-Maradi Boundary Divisions of Nigeria and Niger Republic, C. 1972-1983: A Historical Analyis of Drought Phenomenon and the Need for Stronger Transborder Co-operation. In: Asiwaju, Anthony I./ Barkindo, Bawuro M. (eds.), *The Nigeria-Niger Transborder Co-operation*. Lagos: Malthouse, pp. 211-226.

Schäffter, Ortfried (1991): Modi des Fremderlebens. Deutungsmuster im Umgang mit Fremdheit. In: Schäffter, Ortfried (ed.), *Das Fremde. Erfahrungsmöglichkeiten zwischen Faszination und Bedrohung*. Opladen: Westdeutscher Verlag, pp. 7-28.

Schalken, Wouter (1999): Where Are the Wild Ones? The Involvement of Indigenous Communities in Tourism in Namibia. In: *Cultural Survival Quarterly*, 23(2), pp. 40-42.

Schechner, Richard (1985): *Between Theatre and Anthropology*. Philadelphia: University of Pennsylvania Press.

Schechner, Richard (2013, 3rd edition, orig. 2002): *Performance Studies: An Introduction*. New York: Routledge.

Scheper-Hughes, Nancy/ Lock, Margaret M. (1987): The Mindful Body: A Prolegomenon to Future Work in Medical Anthropology. In: *Medical Anthropology Quarterly*, new series 1(1), pp. 6-41.

Schreiner, O. D. (1967): *The Contribution of English Law to South African Law; and the Rule of Law in South Africa*. London: Stevens & Sons.

Schroeder, Richard (1999): *Shady Practices: Agroforestry and Gender Politics in the Gambia*. Berkeley/ Los Angeles/ London: University of California Press.

Schwarz, Ronald A. (1979): Uncovering the Secret Vice: Toward an Anthropology of Adornment. In: Cordwell, Justin M./ Schwarz, Ronald (eds.), *The Fabrics of Culture. The Anthropology of Clothing and Adornment*. New York: Mouton Publishers, pp. 23-45.

Schweitzer, Peter/ Povoroznyuk, Olga/ Schiesser, Sigrid (2017): Beyond Wilderness: Towards an Anthropology of Infrastructure and the Built Environment in the Russian North. In: *The Polar Journal*, 7(1): pp. 51-85.

Schweitzer, Peter, and Olga Povoroznyuk (2019): A Right to Remoteness? Modernization and Its Discontents along an East Siberian Railroad. *Social Anthropology* 27(2): pp. 236-252.

Scott, Dianne/ James, Bronwyn/ Govender, Nerosha (2012): Aligning national priorities and world heritage conservation: iSimangaliso Wetland Park, South Africa. In: Galla, Ameswar (ed.): *World Heritage: Benefits Beyond Borders*. Cambridge: Cambridge University Press, pp. 203-216.

Searing, James F. (1993): *West African Slavery and Atlantic Commerce: The Senegal River Valley, 1700-1860*. Cambridge: Cambridge University Press.

Sieder, Reinhard (2014): Erzählungen analysieren – Analysen erzählen. Narrativbiographisches Interview, Textanalyse und Falldarstellung. In: Wernhart, Karl R./ Zips, Werner (eds.), *Ethnohistorie. Rekonstruktion und Kulturkritik. Eine Einführung*. Vienna: Promedia, pp. 150-180.

Silvester, Jeremy (2011): *Trading in Tradition: The Development of Cultural Villages in Namibia*. Paper presented at the Commonwealth Association of Museums (CAM) Triennial Conference: Commonwealth Museums: Culture, Economy and Climate Change and Youth conference, 25-28 May 2011, Singapore. http://www.maltwood.uvic.ca/cam/publications/conference_publications/Jeremy%20Silvester.pdf

Singh, Jaidev/ Houtum, Henk van (2002): Post-colonial Nature in Conservation in Southern Africa: Same Emperors, New Clothes? In: *Geojournal*, 58(4), pp. 253-263.

Smith, Laurajan (2011): The 'Doing' of Heritage: Heritage as Performance. In: Jackson, Anthony/ Kidd, Jenny (eds.), *Performing Heritage*. UK: Manchester University Press, pp. 69-81.

Soorae, Pritpal Singh (ed.) (2008): *Global Re-Introduction Perspectives. Re-introduction case-studies from around the globe*. Abu Dhabi: IUCN/SSC Re-introduction Specialist Group.

Sorenson, Marie Louise Stig/ Carman, John (eds.) (2009): *Heritage Studies: Methods and Approaches*. London: Routledge.

South Africa Net (n.d.): *iSimangaliso Wetland Park*. http://www.southafrica.net/za/en/articles/entry/article-southafrica.net-isimangaliso-wetland-park

South African National Parks (2018): *Kruger National Park – Park Management Plan. For the period 2018-2028.* https://www.sanparks.org/assets/docs/conservation/park_man/knp/draft-plan.pdf

South African San Institute (2017): *The San Code of Research Ethics.* Launched on 2 March 2017. http://trust-project.eu/wp-content/uploads/2017/03/San-Code-of-RESEARCH-Ethics-Booklet-final.pdf

Southern African Development Community (1999): *SADC Protocol on Wildlife Conservation and Law Enforcement.* Gaborone: Southern African Development Community, SADC.

South African National Biodiversity Institute (SANBI): National Spatial Biodiversity Assessment 2004: Priorities for Biodiversity Conservation in South Africa (2005)

South African National Biodiversity Institute (SANBI) (2018): *South Africa announces new Marine Protected Area Network.* https://www.sanbi.org/media/south-africa-announces-new-marine-protected-area-network/

Staiff, Russell/ Bushnell, Robyn/ Watson, Steve (eds.) (2013): *Heritage Tourism: Place, Encounter, Engagement.* London: Routledge.

Stander, Philip E./ //Ghau, D. Tsisaba/ //Oma / //Ui (1997): Tracking and the Interpretation of Spoor: A Scientifically Sound Method in Ecology. In: *Journal of the Zoological Society of London*, 242, pp. 329-341.

Stauss, Alexandra von (2012): Intercultural Encounters: the Kalahari and the Zulus. In: Tomaselli, Keyan G. (ed.), *Cultural Tourism and Identity. Rethinking Indigeneity.* Leiden, NL: Koninklijke Brill NV, pp. 85-98

Stronza, Amanda/ Durham, William H. (eds.) (2008): *Ecotourism and Conservation in the Americas.* Cambridge, MA: CABI International.

Stronza, Amanda (2001): Anthropology of Tourism: Forging New Ground for Ecotourism and Other Alternatives. In: *Annual Review of Anthropology*, 30, pp. 261-283.

Sullivan, Sian (2006) The Elephant in the Room? Problematising 'New' (Neoliberal) Biodiversity Conservation. In: *Forum for Development Studies*, 1, pp. 105-135.

Sunde, Jackie/ Isaacs, Moenieba (2008): *Marine Conservation and Coastal Communities: Who Carries the Costs? A Study of Marine Protected Areas and Their Impact on Traditional Small-scale Fishing Communities in South Africa.* India: International Collective in Support of Fishworkers.

Sundnes, Frode (2013): The Past in the Present: Struggles Over Land and Community in relation to the Dukuduku Claim for Land Restitiution, South Africa. In: *Forum for Development Studies*, 40(1), pp 69-86.

Suzman, James (2001): *An Assessment of the Status of the San in Namibia. Windhoek.* Legal Assistance Centre. Report No. 4 of 5. http://www.lac.org.na/projects/lead/Pdf/sannami.pdf

Suzman, James (2002): *Minorities in Independent Namibia.* London: Minority Rights Group International.

Swindell, Kenneth/ Jeng, Alieu (2006): *Migrants, Credit and Climate: The Gambian Groundnut Trade, 1834-1934.* Leiden: Brill.

Tangri, Roger/ Southall, Roger (2008): The Politics of Black Economic Empowerment in South Africa. In: *Journal of Southern African Studies*, 34(3), pp. 699-716.

Taylor, Diana (2003): *The Archive and the Repertoire. Performing Cultural Memory in the Americas*. Durham/ London: Duke University Press.

Taylor, Julie J. (2012): *Naming the Land: San Identity and Community Conservation in Namibia's West Caprivi*. Windhoek: Demasius Publications and Basel, Switzerland: Basler Afrika Bibliographien.

Taylor, Michael (2000): *Life, Land and Power. Constesting development in northern Botswana*. PhD Dissertation, University of Edinburgh.

Taylor, Robert (2008): *The Bushmen of Grashoek, Bushmanland*. http://www.jelldragon .com/theoldways/grashoek.htm

The Economist (2013): *Fool's gold: Black economic empowerment has not worked well. Nor will it end soon*. http://www.economist.com/news/briefing/21576655-black-eco nomic-empowerment-has-not-worked-well-nor-will-it-end-soon-fools-gold

Thomas, Chris D./ Gillingham, Phillipa K. (2015): The performance of protected areas for biodiversity under climate change. In: *Biological Journal of the Linnean Society*, 115(3), pp. 718–730.

Thomas, Elizabeth Marshall (1958): *The Harmless People*. New York: Random House, Vintage Books.

Thomas, Elizabeth Marshall (2006): *The Old Way: A Story of the First People*. New York: Farrar, Straus, Giroux.

Tomaselli, Keyan (ed.) (2012): *Cultural Tourism and Identity: Rethinking Indigeneity*. Leiden/ Boston: Brill.

Tomaselli, Keyan G. (2012): Making Sense of the Indigenous: Who's Looking at Whom? In: Tomaselli, Keyan G. (ed.), *Cultural Tourism and Identity. Rethinking Indigeneity*. Leiden: Koninklijke Brill NV, pp. 17-28.

Touray, Omar A. (2000): *The Gambia and the World: A History of the Foreign Policy of Africa's Smallest State, 1965-1995*. Hamburg: Institute of African Studies.

Tunley, Karen (2009): *State of Management of South Africa's Marine Protected Areas*. WWF South Africa Report Series 2009/Marine/001

Turner, Frederick Jackson (1894): *The Significance of the Frontier in American History*. Madison: State Historical Society of Wisconsin.

Turner, James M. (2014): Rethinking American Exceptionalism: Toward a Transnational History of National Parks, Wilderness and Protected Areas. In: Isenberg, Andrew C. (ed.), *The Oxford Handbook of Environmental History*. Oxford: Oxford University Press, pp. 282-309.

UKDM (2014): Annual Report. http://www.ukdm.gov.za/jdownloads/Annual%20Report s/annual_report_ukdm_-_2013_2014_fy_final_draft.pdf

UNDP (2012): *N≠a Jaqna Conservancy, Namibia*. Equator Initiative Case Study Series. New York, NY.

UNESCO (n.d.): http://www.unesco.org/

UNESCO (2003): *Convention for the Safeguarding of the Intangible Cultural Heritage*, 17 October 2003, MISC/2003/CLT/CH/14. http://unesdoc.unesco.org/images/0013/001325/132540e.pdf.

UNESCO World Heritage Convention (2003): *iSimangaliso Wetland Park*. http://whc.unesco.org/en/soc/2698

UNESCO Office in Dakar (2015): *World Heritage in Senegal: Counting the wildlife in Niokolo Koba National Park*. http://www.unesco.org/new/en/media-services/single-view/news/world_heritage_in_senegal_counting_the_wildlife_in_niokolo/

UNESCO (2016): *iSimangaliso Wetland Park*. http://whc.unesco.org/en/list/914

Urry, John (2002, 2nd edition, orig. 1990): *The Tourist Gaze*. London: Sage.

Useb, Joram (2002): Land Crisis: A San Perspective. In: *Cultural Survival Quarterly*, 26(1), p. 31.

Vermeylen, Saskia/ Dovies, Gemma/ Horst, Dan van der (2012): Deconstructing the Conservancy Map: Hxaro, N!ore, and Rhizomes in the Kalahari. In: *Cartographica: The International Journal for Geographic Information and Geovisualization*, 47(2), pp. 121-134.

Wachira, George Mukundi/ Tuuli, Karjala (2016): The Struggle for Protection of Indigenous Peoples' Rights in Africa. In: Lennox, Corinne/ Short, Damien (eds.), *Handbook of Indigenous Peoples' Rights*. London/ New York: Routledge, pp. 394-413.

Walker, Cherryl (2008): Land of dreams. Claiming the Eastern Shores of Lake St Lucia. In: *Landmarked: Land Claims & Land Restitution in South Africa*. Athens: Ohio University Press/ Johannesburg: Jacana Media, pp. 107-141.

Wang, Ning (1999): Rethinking Authenticity in Tourism Experience. In: *Annals of Tourism Research*, 26(2), pp. 349-370.

Warner, Christopher J./ Sobrevila, Claudia/ Ledec, George C. (2016): Protecting Biodiversity, Rehabilitating Ecosystems, and Promoting Conservation for Development. In: Asad, Alam/ Renosi, Mokate/ Plangemann, Kathrin A. (eds.), *Making it happen: Selected Case Studies of Institutional Reforms in South Africa*. World Bank Group, pp. 151-165.

Watts, Michael John (1983): *Silent Violence: Food, Famine, and Peasantry in Northern Nigeria*. Berkeley: University of California Press.

Wearing, Stephen/ Neil, John (1999): *Ecotourism: Impacts, Potentials, and Possibilities*. Boston: Butterworth Heinemann.

Weaver, L. Chris/ Petersen, Theunis/ Diggle, Richard/ Matongo, Greenwell (2010): *Achievements and Practical Lessons Learned from a Decade of Wildlife Utilization in Namibia's Communal Area Conservancies*. Windhoek: World Wildlife Fund.

Welch, Cameron (2013): *'Land is life, Conservancy is Life': The San and the N≠a Jaqna Conservancy, Tsumkwe District West, Namibia*. PhD Dissertation, Department of Anthropology, McGill University, Montreal, Canada.

West, Paige/ Igoe, James/ Brockington, Dan (2006): Parks and Peoples: The Social Impact of Protected Areas. In: *Annual Review of Anthropology*, 35, pp. 251-277.

Wiessner, Polly (2003): Owners of the Future? Calories, Cash, Casualties, and Self-Sufficiency in the Nyae Nyae Area between 1996-2003. In: *Visual Anthropology Review*, 19(1-2), pp. 149-159.

Wiessner, Polly W. (2014): Embers of Society: Firelight Talk among the Ju/'hoansi Bushmen. In: *Proceedings of the National Academy of Sciences*, 111(39), pp. 14027-14035.

Williams, John J. (2009): *The Everyday at Grassroots level: poverty, protest and social change in post-apartheid South Africa.* 1a ed. Buenos Aires: Consejo Latinoamericano de Ciencias Sociales.

Wilshusen, Peter R. (2014): Capitalizing Conservation/Development: Dissimulation, Misrecognition, and the Erasure of Power. In: Büscher, Bram/ Dressler, Wolfram/ Fletcher, Robert (eds.): *Nature™Inc. Environmental Conservation in the Neoliberal Age*. Tuscon: University of Arizona Press, pp. 127-157.

Wily, Elizabeth A. (1979): *Official Policy Towards San (Bushmen) Hunter Gatherers in Modern Botswana: 1966-1978.* Gaborone, Botswana: National Institute of Development and Cultural Research.

WIMSA (Working Group of Indigenous Minorities in Southern Africa) (2016): *San Rights in Namibia*. Windhoek: WIMSA.

Wimmer, Andreas (2013): *Ethnic Boundary Making: Institutions, Power, Networks*. Oxford: Oxford University Press.

Wöbse, Anna-Katharine (2011): The world after all was one: The International Environmental Network of UNESCO and IUPN, 1945-1950. In: *Contemporary European History*, 20, pp. 331-348.

Wolputte, Steven van/ Hoorelbeke, Els/ Bleckmann, Laura (2015): Fenced Borders and Murky Boundaries: Two Cases from Kaoko, Northern Namibia. In: Wolputte, Steven van (ed.), *Borderlands and Frontiers in Africa*. Münster: Lit Verlag, pp. 151-181.

Wulpe, Christa van der (2016): *Transformation of Communal Lands: Illegal Fences in the N≠a Jaqna Conservancy*. M.A. Thesis, Wageningen University, Wageningen, The Netherlands.

Wynberg, Rachel (2002): A Decade of Biodiversity Conservation and Use in South Africa: Tracking Progress from the Rio Earth Summit to the Johannesburg World Summit on Sustainable Development. In: *South African Journal of Science,* 98 (5-6), pp. 233-243.

Yaar-Waisel, Tal (2018): Bordering on the Impossible: Optimistic Planning of Border Regions. In: *Journal of Borderlands Studies*, DOI: 10.1080/08865655.2018.1531052

Zachariah, Kunniparampil Curion/ Condé, Julien (1981): *Migration in West Africa: Demographic Aspects*. Washington DC: World Bank & OECD.

Zaloumis, Andrew (2010): iSimangaliso Wetland Park, South Africa: Recognizing the people's right to restitution but the state's role in conservation. In: *MPA News*, 12(2), pp. 3-4.

Zaloumis, Andrew (2015): *Andrew Zaloumis received WWF Living Planet Award*. http://www.wwf.org.za/?14601/LPA-2015

Zeller, Wolfgang (2009): Danger and opportunity in Katima Mulilo: A Namibian border boomtown at transnational crossroads. In: *Journal of Southern African Studies*, 35(1), pp. 133-154.

Zhu, Yujie (2012): Performing Heritage: Rethinking Authenticity in Tourism. In: *Annals of Tourism Research*, 39(3), pp. 1495-1513.

Zips-Mairitsch, Manuela (2013): *Lost Lands? (Land) Rights of the San in Botswana and the Legal Concept of Indigeneity in Africa*. Berlin/ Zürich: Lit Verlag and IWGIA.

Zips, Werner (2003): "The Double-Bladed Sword". A Comparative Analysis of the Bond between Rule of Law and the Concept of Justice in Akan Legal Thought. In: Pradhan, Rajendra (ed.), *Legal Pluralism and Unofficial Law in Social, Economic and political Development*. Kathmandu, Nepal: The International Centre for the Study of Nature, Environment and Culture, pp. 393-406.

Zips Werner et al. (2006) Discussion: The concept of indigeneity. In: *Social Anthropology*, 14(1), pp. 17-32.

Zips, Werner (ed.) (2008): *To BEE or not to be? Black Economic Empowerment im Neuen Südafrika am Beispiel der Weinindustrie*. Vienna et al.: LIT Verlag.

Zips, Werner (2011): Fashion Design under a Leopard's Skin. Emerging Forms of Complementary Governance in Botswana. In: Zips, Werner/ Weilenmann, Markus (eds.), *The Governance of Legal Pluralism: Empirical Studies from Africa and Beyond*. Wien/ Berlin: Lit Verlag, pp. 181-212.

Zips, Werner (2015): *The Ambiguous Art of Entertainment: Living Museums and Cultural Villages in Namibia*. Paper presented in a symposium entitled "Thriving Future: Community-Based Research and Planning", Eleventh Conference on Hunter-Gatherer Societies (CHAGS 11), Vienna, Austria, 7-11 September 2015.

Zips Werner (2018) Preface: Stars of their own Show. Close Reading Ju/'hoansi San Performances of Tradition and Culture. In: Ritterband, Salomé, *Tracking Indigenous Heritage. Ju/'hoansi San Learning, Interpreting, and Staging Tradition for a Sustainable Future in Cultural Tourism in the Tsumkwe District of Namibia*. Berlin/ Vienna: LIT, pp. 15-32.

Zips Werner/ Weilenmann, Markus (2011): Introduction: Governance and Legal Pluralism – An Emerging Symbiotic Relationship? In: Zips, Werner/ Weilenmann, Markus (eds.), *The Governance of Legal Pluralism. Empirical Studies from Africa and Beyond*. Wien/ Berlin: Lit Verlag, pp. 7-34.

Zips, Werner/ Zips-Mairitsch, Manuela (2007): Lost in Transition? The Politics of Conservation, Indigenous Land Rights and Community-Based Resource Management in Southern Africa. In: *The Journal of Legal Pluralism and Unofficial Law*, 39(55), pp. 37-71.

Zips Werner/ Zips-Mairitsch, Manuela (2013): *ABORNE Workshop on "Bewildering Borders" – Transnational Conservation and Resource Governance in Africa*. Scientific Meeting – Scientific Report. http://www.aborne.org/uploads/media/2013_Vienna_final_report.pdf

Zips Werner/ Zips-Mairitsch, Manuela (2017). Transborder Game. Re-spatiliazation and Resource Management in Southern African Transfrontier Areas. In: Seiser, Gertraud (ed.): Ökonomische Anthropologie. Einführung und Fallbeispiele. Vienna: Facultas Verlag, pp. 364-381.

Government Publications

Agreement between the Federal Republic of Nigeria and the Republic of Niger concerning the equitable sharing in the development, conservation and use of their common water resources done at Maiduguri, 18 July 1990.

Commission on Restitution of Land Rights Presentation of Annual Report (2009-2010) (2010).

Ministry of Environment and Tourism, Republic of Namibia (2018): *Conservancies*. http://www.met.gov.na/services/conservancies/193/

Ministry of Lands and Resources, Republic of Ghana (2016): *Ghana Forestry Development Master Plan (2016-2036)*. https://www.fcghana.org/userfiles/files/MLNR/FDMP_June%2015%20Final_draft.pdf

Parliament of the Republic of South Africa (1996): Constitution of the Republic of South Africa. http://www.gov.za/sites/www.gov.za/files/images/a108-96.pdf

Parliament of the Republic of South Africa (2001): A People's Government, the People's Voice. https://www.parliament.gov.za/peoples-government-peoples-voice

Republic of Botswana (2009a): National Development Plan 10, (April 2009-March 2016) Volume 1. Gaborone, Botswana: Government Printer.

Republic of Botswana (2015): Botswana Land Policy. Government Paper No. 4 of 2015. Gaborone, Botswana: Government Printer.

Republic of Namibia (2012): Republic of Namibia's 4th National Development Plan (NDP4) 2012/13 to 2016/17. Windhoek: Republic of Namibia.

Republic of Namibia (2016): Harambee Prosperity Plan. 2016/17-2019/20. Namibia Government's Action Plan toward Prosperity for All. Windhoek: Republic of Namibia.

Republic of Namibia (2017): Namibia's 5th National Development Plan (NDP5) Working Together Towards Prosperity 2017/18-2021/22. Windhoek: Republic of Namibia.

Republic of the Gambia (1984): Country Economic Memorandum for the Donors' Conference on the Gambia, 1984 – Vol 1. Main Report. Banjul: Ministry of Economic Planning and Industrial Development.

Republique de Niger (2011): Niger Foreign Policy and Government Guide, Vol 1: Strategic Information and Developments. Washington DC: International Business Publications.

Republic of South Africa, Department of Environmental Affairs and Tourism (1997): White Paper on the Conservation and Sustainable Use of South Africa's Biological Diversity. In: Government Gazette, 28. July 1997, Notice 1095 of 1997.

Legal Instruments: International

African Charter on Human Rights and People's Rights, Banjul, 20 June 1981

African Convention on the Conservation of Nature and Natural Resources, Algiers, 15 September 1968

Charter of the United Nations, San Francisco, 1945

Convention for the Preservation of Wild Animals, Birds and Fish in Africa, 19th May 1900

Convention for the Protection of the World Cultural and Natural Heritage, Paris, 16 November 1972

Convention on Biological Diversity, Rio de Janeiro, 5 June 1992

Convention on Nature Protection and Wildlife Preservation in the Western Hemisphere (Washington), 12 October 1940

Convention on Wetlands of International Importance especially as Waterfowl Habitat. Ramsar (Iran), 2 February 1971. UN Treaty Series No. 14583. As amended by the Paris Protocol, 3 December 1982, and Regina Amendments, 28 May 1987

Convention Relative to the Preservation of Fauna and Flora in their Natural State, London, 8 November 1933

ILO Convention No. 169 Concerning Indigenous and Tribal Peoples in Independent Countries, 27 June 1989

U.N. Convention on International Trade in Endangered Species of Wild Fauna and Flora, Mar. 3, 1973, 993 U.N.T.S. 243 (entered into force July 1, 1975)

United Nations Declaration on the Rights of Indigenous Peoples (UNDRIP), adopted on 13 September 2007. https://www.un.org/development/desa/indigenouspeoples/declaration-on-the-rights-of-indigenous-peoples.html

Legal Instruments: Botswana

Government of Botswana 1979 Unified Hunting Regulations (SI No. 19).

Government of Botswana, 1992 (2008) Wildlife Conservation and National Parks Act, Chapter 38: 01, Article 30.

Republic of Botswana (2009b): Tourism Act 2009. Gaborone: Republic of Botswana.

Republic of Botswana (2009c): Tourism Organisation Act 2009. Gaborone: Republic of Botswana.

Republic of Botswana (2014a): Affirmative Action Framework for Remote Area Communities, 16th July 2014. Gaborone: Ministry of Local Government and Rural Development.

Republic of Botswana (2014b): Supplement C. Wildlife Conservation and National Parks (Prohibition of Hunting, Capturing, or Removal of Animals Order, 2014). Statutory Instrument No. 2 of 2014. Botswana Government Gazette, Volume LII, No. 2, 10 January 2014. Botswana Government Gazette, Gaborone, Botswana.

Legal Instruments: Namibia

Government of Namibia (2006): Promulgation of Nature Conservation Amendment Act, 1996 (Act 5 of 1996). Government Gazette of the Republic of Namibia No. 1333. Windhoek, Namibia: Government of Namibia.

Legal Instruments: South Africa

False Bay Park proclamation 9 of 1944 and 111 of 1952.

Government Notice 1408 of 1956 (Cape Vidal State Forest) (Sodwana State Forest) Eastern Shores State Forest and Nyalazi State Forest).

Government Notice 1479 of 1930 (establishing the Dukuduku State forest).

Mkuzi Game Reserve Provincial Notice 23 of 1912, 28 of 1912, 74 of 1916, 57 of 1917, 266 of 1918, 14039 and 131 of 1941.

Natal Ordinance 35 of 1947 establishing the Natal Parks Game and Fish Preservation Board.

Natal Ordinance of 1939 establishing the Natal Parks Board.

Natal Provincial Notice 108 of 1938 (proclaiming the St Lucia Game Reserve).

Republic of South Africa (2003): Broad-based Black Economic Empowerment Act No. 53, 2003. In: Government Gazette, 9 January 2004.

Republic of South Africa (2008): Integrated Coastal Management Act (No 24 of 2008).

Republic of South Africa (1992): KwaZulu-Natal Nature Conservation Act (No 29 of 1992).

Republic of South Africa (1997): KwaZulu-Natal Nature Conservation Management Act (9 of 1997).

Republic of South Africa (1998): Marine Living Resources Act (18 of 1998).

Republic of South Africa (1998): National Environmental Management Act (107 of 1998).

Republic of South Africa (2004): National Environmental Management: Biodiversity Act (10 of 2004).

Republic of South Africa (2004): National Environmental Management: Protected Areas Act 57 of 2003 (2004): Gazette No. 26025, Notice No. 181. University of Pretoria.

Republic of South Africa (1998): National Forests Act (84 of 1998).

Republic of South Africa (1999): National Heritage Resources Act (25 of 1999).

Republic of South Africa (1999): World Heritage Convention Act (49 of 1999). In: Government Gazette, No. 20717, o. December 1999.

St Lucia Bird Sanctuary Provincial Gazette proclamation 7 of 1927.

St Lucia Game Reserve Provincial Notice 16 of 1897, 74 of 1916, 59 of 1917, 108 of 1935, 140 of 1939 and 35 of 1939.

St Lucia Park proclamation 35 of 1939, 11 of 1944, and 36 of 1957.

Films

Marshall, John (2003): *A Kalahari Family*. Watertown, Massachusetts: Documentary Educational Resources.

Strong, Adrian (2011): *Bitter Roots: The Ends of a Kalahari Myth*. Watertown, Massachusetts: Documentary Educational Resources.

Uys, Jamie (1980): *The Gods Must Be Crazy*. Gaborone, Botswana: Mimosa Films.

Zips-Mairitsch, Manuela/ Werner Zips (2012): *Kalahari San Tunes: The Kuru Dance Festival in Botswana*. Vienna: University of Vienna, Austria (available on DVD, Hoanzl).

Zips-Mairitsch, Manuela/ Werner Zips (2015): *A Living Museum – Ethnotainment in Namibia*. Austria: Documentary Film, Vienna: University of Vienna, Austria.

Zips-Mairitsch, Manuela/ Werner Zips (2015): *The Great Shaman – Healing in the Kalahari*. Austria: Film for 3sat (ORF Content Sales).

Zips-Mairitsch, Manuela/ Werner Zips (2015): *The Ambiguous Art of Ethnotainment: Living Museums and Cultural Villages in Namibia*. Vienna: University of Vienna, Austria.

Zips-Mairitsch, Manuela/ Werner Zips (2016): *Juwel of the Elephant Coast*. Austria: Film for 3sat (ORF Content Sales).

Interviews

!amace, !Kunta. Grashoek, Namibia. Interviewer: Goda Palekaite. Date: 17.01.2014.

//ao, Dabe and //ao, Cwi. Doupos, Namibia. Interviewers: Salomé Ritterband, Silja Strasser. Date: 13.01.2014.

//ao, N!ae. Doupos Namibia. Interviewers: Anna Spitaler, Dora Kemelklyte, Valentina Arienti. Date: 16.01.2014.

Anonymous inDuna. KZN, South Africa. Interviewers: iSimangaliso research group. Date: 01.06.2016.

Anonymous tour guide. Hluhluwe, KZN, South Africa. Interviewers: iSimangaliso research group. Date: 08.06.2016.

Anonymous villager. KZN, South Africa. Interviewers: iSimangaliso research group. Date: 02.06.2016.

Baines, Mary. iSimangaliso Wetland Park, South Africa. Interviewers: Manuela Zips-Mairitsch, Werner Zips. Date: 22.12.2012.

Bhangazi community. KZN, South Africa. Interviewer: Dr. Lisbeth Liden. In: For Whom is the iSimangaliso World Heritage Site, *Africa on the Global Agenda*. Nordic Africa Institute. Date: 2007.

Cgaesje, !uu and Dabe, Tilxo. Doupos, Namibia. Interviewers: Anna-Sophie Tomancok, Silja Strasser. Date: 13.01.2014.

Cgaesje, Xoan//a and Cgaesje, !uu. Doupos, Namibia. Interviewer: Salomé Ritterband. Date: 13.01.2014.

Coplan, David. Johannesburg, South Africa. Interviewers: Manuela Zips-Mairitsch, Werner Zips. Date: 27.6.2016.

Dabe, Tilxo. Doupos, Namibia. Interviewer: Salomé Ritterband. Date: 14.01.2017.

Daqm, Komtsa. //Xa/oba, Namibia. Interviewers: Manuela Zips-Mairitsch, Werner Zips. Date: 16.01.2014.

Daqm, Komtsa. //Xa/oba, Namibia. Interviewers: Dora Kemelklyte, Julia Pucher, Valentina Arienti. Date: 17.01.2014.

Daqm, Komtsa. //Xa/oba, Namibia. Interviewer: Anna Spitaler. Date: 18.01.2014.

Daqm, Tsemkgao. //Xa/oba, Namibia. Interviewers: Eva Erhart, Salomé Ritterband. Date: 16.01.2014.

Daqm, Tsemkgao. //Xa/oba, Namibia. Interviewers: Elina Vestere. Date: 17.01.2014.

Dukuduku South Community Land Claims board member. St Lucia, KZN, South Africa. Interviewers: iSimangaliso research group. Date: 03.06.2016.

Dürrschmidt, Sebastian. Windhoek, Namibia. Interviewers: Valentina Grillo, Veronika Grandy. Date: 09.01.2014.

Dürrschmidt, Sebastian. Windhoek, Namibia. Interviewers: Salomé Ritterband, Josef Wukovits. Date: 13.08.2014.

Ezemvelo staff member. St Lucia, KZN, South Africa. Interviewers: iSimangaliso research group. Date: 09.06.2016

Gaiseb, Willelm. Tsumkwe, Namibia. Interviewer: Julia Koch. Date: 14.01.2014.

Gerrie, Cwi Quinten. Doupos, Namibia. Interviewer: Salomé Ritterband. Date: 13.01.2014.

Govender, Nerosha. KZN, South Africa. Interviewers: iSimangaliso research group. Date: 02.06.2016.

Govender, Nerosha. KZN, South Africa. Interviewers: Manuela Zips-Mairitsch, Werner Zips. Date: 10.06.2016.

Hatzofe, Ohad. Israel Nature and Parks Authority. Personal communication: William Miles. May/ June 2014.

Honorary Ezemvelo officer. St Lucia, KZN, South Africa. Interviewers: iSimangaliso research group. Date: 09.06.2016

inDuna of Khula village and owner of Veyane cultural village. KZN, South Africa. Interviewers: iSimangaliso research group. Date: 01.06.2016.

Intern at iSimangaliso Wetland Park Authority. St Lucia, KZN, South Africa. Interviewers: iSimangaliso research group. Date: 10.06.2016.

Komtsa, N!ae. //Xa/oba, Namibia. Interviewers: Anna-Sophie Tomancok, Silja Strasser. Date: 17.01.2014.

!Kunta, Boo David. Doupos, Namibia. Interview. Interviewers: Manuela Zips-Mairitsch, Werner Zips. Date: 13.01.2014.

!Kunta, ≠Oma. Doupos, Namibia. Interviewers: Manuela Zips-Mairitsch, Werner Zips. Date: 20.12.2013.

!Kunta, Xoan//a. Doupos, Namibia. Interview. Interviewers: Manuela Zips-Mairitsch, Werner Zips. Date: 14.01.2014.

!L/ae, Tsemkgao – Smallboy. Tsumkwe, Namibia. Interviewers: Anna Spitaler, Valentina Arienti. Date: 15.01.2014.

!L/ae, Tsemkgao – Smallboy. Tsumkwe, Namibia. Interviewers: Salomé Ritterband, Josef Wukovits. Date: 01.09.2014.

Librarian in St Lucia. KZN, South Africa. Interviewers: iSimangaliso research group. Date: 08.06.2016.

Lugagu, Phumlani. St Lucia, KZN, South Africa. Interviewers: iSimangaliso research group. Date: 10.06.2016.

Mdletshe, Issiah Mabibi. iSimangaliso Wetland Park, South Africa. Interviewers: Manuela Zips-Mairitsch, Werner Zips. Date: 16.02.2012.

Mkhwanazi, Philip. iSimangaliso Wetland Park, South Africa. Interviewers: Manuela Zips-Mairitsch, Werner Zips. Date: 09.11.2014.

Mkhwanazi, Phillip. Khula Village, KZN, South Africa. Interviewers: iSimangaliso research group. Date: 01.06.2016.

Mngomezulu, Zakithi. iSimangaliso Wetland Park, South Africa. Interviewers: Manuela Zips-Mairitsch, Werner Zips. Date: 10.11.2014.

Mokalake, Kgosi Molatwe. Molapo/ Central Kalahari Game Reserve, Namibia. Interviewers: Manuela Zips-Mairitsch, Werner Zips. Date: 05.09.2009.

Mthembu, Themba. iSimangaliso Wetland Park, South Africa. Interviewers: Manuela Zips-Mairitsch, Werner Zips. Date: 13.11.2014.

N!aice, !amace. //Xa/oba, Namibia. Interviewers: Salomé Ritterband, Eva Erhart. Date: 16.01.2014.

N!aice, /Gao. Grashoek, Namibia. Interviewers: Manuela Zips-Mairitsch, Werner Zips. Date: 11.01.2014.

N!ani, Kaqece. Namibia. Interviewers: Manuela Zips-Mairitsch, Werner Zips. Date: 14.01.2014.

N!ani, Kaqece. Tsumkwe, Namibia. Interviewers: Manuela Zips-Mairitsch, Werner Zips. Date: 19.12.2014.

Nature guide. St. Lucia, KZN, South Africa. Interviewers: iSimangaliso research group. Date: 08.06.2016.

Ncube, Siybane Petros. St Lucia, KZN, South Africa. Interviewers: iSimangaliso research group. Date: 03.06.2016.

Ngorogwe, Gontso Zero. Gudigwa, Bukakhwe Cultural Conservation Trust, Botswana. Interviewers: Manuela Zips-Mairitsch, Werner Zips. Date: 23.09.2005.

Nkosi, Mandisa. iSimangaliso Wetland Park, South Africa. Interviewers: Manuela Zips-Mairitsch, Werner Zips. Date: 06.11.2014.

Nyani, Henry /ui. Grashoek, Namibia. Interview. Interviewers: Manuela Zips-Mairitsch, Werner Zips. Date: 11.01.2014.

Nyani, Henry /ui. Grashoek, Namibia. Interviewer: Veronika Grandy. Date: 13.01.2014.

Nyani, Henry /ui. Grashoek, Namibia. Interviewers: Manuela Zips-Mairitsch, Werner Zips. Date: 12.09.2014.

Pfeifer, Werner. Windhoek, Namibia. Interviewers: Manuela Zips-Mairitsch, Werner Zips. Date: 09.01.2014.

Pfeifer, Werner. Windhoek, Namibia. Interviewers: Anna-Sophie Tomancok, Elina Vestere, Goda Palekaite, Silja Strasser, Veronika Grandy. Date: 22.01.2014.

Receptionist at Umkhuze game reserve. KZN, South Africa. Interviewers: iSimangaliso research group. Date: 04.06.2016

Sangoma, Mabibi Beach. KZN, South Africa. Interviewers: iSimangaliso research group. Date: 11.06.2016.

Security officer, Sodwana Bay. KZN, South Africa. Interviewers: iSimangaliso research group. Date: 11.06.2016.

Shabalala, Thandi. iSimangaliso Wetland Park, South Africa. Interviewers: Manuela Zips-Mairitsch, Werner Zips. Date: 22.2.2012.

Shabalala, Thandi. iSimangaliso Wetland Park, South Africa. Interviewers: Manuela Zips-Mairitsch, Werner Zips. Date: 05.12.2014.

Sibiya, Sizo. iSimangaliso Wetland Park, South Africa. Interviewers: Manuela Zips-Mairitsch, Werner Zips. Date: 10.06.2016.

Tembe, Mduduzi. iSimangaliso Wetland Park, South Africa. Interviewers: Manuela Zips-Mairitsch, Werner Zips. Date: 08.6.2016.

Tjambiru, Zahavara. Puros, Namibia. Interviewers: Manuela Zips-Mairitsch, Werner Zips. Date: 09.12.2013.

Tour guide Heritage Tours. Narrative Drive, KZN, South Africa. Interviewers: iSimangaliso research group. Date: 07.06.2016.

Tsauses, Paulina. Tsumkwe, Namibia. Interviewer: Salomé Ritterband. Date: 04.09.2014.

/ui, Kxore Erna. Grashoek, Namibia. Interviewer: Alicja Khatchikian. Date: 13.01.2014.

Waiter and trained nature guide. KZN, South Africa. Interviewers: iSimangaliso research group. Date: 08.06.2016.

Ya'ari Koch, Elizabeth, Friends of Earth-Middle East. Phone interview: William Miles. Date: 02.06.2014.

Zaloumis, Andrew. iSimangaliso Wetland Park, South Africa. Interviewers: Manuela Zips-Mairitsch, Werner Zips. Date: 11.11.2014.

Zaloumis, Andrew. Interviewer: WWF South Africa. In: *Andrew Zaloumis receives 2015 WWF Living Planet Award*. Date: 2015.

Authors

Peter SCHWEITZER is a Professor at the University of Vienna and Head of the Department of Social and Cultural Anthropology.

David B. COPLAN is Professor Emeritus in Social Anthropology at the University of The Witwatersrand.

Robert K. HITCHCOCK is a Professor of Geography at Michigan State University and an adjunct faculty member of the Department of Anthropology at the University of New Mexico.

Salomé RITTERBAND is an anthropologist at the *Weltmuseum Wien* and graduate of the University of Vienna, Department of Social and Cultural Anthropology.

Alicja KHATCHIKIAN is an anthropologist and graduate of the University of Vienna, Department of Social and Cultural Anthropology.

Paul NUGENT is a Professor of Comparative African History and African Studies at the University of Edinburgh.

William MILES is a Professor of Political Science in the College of Social Sciences and Humanities at Northeastern University.

Jennifer KELLEHER is a lawyer and programme officer for equity and rights at the IUCN and graduate of the University of Vienna, Faculty of Law.

Christian STERKL is an anthropologist and graduate of the University of Vienna, Department of Social and Cultural Anthropology.

Tibor BÖHM is an anthropologist and graduate of the University of Vienna, Department of Social and Cultural Anthropology.

Patrick CASSIDY is an anthropologist and graduate student at the University of Vienna, Department of Social and Cultural Anthropology.

Georg BERGTHALER is an anthropologist and graduate of the University of Vienna, Department of Social and Cultural Anthropology.

Manuela ZIPS-MAIRITSCH is a lawyer and lecturer at the University of Vienna, Department of Social and Cultural Anthropology.

Werner ZIPS is a Professor at the University of Vienna, Department of Social and Cultural Anthropology.

Legal Anthropology and Indigenous Rights
edited by Werner Zips and Manuela Zips-Mairitsch

Salomé Ritterband
Tracking Indigenous Heritage
Ju/'Hoansi San Learning, Interpreting, and Staging Tradition for a Sustainable Future in Cultural Tourism in the Tsumkwe District of Namibia
In *Living Museums and Cultural Villages*, the Ju/'hoansi San of north-eastern Namibia handle their *Intangible Cultural Heritage* as a basis for self-determination and as a strategy to achieve their claims for indigenous rights. On a regular basis, they perform their 'traditional' hunter-gatherer lifestyle for tourists as a means of generating income, while their children playfully practice and re-enact it themselves. After centuries of discrimination and marginalisation, the Ju/'hoansi are moving towards a new position inside the nation state.
Bd. 3, 2018, 294 S., 29,90 €, br., ISBN 978-3-643-90976-3

Erwin Schweitzer
The Making of Griqua, Inc.
Indigenous struggles for land and autonomy in South Africa
With the dawn of democracy in South Africa in 1994, the struggle of indigenous Griqua for land has gained new momentum. Having lost most of their ancestral land in the 19th century due to colonialism, Griqua people are now using new legal opportunities to reclaim land. On their reobtained land Griqua people dwell, farm, celebrate indigenous festivals and create cultural villages for tourists. In doing so, Griqua people are currently contributing to the making of Ethnicity, Inc., the double process of commodification of culture and creation of ethnic businesses.
Bd. 2, 2015, 356 S., 34,90 €, br., ISBN 978-3-643-90577-2

Manuela Zips-Mairitsch
Lost Lands?
Indigenous (Land) Rights of the San in Botswana
Images can be deceiving. The San portrayed on the cover seem to be a remnant from a time when *hunters and gatherers* still roamed vast areas of land in southern Africa. In reality they are actors paid to re-enact the way they once lived. In the Kalahari town of Ghanzi, Botswana, tourists can book so-called "authentic Bushman Walks". More than anything, however, such performances of a foraging lifestyle offer "authentic" accounts of current legal and political living conditions for Botswana's indigenous population: displaced from their land and left without any economic assets, they have to depend on the rampant commodification of their culture.
Now that San communities have joined forces in the international arena of indigenous rights struggles, their voices are getting louder and call for at least some degree of self-determination on the lands they once owned. In many ways, the legal dispute over (land) rights in the Kalahari epitomizes this global justice movement.
Bd. 1, 2013, 432 S., 29,90 €, br., ISBN 978-3-643-90244-3

LIT Verlag Berlin – Münster – Wien – Zürich – London
Auslieferung Deutschland / Österreich / Schweiz: siehe Impressumsseite